STEINWAY & SONS

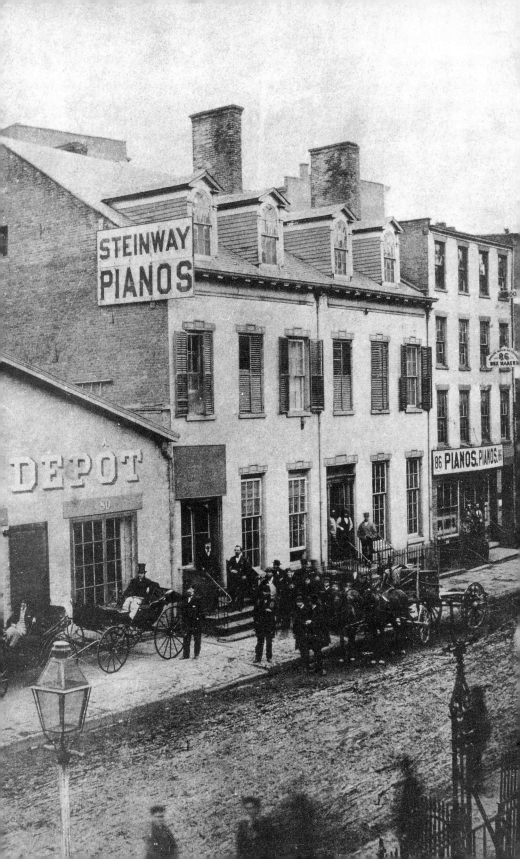

STEINWAY

&

SONS

RICHARD K. LIEBERMAN

Yale University Press

New Haven & London

For my wife, Susan Farkas,
and my son, Samuel,
with love

Frontispiece: Steinway & Sons' retail
showrooms on Walker Street in 1858, with the
Steinway family in and near the carriage and
on the stoop.

Designed by James J. Johnson and set in
Stempel Garamond type by The Composing
Room of Michigan, Inc.
Printed in the United States by Edwards
Brothers, Inc., Ann Arbor, Michigan.

*Library of Congress Cataloging-in-Publication
Data*

Lieberman, Richard K.
    Steinway & Sons / Richard K. Lieberman.
        p.   cm.
    Includes bibliographical references and
index.
    ISBN 0-300-06364-4 (cloth: alk. paper)
            0-300-06850-6 (pbk.: alk. paper)
    1. Steinway & Sons—History. 2. Piano.
    3. Piano makers—New York (N.Y.)—
History. I. Title.
ML424.S76L54   1995
786.2′197471—dc20   95–17330
                                                            CIP
                                                            MN

A catalogue record for this book is available
from the British Library.
The paper in this book meets the guidelines
for permanence and durability of the
Committee on Production Guidelines for
Book Longevity of the Council on Library
Resources.

10   9   8   7   6   5   4   3

Contents

Contents

Acknowledgments

Like the keys on a piano, this book was played upon by many people. My wife, Susan Farkas, had the talent and the light touch to tell me when the narrative was right and when it was wrong. My mentor and colleague Janet Lieberman gave her creative energy. My teacher Tony Gabriele taught me how to communicate and moved the book to completion. And my assistant Eduvina Estrella made it possible for me to have time to write.

I owe special recognition to Henry and John Steinway, who encouraged the company to donate its papers to me at the LaGuardia and Wagner Archives. All photographs in the book not otherwise identified are from the archives. Moreover, Henry Z. Steinway opened his personal collection to me and was available for numerous interviews.

Several colleagues critiqued the manuscript, which resulted in the narrative becoming clearer and more interesting. I want particularly to thank Carol Groneman, Judy McGaw, Julius Edelstein, Danny Lynch, John Chaffee, Dan Ehrlich, Deborah Gardner, Dave Amidon, Sheila Biddle, Josh Freeman, Ted Good, Hans Joachim Braum, and Roy Rosenzweig.

The faculty and staff at LaGuardia Community College/CUNY were supportive of my work, and a grant from the PSC–CUNY foundation helped pay for research assistants. The University Seminars at Columbia University provided financial support for the preparation of the manuscript. I would like to thank the people at the LaGuardia and Wagner Archives: Roberto Ferreiras, Susan Deninger, Aimee Kaplan, Qi-Jian Gao, and David Osborn for their professionalism and cooperation. I am grateful to have had the assistance of Garret Batten, Ruth Cahn, and Dan Wishnoff who tracked down the answers to many questions. Trude Rittman, Harold Herrmann, and Frank Wilkens volunteered their time and did an excellent job translating handwritten Steinway letters.

Special thanks are also due to my agent, Carol Mann, who believed in this book and that good history can be written for a popular audience. She introduced me to Meg Blackstone, who was my first editor. I was very fortunate in finding Harry Haskell at Yale University Press, who, with his colleagues, Noreen O'Connor, Jean van Altena, and Jennifer Kaufman, trimmed a long manuscript into a more manageable-sized book.

To all those who made writing *Steinway & Sons* more enjoyable, thank you.

A Select Family Tree

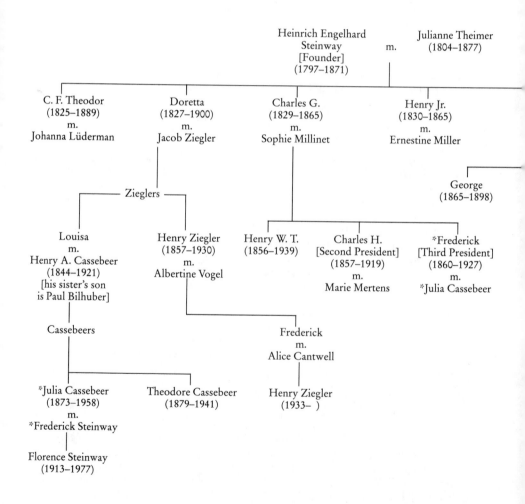

Heinrich Engelhard Steinway [Founder] (1797–1871) m. Julianne Theimer (1804–1877)

C. F. Theodor (1825–1889) m. Johanna Lüderman

Doretta (1827–1900) m. Jacob Ziegler

Charles G. (1829–1865) m. Sophie Millinet

Henry Jr. (1830–1865) m. Ernestine Miller

George (1865–1898)

Zieglers

Louisa m. Henry A. Cassebeer (1844–1921) [his sister's son is Paul Bilhuber]

Henry Ziegler (1857–1930) m. Albertine Vogel

Henry W. T. (1856–1939)

Charles H. [Second President] (1857–1919) m. Marie Mertens

*Frederick [Third President] (1860–1927) m. *Julia Cassebeer

Cassebeers

Frederick m. Alice Cantwell

*Julia Cassebeer (1873–1958) m. *Frederick Steinway

Theodore Cassebeer (1879–1941)

Henry Ziegler (1933–)

Florence Steinway (1913–1977)

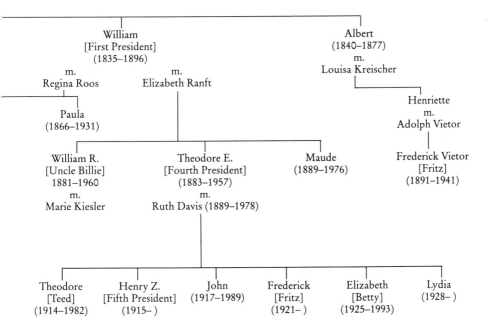

This select family tree highlights the people mentioned in the book. Marriages are included if the marriage or the children are important. Siblings are left out if they were not crucial to the story. Asterisks denote people who appear in two places in the family tree.

Introduction

"I know a fine way to treat a Steinway," goes Irving Berlin's song "I Love a Piano." By 1915 Berlin didn't need to explain the word *Steinway:* it had been the preeminent American piano for more than fifty years. After 1860 most pianos were copies of Steinways. Chickering, Weber, Mason & Hamlin, all came and went; Steinway stayed at the top. *Steinway & Sons* is about the family that manufactured and marketed that instrument.

Starting in 1853, the Steinways saw their piano company through the strains of competition, strikes, and temperamental artists, as well as depressions and wars. Their saga extends from the factory bench to the showroom floor to the concert stage and international trade fairs.

The Steinway story began in Germany in 1835 and went on to span capitalism in America from the days when a weekly wage was $5 to the days when $5 was an hourly wage. The Steinways slogged through the recessions of the 1850s, amassed huge fortunes in the 1880s, were devastated by the financial slump in the late 1890s, recovered with the rest of American business by the turn of the century, and accumulated great wealth before the radio, the phonograph, the automobile, and the Great Depression all but wiped them out. They limped along for the next twenty years and in the 1960s again began to prosper. But when Yamaha captured the world's piano market in the early 1970s, Steinway & Sons' then president, Henry Z. Steinway, decided to sell the company to CBS.

What is astounding is how the Steinways maintained this family business for so long, while all around them privately owned businesses were consolidating into larger stock companies. Few family-owned and operated businesses have lasted long enough to pass to a new generation, yet Steinway persisted under six different family members spanning five generations. This longevity was in large part achieved by having a partnership of an artist and a businessman at the helm. That mix of craft and commerce at the tiller was crucial in establishing the standards and style of Steinway & Sons. Based on a cultural icon, it was not the type of enterprise that could be run by just a merchant or just a maestro. The family was unusually fortunate in having the right mix of skills in generation after generation but ran into trouble when half the mix was missing.

In the 1930s and 1940s responsibility fell solely to an artist with no business sense, who lived more in Steinway's golden past than in its dreadful present. Theodore E. Steinway, grandson of the founder, was forced into the job of president against his will and found himself alone at the top. It was the first time in Steinway's history that the president didn't have a partner. Heinrich Steinway, founder of the company, could not have managed the business without his sons; when William emerged as top man, he called his brother Theodor back from Germany to work with him; after William died, the new president, Charles, consulted daily with his brother Frederick; and when Frederick took over, he had his older cousin Henry Ziegler at his side. But during the Depression and World War II, Theodore had no such support. His older brother Billie was more skilled at making friends and spending money than managing a business, and all Theodore's male cousins and nephews—women were not considered eligible as business partners—were too young. As a result, he made mistakes. He ignored the new, small upright piano market in the 1930s and wasn't astute enough to make money on military contracts during World War II. Lack of collaboration remained a problem into the 1950s and 1960s when his son Henry, who was not an artist but a businessman, ruled the company, again without that other half.

Another reason for Steinway's unusual longevity as a family business in my view is that only twice did a son succeed his father. The presidency usually passed to a talented nephew, brother, or cousin. When the boss died, his eldest son was typically either too young or too incompetent to take over. This meant that the common family business predicament of sons succeeding talented, powerful fathers was circumvented.

But, more than anything, Steinway's resilience was based on the quality of its piano, whose superiority was such that the flow of piano innovations in the late nineteenth century was from New York to Europe. At a time when America was still viewed as a frontier society, better at manufacturing plows than pianos, it was thought, Europeans were shocked to find Steinway & Sons, an American manufacturer, making one of the finest pianos in the world.

The 1850s saw a demand for a more powerful piano as the size of music halls grew to accommodate thousands instead of hundreds of concertgoers. To meet that demand, Steinway, by 1860, was manufacturing a piano with a rich, powerful tone. The volume was increased by introducing new parts, such as a cast-iron plate that could hold the piano wires in tune under tremendous pressure, and by fanning the longer, heavier bass strings out above the treble and middle registers. Henry Steinway, Jr., responsible for these innovations, also added a vibrant soundboard and a more responsive keyboard. These innovations, taken together, were initially called the "Steinway system," but they soon became known simply as the "American system."

Steinway continued to make improvements in its piano after 1860. After Henry, Jr., died and Theodor assumed the role of head of Inventions and Construction, there were hundreds of new patents. Americans loved gadgets and new technology, and Steinway catered to that fascination and used new patents to sell its pianos. On the showroom floor it was useful to be able to say: "And this year we have a new and improved action," or "The strings are now divided differently, to provide a fuller sound." Theodor replaced Henry, Jr., as inventor and in Steinway legend is considered the father of the modern Steinway, although that honor more properly belongs to Henry, Jr.

In the twentieth century, innovations took the form of new models, new manufacturing procedures, and new glues and lacquer finishes. The other major change was that in the 1930s, for the first time, people outside the Steinway family were involved in creating the new technology. Until then, all drawings remained in rough form and were the sole possession of the chief engineer—Henry, Jr., Theodore Steinway, and then his nephew Henry Ziegler. But when Ziegler died and his post went to Paul Bilhuber, the tradition of family secrets ended.

In a family business the story does not stop at the factory gate. Life at home is not separate from work. The Steinway family had all the trappings of upper-class Victorian life—a patriarch, inherited wealth, and ownership of the means of production. But the Steinways' lives did not always conform to our notions of Victorian mores. In addition to some remarkable sexual liaisons, we find novel survival strategies on the part of those attempting to escape a family tradition riddled with addictions to both work and whiskey. William Steinway's first wife, Regina, seems to have slept with almost every man she met in order to assuage her loneliness and compensate for marriage to a workaholic husband; William's nephew, Henry W. T. Steinway, engaged in a decade of court battles, starting in the 1890s, to free himself from his authoritarian uncle, whom Henry claimed was bilking the business of vast amounts of money; William's brother, Theodor, in the 1850s, and his grandson Teed, almost a century later, tried putting as many miles as they could between themselves and the Steinways to save their sanity.

Steinway & Sons is also the story of a search for freedom. In 1850 the family abandoned its homeland and sailed for America. These were people with money, skills, a home, and a business, not potato famine Irish who had no option but to leave. The wealthy Steinways left because they wanted to. In Germany they were stifled by trade barriers, a restrictive economy, disruptive riots, and the failed 1848 revolution which paralyzed commerce. They settled in New York City and within three years were making their own pianos again in the unfettered American economy.

But they also faced hard times in America, and, confronted by strikes and increasing labor costs, the founder's eldest son, Theodor, pioneered a move back to Europe. The first step back to the Old World was the opening of Steinway Hall in London in 1875. This was a showroom for the New York factory and a way into the British market. By the 1880s it had also become a showroom for pianos manufactured in Germany, in Hamburg.

The purpose of manufacturing presence in Hamburg was to exploit the cheaper labor force there. In 1880 the daily wage in Hamburg was less than that in New York. The outcome was that William and his brother Theodor were managing two businesses, 4,000 miles apart, at a time when communication was limited to letters, which took three weeks to cross the Atlantic, or cryptic telegrams sent via the recently laid transatlantic cable. This sort of arrangement was popular in the American colonial period: placing a brother in New York, another brother in Hamburg, and perhaps a trusted cousin in London, and in time a nephew in Berlin.

The Hamburg Steinway evolved into a different kind of instrument from the New York Steinway. Initially, Hamburg did not manufacture its own piano; it was for the most part an assembly plant for parts shipped from New York (rims, plates, actions, and keys), although some parts were made locally. But in 1907 German tariffs on metal parts made it more economical for Hamburg to buy its plates locally. This marked a turning point for the Hamburg operation, and by World War I there were two separate Steinway factories, one in America, the other in Europe. During the 1920s the question was asked—and is still posed today—as to which piano was better, the New York or the Hamburg version. The answer has always depended on whom you ask.

One consequence of operating in both New York and Hamburg was that when Germany and America went to war, Steinway had one foot in each camp. Though Steinway & Sons was an American company, it was allowed to stay in business in Germany, once the family had proved that it wasn't Jewish.

Both factories contributed to the war effort, Hamburg manufacturing bunk beds and rifle stocks for the German military, New York providing gliders, a few coffins, and an occasional upright for the United States military.

The Steinways were as creative at marketing their pianos as they were at making them. In the nineteenth century their strategy was to win fame through medals at fairs, artists' endorsements, and managing their own concert hall. Before Sol Hurok, before Arthur Judson, and long before David Merrick, William Steinway managed celebrated European pianists like Anton Rubinstein and Ignace Paderewski, booked all their concerts in the United States, made their travel arrangements, and guaranteed a minimum income for their national tours. William Steinway was Mr. Music in America. By bringing Rubinstein and, later, Paderewski to small towns across the country, he delivered piano recitals to people who lived in regions barren of classical music. William Steinway did for classical piano music what P. T. Barnum did for the circus. He put it within reach of most Americans. In so doing, he played a significant role in shaping nineteenth-century musical consciousness. Of course, it was all calculated to help piano sales. William knew that if Rubinstein and Paderewski became superstars, more people would want to buy pianos, and that if those celebrities played Steinways, then that would be the piano people would want.

By the 1920s, demand had shifted to the player piano, the phonograph, and the radio. People wanted machines that would generate their music instantly and effortlessly. In those roaring twenties when standards were ambivalent, Steinway decided to sell itself as protector of Victorian values, tradition, and stability. The Steinway piano was marketed as art in the age of machines. With the help of a young copywriter at N. W. Ayer, Raymond Rubicam (who went on to become a founding partner of the public-relations giant Young & Rubicam), Steinway became the "instrument of the immortals," the piano used by the divine artists of the past. Steinway pianos were sold as the real thing, the original, in a world that, more and more, was settling for imitations. The claim was always that "this year's Steinway is the best ever made." It answered the question that was—and still is—on many consumers' minds: "Is the Steinway made today as good as the one made in the past?" The answer was always that it was better. Nothing symbolized this more than the new Steinway Hall on West 57th Street, a palace for the venerated Steinway piano.

If the piano was the "instrument of the immortals" to the public, to the men in the factory making it, it was at the root of a constant battle against wage cuts, long hours, and total control over their work. The 1870s saw the beginning of a move to Queens, in an attempt to keep workers and the factory away from "red hot strikers" in New York City (the city included

Manhattan and the south Bronx only at that time). Management hoped to have more control over the workers' daily lives this way and built a village around the factory, selling lots on some of the 400 acres Steinway owned in western Queens. This was a company town akin to the textile towns and the paper mill villages in New England.

At this time the Steinways were undisguisedly contemptuous of their employees. During a strike in 1864 Henry, Jr., referred to his 400 workers as "swine," telling his brothers to fire them all and not to worry because another 400 swine were ready to take their place. In other strikes police were paid by Steinway to contain the workers, protect company property, and put strikers in jail. Striking men who rented homes from Steinway or were paying off mortgages were dispossessed. Tensions ran high, and during one strike William's life was even threatened. This was not a story of one big happy family. Many workers opted to move on. Being able to say that they had worked for Steinway was a credential that could command a high wage on the outside and was a useful reference for starting one's own shop.

In 1937 the workers formed a factory-wide union and two years later joined the national United Furniture Workers' union, CIO. This was when all shreds of paternalism—company picnics, orchestral concerts at lunchtime, and home mortgages—ended. The strikes continued, but because of close collaboration between Henry Z. Steinway, president of the company from 1955 to 1972, and the union business agent, James Cerofeci, they were limited to an average of two weeks, and the resulting raises were nickels and dimes at a time when Steinway & Sons was making millions. Workers struggling to make ends meet either quit or took a second job. The turnover during the 1960s was 40 percent. Worker loyalty and continuity were traded off for short-term profits.

Customer attitudes changed too. By the late 1960s, technology had come to be regarded with suspicion. What people were now asking was not what was new about the piano being shown them, but whether it was the traditional Steinway. As a result, patents are no longer used to sell Steinway pianos, and the recent marketing plan calls for a limited number of new instruments, based on nineteenth-century models.

Yet, despite labor turmoil, family feuds, depressions, wars, competition from the Far East, and people increasingly wanting their music from records, cassettes, and compact discs, nothing has silenced the Steinway sound, even if what Steinway is now selling is its past rather than any technical innovations. Francis X. Clines, a *New York Times* reporter with a sensitive grasp of city life, as recently as 16 October 1994, referred to the Steinway factory as "a resilient treasure in a city that wonders whether it has lost its soul." *Steinway & Sons* is about what underlies that resiliency.

The Americanization of Steinweg

AS GUESTS DINED ON succulent roasted fowl and mouth-watering marinated oysters, washing their palates with ice-cold champagne, piano music was in the air. The occasion was the opening of the new Steinway factory in New York. In a remarkably short period of time, between 5 March 1853, when they went into business and 1 April 1860, when they opened their new factory, the Steinway family had triumphed in America. According to R. G. Dun & Company, Steinway & Sons was "doing a larger business in their line (piano making) than any other on this continent" and was worth more than $360,000—a substantial amount when compared to the $500 a year average pay of its workers.

The main attraction at the celebration was not the champagne or the oysters, however. It was the 300 workers who would manufacture 1,180 pianos that year. The guests, "literary, musical and artistic gentlemen" (women were invited only to the showroom), were taken on a tour of the factory. Counting the screws, some 40,000 pieces went into making a Steinway, and each piano took about a year to assemble. To the visitors ambling through the Steinway factory that summer afternoon, the transformation of lumber into graceful, 8-foot rosewood pianos must have seemed like magic. The ninety-minute tour was followed by more champagne, music played on three Steinway grands, a demonstration of the private telegraph line connecting the factory to the showrooms three and a half miles away on Walker Street, and speeches. One speaker compared the new factory "with its hundred altars of mechanism" to a temple. Charles, one of the sons, praised the "progressive spirit of America" which aroused in him the irresistible desire

Steinway piano factory at 53rd Street and Fourth Avenue (now Park Avenue) in 1861, with the Steinway family standing by the entrance and workers looking out of the windows. The obstruction in the middle of the photo is a telegraph pole.

to push ahead and come out first in the race for improvement. Editors from more than sixty newspapers covered the event, and, according to one family member, "all the lads were so enthused that we received long laudatory reports in almost all the newspapers, which made our name immensely popular."

A correspondent from a local newspaper declared that there was

no manufactory in the world which combines so perfectly all the elements of creation in so simple working order. It is this gift of arrangement and combination which has placed Steinway, senior, and his four sons at the head of an establishment so complete in the short term of eight years. It is conceded that the Steinway Piano in make, tone, sweetness, precision, and durability, is the most perfect instrument of that class to be had anywhere in the world.[1]

The road to victory had begun sixty-three years earlier, in Wolfshagen, a small forest hamlet nestled in the slopes of the upper Harz Mountains between Hanover and Leipzig in northwest Germany, where Heinrich Engelhard Steinweg, founder of Steinway & Sons, was born.[2] The truth about his origins is difficult to piece together because of the legends that have grown up, fueled by public relations people anxious to use the family history to promote the Steinway mystique. A powerful Steinway public relations machine came into being during the 1920s and continues to this day, perpetuating stories about both the family and the piano.

The first Steinway fable-maker was Elbert Hubbard, a retired soap salesman turned chronicler. In *The Story of the Steinways*, published in 1921, Hubbard described a family of fourteen of which Heinrich, a full-faced boy with deep penetrating eyes, was the sole survivor. The saga includes invasions by Corsicans, then Prussians, and finally by Napoleon in 1806.

Napoleon did in fact conquer and occupy portions of Germany, creating a new kingdom of Westphalia for his brother Jerome out of the states of Hesse-Cassel and Brunswick, where the Steinwegs lived. Napoleon was hailed as "prince of peace" and "regenerator of Germany" in the pro-French state of Brunswick. But French occupation ravaged rather than regenerated the Steinwegs. The family house and land were confiscated while Heinrich's father and two older brothers were away in the army. The remaining Steinwegs fled for safety to the Harz Mountains, where, during the harsh winter, Heinrich watched his mother and siblings (except for one sister) die from exposure. The two youngsters emerged from the forest with the spring thaw, to be reunited with what family remained.

Heinrich's father remarried and had more children, and he and his sons worked for the duke, repairing roads, planting trees, and gathering wood to make into charcoal and sell as fuel. Church records reveal that the Steinwegs, back as far as Heinrich's grandfather, were "kohler Meisters," master charcoal-burners. They lived in the woods and, like most charcoal-burners, were regarded with deep suspicion by townspeople, who rarely saw them. One summer Heinrich, his father, and his half-brother were out in the woods, far from home, when a storm suddenly arose, accompanied by ferocious winds and lightning, typical weather for the upper Harz Mountains. They sought shelter in an abandoned hut, huddling together for warmth and comfort. But lightning struck the hut, setting it on fire. Heinrich was knocked out by the blast, and when he came to, he found the dead bodies of his father and two brothers lying strewn around the shack. He fled by foot to a nearby town for help. A local physician bandaged him up, and the townspeople brought the bodies back. Aged barely fifteen, Heinrich was both an orphan and penniless. He sought refuge in the army.

Two years later, under the Duke of Brunswick's flag, he was fighting against Napoleon at the Battle of Waterloo. Family legend has it that when Blucher and Wellington advanced on Napoleon on that fateful day in June 1815, their charge was signaled by a lone bugler, Heinrich Engelhard Steinweg. According to this tale, he was awarded a bronze medal for "bugling in the face of the enemy." When not heading off to battle, he was in his barracks making mandolins, dulcimers, and zithers and occasionally striking up a tune with the military band.[3]

He stayed in the military until he was twenty-one, which meant that he was too old to embark on the traditional woodworking apprenticeship of five years. Instead, he worked for a so-called wild boss, who agreed to take him on and teach him woodworking in less than the requisite five years. He then served an apprenticeship with the church organ builder in his grandfather's city of Goslar, not far from Wolfshagen, the prerequisites for this being less rigid than for the cabinetmaking guild. His introduction to the piano was through his Jewish friend Karl Brand, the cantor's son. Steinweg learned to build a piano by copying Brand's.[4]

In February 1825 he married Julianne Thiemer, daughter of a propertyowner and well-established glove-maker in Seesen. Heinrich, a cabinetmaker without property, a *Beiwohner* (boarder), was marrying up. Together, he and his wife raised ten children in Seesen, a small city of about three thousand people six miles down the mountain from Wolfshagen.

In Seesen, Heinrich once again found himself up against the guild system's regulations, this time their stipulation that members could start a business only in the town of their birth. But in the very year he moved there, a fierce fire destroyed Seesen, and the chief justice decreed that master builders like Heinrich Steinweg be permitted to establish businesses there and so rebuild the town. He was recognized as a local burgher a year later. He established an organ business and by 1829 had made enough money to purchase a two-story house with a workshop, a large cellar, and a 120-foot fenced-in garden. In 1835 he started a piano business, attaching his nameplate "H. Steinweg, Instrumentenmacher, Seesen" to every instrument.[5]

Within a year he was building one or two pianos a month, as were hundreds of other craftsmen in Germany. Germany's feudal economy meant that piano making was no more than a cottage industry at the time. Thus most piano makers, like Steinweg, were making their instruments at home. But even within that restrictive economy, Heinrich prospered and was able to send two of his sons, Theodor and Henry, Jr., to the finest school in Seesen, the Jacobsohn Hochschule. In the summer of 1839 he exhibited one grand and two so-called square pianos—actually rectangular and looking more like writing tables than what we think of when we think of a piano—at the

Heinrich Engelhard
Steinway at the
Brady studio,
3 July 1862.

Grand piano built in 1836 by Heinrich Engelhard Steinway in Seesen. One of the first pianos built by Steinway, it is now on loan to the Metropolitan Museum of Art.

State Trade Exhibition at the Aegis Church in Brunswick. He won top prize for tone and workmanship and sold a piano to the Duke of Brunswick for 3,000 marks. The talent behind this triumph was Heinrich's fourteen-year-old son C. F. Theodor. He played their pianos at the trade show, so demonstrating both his own talent and the piano's large pure tone. But it was the combination of Theodor's art and Heinrich's craft that captured the prize, secured the sale to the duke, and made Steinweg well known and wealthy.[6]

Although Heinrich had produced about four hundred pianos by 1848, thereby establishing himself as one of the more prosperous manufacturers in Seesen, his economic prospects were bleak. Compared to the rest of Western Europe, Germany was a poor country still subject to an oppressive feudal social order. Each of the thirty-eight German states had its own government, court, and legal codes, it own currency, business laws, weights and measures, and tariffs at its borders. The assortment of regulations, not to mention the licenses that had to be obtained, made trade difficult, and manufacturers like Steinweg sometimes had to pay two or three border taxes or river tolls to get their product to market or seaport. He was part of a small, ailing, urban manufacturing class, and he knew it.

In 1834 the Zollverein was established to promote free trade within the German states and moderate protective tariffs on international trade. But the duties on raw iron and textiles that were being exacted by 1846 discouraged the northern states from joining, which was unfortunate for Steinweg and other manufacturers in the Zollverein because it meant that their products were subject to transit duties en route to major cities in the north; it also made access to the North Sea and the Baltic, and ultimately international trade, costly.

Further, between 1845 and 1847 agricultural failures resulted in a major famine in Europe. Food prices rose by an average 50 percent between 1844 and 1847, and many of the poor wandered through the countryside in search of food and coins from compassionate villagers. Although the downward spiral of the economy and rising costs of food came to a halt in the spring of 1848, enough resentment remained to bring about uprisings in Paris and later in Germany. The revolution of 1848 failed to produce a redistribution of wealth, land, or power, but it did paralyze business throughout central Europe, thereby encouraging businessmen like Heinrich Steinweg to consider leaving.

The inhabitants of the Duchy of Brunswick, where Steinweg lived, had been in sympathy with democratic impulses since the French Revolution. The duke regarded himself as a disciple of the philosophes. The Brunswick middle class, encouraged by the overthrow of Louis-Philippe in France, fostered the socialist movement and supported the uprisings in Paris and throughout Germany. Heinrich's son Charles was caught up in this rally against an absolutist prince and in the fight for popular sovereignty and guarantees of political and civil liberties for the Christian middle class. But when it became apparent that the will of the people was not going to rule in Germany, even in liberal Brunswick, Heinrich and Julianne feared reprisals for their son. Nor were prospects favorable for their piano trade. So they sent Charles south to neighboring Switzerland and from there to Paris, then London, then on to America, where he was to find a safe haven both for himself and for the Steinweg piano business.[7]

In June 1849 Charles landed in New York, center of professional music making in America and of America's piano industry. The other major piano-manufacturing cities were Boston, Baltimore, and Philadelphia, all centers for German immigrants. Pianos had been in America only since the Revolution, most of them brought in from shipwrecks by pirates as part of their booty. The rest were imported by John Jacob Astor, the German millionaire fur trader, who occasionally bartered furs for pianos. By 1849 there were plenty of piano makers in New York, and Charles easily found a job with Bacon & Raven, one of the largest manufacturers in the city and provider of pianos to the composer Stephen Foster.

Charles had come from Seesen, a city with fewer than three thousand inhabitants, to New York, a city with over half a million. He had never seen so many people at once or anything like the traffic on Broadway, especially the lower portion near where he worked. Another visitor to New York at this time wrote: "One of the first things that struck us on arriving . . . was, of course, Broadway. It is a noble street and has a thoroughly bustling, lively and somewhat democratic air." It was also littered with most of the rubbish and dead animals of the city. But to escape the throng and trash of the metropolis, Charles could stroll under the trees in Washington Square Park or visit Barnum's Museum at the corner of Broadway and Ann Street. For a young man it was an exciting, if dirty town, and Charles wrote to his family urging them to join him immediately.[8]

What he didn't tell them was that New York was in the grip of one of the worst cholera epidemics in its history, caused by the mixing of drinking water with sewage, and that people were dying all around him. In 1849 New York had neither a sanitation department nor a board of health. Even the new Croton Water System bringing fresh water from the Catskills to the city did not prevent this flu-like fever from claiming thousands of lives. Nor did he tell them about the class and ethnic warfare that was tearing New York apart. In early May 1849, a month before Charles arrived, working-class Irish had stormed the Astor Place Opera House in protest against a celebrated English actor playing Hamlet. They were eventually overpowered by the New York police force and the New York State militia, but not before twenty-two people had been killed and more than a hundred seriously wounded.

Charles must have heard about the scene at the opera house and witnessed some of the cholera deaths on the streets. He must have seen the carloads of coffins of those whose families could afford burials and the bodies of the less fortunate lying in the gutters and being eaten by rats, dogs, and wild pigs, New York's undomesticated street cleaners. But none of this found its way into his letters back home. If it had, it is unlikely that his family would have come. Charles was highly selective in what he divulged.[9]

In the spring of 1850, Heinrich, then 53, and Julianne, 46—old to be setting out on a new life—on the strength of Charles's reports, sold their home, paid off their debts to the local pawnshop, and, together with three daughters and five sons, set out for America. Only Theodor, their firstborn, stayed in Germany, moving to the nearby town of Holzminden, where he repaired violins and tuned pianos. The rest of the family embarked for New

York on the maiden voyage of the most modern ship then sailing, the *Helene Sloman*, one of the first steam-propelled three-mast boats to cross the Atlantic. Unfortunately, the ship broke down outside Deal, in England, delaying the voyage for nine days. What should have been a three-week voyage took almost five weeks.[10]

It was almost summer when the family sailed into New York's lower bay. They were among 213,000 who left Europe for America in mid-century. Some 82,000 people emigrated from Germany alone in 1850, almost half of them headed for America. By 1860, one out of every four New Yorkers was German-born, only Vienna and Berlin having more German speakers than New York City, and in time Germans became the principal immigrant group in America. When the Steinwegs arrived, they faced no restrictions, no questions, no Castle Garden, no Ellis Island, and no Statue of Liberty. Immigrants arrived and either settled in New York or boarded trains, wagons, or other boats and headed west.

These Germans brought with them a classical music culture which didn't exist in America. In New York and across the country they formed singing societies and orchestras to perform classical music the way they believed it was supposed to sound, and those who didn't play an instrument sat in the audience and listened. During the next five years the Germania Orchestra, a group of twenty-four young Germans, toured the country, playing more than eight hundred concerts and bringing Germanic renderings of the masters to America. German musicians dominated concert life in America in the 1850s, thanks to the large number of talented German musicians who had emigrated and the thousands of Germans scattered throughout the country wishing to buy concert tickets. German music became so pervasive that in 1854, when the New York Philharmonic Orchestra scheduled only the music of German masters for the entire season, nativists complained.[11]

The Steinwegs were part of this music migration. They had an obsession with craft, an enthusiasm for experimentation, a passion for publicity, and enough money to start their own piano company. But they did not go into business right away. Instead, they decided to work for others until they got their feet on the ground and had learned some English and New York methods. Henry, Jr., estimated that there were some two hundred piano shops in New York to select from and the same number in Boston. In fact, there were only 204 such establishments in the whole country. But Heinrich and his sons selected the best New York piano makers to work for, so that they could learn the latest and finest techniques.[12]

Henry and Charles wrote to their brother Theodor that their father was earning all of $6 a week making soundboards for a German instrument maker by the name of Leuchte. This was substantially below the average

New York artisan's salary, which ranged from $10 a week for barbers to $25 for cigar makers. With rent at about $4 a week and groceries averaging $12, Heinrich's meager salary didn't go very far. In 1853 it was estimated that a family of four needed $600 a year to meet expenses. Heinrich was earning only $312. He could have earned twice as much had he worked for an American, but he didn't speak any English and refused to learn. This was not a political statement. At fifty-three, Heinrich was illiterate in German as well and was just too old to be bothered with a new language. In Germany he had signed contracts with an "X." Moreover, English was not crucial for business. Piano making in New York was dominated by Germans. He could conduct most of his affairs in German, especially those with his workers, and leave the part of the business that required English to his sons and daughters. The following year he went to work for Bacon & Raven, who were then hiring many Germans, including Jacob Decker, Frederick Hazelton, and Otto Schuetze who, like Steinweg, would soon be establishing their own piano factories.[13]

Heinrich's sons earned more than he did. Henry, Jr., aged twenty, earned $7 a week making keyboards for James Pirsson, an Englishman who played double bass in the Philharmonic Orchestra and manufactured three or four pianos a week. He had made his name by introducing the "American double-grand pianoforte." A strange-looking rectangular instrument with keyboards at each end, it was essentially two pianos joined at the hip, so creating a fourteen-octave instrument that could accommodate two pianists. "With that stupidity," Henry, Jr., contemptuously commented, Pirsson had "acquired such a reputation that all the world was now coming to him." Henry could have left and made more money as a piano tuner, but he didn't enjoy tuning all that much, and he did enjoy watching Pirsson's experiments, especially his use of iron as a replacement for wood for the piano frame.[14]

Charles, just turned twenty-one, and his younger brother William, barely sixteen, worked for the English piano maker William Nunns & Company. Charles worked for the miserable wage of $3 a week, and the moving of pianos was so strenuous that it gave him chest pains. He wrote to Theodor that he had had to stop working and was thinking of returning to Seesen for six months to regain his health but was afraid of getting "into trouble in Germany because of the military." He didn't like New York because of the exorbitant cost of doctors and because of his belief that the climate caused chest or lung diseases, thereby killing many Germans. Charles told Theodor to warn people who did not know a trade against going to New York.[15]

When William Nunns & Company subsequently went bankrupt, they owed William $300. They had withheld some of his salary under the so-called truck system, a scheme that, as William later described it, gave the employer the right to act as a "savings bank without paying interest and sometimes not even paying the principal" back to the worker. In 1860, William generously forgave Nunns, then seventy years old, the debt, and for the next ten years he sent his former employer monthly contributions to assist him in his retirement.[16]

After three years the Steinwegs, tired of being exploited by others, reckoned that they knew enough about New York piano making to launch out on their own. On 5 March 1853 they established an informal partnership called "Steinway & Sons" with an investment of $6,000. They appear to have thought that anglicizing their name would improve sales. In the 1850s English pianos such as Broadwoods were still regarded as the best instruments on the market, so no loss of prestige was entailed in being less German. Only after the Civil War would German and German-American pianos become predominant. Moreover, Steinway wanted to let it be known that they were in America to stay. Privately, however, they were still Steinweg and would remain so legally until 1864.[17]

In their new business, they planned to manufacture pianos and to sell both their own pianos and small imported instruments. It was a good time to be in the piano business. A definable middle class was emerging, consisting of consumers prepared to buy all the products which industrializing America was setting about making. Membership in this class was demonstrated by size of house, and a piano dominating the parlor served both as a symbol of social respectability and responsibility and as a reminder of the genteel life. Musical life in America was flourishing, and the piano was at the center of this increasing interest in music. It was in the home that most people played and heard piano music. Music in the home was seen as medicine for the soul and stimulant of romance. Most piano pupils were women, other instruments being seen as detracting from feminine attractiveness. The cello demanded that a woman spread her legs, and the harp ruined her posture. But at the piano she could sit demurely with her feet together. By mid-century every young middle-class woman was expected to learn to play the piano; even courtship increasingly took place at the keyboard. This shift to the piano was as far-reaching in its own way as the advent, sixty years later, of the radio and the phonograph as sources of music in the home.[18]

In the very same year that Steinweg set up shop, the firms that would become its chief European competitors also went into business: Carl Bechstein in Berlin and Julius Blüthner in Leipzig. Further, Jonas Chickering, whose Boston piano company made one out of every nine American pianos, had just rebuilt his factory after a devastating fire that had caused $250,000 worth of damage. Chickering, the leading piano manufacturer in the United States, now had a new five-story factory that was reputed to be the second largest building in the country; only the Capitol in Washington, D.C., was bigger. Chickering's factory housed five hundred workers who manufactured two thousand pianos a year. It had elevators to move the pianos from floor to floor and eleven miles of steam pipes to keep them warm in the winter. Chickering died before his super-factory was finished, but his sons, who took over the business, remained Steinway's major competition in America until the 1870s.[19]

By contrast, the Steinway shop was in a small rented building on Varick Street, below Canal Street on the west side of Manhattan, and the eleven pianos sold during their first year in business were handmade entirely by the family. William always put in the soundboard, Charles regulated the action (the part of the piano that translates the touch of the fingers to the hammers hitting the strings), and Henry, Jr., did the finishing work on the action. During the first year they made only square pianos. According to William, 97 percent of all pianos made in the United States until just after the Civil War were square pianos. They did not manufacture their first grand until 1856.

In 1854, Steinway hired five assistants and moved to larger premises on Walker Street, now the middle of Chinatown but then New York's piano row. Charles and William had worked for Nunns in this very spot. Pirsson, Henry's former employer, had also once had his factory there. The building at 88 Walker Street was therefore already set up to manufacture pianos. Proud to be in business, the Steinwegs painted "Steinway Pianos" in large letters on the side of the building.[20]

It was a difficult year to be starting a business. The country was in recession, and half the piano workers in the city were either unemployed or working only part-time. Fortunately, the rent on their new Walker Street shop was not due until 1 May, six months rent free being a typical inducement to sign a lease in New York, with 1 May the traditional "moving day." For Steinway & Sons the few months of free rent was a matter of survival: if business continued this way, they would soon be heading back to Seesen.

But it didn't continue this way. Moreover, this was a family that pulled together. They all lived nearby at 199 Hester Street, a German neighborhood at that time, and in all probability used the front parlor or bottom floor of their home as a salesroom. In addition, they all worked, even if only the adult men were partners. And by contrast with other family businesses, in which it was common to find daughters in the office, behind the counter, or out milking the cows, some of the Steinway women held positions of responsibility. Julianne, Heinrich's wife, was also his counsellor and secretary and was in charge of all correspondence. And Doretta, their twenty-six-year-old daughter, constituted the entire sales force for Steinway & Sons, selling all that her father and brothers produced and sometimes offering free piano lessons to close a deal.

After a year, Charles remarked that they were "doing quite splendidly." During the opening weeks of 1854 they were making two pianos a week and needing to make three to meet demand. Their economic success was noted in an R. G. Dun and Company report of 1854 which characterized the Steinways as honest, industrious, "said to pay promptly," a group of "worthy men" conducting a small business in good credit. In the 1850s paying on time was a more important measure of credit than having a lot of money. The scale of operations was small, so enormous amounts of capital were not needed to stay in business as long as customers paid their bills.[21]

The Steinways' future depended first on skill, then on national recognition to boost sales. In an attempt to put their fledgling company on the map, they entered the 1855 American Institute Exhibition held at New York's Crystal Palace. The Crystal Palace, an enormous iron and glass structure, towered more than 750 feet above Sixth Avenue, spreading out over five acres at 42nd Street. Modeled on a greenhouse, its 15,000 panes of glass shimmered in the sun by day and glowed by gaslight at night. It had been built in 1852 at a cost of more than half a million dollars as a replica of London's popular Crystal Palace, site of the first, spectacularly successful international exhibition of 1851. New York's Crystal Palace had a glorious, if short, history. In 1853 it was the site of the first World's Fair in America. Five years later an arsonist burned it to the ground, sending six Steinway pianos, worth $4,000, and $1.5 million worth of art, inventions, and rare gems up in smoke.

In an era when advertising was vestigial, fairs were major opportunities to promote one's wares, and winning a prize constituted the biggest market boost going. For the 1855 fair, Steinway decided to build a piano such as no one had ever heard or seen before.[22] Surprisingly, this new piano was the brainchild of Henry, Jr., not his father or his older brothers. Henry had been encouraged by the Steinway winning first prize at the Metropolitan Mechanics Institute fair in Washington, D.C., the previous March, the first time a Steinway had been shown at an American fair, but the November exhibition at the Crystal Palace would be the critical contest.

Initially, the judges at the 1855 exhibition were not overly impressed by the Steinway instrument. But as luck would have it, one day while they were casually walking around the exhibition floor, they suddenly "came upon an instrument that, from its external appearance, solidly rich yet free from the frippery that was then rather in fashion, attracted their attention. One of the company opened the case, and carelessly struck a few cords. . . . One by one the jurors gathered around the strange polyphonist and without a word being spoken, everyone knew that it was the best pianoforte in the exhibition." A reporter from *Frank Leslie's Illustrated Newspaper* applauded its "great power of tone, a depth and richness in the bass, a full mellowness in the middle register and brilliant purity in the treble." This acclamation was exactly what Steinway & Sons needed. New York could not yet compete with London or Paris, but it was up and coming and was certainly the most important city in the United States, and such acclaim in New York boosted Steinway sales both nationally and internationally.[23]

Total sales in 1854 were 74 pianos; a year after the fair, in 1856, they had almost tripled, to 208. In May 1856 Steinway determined its worth as $24,000, four times what it had invested three years earlier to start the business. An R. G. Dun & Company report that year complimented the company on its extensive business but cautioned that it might be expanding too quickly given its small capital base.

The following year, 1857, the failure of the New York City branch of the Ohio Life Insurance and Trust Company, following years of real estate and railroad securities speculation by other investors, precipitated a severe financial panic. The nation was hit by bank and business closures. But Steinway was not in fact overextended, and it had this exceptional piano. It therefore felt invulnerable and rehired its eighty workers within the year—this at a time when most piano factories had fewer than thirty workers. Steinway not only prospered but, in 1857, during the worst depression in antebellum America, shipped more pianos (413) than it had in all the previous years combined, thereby demonstrating that something remarkable had indeed been set off at the Crystal Palace fair. The company's net worth tripled to $75,000, and by the end of 1858 Steinway had doubled its showroom space and almost doubled its sales for the third year in a row, all the while keeping the average wage in the factory below $2 a day.

In addition to producing an outstanding piano, another cause of Steinway's success was a new group of consumers emerging. A middle-class domestic revolution had taken place in America from 1830 to 1860, and members of this class were anxious to cover the floors, paper the walls, and stuff their parlors with furnishings. Balloon-frame construction enabled them to build large Victorian houses away from the center of the city to house and display the goods. The men in this group commuted to work each day on streetcars and ferries. The women commuted to attractive downtown retail shops to buy an array of goods, but would usually bring their men for the more expensive items like a piano, which, according to one contemporary, "was a requisite to parlor equipment."[24]

Increasing sales and hence pressure on production triggered a search for more space. The company subsequently expanded into a warren of rented shops on Mercer, Crosby, and Walker Streets and a lumberyard on 23rd Street. The shops lacked circular saws or planing machines to do the rough woodcuts and elevators to haul pianos from floor to floor. The pianos were carried up and down two and three flights of stairs on workers' shoulders. Before long, they had decided to turn their several shops into one large factory and their craft into an industry. This capacity for imaginative thinking, together with a willingness to experiment, was atypical of their trade and their time.[25]

William, aged twenty-three, was soon given the task of buying land for a new factory. Piano making required a lot of space, and by 1858 it had become prohibitively expensive to keep expanding downtown, where land was costly. So Steinway and many other manufacturers left their showrooms downtown in the commercial and shopping district and moved their mills uptown or out of town to the Bronx, and later Queens, where land was cheaper and more plentiful. In 1858 he purchased a large site along the Harlem and New Haven Railroad line between Fourth (Park) and Lexington avenues from 52nd to 53rd streets.

Heinrich Steinweg oversaw the construction of the new, 175,000 square foot, five-story, L-shaped, brown brick factory. It was designed by architect Louis Berger and cost $150,000. The back door to Heinrich's house opened onto the factory courtyard. His sons noted that "he was out there every day and every now and then he also quarreled with the construction workers when things were not done according to his wishes. . . . He was entirely in his element there."[26] To Heinrich, building a factory and building a piano required the same care.

He supervised the installation of three enormous steam boilers in the yard. He would not allow fire of any kind inside. These boilers were so big that they generated enough steam to warm the entire factory, heat four kilns in which 250,000 feet of lumber dried for three months, power four elevators, and drive the fifty-horsepower Corliss engine that ran all the saws, lathes, and planes in the basement.[27] Not since Chickering's 1853 piano factory in Boston had any piano maker put so many line-shaft-driven tools under one roof. Steinway was the first in New York to mechanize on such a grand scale, and certainly one of only a few woodworking outfits to use steam power, which, except for transportation, was not in wide use in America until much later in the century. Furniture makers in New York, Boston, Baltimore, and Philadelphia were reluctant to introduce steam power into their factories and continued to depend on water, wind, tide, and hand power to run their machines. Unlike woodworkers in midwestern cities like Cincinnati, New England and the Middle Atlantic region, which accounted for three-quarters of the nation's manufacturing employment in 1850, stayed

The three Steinway brownstones on 52nd Street, near the factory, in 1861. Standing on the stoops are (*left to right*) Heinrich and Julianne, Henry, Jr., and Ernestine, Regina and William. In the carriage are Charles G. and Sophie, who had a house around the corner.

with hand-powered tools. As late at 1880, only one out of every five Philadelphia furniture manufactures used steam power.[28]

Steinway had precision machinery on the third floor for making scrolls and rounding corners, but most of the machines, used primarily for rough woodworking, were in the basement. But despite all the milling machines in the new factory, production time, far from decreasing, increased. This was probably because Steinway workers were new at this rough carpentry and were probably not as efficient as the mill hands in the lumberyards where Steinway had previously bought wood already cut into planks—as it turned out, it paid to buy wood from the lumberyard already milled. In addition, Steinway had had to hire hundreds of new workers in a very short period of time, so the new factory was filled with inexperienced apprentices.

The net result was that the new factory was not as productive as the old ones. On paper the plan looked good, but it didn't work out that way, an experience that was to be repeated when Steinway modernized in the 1960s. The bottom line was that the number of pianos produced per worker per year went down. In 1858 a hundred piano makers had produced 712 pianos, whereas five years later, after moving into the 53rd Street factory, 400 piano makers manufactured only 1,623 pianos, a decrease of three pianos per worker per year. In their catalog Steinway & Sons claims "that from careful and moderate estimate, they replaced the hand labor of at least 900 workmen" in their new factory. But an audit of Steinway's sales and production figures from 1853 to 1863 proves that this was just not true. Moreover, a special study conducted under the Tenth Federal Census concluded that the mechanical improvements made by Steinway & Sons between 1853 and 1886 had brought about "no perceptible change in the efficiency of labor." More men and more machines did not increase productivity at Steinway & Sons or at any other woodworking factory in the nation. In the 1860s the bulk of the fine work was still done with hand tools. As Alfred Chandler pointed out, by the Civil War most woodworking shops had already substituted machines for the rougher hand operations; hence output could be increased by more men and more machines, but not productivity.[29]

One of the finishing rooms in the new 53rd Street factory. From *Frank Leslie's Illustrated Newspaper*, 28 May 1864.

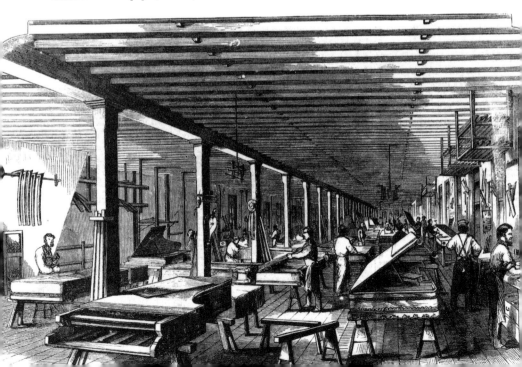

Steinway's rapid rise is nevertheless remarkable. Between 1854 and 1860 the company had gone from barely managing to pay the rent to being the most successful piano makers in the country. What had Henry Steinway, Jr., put into his piano that made it so extraordinary?

Inventing and Marketing
the Modern Piano

H ENRY THREW HIS
soul into the Steinway piano. He was constantly drawing up new plans and
sending them to his brother Theodor, who stayed in Germany largely because his wife, Johanna, hated New York. Even when they did visit finally, in
1864, for the inauguration of Steinway Hall, she insisted that under no
circumstances would they stay longer than a month. Nor did Henry visit
Theodor, because he was afraid of being "badgered by the police and stuck
into the army." The consequences of this fourteen-year, 4,000-mile separation constitute a gold mine for historians, since more than a hundred of the
letters that passed between Henry and Theodor have been saved by the
family.[1]

In these letters, Henry delighted in informing his brother about new
techniques, inventions, ideas, and developments.[2] In them we also read how
Henry worked on a series of problems facing piano manufacturers in the
nineteenth century. One was the plate, which couldn't hold the tension
because it was either made of several pieces of metal or in some pianos still
made of wood. The plate has the appearance of a harp, and its main purpose
is to hold the strings. The trouble with a plate made from several pieces of
metal and even more so a plate made out of wood was that a piano would
need to be tuned during the intermission of a concert because the plate could
not hold the tension of the strings for more than an hour. The plate also
restricted the piano to six and a half octaves. Composers and pianists alike
argued that manufacturers owed them a seven-octave piano. But an additional half-octave, at the treble end of the range, would increase the tension

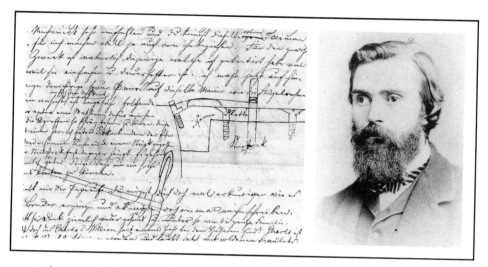

Left: a page of a letter from Henry, Jr., to Theodor, 23 September 1859, showing the pinblock assembly with flanged plate, viewed from the side. "The result," he says, "is a magnificently firm treble since the iron block and the iron frame are moulded in one piece and the wrestplank is firmly pushed against it." *Right:* Henry Steinway, Jr.

on the weakest part of the plate. Moreover, the North American climate, with its extremes of temperature and humidity, played havoc with the wooden plate, causing the wood to expand and contract so much and so often that the plate would literally be pulled apart at the joints and become warped.

As performances shifted from salons accommodating hundreds to concert halls holding thousands, artists and their audiences began to demand a louder, richer, stronger tone from the piano. But the only way to increase the volume was to increase the tension on the strings, and the existing plates could not sustain this.

A full cast-iron plate was one solution. (Other materials were considered suitable, but cast iron was the best and the cheapest.) It could hold the strings under greater tension, thus increasing the length of time a piano could stay in tune and providing a larger, more penetrating tone, and it could resist changes in humidity and temperature better. In 1825 Alpheus Babcock, a Boston craftsman, patented a metal plate cast in one piece for a square piano. For the first time a single piece of cast iron circumscribed the interior of the piano. This meant that thicker, heavier strings could be used, and this, combined with the higher tension, produced a more brilliant, more powerful tone. But there was a drawback: cast iron made the tone thinner and disagreeably tinny. Furthermore, a knocking sound developed as the tuning pins worked their way loose from the plate.[3]

Henry Steinway, Jr., improved the metal frame. First, he changed the shape of the plate, creating a "downward projecting flange" which ran all along the bottom of the plate, overlapping and abutting the tuning-pin block. This situated the plate more solidly in the piano and gave it a firmer grip on the tuning block and pins. Metal studs, called "agraffes," through which the strings passed after leaving the tuning pin, were then screwed into the flange. This constituted a significant start in eliminating the wiry nasal tone and the knocking sound. But Henry didn't stop there.

His big contribution was figuring out how to over-string a grand piano with a one-piece frame and a single soundboard. Over-stringing is the arrangement of the bass strings in a tier above the treble and middle strings, which allows the bass strings to be longer. Henry was not the first to try over-stringing. Henri Pape had experimented with it in tiny uprights as early as 1828, and many American piano makers had tried it in square pianos during the 1830s. But in 1859, when Henry succeeded in making over-stringing work in a grand piano, he was the first.

Henry's over-stringing brought the bridge to the center of the soundboard. Because the center of the soundboard is more elastic than the periphery, placing the strings closer to it produced a richer tone. (In the percussion

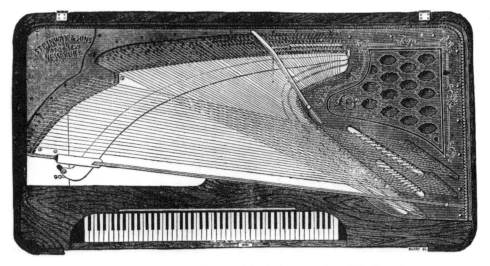

Over-strung scale in square pianos, invented by Steinway & Sons. The first piano so constructed was exhibited at the fair of the American Institute, Crystal Palace, New York, in 1855, and was awarded the first prize, a gold medal.

instruments, hitting the center of a drum creates a more resonant sound.) The bridge is the strip of wood on which the strings rest which transmits their vibrations to the soundboard. All these modifications combined to produce a fuller, stronger tone than that characteristic of other pianos with cast-iron plates.[4] At the same time he fanned the strings out instead of running them parallel to each other. This kept the strings further apart, so that the vibrations of one string did not affect another.

He also overhauled the action. In the early eighteenth century, when Bartolomeo Cristofori "invented" the pianoforte (now called the piano), what he really invented was the action. For this was what transformed a harpsichord into a piano. On a harpsichord the tone is produced by the pressure of the finger on a key which pushes a quill on the other end of the key shaft to pluck a string. By contrast, Cristofori's action set in motion a hammer, a small wooded knob of tightly rolled parchment glued into a cup of wood and covered with deerskin, in free flight at the string. The force with which the hammer hit the string was controlled by the pressure of the player's finger on the key. This enabled the player to produce not only loud and soft tones but also gradations of tone from soft (*piano*) to loud (*forte*)— hence the piano's original name, "un gravicembalo con piano e forte," a harpsichord with soft and loud. On such an instrument the player could diminish the tone gradually and then return to full volume, something easily done with the bow on a violin, hammers on a dulcimer, or the human voice, but not on a harpsichord.

In 1821, Sebastien Erard, a native of Alsace, invented what he called the "double-escapement." Even as his action propelled the hammer toward the string, the hammer was ready to be thrown again, while the key was still coming up. So if the pianist struck the key before it had come all the way back up, it would deliver the hammer with the same force and produce the same delicate (or thunderous) sound again and again and again. Without Erard's invention, according to musicologist Rosamond E. Harding, "the art of pianoforte playing could not have attained the state of perfection to which it has now risen; in fact we may say that modern pianoforte technique was built upon it."

Henry Steinway, Jr., was the mid-century master at making actions more responsive. Four of his six patents were for inventions that provided a very quick, very easy repetition of the blow of the hammer. Some critics insisted that Erard's pianos were unapproachable, but Henry's action was fully equal to Erard's action.[5]

With all these improvements in place, Henry bragged in 1859 that "nobody ever built one like ours." Several contemporary accounts refer not only to the "great power of tone" of the Steinway but also to the "depth and richness in the bass, a full mellowness in the middle register and brilliant purity in the treble." Charles summed up what was becoming evident to all when he said: "our over-strung grand pianos are really fabulous; they have a fuller and stronger sound than the regular grand pianos that we made. . . . Other piano makers are already imitating us."[6]

The so-called Steinway system included all Henry's achievements: a cast-iron plate with a downward projecting flange, longer and heavier over-strung bass strings fanning out over the center of the soundboard, a vibrant soundboard with the bridges closer to the center, and a responsive action that gave performers more control over the new power at their fingertips. Some of these things were his own invention, some the result of heavy borrowing from others. Whenever another manufacturer had come up with a new piano, Henry had hardly been able to wait to open the lid, examine the mechanism, and draw the parts that interested him. But nobody had ever put it all together like this before. This was the modern piano, and it has not changed much since 1859. By the end of the century most of the major piano manufacturers in the United States and Europe were imitating Henry's construction, and all pianos today use the Steinway system, although the term is no longer used, because there is no alternative around.[7]

Henry had produced the finest piano ever made. Now he had to convince the public. He started with the old and honorable practice of soliciting artists' endorsements, a practice that goes back to Bach, who in the 1740s played and praised Silbermann's improved piano at Potsdam, thereby promoting a sale to Frederick the Great. In 1777 Mozart privately praised Johann Andreas Stein's piano, proclaiming in a letter that Stein's love of music had enabled him to produce the finest instrument going. John Broadwood, the English piano maker, sent an instrument by ship from London to Trieste and then had it carried by horse and wagon 360 miles over the Alps to Vienna for Beethoven's approval. Even before the piano arrived, Beethoven wrote to Broadwood: "I shall regard it as an altar upon which I will place the choicest offerings of my mind to the divine Apollo. As soon as I shall have received your excellent instrument, I will send you the fruits of the inspiration of the first moments I shall spend with it." By the opening years of the nineteenth century almost every European piano manufacturer was seeking acclaim by association.

In America Sigismond Thalberg, one of the most celebrated pianists to visit that country in the 1850s, performed regularly on a Chickering, so launching artists' endorsements on the other side of the Atlantic. During Thalberg's 1856–58 seasons Chickering shipped specially selected pianos to cities on Thalberg's fifty-six-concert itinerary. Local dealers oversaw each instrument's placement and tuning in the concert hall, at no charge to the artist. They displayed the piano before the concert and put it on the show-room floor for sale after the performance. Although there was no written agreement, concert advertisements and programs associated Thalberg with Chickering.[8]

In 1859, Henry Steinway started soliciting testimonials, too, sending pianos to the most influential artists in Europe for their endorsement. Later, he instructed Theodor to send a grand piano to Franz Liszt in Weimar, "to prove that musically we're not so far behind here as one generally assumes in Europe." He realized that it would be expensive to do this but believed, like many other piano manufacturers at the time, that an encomium from Liszt would pay for itself ten times over. Indeed, Liszt had so many unsolicited pianos that his homes looked like piano showrooms. In 1861, Liszt told music historian C. F. Weitzmann:

> As for the pianos in my possession, in Altenburg (near Weimar), [he had not yet received his Steinway] there [were] the following instruments: 1 Erard in the reception room on the first floor, 1 Bechstein in the little salon next door - 1 Boisselot (Marseille) in [his] study and workroom. . . . In the so-called music room (2nd floor) there [were] two Viennese grand pianos by Streicher and Bösendorfer, and in the other room there [was] a Hungarian one by Beregszay.

Fifteen years later a Steinway was added to the inventory.[9] In 1872 Steinway & Sons sponsored Anton Rubinstein's first and only American tour and by the end of the century was managing Paderewski in America, providing him with pianos and tuners in exchange for his endorsement.

Back in 1866, the Steinway & Sons catalog boasted a fifteen-page section of what were entitled "certificates." William Mason, pianist and teacher, and Carl Bergmann, conductor of the New York Philharmonic, in addition to twenty other distinguished artists, exalted the depth, richness, and volume of the Steinway. They showered praise on the elasticity and promptness of its action and on its durability under the severest trials. They judged that "the Steinway pianos, in all respects, [were] the best instruments made in this country or Europe." There was also a statement signed by twenty-four "artists of the Italian and German opera and other celebrated vocalists," claiming that they had "never met with any instruments, not even of the most celebrated manufactories of Europe, which have given us such entire satisfaction, especially as regards their unequalled qualities for accompany-ing the voice, and keeping in tune for so long a time."

Henry also courted newspapers, critics, and sheet music publishers and expected his brothers to do the same. He was irate when Theodor failed to get a statement from Henry Litolff, a pioneer in publishing inexpensive classical sheet music, but was delighted when Charles "made the acquaintance of a certain Mr. Gottschalg from Weimar, [who was] good friends with Franz Liszt. [Gottschalg] wrote for several newspapers and was the publisher of a musical dictionary." At that meeting Charles bribed Gottschalg, whom Henry called a "hungry penny-a-line scribbler," to get a "very favorable" review in the *Allgemeine Zeitung*. This would not be the last time Steinway paid for a first-rate review.[10]

In a letter to their agents and dealers, Steinway asked them to subscribe to C. B. Seymour's new journal the *New York Musical Review* and solicit subscriptions from friends and the public. Seymour was the music and drama critic of the *New York Daily Times*. Steinway & Sons emphasized that Seymour "has contributed vastly to our success through the medium of his pen in the columns of the leading papers in the U.S."[11] This practice was probably more widespread than is documented. Paying off the music critics was good for business, and it's a fair supposition that Steinway & Sons wasn't the only company doing it.

In search of the ultimate testimonial, a European gold medal, Henry Steinway, Jr., entered his piano in London's great international exhibition. On a blustery March evening in 1862 he and his brothers packed two square pianos and two grands for the voyage to England. To safeguard against disaster, they split the shipment, sending two pianos to Liverpool and the other two, with Henry, on the steamer *City of New York* to London.

Henry Steinway, Jr., was one of almost a hundred American exhibitors, a small but significant number given that the United States was in the midst of the Civil War. (Steinway & Sons was listed in the official directory as from "North America—Federal States," because the States were not United in 1862.) The *London Musical World* remarked how curious it was that, with war in the United States and peace in England, Birmingham should be manufacturing arms to send to America, while New York was making pianos to send to London, and expressed its delight that "the peaceful arts still flourish" across the Atlantic.

These international fairs were breeding grounds for new technology and meeting places for both technicians and manufacturers from Europe and North America. More than six million people attended the London exhibition of 1862. Many came to buy something from the 26,239 items on display, which included 269 pianos from all over the world. But on some days it seemed as if everyone was at the Steinway booth. According to one eyewitness, the best pianists in London flocked around the Steinways and played on them from morning til night. Artists lined up both to play and to look inside. If they couldn't find someone to unlock the top for them, they would break the instrument open. Steinways were being devoured.

Then it was the jury's turn. Its members were impressed but were not as ecstatic as the crowd—or as they should have been. They awarded Steinway & Sons a medal for "powerful, clear, brilliant, and sympathetic tone, with excellence of workmanship, as shown in grand and square pianos." They recognized Steinway as ahead of all the other manufacturers from the United States and as among the top eight, along with Broadwood, Pleyel, Bechstein, and others. Steinway was number one from the United States, but only first in a field of four. Furthermore, they were not unusual as Americans doing well in London. Of ninety-eight American exhibitors, eighty won prizes. Almost all of them went home with some kind of medal and some sort of praise. But the medal for the best piano in the exhibition was awarded to the English manufacturer Broadwood. The judges praised its iron plate, which, unlike Steinway's, was not cast in one piece, and awarded Broadwood a medal "for excellence in every kind of piano power and quality of tone, precision of mechanism, and solidity." The jury erroneously concluded that Steinway's over-stringing was like that seen in Russian pianos exhibited at the 1851 London exhibition. But they had overlooked the revolutionary nature of Henry's piano. Reviewers were mistakenly confident that England was still the center of the piano-manufacturing world, and the judges were trying to prove England's preeminence by giving Broadwood the gold. They didn't realize that this very moment marked the end of England's dominance in the field.

Piano maker Johann Baptist Streicher recognized that Broadwood would no longer set the standard and went back to Vienna to begin making copies of the Steinway. The Vienna press insisted that "Steinway's method seems to us to have the greatest capacity of development, the most of the future in it." In another account Steinway's medal, albeit not a gold, was viewed as one more sign that America was superseding Europe. The Steinway piano was placed on a growing list of American triumphs: the yacht *America*, the chess master Paul Morphy, and the Singer sewing machine.

At home Steinway was praised for its "quality of tone, touch, excellence of workmanship, and elegance of appearance." The United States Official Report placed Steinway & Sons "at the head of the whole list of instruments of that class." Predicting a reversal in the flow of high culture, not recognized by the jury at the fair, the *New York Times* reported that "the folly of sending pianos from America to Europe nearly excited laughter"; but when the cases were opened and people heard the sound of a Steinway, it became evident that these German-Americans had set the standard for piano construction

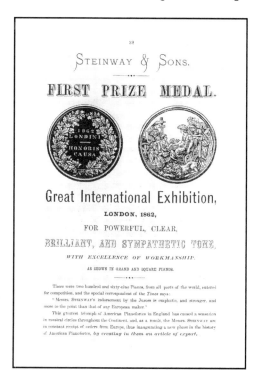

Steinway & Sons' first prize medal from the 1862 London exhibition. From the 1870 sales catalog.

and tone. In October 1862, however, it didn't look all that hopeful for Henry Steinway, Jr. His piano had not been the smash international hit with the judges that he had hoped for or that it should have been. At the end of the exhibition he sold all four pianos, took orders for more, and sailed home to suffer the upheavals of his adopted country, which was at war with itself, a battle with his workers, and the sickness raging in his own body.[12]

THREE

Riots, Strikes, and Domestic Tragedies

THE CIVIL WAR CREATED
hardships for both those on the battlefield and those at home. Piano manufacturers in the North lost all instruments on loan to dealers in the South and all claims against them. At the same time supplies crucial to piano making, like lumber and metal, were in short supply because they were being diverted to the war effort. Limited supplies, not only for piano production but for everything, increased prices, as the same dollars chased fewer goods. This national inflation bred disgruntled workers whose salaries were not keeping pace with wartime prices. As workers demanded and obtained higher salaries, manufacturers either decreased their payrolls by laying off people or increased the price of goods. In the summer of 1861 some thirty thousand people roamed the streets of New York City looking for work. At Steinway & Sons, pay cuts and layoffs occurred in every department; only the office clerks, salesmen, and foremen were unaffected.[1]

In October 1862, when Henry, Jr., returned from the London exhibition, all dealers were notified that retail prices of pianos would increase by $25 due to increases in the costs of materials. This increase did not cover the 30 percent rise in manufacturing costs, the higher tariffs, a national tax of 3 percent, and the new income tax. In 1859 Steinway's cheapest piano had sold for $275; by the end of the war a Steinway couldn't be had for less than $500.[2]

Charles Steinway was in New York's mostly German 5th Regiment from April until August of 1861. Henry, although a strong supporter of the party of Lincoln, was against all "military humbug." Charles, about to go off to battle during the opening weeks of the Civil War, scribbled a touching "auf Wiedersehen" to his family:

> Right in this moment I am sitting here in uniform and sabre to wrap up my figures and invoices, just in order to leave for Washington as the paymaster of the 5th Regiment of the New York militia. Tomorrow around 1 o'clock we will leave on the steamer Baltic for Annapolis, Maryland. From there on foot and via railroad to Washington. My wife is of course very sad but calm and collected! Let's hope that I'll return to tell you all about the experiences of life in war and in the field. If I shouldn't return, well farewell to you and your sweet Johanna [Theodor's wife]! And remember your brother as often as you can. I love you all very dearly![3]

In May 1861 his regiment took part in the occupation of Arlington Heights, Virginia. Fearing that Charles might die and leave his share of the partnership to his wife, the family modified the copartnership agreement to restrict the rights of Steinway women: they could inherit the value of their husbands' share in the business but could not become partners in Steinway & Sons. The family's apprehensions were twofold: they didn't want women controlling the company, and they wanted to keep Steinway & Sons shares in the bloodline and out of the hands of in-laws.[4]

On 3 July 1863 Albert joined the war in Pennsylvania, serving as a first lieutenant with the 5th Regiment at Harrisburg, Marysville, Carlisle, and Chambersburg, all about thirty miles from Gettysburg. When his regiment left town, the horrifying news of the three days' bloodshed battling Lee's army in the open fields of Gettysburg was probably just trickling in.[5] A week later, to fill the ranks of the decimated Northern military, the draft began in New York City. To start the draft on a Saturday, 11 July, when New York troops were still in Pennsylvania was dangerous. It gave people all day Sunday to gather in saloons and complain about a war that was not going to benefit them.

The Irish did not want any part in the Civil War. They were against the draft and against a war that, as they saw it, would free African-Americans to come north and take their jobs. Living in the worst housing, plagued by the highest infant death rate, and starved by the lowest wages, the Irish were angry and were ready to revolt against what they saw as a "rich man's war and a poor man's fight." The idea of conscription was un-American; wars were fought by patriotic men. Until that summer of 1863 all wars in the United States had been fought by a volunteer army. The Civil War had in fact

begun with volunteer armies, but by 1863 both North and South had re-
sorted to the draft to fill their ranks.[6]

They started protesting on Sunday, and by Monday, William Steinway
noted in his diary, there was "terrible excitement throughout the city, resis-
tance to the draft. Row of buildings on Third Ave. burning down, also on
Lexington Ave. Various other buildings fired by the mob."[7] The focus of the
violence quickly shifted from the draft to race. African-Americans were
hunted down all day, beaten, and lynched. The mob held the city from
Union Square (14th Street) to Central Park (59th Street). The leaders incited
the crowd to plunder. Residences of abolitionists were burned, the households of the wealthy were sacked, and stores like Brooks Brothers were
raided.

Late in the afternoon the mob reached the Steinway factory gates. William anxiously noted: "Charles speaks to them and with the aid of Reverend
Father Mahon [and Mr. O'Connor] they draw off towards Yorkville where
late in the eve[ning] many buildings [were] fired. Father, Charles [and Wil-
liam] stay in the factory office till 1 A.M. then go to bed." During his meeting
with the mob Charles gave the ringleaders $20 to $40 cash and one a check
for $30, about a month's wage for most laborers in 1860. The payoffs were to
prevent the destruction of the factory. As it turned out, a thunderstorm
ended the first day of rioting, keeping everyone off the streets that night.[8]

The next day rioters attacked factories, station houses, gun stores, railroad tracks, and telegraph lines. The owners of factories, like Steinway, tried
to buy peace, but the mob continued to sack houses, taverns, and stores,
taking jewelry, furniture, silver, food, and weapons. Stores and boardinghouses known to serve the African-Americans, although run by Germans,
were pillaged and burned. The rioters tried to destroy the colored church on
30th Street between Seventh and Eighth Avenue. Some five thousand rioters
assembled near Eighth Avenue and 32nd Street and proceeded to pillage
houses and hang African-Americans. Wealthy white New Yorkers crowded
boats and trains leaving the city. But the Harlem Railroad (which ran along
Fourth [Park] Avenue) and Third Avenue tracks, on the east side of town,
were soon torn up by the mob, as was the west-side Hudson River Railroad,
which slowed the exodus. At the end of the day, Steinway recorded "heavy
fires in the evening. Factory stopped work yesterday and today. All business in the upper part of the city suspended. Negroes chased everywhere
and killed when caught." Most of New York's thirteen thousand African-
Americans tried to leave town; many of those who couldn't were beaten,
burned, or lynched.[9]

William, so upset that he couldn't eat, walked down to the store on
Walker Street that evening to keep watch over the building. He stayed there

Rioters chasing an African-American family through vacant lots on Lexington Avenue. From *New York Illustrated News,* 1 August 1863.

all night. Only after four days of rioting did army regiments reach the city. On arriving, the 7th and 31st regiments fortified the town with a force of more than fifteen hundred policemen, five hundred volunteers, and a thousand patrolmen. With such an armed presence, William reported "comparative quiet in the city. . . . All the cars and stages resume running and some shops working. No more fires. Charles stays up till 1 A.M. watching in the shop." A heavy storm quieted the city that night.[10]

On Friday most Steinway workers returned to the factory. By Monday even the Irish had come back. In the shop William found to his horror "that all the knapsacks of the 5th Regiment [Charles's and Albert's Regiment] had been moved to the basement," transferred there with Albert's or Charles's endorsement, apparently. Soldiers were sent to the showroom on Walker Street to retrieve the 5th Regiment's knapsacks. William went to the armory, Lafayette Hall, to see Albert and his company on duty there. A few days later Albert mustered out of his regiment.[11] One of the worst riots in the history of American cities was over. More than a hundred people had died, and many more had been injured.

The discontent remained, however. At the local level jobs and income remained critical issues, certainly for the piano workers. In 1859 some workers had organized into a union named the "United Pianoforte Makers." But, according to a *New York Herald* report, they had attracted only 250 of the 1,200 piano makers in the city because the proceedings had been conducted in German. Those of other nationalities refrained from joining, and the union became known as the "German Pianomakers' Society." This was not the only German-American union in New York City: the German Joiners claimed 1,000 members, and the German Cabinetmakers 550. By 1863 the proceedings were being conducted in English, and a larger society of some three thousand New York City piano workers was formed, the Piano Makers' Union.

In October the new union presented a set of demands: a 25 percent pay raise, the right to review all firings, 100 percent union membership of workers (closed shop), full employment throughout the year (even during the slow seasons), and weekly inspection of the factory ledgers.

Charles Steinway, along with the other twenty-two piano manufacturers in New York, presented a united response to these demands. They formed the "Pianoforte Manufacturers' Society of New York," uniting the employers. Each member was required to place in a fund $20 per worker, which would be forfeited if he broke the alliance. The owners explained to the union that no such wage increases had been awarded in Boston, Baltimore, or Philadelphia and that if they gave in, it would lead to an increase in piano prices, thereby insuring a loss of sales and then jobs. One manufacturer, Albert Weber, sarcastically added: "Gentlemen employees, your demands are exceedingly moderate; but in your very modesty you have omitted your most important point." When the spokesman of the employees inquired what that might be, he replied: "Simply this, that every Saturday afternoon, when you have looked over the manufacturers' books, the employees shall go bowling, and that the bosses should be made to set up the ten-pins for their workmen."

According to William Steinway, the "unanimous roar of laughter" after Weber's quip broke the ice in the negotiations and persuaded the workers to accept an immediate 15 percent raise, with a promise of 10 percent more when business improved. All agreed on the new pay scale. Within a month Steinway raised the prices of its pianos: a 6⅞-octave rosewood square piano that had sold for $218 (wholesale) in 1862 would now sell for $288, an increase of 32 percent, which more than covered the increased labor costs. Nor did the price increase decrease sales as the manufacturers had predicted.[12]

Henry did not take part in the labor negotiations. He had returned from the London exhibition with a debilitating cough, and, not long after, his wife Ernestine had found him one night roaming the house, spouting irrational phrases. She had run next door to William, describing her husband as "deranged." Henry was sane but very sick. Later in the week, William was startled to find his thirty-three-year-old brother "flushed & tinctured with small red spots all over." The doctor diagnosed his condition as chronic rheumatism and confined him to bed. But when winter set in, two months after the strike was settled, Henry was shipped off to Cuba for six months' rest and recovery.

Henry described Cuba, with its healing, warm south wind, as the "Eldorado for all spitters and sufferers from consumption." He and his wife, pregnant with their third child, stayed at the Hotel Inglaterra, which was "situated on the most beautiful park with a view on the Gulf of Mexico." It cost them $15–20 a day, more than the average weekly salary of most piano workers. There were some four hundred Germans in Havana, enough to support an exquisite German club outfitted with billiards, fencing, foreign newspapers, and an assortment of Rhine wines. Henry wrote to his brother Theodor that, "since they all know our firm and our renown, I had a friendly acceptance!" When not in his club or hotel, he found life in Havana dirty, expensive, and exotic.

His cough improved, but only when the south winds were blowing. After five months in Cuba Henry realized that the illness was deeply rooted in his system. A slight cold spell—anything under 75 degrees—could bring on a cold, a cough, and eventually pleurisy. He was never sure whether his ears were better or whether he had simply become used to the hammering and buzzing sounds.

In spite of his ailments, Henry sent lengthy letters back to New York about life in Cuba, where northerners and southerners recuperated side by side and shared Civil War stories. In January 1864 Henry reassured his brothers that "if you think that my confidence in our government's ability to bring the war to a successful conclusion is shaken, you are absolutely wrong. That we are on our way to success you can't see more clearly than right here when you see the doleful, downright depressed faces of the 'Chivalry' here after they have received the so-called Southern mail (via Wilmington and Nassau); then one can see how things are, and the candid ones do not conceal it anymore."[13] In other letters Henry made serious suggestions as to how to improve the action, modify the stringing, preserve the finish, and enrich the tone on Steinway pianos. He also worked on a few Steinway pianos in Cuba, had a grand piano sent to him so that he could drum up some business, and advised his brothers on arbitrating labor unrest.[14]

The piano business had recovered, but the employers did not keep their promise with regard to the extra 10 percent wage increase. Most workers accepted the postponement, but not those at Steinway & Sons and Decker Brothers. And by the end of the month the rest of the piano workers had joined them. Some twelve hundred went out on strike for a 10 percent increase. Nor were they alone. House carpenters, laborers, mechanics, carvers, cabinetmakers, and other woodworkers also went on strike. New York City saw more than a hundred and fifty strikes during this period. Increases in workers' living costs had outstripped increases in wages, so that by 1864 they had lost more than 30 cents a day in real terms. In 1864 manufacturing wages were around 97 cents a day, down from $1.30 in 1860.

Henry, revealing a surprisingly strong resentment of his workers for a company that had always prided itself on being one big happy family, advised his brothers to ignore the strike. He had more faith in the skilled labor pool in New York than his brothers, who were reluctant to thumb their noses at all four hundred of their piano workers. However, he too feared that the workers might find other livelihoods and so ruin the New York piano business. By early March the strike was in full swing, and Henry, ensconced in Cuba, followed it with "great suspense and excitement." He pleaded with William to "send me everything that is written about the strike, cards and rejoinders. You only sent me your response this time, but I would like to know what they have to say." He suggested to Charles that he use the down time to renovate the machines and the boiler rooms. He cautioned William not to take the workers' bluff too seriously: "Don't let yourself be concerned, even if [the workers] move everything out of the shop, that doesn't mean anything, they'll move it all back again." Henry considered the men to be "completely untrustworthy" and advised his brother to stop trying to appease such a boorish bunch. They will "blame us for everything," Henry concluded, and hate us, no matter what we do.[15]

After four weeks William and Charles were concerned that the strike had gone on so long. They had just opened Steinway Hall on 14th Street, orders were going unfilled, some of the Steinway workers had formed their own business, the "New York Piano Company," and dealers were pressuring them about unfilled orders. They proposed to their fellow manufacturers that they give the workers a 10 percent increase; but, as William recorded in his diary, the others were resolved "not to offer any advance." Then, in the fifth week of the strike, they resolved that each boss be free to settle with his own men but not to exceed 10 percent and not to take each other's workmen.[16] William, clearly more paternalistic than Henry, translated all these decisions into German for his workers. And on 11 April, after twelve hundred workers had been out for seven weeks, a mass meeting was held to celebrate piano worker stamina and the winning of the 10 percent increase. Steinway again raised its prices to cover the increase in the cost of labor and materials. The cheapest piano, a rosewood 7-octave square, increased in price from $385 (retail) to $410, and the most expensive, a large rosewood 7⅓-octave grand, from $1,200 to 1,300.

Henry recognized that the manufacturers had been foolish to renege on the 10 percent increase in the first place and that the workers would "never make up for these eight weeks of not working and using up their savings," adding that "if our army will be beaten this spring instead of being victorious and the long feared and predicted money and business crisis (which showed already some symptoms) actually happens: then in a single blow it will be all over" for the North—employers and workers.[17]

Feeling better, and bored with being a deck-chair piano maker, Henry returned to New York during the warm month of May 1864. He discovered that his brother Charles, who had been very busy managing the factory, had been suffering from earaches and chest pains since Christmas. Ironically, it was Charles, back in 1853, who had foretold that New York would kill Germans with chest or lung diseases.

On Christmas Day 1863 Charles had fallen ill and been confined to bed for two weeks. According to William, the next few months were fine, but then in early May 1864, just before Henry came back, Charles's ear had swelled enormously, causing him intense pain. Subsequently he was operated on, but it did not help, and the pain became unbearable. In early July he and his family sailed for Europe in search of a cure for his inflamed throat and ringing ears.

Doctors in Germany diagnosed his symptoms as reflecting no more than an infection of the mucous membrane and catarrh. He was told to wash his ears with warm soapy water, gargle with herbal concoctions, and wait. Theodor confessed to William that he had misgivings about Charles's health and didn't think that he would be returning to New York too soon. "His nervous system was quite seriously destroyed and all doctors had maintained that his ear problems would recur as surely as somebody who has once had the sniffles would get them again with the next cold."[18] Ironically, Henry and now Charles, the most talented piano makers of their time, were racked with earaches. Like Beethoven, these men who had brought beautiful music to millions were doomed to listen to an endless buzzing or knocking in their ears.

Henry, faced with frigid New York winter winds, became incapacitated once again. On Christmas Day 1864 William reported that Henry was low with rheumatism and suffering dreadfully. His condition grew worse in

January and February: his feet and hands were swollen, and his lungs ravaged by fits of coughing. On a gray winter's morning in early March 1865, the greatest piano maker of his time died of tuberculosis.

Henry was only thirty-four when he died. Pastor Steins of the German Presbyterian Church officiated at his funeral and the Arion Society sang. There was a long funeral procession of people from the music world and a ferry-boat ride to the Steinway plot at Greenwood Cemetery in Brooklyn. The *New York Times* obituary summed up Henry's achievements thus: "Mr. Steinway had reduced the manufacture of piano-forte to a science and it is probable that few men ever lived who were better acquainted with the construction of the instrument."[19]

His wife Ernestine was left with three daughters, Lilian, Anna, and Clarissa, all under five. According to the copartnership agreement of 1863, Ernestine couldn't inherit her husband's share of the business, but, in lieu of a partnership in Steinway & Sons, she was paid a cash equivalent which in 1865 amounted to $200,000. The money was invested in mortgages and became the trust fund of Henry's estate. Two-thirds of the interest went to the children's education and support and one-third to Ernestine. Each daughter would take control of her share of the estate from its executor and guardian, William, as she came of age.

Within seven months of Henry's death Ernestine married Charles J. Oaks and left for a clandestine honeymoon in Europe. When William found out, a month after the wedding, he was embarrassed by the secret marriage to Oaks and the rumors building around the hasty wedding. Ernestine had met Oaks three or four months after Henry died, while she was living with her sister-in-law Wilhelmina Steinway Candidus on Staten Island. Oaks was a coachman, and, according to one of the servants, they would frequently go out on horseback rides into the wilds of Staten Island. William suspected Ernestine of having had a long-term love affair with Oaks, going back before her husband's death, and Oaks of being a fortune hunter, intent on living off the interest of Henry's estate. In William's eyes, Oaks was not the man to raise his brother's children. But most of all, William was annoyed because Ernestine, then twenty-three years old, was not deferring to him as the patriarch he thought he had become at the age of thirty.

Under the terms of the will, William and Theodor authorized Charles Koch, Theodor's old friend and "counsel for the crown of Brunswick," a state prosecutor, to find a "proper" home for the girls. Koch decided that the babies should stay in his own household until "Mrs. Oaks has established a new home, and her husband has proven to be a 'gentleman' who knows more than to sponge on his wife's money," and that she should be permitted to visit the children occasionally, after an appropriate amount of time had passed for friends of the Steinway family to come to terms with her remarriage.

Ernestine's response, according to Koch, was to admit that she had failed and deserved to be reproached, but to plead against having her children taken away. Throwing herself on William's mercy, she appealed to him to forgive her rush to the altar, explaining, "I may have walked the world for years and may not have found one that I cared so much for as I do for him, can I help that he was thrown in my path so prematurely?"

Having initially agreed that giving up her children for a while might be the best solution for them, she then changed her mind, telling William that it was impossible for her to give them up. William could see that the only way to spirit them away from her was to tighten the purse strings. As executor of his brother's will, he sent a letter to Ernestine's landlord in January, stating that until she "complied with the instructions and wishes of the guardian with reference to her children" he would under no circumstances agree to any advance payments or pay any debts she might incur. Ernestine had no other income, and the support payments to date were not even covering her expenses. She had already taken advances on the July payment. Moreover, William suspended child support. Through Koch, he threatened her with eviction from Brunswick as a vagrant, unless she handed over her children to Koch. By January 1866 Ernestine was out of money and gave up her girls, Lilian, Anna, and Clarissa, to Koch. The next month she and Charles Oaks sailed for New York. She wrote to William that the reason she had returned from Europe was "to hear from your lips what you intend to do in regard to my children, whom you have taken and given to the care of strangers. I will say nothing of the means you employed, to get them." What she wanted to know was whether William intended to restore her children to her or not. She also wanted an allowance of $250 per month.[20]

After living in New York for more than two years without her daughters, amid rumors that they were playing in the streets of Brunswick unattended, Ernestine renounced her subservient, apologetic demeanor, which she had thought would persuade William to give her back her children. On 6 May she sued William for custody, claiming that "her little ones were wrongfully and fraudulently withheld from her." She also claimed that William, as executor, was selling off her dead husband's property to himself and other family members at bargain prices. Steinway Hall, she claimed, was worth $400,000 (it was probably worth at least $200,000) and had been sold to the family for $82,000. Her share would be a quarter of that. William responded in June, and the case came before the Brooklyn Supreme Court that summer. After hearing testimony from William, his father, Heinrich, who testified in German through an interpreter, and other family members, the judge decided that "to take the children from her would be an act of cruelty." She was their mother. Although William was acting "from the best motives," he had nevertheless committed a legal wrong. The court judged that Henry's will did not give William any "legal or equitable right to the custody" of his brother's children, who were to be given exclusively to Ernestine.

Henry wasn't the only brother William lost in 1865. Less than a month after Henry died, Charles too went to his grave. The tragedy was that, having recovered from his ear and chest pains, he decided to visit the principal cities of Germany before returning home.[21] The trip killed him. In the course of it, he consumed some contaminated food or water and subsequently died of typhoid fever in Theodor's home.

He was only thirty-six when he died. His death "aged me by five years," Theodor later recalled, "and my health was very precarious at that point." Theodor decided to delay the bad news. Instead of a cable reporting Charles's death to the family, he sent a letter, which he knew would take at least three to four weeks to cross the Atlantic. He wanted time to think, and he wanted to give his parents a bit of time before reporting another son's death. He was stunned by his younger brother's sudden end, concerned about the health of his other brother, William, and anxious about the anticipated call for him to come to New York.

General Robert E. Lee had recently surrendered at Appomattox Court House, and Lincoln had just been inaugurated for a second term. Steinway & Sons had participated in the parade to celebrate the Northern victory with three carriages, one carrying the Steinway piano. But the celebration was short-lived, because on 14 April Lincoln was assassinated at Fords Theatre in Washington. The following Monday there was gloom throughout the country as businesses shut down and the nation mourned the loss of its president.[22] On 24 April Lincoln's funeral train arrived in New York for public viewing, only a day before the arrival of Theodor's letter on the twenty-fifth.

The letter was addressed to William, to whom it fell to tell his parents that they had just lost another son. William felt overwhelmed and incapable of running Steinway & Sons alone. Moreover, Papa, now sixty-eight, was not well.

William, who had just turned thirty, finding himself with sole responsibility for Steinway & Sons, the preeminent piano house in the nation, with total assets of almost three-quarters of a million dollars, appealed to Theodor to sell his business in Brunswick and join him in New York as a partner. Theodor resisted. He feared that the pace in New York would kill him the way it had killed his two brothers. He pleaded with William to allow him to stay in Brunswick and lead the life that their dead brother Charles always envied. He had three times as many orders as he could fill, a comfortable house, and was too accustomed to his routines to change. And for the first time he was making money. He thanked William for the generous offer but refused, explaining that "I do not see how I could close down my business here without the most tremendous losses." He advised William to either make Henry Kroeger, the factory foreman, a partner or sell out. If the latter, he could take the capital from the sale, "which will be respectable under any circumstances" and "retire to Europe from that land of iniquity where the worst is yet to come." At the very least, Theodor argued, Charles's widow, Sophie, and three sons should move to Brunswick "so that these youths, on whom, for the time being, rests the entire continuous existence of the family, will receive a good education."[23]

William said no to this last possibility. After fifteen years he was too much an American to return to Germany. He put pressure on Theodor to come to New York and help him save the business. He pointed out that Theodor owed everything to his family: they had given him money, machines, and pianos for the past ten years. He had been floundering on his own and had only recently begun to make a living. Charles had jested at the 1860 opening of the 53rd Street factory about their immense business in Brunswick which was producing all of ten pianos a year. As recently as 1863 Theodor's cash on hand barely equaled the amount of money he had borrowed from his family.

Theodor recognized his obligations and agreed that if it were unavoidable, he would give up his business and move to New York. William collected on that debt. In October 1865 Theodor joined William in New York and that January became a full partner in Steinway & Sons. He sold the Brunswick business to his three employees F. Wilhelm Grotrian, Adolph Helfferich, and H. G. W. Schulz, allowing them the privilege of continuing for ten years under the name "Successors to C. F. Theodor Steinweg." As the Steinway name became more distinguished, Theodor's agreement to give these non–family members, now competitors, permission to use the Steinweg name, models, measurements, and scales (the whole plan and proportions of the instrument) became grounds for Grotrian continuing to use the Steinweg name after the ten years were up. Indeed, the issue of Grotrian-Steinweg selling pianos under the illustrious Steinweg name lasted in and out of court for more than a hundred years.[24]

Theodor took over Henry's post. He contributed a great deal to Steinway & Sons, filing forty-five patents during the next twenty years. His productivity was impressive compared to that of Henry, Jr., in part because he lived longer. One of his most important patents was for a wood-bending contraption for forming the curved shape of a grand piano case. He also experimented with dividing the strings to elicit a richer tone. At the same time he intentionally erased the name of Henry, Jr., on all Steinway improvements. Several decades later his assistant and nephew Henry Ziegler said that he always suspected that Theodor had destroyed traces of Henry's work.

William supported this elimination of Henry's name from Steinway ledgers and promoted Theodor's patents as if each one were a holy grail. Together they rewrote the history of Steinway & Sons, substituting Theodor for Henry in the star role. After all, Henry, Jr., was dead, and William needed a live Steinway as public guardian of quality and innovation. But although Theodor refined Henry's work, his own work never warranted him the title "architect of the modern Steinway." As it was, however, with Albert and the founder dead, it remained for Theodor and William to take Steinway & Sons to the end of the century.[25]

FOUR

Steinway *Becomes a Household Word*

ILLIAM STEINWAY loved music. He played the piano, had a captivating tenor voice, and even with his extremely busy schedule always found time to sing several times a week with the Liederkranz, one of the oldest and largest musical societies in the country. He was its president for fourteen years, and when he and his family sailed for Europe, which was often, members of the Liederkranz would sometimes see them off at the dock and sing as they boarded the ship. William was also a patron of music. He supported most of the concerts in the city and helped finance the Metropolitan Opera, the New York Philharmonic, and the symphony orchestras of Theodore Thomas and Walter Damrosch. He associated with major New York-based pianists such as William Mason, Sebastian Bach Mills, and Leopold de Meyer. William Steinway was Mr. Music in late nineteenth-century New York City.[1]

William assumed that linking the Steinway name with the development of musical taste in America would define Steinway & Sons as both patrons and makers of the preferred piano on the concert stage, thereby establishing it as a household word synonymous with culture. He expected this to breed a loyalty, give a certain panache to his pianos, and increase sales. According to Henry T. Finck, music critic for the *New York Evening Post* from 1881 to 1924, everybody looked to William Steinway. "Every orchestral or chamber music association was backed by him, nor did he overlook even the opera companies; he once helped Abbey, [Schoeffel], and Grau [the management company who handled the Metropolitan Opera 1891–97] to the tune of $50,000." He was even generous to Finck, giving his bride an upright piano

William Steinway, 1868.

at cost as a wedding gift. Theodor Steinway did not think these investments would pay off. He complained that "the damned artists consider piano makers a cow to be milked. I wish I could invent a piano which makes you stupid and seasick—I would donate one to each of them."[2]

To provide a shrine for his piano, William supervised the building of the second largest concert hall in New York City, locating it directly behind Steinway's elegant showrooms, which had opened two years earlier, in 1864. It was not a new idea. Johann Streicher had built a public concert hall in his Viennese piano factory, and in Paris, Erard and Pleyel had built their own concert halls. All Steinway pianos, no matter what their destination, whether dealer, public school, or private customer, came through the showroom to receive its finishing touches and would now be blessed by the hallowed music going on upstairs. This was all part of the marketing strategy to make Steinway the piano with a cultural mission—to make it *the* piano.

William called his white marble emporium Steinway Hall and moved in next door with his wife, Regina. The hall was located in the heart of New York's music district, on East 14th Street between Union Square and the Academy of Music. Its main entrance was adorned by a marble portico with four corinthian columns. Inside, to the left, were large showrooms exclusively for square pianos; to the right was a small room filled with uprights. The main entrance hall was quite formal, with solid black walnut doors,

Steinway Hall on East 14th Street, c. 1900.

The salesroom at Steinway Hall.

stairs, and wainscot, which, when oiled and waxed, contrasted starkly with the Italian marble mosaic floor. At the top of the elegant staircase were the largest rooms of all, housing uprights and the grands. Nearby were two huge walnut doors to the main floor of the 2,000-seat concert hall. With its 42-foot ceiling and arched galleries housing private boxes, it had the feeling of a palatial opera house. There was also a smaller hall, seating 400, on the far side of the stage, which by means of a colossal sliding partition could be opened up as an annex to the concert hall. The two floors above the concert hall consisted of studios and rooms for music lessons and were given over to Steinway artists.

It was one of the few large concert halls in the country devoted to classical music. The largest such hall in New York was at the Academy of Music and seated 4,000. Other popular but smaller halls in New York at that time included Dodworth Hall, Irving Hall, New York Assembly Rooms, Woods Theatre, and Niblo's Saloon. Concerts were also given in churches. The inaugural concert took place on Halloween with Theodore Thomas conducting his orchestra before a packed house. A review of the "Amuse-ments" section of the *New York Times* for 1866 reveals that Steinway Hall quickly came to dominate the music world of New York.[3]

In years to come, performers included Walter Damrosch, the Yale Glee Club, the Boston Symphony Orchestra, Jenny Lind, and F. Boscovitz's "Popular Airs and Melodies," piped into the hall all the way from Phila-delphia by Bell's recent invention, the telephone. During the music season there were between forty and seventy major concerts. But Steinway Hall did not cater only for music. It was rented out for special events. Readings by Charles Dickens, commencement exercises of the New York Medical Col-lege for Women and the National Women's Suffrage Convention took place there when the likes of Theodore Thomas and Walter Damrosch vacated the stage.

The hall was also rented by esoteric groups. "Lectures on the Moon," mystical seances conducted by "celebrated mind readers," and "the World's Greatest Prestidigitateurs" were featured at Steinway Hall. Clearly, the com-pany was not concerned that its image might suffer from association with moon people and magicians; what mattered was renting the hall. Whatever the occasion, whether a symphony concert or a demonstration of the effects of anesthesia, the crowds would pass through the Steinway showrooms downstairs to reach the hall, an excellent way to advertise pianos. It worked. Sales increased by more than four hundred instruments in 1867 and, except for an occasional slump, stayed above two thousand instruments a year for

Piano music transmitted by telephone wire from Philadelphia to Steinway Hall.

the rest of the century. Having showrooms and a concert hall in the same building proved so successful that other piano manufacturers like Weber and Chickering followed suit and built their own halls.[4]

But capturing the domestic market was not enough. The real music, the real musicians, the real measure, in William's view, were still in Europe. He must prove there too that he had the best piano. William's first international test was in Paris at the Exposition universelle of 1867. There his piano would be up against more than four hundred pianos from all the celebrated manufacturers of Europe. William coveted the gold medal and spent a fortune ensuring that it would be his.

The Paris fair opened in April on a brilliantly sunny day; but even with such sparkling weather, no one much showed up. The emperor spoke to a room of echoes. The *New York Times* reported that "never before was a great public enterprise so silently inaugurated." Most of the exhibits, except the French and the English, were still in boxes because their buildings were not finished. The American section, where Steinway was to be, was reportedly "wild and chaotic" and looked as if it would be the last to be finished. The U.S. Congress had delayed appropriating funds, and those intending to exhibit had failed to furnish inventories of what they planned to bring. The result was a jungle of unpacked boxes, with Americans particularly exasperated because most of them knew no French. While exhibitors unpacked, guests and sightseers roamed the hallways bewildered, as at a housewarming where only the basement is finished. Moreover, it was very expensive—no place for the impecunious or those seeking relaxation.[5]

Amid all the confusion, Theodor, who was representing Steinway & Sons at the fair, unpacked two concert grands, a square piano, and an upright. As he adjusted the instruments in their new venue, he explained to John F. Petri, the first non-family employee with any authority in the inner circle, that they had to make sure, using whatever influence was needed, that Steinway won "a medal and cross" and that no medal went to Chickering, Steinway's arch rival. The medal was worth 2,000 francs ($400) in advertising, Theodor explained. It was obviously worth much more, because Steinway and Chickering each spent 400,000 francs ($80,000) in just two months of self-promotion in their attempts to win the gold in Paris. The money, spent on advertising at home and abroad, mailings, broadsides, special catalogs, and entertaining people who might be influential when the judging started, was budgeted even before the tents were pitched in Paris. The amount was more than the average Steinway worker would make in a hundred years. The battle would be bloody, but in the end Steinway and Chickering would both benefit.[6]

Although American industry was underrepresented at the Exposition

A lithograph by
Amédée de Noé
("Cham") showing
the excitement over
the Steinway piano
at the 1867 Paris
Exposition. The
pianist is Desiré
Magnus.

universelle, more than half the Americans who did exhibit won awards: McCormick for his reaper, Cyrus Field for the Atlantic cable, and Wood for the mowing machine. American machines that made screws, peeled apples, beat carpets, and cleaned glasses were also admired. But what captured everyone's attention was the American piano, especially the Steinway and the Chickering.

In May, in one of the earliest messages transmitted over the recently laid transatlantic cable, Theodor telegraphed William the good news that Steinway & Sons had been awarded the first gold medal. By the end of June William had the official list of medals awarded to Americans and noted proudly in his diary that "we head the list." Back in New York, William waited almost seven more weeks for additional news. He was almost in despair when, at noon on 3 July, a telegram finally arrived stating that Steinway "got gold medal before Chickering." William immediately dispatched the news to his principal agents. The next day a second telegram brought more good news, that Steinway & Sons had won the grand annual testimonial medal and honorary membership in the Société des Beaux Arts. At the end of the month a telegram from Theodor proclaimed that the jury had classified Steinway & Sons' piano as superior to Chickering's. He added—what didn't seem crucial then but later became decisive—that

Chickering had made a personal, written application to the French government for the Legion of Honor ribbon. William waited anxiously for the official certificate stating that Steinway had beaten Chickering. When it finally arrived, it became a staple of Steinway advertising.

In July, however, Chickering also won a gold medal. The company declared a holiday, and the Chickering workers marched through the streets of Boston waving French and American flags. With a gold medal and selection for the "Cross of the Legion of Honor," Chickering claimed to have done best in the show. It even had a testimonial from Franz Liszt certifying his highest regard for the Chickering piano. "I never thought a piano could have such qualities . . . I congratulate you," Liszt had reportedly said while grasping Chickering by both hands. In fact, Liszt was just as enthusiastic about the Steinway piano. In the Boston papers Chickering advertised that, like Steinway & Sons, it was among the five gold medal-winners. It went on to report that on published lists Steinway was placed fourth. Steinway responded vehemently, noting that the list that placed it fourth was from an obscure Paris music journal (the *Gazette musicale*) and that it had been placed first on the "official" list.

This led to a ferocious advertising war between the two firms, each attempting to prove that it had won first place. Chickering highlighted its "Cross of the Legion of Honor," although this was completely outside and unrelated to the official awards at the exposition, insisting that this was a higher award than a gold medal. Nevertheless, Chickering placed a larger-than-life replica of the medal on the top of its building on 57th Street. The medal is still there, a block from the current Steinway Hall.[7]

William, angered by Chickering's "Legion of Honor" award, set out in search of his own royal recognition. Praise came in from various court pianists. A letter from His Majesty the King and Crown Prince of Prussia's pianist proclaimed the Steinway to be "the perfect piano," and another from the Emperor of Austria's pianist thanked William for "the splendid Concert Grands which you furnished for my use during my present Concert trip in the United States." There were certificates recognizing Theodor's accomplishments from the Royal Academy of Fine Arts in Berlin and the Royal Academy of Fine Arts in Stockholm. William himself received an honorary gold medal from King Charles XV of Sweden. The Queen of Spain bought a Steinway, and later the Empress of Russia, the Sultan of Turkey, and the Queen of England would buy or be given Steinways.

To put Chickering in its place, William advertised extensively, using statements by royalty that Steinway was their choice. A quote from Wilhelm Kruger, court pianist to the King of Württemberg, placed Steinway as number one at the Paris fair. "It was now [a] universally established and recognized fact," Kruger proclaimed, "that the appearance of your matchless instruments at the great Universal Exposition in Paris has created the second great revolution in the construction of pianos throughout the world." Interestingly, his letter goes on to list as the "chief advantages" of the Steinway all the inventions of Henry, Jr.: the over-strung bass, the iron frame, and the new arrangement of the soundboard, all of which gave it, he said, a huge tone, so making it suited to large concert halls. He made reference to the competitiveness at the fair, saying that Steinway had emerged victorious from the "hot competition . . . though envy and intrigues of all kind[s] have vainly endeavored to frustrate the conferring on you of the highest distinction."[8]

Royal purchases and appointment meant prestige and sales. Every palace had rooms that could house pianos, and, once the first instrument had been purchased or presented as a gift, orders for several more usually followed. William's nephew Charles later remembered that the Sultan of Turkey, Abdul Hamid, bought eight pianos, each one "beautifully decorated, each succeeding one handsomer than the last," to present to his favorite wives. Charles mused: "We were almost able to see some mitigating circumstances in polygamy!" The competition in Paris and the endorsements and advertising that followed brought customers streaming to Steinway dealers across the country. When the figures were tallied and published by the Internal Revenue Service, Steinway's sales were reported to nearly double those of the next largest piano manufacturer in America and exceeding those of the twelve largest piano makers in New York combined.

Steinway was now way ahead of Chickering in sales, and within a few years Chickering would no longer be its chief competition. But Steinway's victory was far more than a triumph over Chickering. The jury's written report, combined with artists' and royal letters of tribute after the fair, had established the supremacy of the Steinway in Europe. The Steinway system had become the new standard by which all other pianos throughout the world would be measured. Probably because the 1867 Steinway was still the instrument of Henry, Jr., Theodor later condemned it as an "atrocious" piano while emphasizing his (failed) attempt to make it better. Writing to his sister Doretta, he maintained that "the grands of 1867 had a quite new superior full, round tone, but the treble was dull and I made it brighter by giving it a more solid foundation. However that made them glassy and thin. Yet the frame was so atrociously ugly that I really fear the grands from the sixties will all go to the devil."[9] Theodor's criticism notwithstanding, the 1867 Steinway of Henry, Jr., revolutionized expectations of what piano music should sound like. By 1873, at the Vienna exhibition, over two-thirds of the pianos exhibited were imitations of Steinways.

At a time when America was still seen as a frontier society, capable of leading only in farm machinery, small arms, and such like, this was truly remarkable. Charles later described it as "a matter of national pride" that European palaces were then equipped with "instruments of American make, when 'American' had so long been the synonym for all that was merely commercial." Steinway had overcome a deep-rooted prejudice against the New World. Its piano had become the standard for the whole world; and it was art made in the United States.

In 1871 the company's founder, Heinrich Steinweg, died. He had been inactive since the Paris fair and had spent his last five years watching his son William build up the business. According to one R. G. Dun and Company report, Steinway & Sons' profits were more than a quarter of a million, the company was worth almost two million dollars, and William alone was worth more than one and a half million—a lot of money when compared with the average daily wage of its workers: $2.85.[10]

William had raised what Cyril Ehrlich in his book *The Piano, A History* called the "familiar German pattern" of marketing, "excellent catalogue endorsements and . . . royal patronage," to a new level. Now he would revolutionize the third aspect of that marketing pattern, performances by leading virtuosi. In 1872 he financed, managed, and delivered the acclaimed Russian pianist Anton Rubinstein to the American concert stage, guaranteeing $40,000 in income for 215 concerts.

Inheritor of Liszt's glowing crown as the most celebrated of European pianists, Rubinstein looked and played like Beethoven, with immense power. He was a big man with thick unattractive hands, and each finger seemed bigger than the keys on which it rested, which may explain why he hit the cracks so often. His most famous student, Josef Hofmann, described Rubinstein's little finger as being as thick as his own thumb. Rubinstein was conservative in his choice of music. His programs included Bach, Beethoven, and Chopin, rather than Thalberg or other more trendy composers. Rumors abounded that he was a gambler, a womanizer, and the illegitimate child of Beethoven. He did not remind people that he was born in 1830, three years after Beethoven's death.

Rubinstein arrived in New York on 10 September 1872. Colleagues and devotees were so anxious to welcome this maestro from Moscow that the Philharmonic Society of New York led "a large concourse of people" to his hotel, where, from below Rubinstein's window, they serenaded him with the Andante to Beethoven's Fifth Symphony, among other things. The Philharmonic had not done such a thing since the "Swedish nightingale," Jenny Lind, came to town in 1850. Responding to the loud calls and music from the

Caricature by Joseph Keppler (*lower right, holding top hat*) of Anton Rubinstein playing the piano at Steinway Hall in 1872. *Upper left:* Theodore Thomas; *second from the left:* Carlotta Patti. Henri Wieniawski is next to Rubinstein, holding his violin.

street, Rubinstein appeared on his balcony, briefly expressed his gratitude, and retired.

His debut, on 23 September at Steinway Hall with Theodore Thomas's orchestra, lasted until the early hours of the morning. It was Indian summer in New York, and Steinway Hall was intolerably hot. But this did not stop 3,000 people from cramming a hall that normally held 2,400. They had come to hear music more powerful and more expressive than they had ever heard before. Nor were they disappointed. When he played the opening chords of Handel's D Minor Concerto, the audience went wild and stood up and shouted. He then overwhelmed them with a rondo in A minor by Mozart, an arrangement of the march from Beethoven's *Ruins of Athens,* Schumann's Etudes symphoniques, and three of his own works.

Although it was somewhat cooler a few days later, when the second Rubinstein concert took place, the atmosphere in the hall was "simply murderous." People had to leave, and those who stayed became ill. The air was intolerably hot and foul-smelling. It was not a new complaint. Audiences had complained about the air in Steinway Hall during the previous spring and winter. A contemporary writer had said that the "much abused public" was "thoroughly sick and tired of sweltering in the unwholesome stew that usually constitutes the atmosphere of the Hall." But the warm weather of the past few days had become trapped and was now heated by 3,000 concert-goers and 700 gaslights.

After New York, Rubinstein set out for Boston and a grueling schedule of 215 concerts in 239 days. Buffalo followed Boston, then Montreal and Toronto. He toured with two singers, a small instrumental ensemble, and his colleague from Moscow Conservatory, the Polish violinist Henri Wieniawski. When he was not traveling or performing, he was racing to his hotel room for a few hours' practice. He became so exhausted that on 24 May 1873 he wrote to William that "each day I feel unhappier. I think often of breaking my contract. The tour has no end and becomes daily more difficult, more unbearable." There were too many concerts, he had no time to practice, and his repertoire was exhausted.

On his return to New York, he gave seven farewell concerts at Steinway Hall in nine days. They were all solo recitals and grossed more in box office receipts than any of his other concerts. On his final night, after the applause and the bows, the audience rushed the stage to tear clothing and buttons off the maestro for souvenirs.

This concert tour netted him not $40,000 but $80,000, which he was glad to get, so that he could pay off the debts incurred by the extravagant life-style of his wife, Vera. But he never returned to the United States, not even with a guarantee of half a million dollars. He hated going from town to town with his piano and recalled that under such circumstances "there is no chance for art. One simply grows into an automaton, performing mechanical work; no dignity remains to the artist. . . . The receipts and the success were invariably gratifying, but it was all so tedious that I began to despise myself and my art. So profound was my dissatisfaction that when several years later I was asked to repeat my American tour, I refused point blank."[11]

Nevertheless, Rubinstein had had a major impact on American music. One reviewer marveled at Rubinstein's "touch of inexhaustible variety, marvelous power and delicacy of wrist." He had received more press coverage than any musician before him. And, of course, the publicity and prestige for Steinway & Sons were enormous. Never before had there been a concert tour like this, on such a scale and with so much fanfare. William was making news, making the piano a topic of conversation, creating a national celebrity, and putting the Steinway name up front and next to that of Anton Rubinstein. At the same time, he was encouraging an awareness and appreciation of classical piano music throughout late-nineteenth-century America. The Rubinstein tour was an extraordinary musical experience for people across the country who would otherwise not have had access to this powerful Russian artist.

Having captured the American market, William then set his sights on the British Empire. In 1875 he signed an agreement with William M. Yandell Maxwell to sell Steinway pianos through Anglo-Continental Pianoforte, Limited, in London. Two years later Maxwell and Steinway bought Anglo-Continental and founded Steinway & Sons, a London partnership. It was established at 15 Lower Seymour (now Wigmore) Street in what came to be known as Steinway Hall. (The building is no longer standing, but the site is around the corner from the present Steinway Hall on Marylebone Street.) The concert hall, previously the Quebec Institute, where Carlyle, Thackeray, Charles Dickens, and other luminaries used to lecture, reopened as Steinway Hall in 1878, with exquisite acoustics and a seating capacity of four hundred.

The Steinway–Maxwell venture was not very profitable, because, according to William's nephew Henry W. T. Steinway, the New York factories could not supply it with pianos cheaply enough and in any case, pianos manufactured in New York did not do well in the English climate, neither the wood nor the varnish lasting well in the moister atmosphere. In 1884 William considered selling the London store to Maxwell, but when he discovered that its assets had been trumped up by court claims against Bluthner and debts owed by Yandell Maxwell of New York and that Maxwell had been using company funds for personal expenses, he decided to buy Maxwell out. He dissolved the partnership but retained Maxwell as a salesman and as business manager of the London branch. A year later he discovered that Maxwell had not only been dishonest but also disloyal. He had taken out a music license in his own name, which signaled to William that he was planning his own business. He fired Maxwell and with his brother Theodor started making pianos in Hamburg. These were less expensive than those made in New York and more suited to the European climate. The result was that Steinway Hall in London became profitable and an important showroom for the British piano trade.[12]

Back in New York, William formally established the Concert & Artists department in Steinway Hall, with Charles F. Tretbar in charge. Tretbar, a native of Brunswick who had been with William since 1865 and was then secretary to the board of trustees, was to make sure that all the Rubinsteins of the world used and endorsed Steinway pianos.[13]

Steinway & Sons in America's Centennial Year

HILE WILLIAM WAS
cultivating Steinway's name, Theodor was designing a modern upright piano
and trying to persuade his brothers to make it part of the Steinway line.

Uprights first appeared during the middle of the eighteenth century, and
by the end of the century the large upright made by Robert Stodart looked
very much like a bookcase with a keyboard. In 1811 Robert Wornum patented one of the first small uprights, "cottage pianos," and the shape of the
modern upright was born. By the 1860s Theodor, in Brunswick, had constructed an upright with a cast-iron plate which produced a brilliant tone,
surpassing most square pianos on the market and bringing uprights to a new
standard of excellence. He was so thrilled with his "pianino" that, as early as
1859, he was urging his brothers to put everything else aside and start an
upright line in America. He predicted that "thousands of ladies will buy one
for their drawing room, especially in New York where space is so scarce and
expensive." He believed that it was more important for Steinway to make an
inexpensive piano than to promote the concert grand as the instrument used
by all serious pianists. But his family in New York disagreed. New York
homes were larger than European homes at the time, so the upright's smaller
size did not guarantee a market. Furthermore, the New York Steinways were
determined to establish Steinway & Sons as a "grand" house. Uprights and
the low end of the market were not what they were seeking. The profit
margin was also greater for grands than for uprights. They didn't make their
first upright until 1862, insisting that "Americans don't know upright pianos

and therefore they don't love them." When Steinway Hall opened, only a small room was devoted to the display of uprights.

By 1865, when Theodor arrived from Germany, uprights had already surpassed square pianos in Europe but were rarely made in the United States. Nevertheless, Theodor brought with him from Germany workmen who were skilled in making uprights. Present in person and with this nucleus, he persuaded William to establish an upright department and proceeded to make such instruments on American soil. Theodor insisted that his upright was "fully as beautiful in tone and as durable for use as the square and grand pianos." Although always a stepchild, his Steinway upright subsequently became a permanent feature of the Steinway line. Only Steinway and one or two other manufacturers were making uprights at that time. But in 1872 William increased promotion of the upright by giving it more space in the catalog and the company promoted the "boudoir piano" a 3-foot, 10-inch upright with a new detachable front portion, the action, keyboard, legs, and feet being separate from the case, thereby permitting the piano to be transported up the narrowest of stairs and through the smallest of doors—the perfect piano for peripatetic city people.[1]

Theodor's work on uprights and his refinements of grands and squares entailed more than mere tinkering. Living at a time when scientists were investigating the physics of sound and had discovered that sound waves traveled better *along* the fibers or grain of wood than against it, Theodor was anxious to apply their findings to the piano.[2] He was an avid reader, of Sir Isaac Newton on sound waves, Sir Charles Wheatstone on vibrations, Monsieur Marloye on vibrating strings, and Hermann von Helmholtz on tone.

On the basis of his reading of Helmholtz, Theodor developed a new way of stringing the piano that utilized portions of the string that had previously been left out of account. In Theodor's design the segment of the string between the bridge and the hitch-pin in the back of the piano was assigned a length determined scientifically in proportion to the length of the main part of the string so as to vibrate sympathetically with it. The double vibration of the string or, as he called it, "the duplex scale" (*scale* in piano language generally refers to design of the stringing) created, according to Theodor, a fuller, richer sound that was particularly noticeable in the treble notes.

He received a tremendous boost in 1871 when Helmholtz, then chairman of the acoustics department at the University of Berlin, examined several pianos and selected the Steinway for his experiments and lectures. He wrote to Theodor thanking him for "the superb grand" he had sent. He professed himself most impressed by the "prolonged vibration of its tones, by which the instrument becomes somewhat organ-like" and by the "light-

Illustration of the boudoir piano, from the Steinway catalog of 1866.

ness and delicacy of the touch." Liszt confessed that, "owing to my igno-rance of the mechanism of piano construction, I can but praise the magnifi-cent result in the volume and quality of sound." When Steinway refrained from exhibiting at the Vienna World's Fair in 1873, by agreement with Chickering, in order to save on expenses, the jury expressed its regrets that it had not been given the chance to applaud the Steinway piano.[3]

Theodor had read that a string stretched to its limit produces the purest tone. After years of experimenting with metal alloys, he developed a metal for the frame which made it very strong. It possessed valuable musical vibrations but was almost twice as strong as ordinary cast iron. While most manufacturers were still struggling to prevent a harsh metallic tone from a frame that could barely hold a tension of 25,000 pounds, Theodor had come up with a metal that had a pitch so low that it added to the sound and could withstand a tension of 75,000 pounds under all circumstances in any climate. This alloy was later produced in Steinway's new foundry in Queens, which was especially built for casting iron frames for its pianos.[4]

Theodor had produced a piano with strings pulled tighter that stayed in tune longer than any previous instrument, but Steinway had few customers at the time. The bank panic of 1873 had stalled the United States economy,

C. F. Theodor Steinway, c. 1875.

taking the piano business with it. By 1874, Steinway sales were down, the factory was running only half-time, and the firm was short of ready cash. Production and sales had not been as low since the Civil War, and in 1876 William mortgaged Steinway Hall and the factory to raise $175,000.[5]

The centennial international exposition in Philadelphia that year was a chance to show off Theodor's accomplishments in a grand way. William also hoped it would improve business. Toward the end of April Steinway shipped nine pianos—five grands, three uprights, and a square—in a special railroad car to Philadelphia. As well as exhibiting his piano with its duplex scale in the Main Building, Theodor sent metal castings of various parts of the piano for exhibit in the Machinery Hall.

Four years in the planning, the Centennial exposition opened on a hot, humid May 10. Albert and his wife were there, along with some two hundred thousand others, as well as President Grant, who declared the exhibition open. Theodore Thomas led his 150-piece orchestra and a chorus of almost a thousand Philadelphians in Handel's "Hallelujah" chorus.[6]

William went to the Philadelphia centennial feeling depressed. He had just seen his wife, Regina, and son Alfred off on a one-way trip to Europe and was suing her for divorce on grounds of adultery. A year earlier, confronted by his brother Albert with stories of her infidelities,[7] William learned that while he was away, his wife was enticing other men into their bed, dressing them in his nightclothes, and demanding that the servants fetch ice cream and champagne to supplement her nights or afternoons of sexual pleasure. Regina's paramours included Steinway employees, neighbors, and friends of the family.

After the initial shock and shame, William began to wonder whether he had even fathered his own children. His son Alfred was born in early October 1869, so, in search of evidence as to whether "little Ditz" was his or not, he examined his diary for the nine months prior to that. William kept track of everything, including his wife's menstrual cycle. He found his code for the onset of Regina's period on 7 January. He then discovered that on 1 March his wife had told him she was "pops"—his code word for pregnant. Between 7 January and 1 March there was no dot on any page to indicate that they had had sexual intercourse. Ergo, six-year-old Alfred was not his son.[8]

When confronted, Regina admitted that Alfred's biological father was Louis Stern, who lived across the street from them. Shortly after she met Stern, the maid noticed "Mrs. Steinway standing in her night dress in the window and throwing kisses to Mr. Stern, which he returned." When William was out of town, Regina and Stern signaled each other from their windows. Stern would then meet Regina in a brothel on 16th Street or come across the street for the usual: ice cream, champagne, and sex.[9]

The Steinway nursemaid, Augusta Krauss, later recalled:

On the 4th of June 1869 at about 10 o'clock in the evening Mrs. Steinway [then five months pregnant] let Mr. Stern into the house. This was the birthday of the eldest son George. Mr. Steinway was away to Buffalo and remained there until I left June 8th or 9th. On the evening of the 4th when Mrs. Steinway let him in she whispered to him not to speak. She had told me to go to bed early. I was the nurse and slept in the nursery right off her room. The doors communicated. She took him into her bedroom and locked the door leading into my room. I was not asleep. I got up and looked through the keyhole. I saw them undress and go to bed together. Mr. Stern put on one of Mr. Steinway's nightshirts. I found it on the bed in the morning. He stayed until about four o'clock in the morning. The same thing occurred every night until June 8th or 9th when I left.[10]

William Steinway's family, 1874. *Left to right:* George, Regina, William, Paula, and Alfred.

Regina later confessed that she did not know why, but she always felt that she must have another beau besides her husband.[11] But William did not want to lose her—in part because their active sex life, or at least the memory of it, was hard to give up. In the early years of their marriage they were having intercourse every night and sometimes four to six times a night, and William didn't want to lose his passionate bedmate. Further, divorce would be time-consuming, embarrassing, and disruptive. It would be easier just to stay married. He finally decided that if she would stop her affairs and vow to be faithful, he would try to cover up Alfred's illegitimacy and raise him as his own. But he soon found out that there was too much to hide.

He discovered that on Regina's recent trip abroad with her niece Reinel they often had sex with the same man. In Germany they shared their bed with Carl Seyffert, director of the Thalia Theater in Munich. A few weeks later Theodor, through his contacts in Germany, obtained five love letters that Regina and Seyffert had exchanged and handed them over to William. After reading them, William wrote in his diary: "no language can describe the mental tortures I endured on reading these horrible depraved and un-alterably imprudent missives." The bizarre ending to the Seyffert story was that after Reinel became engaged to him, she discovered that he already had a wife and children.[12]

With Regina's help, Reinel then picked one of their other lovers to marry, Louis Ehrenberger, a young Cavalry lieutenant, who later blackmailed Regina with letters she had written to him about their trysts. This developed into a quite absurd situation, because at the very time that Ehrenberger was demanding $1,500 per year from William to keep the ménage à trois quiet, he was also asking the family to approve his marriage to Reinel. Regina eventually gave Ehrenberger $1,000 for the letters.[13]

The adventures with Seyffert and Ehrenberger were just a few items on an ever expanding list. It seemed to William that he was discovering lewd stories about his wife every day. For example, he met a former household servant, Laura Nyncke, for lunch, and she told him about Regina having sex with Henry Reck.[14]

Henry Reck was an architect and one of William's closest friends. He had been given an office and a bedroom in William's house, which was right next to Steinway Hall. When William moved into his new home at 26 Gramercy Park, it was Reck who did the decorating. When the Steinway family decided on Greenwood Cemetery in Brooklyn as where they wished to be buried, it was Reck who designed the mausoleum. Henry Reck was in William's house all the time. When they played cards, Reck was there. And on Christmas Eve, Reck would be decorating the tree along with the family. And when

William was not around, Reck was sleeping with Regina, it now turned out.[15]

Louis Dachauer, a well-known organist, was also on Regina's list. In suing her husband for divorce, Maria Dachauer claimed that her husband had committed adultery with Mrs. Steinway both at the Steinway house in Gramercy Park and at the Dachauer house.[16]

After hearing about all these "crimes of the depraved creature [Regina], I loved so deeply," William had his lawyer, George W. Cotterill, draw up a plan for divorce. They mapped out the end of the marriage and a new life for Regina in Nancy, France.[17] On 20 May 1876 Regina and little Alfred set sail. The letters of credit, passports, and legal agreements were all arranged. The only problem was that William was still in love with her. In his diary he poignantly described his last moments with Regina and Alfred:

> lonely day. . . . At 1:40 wife takes leave of the children Georgie and Paula a most affecting scene, only little Ditz (Alfred) laughs. Wife, Mrs. Krüsi, Margaret, & I, also little Alfred drive to steamer "Labrador," I cry bitterly on the way. On the steamer wife gives me a little package begging me to open same, when I get home. After drinking some champagne together I kiss little Alfred with bitter tears in my eyes, I kiss my wife and take leave. The steamer starts at 3 P.M. precisely. I catch a glimpse of them and they of me, and I see that wife weeps bitterly. I then break down utterly, so that Fritz Sterns has to support me. I get home in car, to office, Theodore there, open package, wherein wife returns me our wedding ring with a few affectionate and poignant words. I again break down and sob as though my heart would break.[18]

Four days later, William, with an entourage of eleven people that included his children and nephews, arrived at the centennial exhibition feeling "sick and dejected beyond description." But he tried to forget his personal crisis and tend to his business problem, Albert Weber.

During the 1850s and 1860s Chickering had been Steinway's major competitor; but by 1876 Weber had emerged as Steinway's chief rival. Neither company was doing well at the time, however, and most manufacturers were looking to the centennial exhibition to boost sales. They all wanted to claim victory at what was billed as "the nation's birthday party."

At the trial performances on the evening William arrived at the fair, the Steinway on the platform of the great rotunda was played by Frederick Boscovitz, the Weber by John N. Pattison. Later that night William returned to his hotel room and the more sober reality of trying to comfort young children who had just lost their mother because of divorce. He jotted in his diary that his eleven-year-old son Georgie "sleeps with me . . . very affectionate, kissing me very often," and missing his mother in the worst way.[19]

The next day they all went to the fair. The fairgrounds covered more than 450 acres in Philadelphia's Fairmount Park, and there were more than thirty thousand exhibitors. Aware of an intense patriotism, foreign manufacturers stayed away, for fear of favoritism to "made in the USA" and of the unstable American economy. Two-thirds of the exhibitors of pianos were from the United States. The turnout (64) was low compared to that at the fair in Vienna three years earlier (139) and that in Paris (178).

A special trolley line had been set up to take people to the centennial. Three hundred cars, pulled by horses on newly laid track, carried some twenty thousand people per hour to Fairmount Park. By 10 November, when the centennial exposition closed, almost ten million people had roamed the Avenue of the Republic, beheld the Catholic Total Abstinence fountain, and examined the exhibits in the Horticultural, Machinery, or Main Halls. In Machinery Hall the exhibits ranged from a machine that made 40,000 bricks per day to a chewing-tobacco invention run by four African-Americans singing hymns to a typewriter described as "an ingenious machine for printing letters or manuscripts instead of writing them with the pen," and a fellow named Bell had brought his latest contraption, the telephone.

For most people who attended the fair, it was a matter of exhibits, food, and fun. For William and his fellow piano makers, it was work. The nation's attention was on the fair, and winning would be priceless for advertising. Steinway and Weber, in fierce competition for the crown, would—and did— do anything to win.[20]

Main Building, where the pianos were exhibited, was billed as the largest structure in the world, covering twenty acres. The Steinway concert, with Boscovitz playing, took place on the bandstand in the center of Main Building. In line with what other manufacturers were doing and to make sure that the surrounding area was filled with Steinway fans, William hired two large trains, at a cost of $4,000, and on that rainy morning transported all his workers to Philadelphia. When they arrived, all the Steinway men assembled by the front entrance to the fair and marched, in the rain, to the Grand Plaza, led by a blaring band.

On 7 June the judging started. William, Albert, and Theodor took the 7:30 A.M. train back to Philadelphia and went straight to Judges' Hall, where the pianos were brought for the trials, and all the other manufacturers were standing around nervously in the entranceway. The Steinway brothers went before the four judges to highlight the more extraordinary features of

Steinway & Sons' exhibit at the centennial exhibition in Philadelphia. From the *Daily Graphic,* New York, 29 December 1876.

their piano, feeling fairly confident. In the evening William and Albert walked over to the home of one of the judges, Julius Schiedmayer. He headed one of the oldest German piano houses and was a veteran international judge known to have a preference for Steinways. William knew that two other judges were not in his pocket: George F. Bristow, the pioneering American composer and violinist, who was a Weber supporter and featured in many of their advertisements, and General Henry Kemble Oliver, an elderly Salem, Massachusetts, statesman, organist, and composer, who was incorruptible.

William had turned to Schiedmayer for support at the fair in Paris. Schiedmayer had certified that Steinway was better than Chickering then, now William wanted his help to beat Weber. They hatched a plan, one that they didn't want to get out of the room. Before William and his brothers went back to New York, they would give Boscovitz $1,000 to pay off the fourth judge, F. P. Kupka, an amateur musician who had a reputation for accepting bribes. Apparently he had fixed the sewing machine awards at the Vienna fair.[21]

A month later the close relationship between Steinway & Sons and Schiedmayer became an issue, with the former accused of trying to influence the judges. Rumors circulated that Schiedmayer's report was handed out of a window, rewritten by Steinway, and then handed back. In its Sunday edition the *New York Herald* printed a scathing indictment of Schiedmayer, Steinway & Sons, and various other judges and manufacturers, accusing them of collusion, bribery, and using prostitutes when money wasn't sufficient to attain their ends. The Steinway–Schiedmayer relationship was singled out as being "peculiarly close," thereby rendering Schiedmayer "utterly unfit . . . to be a member of the jury." The *Herald* quoted a Philadelphia piano manufacturer's claim that Schiedmayer and Kupka were in cahoots and, by inference, funded by Steinway & Sons. Other newspapers started writing about the Steinway–Schiedmayer connection, and reporters pestered William for information. He sequestered himself with Tretbar and John C. Freund, owner of *Music Trades* magazine, to write a response. In it he focused on Schiedmayer's integrity and said nothing about himself or Steinway & Sons. The *New York Herald* printed it, accepting it as if a reporter had written it. Both the *Herald* and the *World* supported William Steinway's integrity and denied any wrongdoing on his part. William was pleased. He believed that his name and that of Steinway & Sons had been cleared by the articles in those two papers. Over lunch one day he urged Schiedmayer to stick to the official story—that they had done no wrong. The centennial commissioner from New York then asked William to make a public statement about the rumors surrounding all the wrongdoing at the fair. William responded, by priority mail, with "a positive statement that we never paid any money to any of the judges." The fact that this statement of innocence was accepted, despite it being known that he had been in collusion with Schiedmayer and in all probability had paid off Kupka, illustrates his hold over the local press and the music trade.[22]

In October the Centennial commission issued its report, granting Steinway & Sons two awards: one for the "highest degree of excellence in all their styles of pianos," the other for their iron works, which were said to display the "highest perfection of finish and workmanship." The *Tribune* reported that Steinway & Sons had won the "highest honor of the forty competitors." The *Herald*'s headline announced: "Steinway & Sons proclaimed the standard pianos of the world."

But the headline in *Harper's Weekly* read: "Weber, of New York, Receives the Highest Award at the Centennial Exhibition," and its article proclaimed Weber "the Piano Maker par excellence of the world." Apparently Weber had engaged in some jury tampering of his own. The judges' reports had gone to the Centennial Commission for review and publication. But somewhere between the judges' chambers and the Commission's printing press the report was changed so as to favor Weber. Steinway received a copy of the judges' report and realized that the changes could only have been the work of Weber.

The award system at the centennial did not follow the established gold, silver, bronze distinctions of previous fairs. There was only one level of award, and this, in the words of General Francis A. Walker, chief of the Bureau of Awards, "simply declared that an article is good; the report tells what it is good for, and how good." The outcome was that most of the exhibitors won awards, so it was the wording of the reports that was decisive. It was a "bare-faced fraud," recalled an irate James C. Watson, secretary to the music group judges. The report had been altered to entirely change its meaning, and undoubtedly somebody had been paid by Weber, he claimed, to change it so that Weber would appear to have won, not Steinway & Sons. Inside the jury room, according to Watson, "Steinway & Sons stood first in the estimation of the judges."[23]

This set the stage for a battle over who really won in 1876. Weber's pamphlets, fliers, and one-page spreads in playbills claimed a "complete triumph at the centennial exhibition." Patronizing Steinway & Sons, Weber maintained that Steinway won for "largest volume, purity and duration of tone," which was fine for the "pioneer epoch" of piano making, but that loudness at the cost of "sweetness, delicate nuances and clearness" was no longer acceptable. The "world of art" wanted "sensibility and expression." Weber declared that, "according to the World's Judges at Philadelphia," his piano had finally brought about that "alliance of Sensibility, Sympathy and Power. In short, a soul." Weber quoted George F. Bristow as pronouncing "Weber's pianos unquestionably the BEST PIANOS in the exhibition."

William was outraged. He directed Charles Tretbar to help him contact every judge in the larger group of judges, of which the piano section was only a part, and obtain from each a certificate of superiority. William also hired Herbert VanDyke to investigate the transactions among George F. Bristow, officials of the centennial exposition, and Weber. His goal was to uncover enough fraud and corruption to force Bristow to change his report to benefit Steinway & Sons. VanDyke reported back to William on Weber's sales, finances, creditors, wages, worker relations, material costs, those "with whom he associated, either at his house, factory or store; his relations with different parties, especially with J. P. Hale [the mass producer of inexpensive pianos], Chickering & Sons, and John C. Freund." Hiring spies was nothing new to William. He had hired informers during strikes and to spy on his wife and her lovers. But he would later deny hiring VanDyke—even though his diary records a series of payments, notes, and "affidavits" received from him.

By November 1877 Steinway had rounded up ten of the judges from the larger group. He then published a certificate signed by them, stating that the Steinway pianos "at the Centennial Exposition at Philadelphia in 1876 presented the greatest totality of excellent qualities and novelty of construction and in all points of excellence they received our highest average of points." It also said that Steinway was "rated highest and far above all other competing exhibits [meaning Weber], in each and every style." This certificate occupied a prominent place in Steinway catalogs and advertising for the next twenty years.[24]

This didn't silence Weber. He pointed out that it had taken Steinway & Sons more than a year to twist the arms of the signatories to revise their reports. He invited the judges to make their statements in court, where perjury was punishable by a jail sentence. Three years later Steinway was still battling Weber, this time in the corridors of the Westminster Hotel in Philadelphia. James Henry Mapleson, the English impresario, had brought his opera company to Philadelphia. He recalled that "every artist in the company had had a magnificent Steinway placed in his or her bedroom; this in addition to the pianos required in the theatre." All this was quid pro quo for their unqualified, glowing endorsement of Steinway's piano as "above all others." Weber had been frantic about the Mapleson troupe endorsement, and upon discovering that there were Steinways in the hotel rooms, had sent his piano movers to put the Steinways out in the hall and Webers in the rooms. William, hearing that the singers had come back from dinner to discover Weber pianos in their rooms, sent his movers to reinstate the Steinways. The two moving squads met in the hallways and unscrewed the piano legs, and a battle like something out of the Middle Ages ensued. The Weber men won the day, and after the opera Weber invited the cast for dinner, where "sundry bottles of 'Extra Dry'" flowed and his guests gladly signed a letter stating that Weber pianos were the best they had ever known. It was one of the more dramatic Steinway–Weber battles and was to be their last. Albert Weber died at the age of fifty—some claim he worked himself to death—in June 1879.[25]

SIX

Escaping the "Anarchists and Socialists"

ILLIAM'S SUCCESS IN
promoting his brother's piano pushed sales a year or two ahead of supply.
There were simply not enough skilled workers to do the job. Not only had
immigration from Europe stopped, but more than six hundred thousand
soldiers had lost their lives during the Civil War, and another four hundred
thousand were disabled—a million casualties overall in a nation of only
thirty-one million.

Moreover, a labor shortage during a time of increasing sales gave workers
the courage to fight for more time off. Immigrant workers saw it as their due
to have leisure time to relax with family and friends. They wanted to work
no more than eight hours a day, not the exhausting ten or eleven hours that
they *had* been working. Having survived the Civil War, they were resentful
that they were still only eking out a living in a land that had promised them
prosperity. They saw fortunes being made as the nation put itself back
together again—but only by the favored few.

Most shops were on a ten-hour day, even though the eight-hour day
movement had started six years earlier, in August 1866, with the setting up of
the National Labor Union in Baltimore. In 1868 Federal Government employees were granted an eight-hour day, but by 1872 the movement was
almost moribund. Its place was taken by the Knights of Labor, who had been
meeting secretly in Philadelphia since December 1869. Led by the Grand
Master, Terrence Powderly, they too pushed for an eight-hour day.

In spring of 1872 carpenters in New York City went out on strike, and
within a week William Steinway was recording in his diary that the strike had

been very successful. Three days later, five hundred piano workers met at the German community meeting halls on the Bowery and voted to fight for an eight-hour day, which was tantamount to fighting for a 20 percent increase in piecework rates to generate the same income. Of those who attended the meeting that Monday, none worked for Steinway.[1]

At that time Steinway & Sons was worth well over a million dollars, William himself owned almost half the company and controlled assets of over $700,000, while the workers were making, on average, less than $900 a year. The company had sold 2,553 pianos in 1871, making it the best year ever in terms of sales. Its new piano, the "school" piano, which was just like its other 7-octave instruments except that it had a plain case, so sold for less money, suited limited school budgets, and many institutions were sending in orders for it. According to one account, Steinway couldn't fill half the orders it received that year, even though it claimed to be making one piano every working hour—ten pianos a day.

William told his men that he could give them a 10 percent increase or a nine-hour day, but that to meet their demands for an eight-hour day would mean raising the price of pianos by a third. This, he claimed, would ruin sales. The workers voted to talk it over with him. The notion of even talking it over brought three thousand striking woodworkers from other shops to the Steinway factory, these workers "having been thrown into the wildest excitement by the report that Steinway men would probably accept a compromise." With the strikers approaching his factory, William sent for the police, closed the gates, and admitted no one but representatives of the press and his workers. The pressure on the Steinway workers from the woodworkers in other factories was so great that the former joined the eight-hour-day movement. William's response was to walk away quietly, insisting that he had no more to say.[2]

That night he confessed to his diary that he was "much worn out" and very worried. He was reminded of the strike just three years earlier. At that time he had attempted to cut wages, arguing that unless he lowered prices, Chickering would have the edge over Steinway. The workers had stood firm and won. William knew he would lose again; so did his men. He needed them more than they needed him, since they could always find work in other woodworking shops.

He decided that the only thing to do was to raise the price of pianos to finance the eight-hour day. That evening, he drafted a circular to his agents, telling them that the power of the workers is "so formidable in its character that there is hardly a doubt that they will be successful" and asking them to raise their prices to compensate for the increase in wages that he was going to have to agree to. The price of pianos was not the same for all dealers. Smaller dealers paid more per piano than high-volume dealers who sold a hundred or more pianos a year. Moreover, dealers had the right to charge what the market in their area would bear. Never was there any mention of less profit for Steinway or introducing labor-saving techniques. The plan was simply to pass along the wage increases to the dealer and ultimately the buyer.

Steinway's dealers promptly reported that they were unwilling to raise the price of pianos. William therefore put his earlier proposal to his workers: a ten-hour day with a 10 percent wage increase. The varnishers would get $2.75 a day, tuners $3.30, foremen $4.59, laborers $2.01, and so forth. Compared to William's salary, this wasn't much: he made more in a week ($1,145) than his laborers did in a year. But, given that the average national daily manufacturing wage at that time was a mere $1.50, it wasn't a bad deal. The Steinway workers agreed, and next day William was delighted to be able to write that "our men met and resolved [at the factory] with strong majority to go to work tomorrow morning at 10 hours and ten percent advance." The strike was settled—or so he thought.[3]

But that night the piano workers at other factories, who were still on strike, attended a frenzied meeting at the German assembly rooms in Manhattan and decided to storm the Steinway factory at 6 A.M., to prevent Steinway employees from returning to work. The next morning, shortly after 6 A.M., William approached his factory only to find it surrounded by forty policemen and, in spite of heavy rain, "an immense crowd of men in front on 53rd Street, who yelled at every man who entered the factory." At William's request, the police chased the crowd away. But in order to protect the 150 returning workers, 300 policemen had to occupy the factory all day, with meals provided by Steinway & Sons. Interviewed by *The New York Times*, William insisted that the strike was not in the workers' interests. This was the slow season for piano orders, and business would not be brisk again for another three months. But although the manufacturers didn't really need the workers now, he concluded, they would eventually, and the higher wages and shorter workday would force the piano manufacturers of New York to emigrate. Even now, some dealers had gone to Boston, he claimed.[4]

William was alarmed. He noted in his diary that the "whole city was in a blaze of excitement about the strikes." He hired one of his workers, Zielfelder, to spy on the other striking piano workers. He especially wanted to know about the "grand demonstration to take place next Monday by all the working men." Some two thousand people demonstrated for the eight-hour day on the streets of New York that Monday, a far cry from the forty thousand that the unions had anticipated, but, nonetheless, not a small crowd. The Steinway workers were not among them; most of them were back in the factory. The unions believed, however, that they must convince the workers at Steinway, the largest and most prestigious piano house, to join them or else the whole effort would collapse. About two hundred strikers tried to take over the Steinway factory but were pushed back by the police. Three days later William's spy informed him that the strikers had met again and had agreed to move immediately on the Steinway factory. The cabinet-makers and the iron men had promised to take part in the demonstration. In response to a call by William, the police surrounded the factory.[5]

The next morning, Saturday, William walked up Lexington Avenue to 40th Street and watched about two hundred strikers assemble on Fourth Avenue (now Park Avenue) and 42nd Street.

> There being from 300–400 policemen around our factory [on 53rd Street], they did not dare to go up there, but marched across to Jackson & Steinmetz Piano Company and commenced to take possession of the place. The proprietor sent for the police and Captain Gunner arrived with about 80 men. [They] charged on the strikers and clubbed them on the arms and legs, they running as fast as their legs can carry them. Very little trouble takes place near our factory.[6]

The version in Sunday's *New York Times* was a little different. Their headlines ran: "Strikers Clash With Police . . . Some Strikers Return To Work; Some Attack (Steinway) Factory . . . The Police Intervene." According to the then anti-union press, the workers became so threatening that the police "were compelled to interfere." The workers' plan, according to the paper, was to gain access to the Steinway factory, "clean it out . . . and block all the approaches to the factory and prevent the workmen from entering." Two hundred and fifty policemen showed up and ruthlessly put an end to all that.[7]

According to William, the clubbing of the strikers by the police was not a brutal but a defensive act. This was not the workers' view. They wanted Gunner and his squad brought up on police brutality charges. According to Zielfelder, who was present at the strikers' meeting at the Cooper Institute at which they resolved to hire a lawyer, Steinway had nothing to fear at present. In this he was right. At the trial the officers' conduct was commended, and the complaint dismissed.[8]

On Monday, 24 June, the citywide strike ended, with only Steinway & Sons and Weber Company agreeing to a 10 percent wage increase. For William the eight-hour-day issue was over for now. He had met the men half way, and the police had protected that compromise.

But suddenly the nation plunged into one of the longest slumps in its history. Precipitated by the investment failures of Jay Cooke & Company, a bank panic in the fall of 1873 revealed a seriously overextended economy. Cooke and his partners eventually regained their fortunes, but the rest of the country was consigned to six years of rising unemployment and low wages, resulting in a severe setback to the union movement. Union membership nationwide plummeted from about three hundred thousand in 1873 to around fifty thousand in 1878. The average Steinway worker's wage, which had been steadily increasing since 1858, dropped 18 percent from a little over $3 per day in 1872 to a bit under $2.50 per day six years later. Even so, Steinway workers were doing better than most city workers, who saw their wages drop 25 percent, and the national average daily wage in manufacturing went from $1.50 to $1.30 during the same time period. This was a time when employers attacked labor, and labor lost. It was also the time of the Molly Maguires, the suspicious trials in eastern Pennsylvania at which Irish Catholic miners were accused of murdering their Welsh and Scottish Protestant employers. Although the evidence presented at the trials was questionable, ten "Mollies" were hung, and fourteen went to jail.[9]

William Steinway blamed other "red hot strikers" as he called them, not his workers, for his labor difficulties. He was a firm believer in the influence of the "social environment" on human behavior. His workers had been willing to settle for a nine-hour day in 1872 and, according to William, had been dragged into the strike by other unions. In 1870 he had started looking for land for a new factory site, away from the city, yet within easy access of it. "We sought a place outside the city," he later explained, "to escape the machinations of the anarchists and socialists . . . [who] were continually breeding discontent among our workmen, and inciting them to strike." He bemoaned the fact that the strikers made Steinway, the largest, most prestigious piano house, the "target for their attacks." Before a Senate Committee on relations between labor and capital William lamented the "baneful" effect of tenement house life upon the morals of his workers and testified that the only thing he could do to stay in business was "to remove [his] very large factory requiring much room and many men from the City of New York to the suburbs." William was not alone in feeling this way. Other industrialists, in the wake of the 1870s strikes, were experimenting with providing housing as a way to avert strikes and, hopefully, socialism.[10]

His piano business demanded more efficient, continuous production. In addition, Theodor's new piano frame required a foundry where he could smelt his own iron. The new site must be spacious enough to store more than five million square feet of lumber for two years before kiln drying, have corridors and doorways wide enough to allow for moving 7-foot pianos with a gross weight of 1,400 pounds, equal to that of a baby elephant. Steinway needed a factory large enough to produce at least twenty-five hundred of these unwieldy instruments per year. William found the ideal site just four miles away from his Manhattan factory, across the East River on the north shore of Queens, opposite 120th Street. (Queens, Brooklyn, the North Bronx, and Staten Island did not join Manhattan to form Greater New York City until 1 January 1898.) Now all he had to do was buy up most of northwest Queens.[11]

In 1870 he purchased the largest nursery in Astoria. Wilson's farm produced 50,000 camellias, 50,000 Marshall Neil roses, and 100,000 other choice roses and miscellaneous flowers annually. He also bought the Benjamin Pike estate. A year later he acquired a total of 400 acres of woodland, tidal swamp, meadows, and open fields. His property bordered more than half a mile of waterfront—perfect for a factory that needed millions of feet of lumber and tons of sand and pig iron delivered by barge.[12]

In the middle of this wilderness, overlooking Bowery Bay on Long Island Sound, was the Pike mansion, which William claimed as his summer home and which later became a Steinway & Sons' presidential perquisite. From its tower one could see the old Bowery Bay Road heading toward the ferry slip and along its route a few farmhouses and outbuildings. Benjamin T. Pike, Jr., who owned an optical supply business, aspired to the trappings of the landed elite and had constructed an impressive stone mansion for summer retreats. He sold the mansion to William for $127,500.[13]

By 1873 a sawmill, iron and brass foundries, and metal works had been built at the Queens site, and the main street had been renamed Steinway Avenue. A private telegraph line linked the Queens factory with the Manhattan works and Steinway Hall. In 1884 Steinway installed a telephone link. A waterway near the factory was converted into a holding basin as big as a football field, capable of storing millions of square feet of logs in the water. A steam-engine house and a large building for drilling, finishing, and japanning (high-gloss finish) iron frames were also erected on the new property.

William was so proud of his new plant in Queens that he hired an artist to produce a lithograph of a bird's-eye view of the sawmill and foundry in Queens, the factory in Manhattan, and Steinway Hall. Almost four feet by six feet, mounted and framed in black walnut, William sent copies to all dealers and agents to hang on their walls. Steinway boasted that "every portion of their pianos [was] made in their own factory, and every iron frame [was] cast in their own foundry, under the direct supervision of the Messrs. Steinway." They even made the brass key that opened the lid covering the keyboard. Only the ivory to cover the keys was made by another firm.[14]

The four hundred workers produced actions, hammers, iron frames, keyboards, legs, lyres, and cases. The pianos were then shipped across the

Steinway mansion in Astoria, Queens, c. 1881. On the porch, *from the left:* Richard Ranft (Elizabeth's brother), William Steinway, daughter Paula, wife, Elizabeth, and son George.

East River to the 53rd Street factory, where another six hundred workers fitted the soundboard, regulated the action, and varnished and polished the exterior. Even though their factories were on either side of the river, Steinway insisted that operations were still under the watchful eye of Theodor, who was constantly sailing back and forth to Germany, and his nephews, who were then apprenticing.[15]

William established a village around his factory, for two reasons. One was to try to control his workers, especially during times of discontent. The other was to sell land and sell or rent homes on the 400 acres that Steinway & Sons now owned in western Queens.

The idea of the company village in America goes back to 1790, when Samuel Slater built his cotton textile town in Pawtucket, Rhode Island. Perhaps the most famous, as well as the largest, antebellum New England textile town was Lowell, Massachusetts. In Lowell workers were provided

CASE MAKING BUILDING AND DRYING KILNS.

STEINWAY & SONS PIANOFORTE FACTORY, FOUND

MANSION.

STEINWAY & SONS.

FOUNDRY, METAL WORKS AND SAW MILL.

DRYING KILNS.

STEINWAY & SONS.

BATH.

COAL DOCK.

METAL WORKS AND LUMBER YARDS, ASTORIA, N. Y.

with boardinghouses, a dispensary, a hospital, and tree-lined streets. Like Lowell, most of these towns were built near a natural resource—coal to be mined or waterpower for a mill—and the building of a town, especially houses, was as much a matter of necessity, to attract workers in the first place, as to oversee them. In a few cases, like Pullman, Illinois (famous for its exquisite railroad cars), social control was more the motive. In all these towns employers could threaten to withdraw the services they were providing. But, for the most part, workers got on with their own lives, continued to protest against wage cuts and long hours, and were not total victims of the "boss." Company towns took many forms and had benefits for both workers and owners.

William Steinway's village was, up to a point, like a Berkshire paper mill town. On the edge of Bowery Bay, in a sparsely settled area of Queens, he built houses, financed a church, and maintained the streets. This gave him some power over his workers by enabling him to evict strikers from their houses, foreclose on their mortgages, or restrict their credit at local stores. But only a small percentage of his workers lived in Steinway Village; most still lived in Manhattan or the South Bronx and commuted to Astoria, which limited his influence. Although some workers later claimed that buying or renting a house from Mr. Steinway was a prerequisite for a job, a survey of where workers lived contradicts this assertion. Steinway Village was similar in spirit to other company towns; where it differed was in being located just across the East River from the largest city in the nation.

William was also in the real estate business in a more general way. He encouraged people other than Steinway workers to move to his village by building a variety of houses, some of wood, and others of brick, most of them two-story family houses. Eventually he established a land office, the Astoria Homestead Company, at the Steinway factory in Queens, to attend to maintenance problems of houses being rented out and to sell land and houses that were owned.[16]

William financed most of the public services in the village. He purchased hundreds of thousands of dollars' worth of municipal bonds to pay for paving Steinway Avenue. He supported the grading and macadamizing of other streets and sidewalks and the planting of shade trees. He bought $10,000 worth of Long Island Shore Railroad stock to encourage the company to extend its lines from the ferry to his factory and run cars every fifteen minutes. By 1893 he had set-up the Steinway Railway Co. and owned most of the trolley lines in western Queens. He used power from the plant at his

Preceding illustration: Print of the Steinway & Sons piano factory, foundry, metalworks, and lumberyards in Astoria, from an 1881 Steinway pamphlet.

Steinway houses in Astoria.

piano factory to electrify them, and his lines were among the nation's first electrified trolley lines.[17] He also sat on several boards and committees encouraging bridge and rail links to Manhattan. In 1891 William became the largest stockholder in the New York & Long Island Railroad Company (NY & LIRR), championing the tunnel it intended to drill under the East River to carry freight and passengers between Manhattan and Queens. But a work-site explosion of eighty-seven pounds of dynamite on 28 December 1892 caused five deaths, and legal claims for personal and property damage ruined the NY & LIRR and stalled the project for a decade. It was not completed until 1915, long after William's death and following years of legal disputes, but it is now a vital subway tunnel between Manhattan and Queens and bears the name "Steinway Tunnel."[18]

Moreover, ten years before George Tilyou invented Steeplechase Park, before Lunar Park, before Coney Island, William Steinway developed the largest amusement park and bathing beach in the city: North Beach Amusement Park—today the site of LaGuardia Airport. It was a brilliant investment and made money from the day it opened, in summer of 1886. By 5 P.M. that day the concessions were out of beer, and the crowds were off to downtown Steinway Village to drink it dry.

On a typical summer weekend some fifty thousand New Yorkers went there. Most went to drink, dance, and listen to music at hotels and saloons called "The Tivoli" or "Corey's." There were several concerts every evening, and on warm starlit nights there was dancing outdoors at the pavilion.

Sailboats, steamboats, and rowboats could be hired for cruising or fishing on Bowery Bay. For those who preferred calmer waters, the man-made Silver Spring Lake was available for a swan boat or gondola ride. Miles of grounds covered with beautiful shade trees and grassy lawns provided a tranquil space where thousands strolled or stopped to picnic.

There were also rides: a switchback railroad (today's roller coaster), a tall Ferris wheel, and George W. Kremer's carousel (which featured wooden animals carved by Kremer himself). In addition, daily spectacles, such as balloons dropping women into the bay from heights of 400 feet, and weekly fireworks displays added to the carnival atmosphere. The fireworks included the usual pinwheels and star bursts and, on the Fourth of July, the American flag. But the two displays that regularly drew the most applause were an exploding glass of beer replete with foam and a blazing sign that read "Welcome—W. Steinway & Sons."

North Beach was where most New Yorkers saw electric light for the first time. William reported in his diary that in July 1895 "North Beach was for the first time lighted up with electricity." All the hotels, saloons, waterways, rides, and walkways were lit by electric lamps, hundreds of them, the electricity provided by William's latest investment, the Steinway power plant. Tenement house-dwellers, accustomed to gaslight, were dazzled.

For safety, William built a firehouse and fitted it out with one of the best steam engines and hook-and-ladder carriages in town. For piety and schooling he donated land to the Protestant Union Church and in 1879 took delight in singing "Tag des Herru" (The Day of the Lord) at the dedication of the new Steinway church that was built there, which he referred to as "our little Church."

In 1889 when the building, which held five hundred people, became too small for its original purpose, Steinway converted the basement into a public kindergarten and the upper floors into the Steinway Free Circulating Library. He then arranged for a free piano and more land for a bigger church building. With money from the sale of the old building to Steinway & Sons and an inheritance from Theodor's will, the congregation erected a magnificent new church in 1890 on Albert Street, so named for William's dead brother. That same year Steinway closed its concert hall and donated the cathedral organ that was in it to the church. All expenses for the Steinway kindergarten and library were paid for by the company. An instructor was available three times a week to teach German to English-speaking children, English to Germans, and music to everyone.

In 1890 Steinway & Sons leased for a dollar the kindergarten and library building to the Public Library of Long Island City, to accommodate the hundreds of children in Steinway Village for whom there were not places in

Steinway Village kindergarten children in 1911. The boy at the back in the sailor suit is Charles Roekell, who, like his father and uncle, later worked for Steinway & Sons.

the public fifth ward school. Steinway also picked up a share of the kindergarten teacher's salary. But the following school year William made a profit on the deal, and in 1892 the Board of Education issued a rent check to Steinway for almost $3,000.[19]

"Steinway," as the village in Astoria came to be called by the United States Post Office, was complete and independent, with a population of seven thousand, by 1895. Although not everybody in the village worked for Steinway, all benefited from the company's presence. Nor could they fail to be aware of it as they walked down Steinway Avenue or side streets named after Theodor and Albert or sailed on Bowery Bay, from which could be seen an enormous wire sign on top of the case-making building—"Steinway & Sons."[20] The firm even served as time-keeper for the whole village, as Joseph J. Duffy, remembering his grandfather, who was an engineer at Steinway from 1878 to 1926, recalls: "One part of Grosspop's job that he relished was blowing the whistle, a warning at 7:00 A.M., a starting whistle at 7:20 A.M. and a closing whistle at 5:00 P.M. . . . . He was very proud of the accuracy of his watch since the whole village of Steinway set their clocks by his whistles."

The town grew but never provided William with the control over his workers which he had hoped for.

SEVEN

The Piano Workers Strike Back

B Y 1878 THE PIANO business had started to come out of its slump. Railroad tracks were linking small towns together into a national marketplace, and among the beneficiaries were piano manufacturers. Farmers, city clerks, and mechanics were enticed by both the ease of delivery and the new way of paying—the installment plan: play now, pay later. Steinway, wishing to capitalize on the new demand, introduced a smaller, 6-foot grand, model "A," suited to city apartments. Midwestern farmers especially liked the enormous, elaborately decorated, highly polished uprights. Traveling salesmen used to say that farmers bought their pianos like they bought their hogs, by the pound. On the farm and in city apartments pianos tended to be used more as an accompaniment to romance than for formal parlor recitals. "I Dream of Jeanie with the Light Brown Hair" and "Bedelia, I'd Like to Steal Ya" were more likely to be heard than Beethoven, Brahms, or Chopin.

The rich were buying Steinway pianos for the prestige and the finish on the case as much as for the music they produced. For a price, Steinway would make the case to fit any decor. Curled maple cases engraved in gilt or silver could be bought off the showroom floor, but from a customer with deep pockets, special orders were taken for cases with unique carvings and unusual paintings. An "up-town [gent] whose palatial home boasted of a music room tinted in chocolate" had his concert grand finished in "light chocolate enamel." W. K. Vanderbilt ordered a piano, for his new yacht *Alva,* of solid mahogany with "fretwork panels representing different musical instruments . . . made to match the trimmings of the cabin." One New Yorker purchased

Steinway's art case piano department on the second floor of Steinway Hall, c. 1885.

"an ebony-cased piano, ornamented with Japanese fretwork and titles and inlaid Japanese ornaments" for the Mikado music room in his summer home in Newport, Rhode Island. Steinway called such instruments "art case" pianos. Salesmen were always on the lookout for a notice that a wealthy family was building a new home, in the hope that a special piano might be required. The made-to-order trade was to be a growing part of Steinway's business for the next fifty years.[1]

With the rich enjoying homes in Newport and pianos with inlaid pearls, the nation's workers were not about to sit idly by. From 1872 to 1878 the national daily wage for laborers had dropped from $1.64 to $1.23. In July 1877, while the nation was still in a depression, demonstrations protesting wage cuts spread across the country, becoming violent at times. Strikers derailed trains and burned rail yards, paralyzing two-thirds of the country's tracks. A year later piano workers in Manhattan reached across the East River and penetrated Steinway Village.

At that time William was raising prices on most models and trying to reduce wages. The result was "a revolution in the shop against the proposed reduction" in pay, and when William tried to enforce it, "a perfect pandemonium" broke out. Racing off to the factory in Queens to stop the protest, he found it partially shut down by the casemakers, machine men, and blockers. There he met a "delegation of our workmen who demand 10 percent more wages and Blockers and Machine Men 15 percent. After lengthy conversation I agree to allow them an average advance of 10 percent to be at once deducted again if the trade cannot stand it." The 10 percent increase across the board brought the factory-wide average pay up to $2.66 a day, which restored salaries to what they had been more than a dozen years earlier.

William wrote a confidential letter to his dealers and agents reporting on the militance of the workers, the increase in wages, and probable future labor problems. At the end of the year, when the keymakers were out on strike and a citywide piano makers' strike threatened, William recounted in his diary that it had "been the most prosperous (time) in business for 7 years past, and though almost crushing me with immense loads of work and responsibility, yet spared us any serious sickness or death in the Steinway family." In reaction to the keymakers' strike, he started to buy parts of the keyboard from Pratt, Read & Company in Connecticut.[2]

Within six months the varnishers were demanding a 12–20 percent raise beyond the 10 percent they had just received. Entailing about sixty-five men, varnishing was one of the largest operations in the factory. Every grand piano case was given six coats of varnish to fill in all the pores, and each coat

Steinway varnishers, early twentieth century. The varnishing process had not changed since the 1870s.

Steinway rubbers, early twentieth century.

needed eight days to dry, a bit longer on rainy days. The factory was producing more than two thousand pianos per year, which meant that about six
hundred pianos were always on the floor being varnished. After the fifth
coat, they were put away for two to three months before final rubbing and
polishing and the final coat of varnish. This sixth and last coat after the case
had been rubbed smooth and polished to mirror brilliance was applied with a
camel's hair brush, and great skill was required to insure that no streaks, no
drip marks, and no camel's hair remained on the piano.

The varnishers and the polishers claimed that they worked harder than
anyone else in the factory and were paid less and that, with the cost of living

rising, their real income was going down. There were also a lot of entry-level boys in the varnishing, polishing, and rubbing departments, because the pianos had to be moved after each coat, a job that required more brawn than brain. These recently hired, unskilled workers had less loyalty to the foremen and usually the lowest salaries in the department, so they were the most likely to walk out. The more skilled varnishers were also less prone to knuckle under. Every woodworking shop needed varnishers, from furniture makers to railroad car manufacturers, and they could find work elsewhere.

On a rainy Friday the thirteenth, in 1880, they stopped work at noon, went out to lunch, and never came back. William told them that he expected them back in the factory on Saturday morning at 7 A.M., and that if they were not back by Monday, they would all be fired—all to no avail. Within a few days, almost the entire workforce followed the varnishers out the factory gates. They demanded a closed shop. William tried to pressure them into returning by means of his power in the village, warning the local merchants in Astoria against giving credit to the strikers, since they might never get their money back. The strikers met at Albert's Astoria Assembly Rooms, and their speeches reflect how they felt about living in Steinway Village. "One speaker compared the firm [Steinway] to the coal owners of Pennsylvania and said that though the firm did not trade in provisions, they banished the men to God-forsaken Astoria and compelled them to hire their houses if they wished employment."[3]

William realized that strikes were going on all over the country and that his problem was part of a national issue of labor unrest. To end the strike, he needed more muscle. So, as he had done before, he turned to the other New York piano manufacturers. They decided to lock out all thirty-five hundred piano workers in the city on Monday the 15th, if by the 13th Steinway's men had not returned to work. That wet and gloomy day Steinway workers were given quite a jolt when nearly all the piano manufacturers of New York locked out their workers. The workers received immediate financial aid from unions in Baltimore and New Haven. Meanwhile the manufacturers considered hiring Chinese laborers for fifty cents a day. The lockout lasted a week, after which a few manufacturers broke ranks as orders piled up and they saw their more skilled workers take other jobs.

William offered his men a 10 percent raise. They agreed, and he dropped his threat to fire the instigator of the strike, supposedly on account of his family, which included six children. The six-week strike ended on Easter Sunday with considerable fanfare as the Steinway men returned to the factory in a parade, with the band playing "Hail Columbia." There Theodor gave a speech, and the men gave him three cheers and celebrated with beer offered by the foremen but paid for by William.

William wrote to his dealers that "after six weeks of intense excitement and trouble of the gravest kind, and at a direct cash loss to us of over $40,000, the strike in our factory has come to an end." He lamented the loss of power of the Piano Manufacturers' Society, which, as he saw it, had "triumphed completely during the great strikes of 1864 and 1872." The average salary went from $2.66 to $2.77 per day. The Steinway workers were doing pretty well compared to blacksmiths earning about $2.31, machinists $2.45, and locomotive engineers $2.15. Meanwhile, William passed the extra costs along to the dealers by increasing wholesale prices while insisting that they hold the line on retail prices.[4]

During the strike many of Steinway's better workers were lured away by smaller factories offering higher wages. In addition, according to William, piano manufacturers throughout the country bought New York pianos to give New York piano manufacturers the impression of an increasing demand. Apparently they hoped that the New York companies would increase their wages and settle the strike, so making New York pianos more expensive and less competitive on the national market.

Frustrated that his move to Queens had not prevented the walkouts, William sent his nephew Henry W. T. Steinway to buy the piano case factory of L. W. Portes in Leominster, Massachusetts, a factory town forty miles northwest of Boston. The plan was to move part, or perhaps all, of Steinway & Sons out of New York. Within six months the scheme literally went up in smoke. Charles H. Steinway reported to the Board of Trustees "that the old factory at Leominster was totally destroyed by fire with all its contents."[5]

Nor was William satisfied with his own financial success. He wanted a new family. Theodor introduced him to Elizabeth Ranft, the dour twenty-seven-year-old daughter of a wealthy German felt maker. In July William, aged forty-six, went to Dresden and a month later married her. It was pretty much an arranged marriage and certainly did not have the love—or the problems—of his first marriage. Ellie was as practical as Regina was passionate. A year later their first child—William Richard Steinway, "baby Willy" as they called him—was born. William and Ellie had a second child, Theodore, and then a girl, Maude.

William was now a millionaire, one of four hundred in New York listed in *New York World* for 1880. Moreover, his fortune was growing. In 1881 Steinway & Sons manufactured more than twenty-six hundred instruments, the most they had ever made in a year. The corporation had a surplus of almost half a million dollars. An R. G. Dun and Company investigator summarized its status as "rich and safe." From 1883 to 1893 Steinway & Sons dividends ranged from 10 to 20 percent per year, a bonus that gave William an extra $60,000–120,000 a year, more than his workers would make in a lifetime.[6]

But this prosperity did not escape the workers' notice. They saw pianos flying out the door and also saw that they were needed to keep up the flow. Fired with a sense of their own worth, they went on strike again in September 1882. This time the issue was who controlled the workplace.[7] The men hated the new superintendent, Conrad Sommers, and wanted him out of the factory. What precipitated their ire was his refusal to pay two top-makers for repair work. The top-makers were under contract to "repair all tops [the lid of the piano] which crack after leaving the shop before being used." In this instance a number of tops were returned, and the workers claimed that when they scraped them down, they found that the fault was in the wood, not the workmanship. They asked Sommers to pay them for their time, and he refused. The men then appealed to young Charles H. Steinway, second son of William's late brother Charles, and claimed that he agreed to pay them.[8]

Sommers claimed that Charles Steinway had never acquiesced and said that the workers would not be paid. At that point the three hundred Queens piano men walked out and demanded that Sommers be fired. Workers at the 53rd Street factory then held a meeting, and the four hundred workers in Manhattan decided to join their brothers in Queens and to remain out until Sommers was discharged. The next day, Charles cabled William in Berlin that "both factories are out striking for A. Sommers' discharge." William telegraphed back: "we will not be dictated to and [to] close both factories till I return."[9]

Sommers had worked at the 53rd Street factory for three years and had only been at the Queens plant for a year and a half. He had never been popular with the men, who claimed that he was always making them do extra work without extra pay. A meeting to discuss Mr. Sommers attracted some four hundred Steinway workers to Fernando's Hall, a meeting place near the Manhattan factory, on 55th Street and Third Avenue. After listening to speeches in both German and English, they demanded that "Mr. Sommers be discharged, that the men at work in the store [Steinway Hall] be discharged and that the men shall not be considered responsible for work which has left their hands and been approved by their foremen." They then waited for Charles to answer their charge.

Charles responded that it was one of the rules of the shop that faulty work be repaired at the expense of the workmen and that the firm did not propose to allow its workers to dictate the management of the business.[10] He kept William informed through a series of cables until finally, in desperation, William cut his trip short and sailed for New York on 1 October.[11]

Upon arrival, William met immediately with other piano manufacturers —Weber, Haines, and Behr—who promised not to employ any Steinway men. He also arranged for two detectives to watch his workers. He then met with a committee of fifteen strikers and representatives of the union, who demanded the immediate removal of both Sommers and the scabs. William reported that he gave "them a fearful talking to and in writing refused their demands in total and discharged them all." At the end of the month he sent out a notice that all workers who did not report to work should consider themselves no longer employed by Steinway and should remove their tools from the factory. The twenty-eight men who were considered ringleaders were rudely reminded that William was father of the village when they were told to vacate their Steinway-owned homes and their tools were moved to O'Reilly's storage room. Workers were jailed and dispossessed of their homes. William received a letter threatening that unless he paid $1,500, he would be murdered. But at every meeting William stood firm, consistently telling the union, the workers, and the press that he would not give in to any of their demands.[12]

A week later, on Election Day, William had a long talk with Sommers, and they decided that it would be best if Sommers took his family to Germany and worked in the Hamburg factory until the New York strike was settled. What happened in fact is that, within six months, he resigned.[13]

With Sommers gone, many workers returned to the bench, and the press predicted that the strike would soon be over. But those still committed to the strike started to attack scabs on their way to the factory. According to William, "Strikers at Astoria [are] getting desperate and boycotting and hooting at those who work." In the afternoon of 9 November a committee of action makers from Astoria called to inform William that their branch had decided to return to work the next day, which of course he approved.[14]

Those still on strike, like Isaac Oehler, were hauled into court and fined for fighting with the action men returning to work. Oehler himself was accused of throwing sand in the face of action maker August Stumpf. According to Justice Kavanagh, the Steinway men had every right to strike but no right to stop other men from working for a living. He fined Oehler $10.[15]

By 20 November, after nine weeks of turmoil, the strike was over. William was elated and quickly cabled Theodor in Hamburg: "Constant stream of old employees coming back . . . Union declared strike officially ended." Most of the workers returned to the factory, but William refused to take back the ringleaders. William jotted down that "John Heis, the striker from Astoria calls . . . [I] tell him he remains discharged, also Begriebring." Nor did he rehire the twenty-eight men who had been served with dispossess notices "and who [were] considered to be the ones principally responsible for the continuance of the strike."[16]

William proclaimed: "Our victory is complete, and the men are very much cowed down." According to the *Staatszeitung, Tribune, World, New York Times, Sun,* and *Star,* Steinway had beaten the workers and their socialist leaders: "Right and justice have triumphed . . . over the dictatorial and unreasonable attitude so frequently taken by the leaders of trade-unions." What they didn't know was that William had paid the police more than $2,000 "as a reward for their help" during the strike. The police force in Queens remained on the Steinway payroll until William's nephew Charles raised the issue at a board meeting in 1888, proposing that they change their arrangements for police protection so as "to show that such police are in no manner in our employ."[17]

A confidential company letter maintained that the firm had won its battle to keep the foremen as strong representatives of management, not "pliable tool[s] under the dictation of the Trade Union." William also wrote that the "whole piano trade of the country ought to be thankful to us." With the strike over, business picked up, and William took advantage of the victory spirit by drawing up new shop rules.[18]

It wasn't an absolute victory, however. The nine-week strike had cost Steinway $60,000, and the firm had to increase wages to attract men back to work. As a result, it also had to raise prices. Fewer than two thousand pianos were shipped that year, making it Steinway's worst year since the Civil War.[19]

Due to all the strikes, the New York factory had not been able to supply the London showroom with enough pianos at a competitive price. Moreover, the problems with regard to American varnish not holding up in the damper European climate had not been solved. One solution was to replace rosewood, the wood that Steinway had used for cases since 1853, with an ebonized cherry-wood veneer. William told his dealers that he recommended the ebony case because with rosewood, the varnishing process was so expensive. Switching from rosewood to ebony would also ease his problems with the varnishers, since he would no longer need as many of them or be so dependent on them. This would entail a major change in appearance. William assured them, however, that the ebonized cherry veneer, with its far smaller pores, was "absolutely impervious to the effects of a damp atmosphere" and, with its "evenness, and unbroken length fibers," exerted "a most beneficial influence and effect upon the vibration and sound of the instrument." In Europe ebonized pianos became—and remain—the rule.[20]

The increasing value of the American dollar in 1880 added to Steinway's problems abroad, making even those cracking Steinway pianos expensive.

Moreover, European customers wanted "embellishment, carving or incising" on a piano, the costs of which were several times greater in New York than they would be in Europe because wages were higher.

Theodor proposed opening a factory in Germany to serve Europe and South America. He never cared for New York and, like his wife, Johanna, always yearned to be back in Germany. They had commuted back and forth a lot, sometimes staying in Brunswick for extended periods of time.[21] The idea of setting up shop in Germany was not new. In 1874 Theodor had even put down a deposit on a factory in Brunswick, but William had said positively no. William once told Charles that a business headed by Theodor would be bound to fail, because although Theodor was a great inventor, he was not a good businessman.

Notwithstanding, in March 1880 William was prepared to listen to Theodor's proposal. Many American companies were seeking a European market by setting up a sales agent there and later establishing an assembly plant. In 1879 Westinghouse established a factory in Paris to manufacture brakes. By the 1890s American manufacturers of all kinds of things, from sewing machines to elevators, had investments outside the United States and were capitalizing on the cheaper labor and trying to sell their product to new markets. Like many other American businesses going abroad, Steinway had set up its first showroom in London, where it was easier to handle worldwide trade because of British sophistication in the piano business. Also like many other American manufacturers, its next move would be to establish a finishing plant in Germany, where hostility to foreign trade was so intense, tariffs so high, and the German patent law of 1876 so framed that it made sense to manufacture there.

William thought that there would be great advantages to "rendering us more independent and not so helpless as . . . at present from the trades unions and strikers." Theodor added that if Steinway owned and operated a plant in Germany it could provide London with pianos that would be 20 to 45 percent cheaper and have a French polish finish to protect them from the moist European climate. "French polish" referred to a way of applying shellac without a brush, by rubbing it on, over and over again, with a cloth. The finish was magnificent and did not crack or swell with changing humidity, because shellac, being a secretion of the lac bug, can breathe, unlike varnish, which put a hard, glossy, thin film on the wood. But the rubbing process was labor-intensive and prohibitively expensive in New York. On 28 March William wrote in his diary: "Briefly inform Holwede of Theodor & I intending to have our own business in Hamburg & him as manager at which he is very much rejoiced." Arthur von Holwede had worked with Theodor in Braunschweig and had come to America with him in 1865. He was a tuner-technician who had traveled with Steinway artists in the United States and had maintained the Steinway pianos at the 1876 fair. Von Holwede was to be put in charge of the daily factory business, and Theodor would be the overseer.

At that time William and Theodor owned or controlled 86 percent of Steinway & Sons, but the move back to Germany nevertheless had to be formalized at a family council. This took place over dinner at Mrs. Albert Steinway's house in late May 1880, at what was billed as a going-away party for Theodor and his wife, who were about to sail for Germany. The family, meaning all the stockholders, discussed the project and gave their blessing to the decision to start making pianos in Germany again.

In June 1880 Theodor and William rented an old sewing machine factory in Hamburg, a free port at the time, with no duties on imported material and shipping lanes to continental Europe, Great Britain, and the "tropical countries" of Australia and South and Central America. There was one problem with Hamburg, however. There were no other piano manufacturers there, hence no supply of skilled piano makers. Still, the factory gates opened in November. The new company was legally independent of the New York business. Steinway's Piano Fabrik in Hamburg bought plates, action frames, lumber, and unfinished pianos from the New York factory, assembled the instruments in Hamburg, and shipped finished pianos to the London showroom. If a customer like the Turkish ambassador to the United States, who bought several expensive pianos, insisted that his piano be finished in New York, where it would be treated so as to protect it against the moist climate of Constantinople, Steinway would then ship the finished piano to Germany.[22]

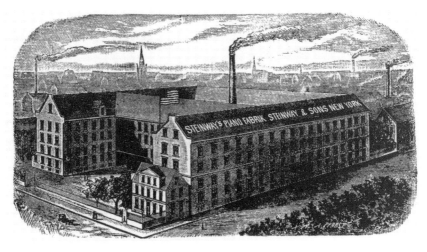

The Hamburg factory. From the Steinway catalog of 1888.

In addition to overseeing the Hamburg operations, Theodor had authority to manage Steinway affairs in Great Britain and Europe. After his wife died, Theodor moved back to Brunswick, about a hundred miles south of Hamburg and only a short drive from where he grew up, in the Harz Mountains. By spring of 1884 he had made it his permanent home, never returning to the United States. That was when the Hamburg factory started to make a profit.

Like his brother, Theodor was a wealthy man. His estate in Brunswick was worth $1 million, and he had at his beck and call two servants and a cook. His house was crammed with paintings, antiques, books, and overstuffed furniture, as well as ancient and modern musical instruments from all over the world and wood specimens gathered from his trips to Asia and Africa, which found their way into parlors, guest rooms, his music room, and his library, where he spent most of his time. He loved to read, from scientific treatises on acoustics to sensual French novels. In the middle of the front doors to his palace his initials were artistically placed, one on top of the other.[23]

Theodor loved living in Brunswick, although, as it turned out, he didn't have too many years left to enjoy it. Anticipating his own demise, he wrote to William in 1887 that "as soon as the C grands have become good pianos and all improvements have been made, I shall resign as Director, as at the age of 63 I experience a marked decrease of my strength and shall probably not be able to do anything useful any more for the company." His nephew Fred quickly responded that the family was against his retirement, since they realized that the "improvements and inventions" he had made in the field of piano making had resulted in "the huge success and outstanding position of our company among all other piano makers."[24]

He accepted their verdict and continued working. On 27 February 1889 his sister Doretta sent a distressed telegram: "Theodor very sick, asthmatic. Wish suggestions. I'm here to take care of him." She had rushed to his side, from Stuttgart, when a cold had developed into what he described as shortness of breath, "inflammation of the intestines and heart cramps." On 26 March he died in his sister's arms. He was a cigar smoker to the end, and according to his obituary, tobacco poisoning had probably hastened his death.[25] This left only William and Doretta of the Steinways who arrived in New York harbor in 1850. Who would run the show after they died?

EIGHT

Family Feud

WILLIAM BEGAN TO take serious stock of the next generation of Steinways. His son George, who was only twelve at the time of the divorce and had suffered a lot through being separated from his mother, was continuously ill, low, and despondent. William took him into the business when he was nineteen, but he lasted only three years. In 1888 George married a sixteen-year-old girl and within nine months was father of a baby girl. Subsequently he entered a sanatorium suffering from what William described as a "peculiar malady"—memory losses and an unsound mind. His wife divorced him on the grounds of his drunkenness and immediately remarried, and George was sent abroad to travel, spare the family embarrassment, and die. He did all three, dying at the age of thirty-four.[1]

William's other two sons were too young to be considered. The front runners among the nephews (nieces were not even on the list) were Charles H. and Fred, middle and youngest sons of William's late brother, Charles G., who had died unexpectedly in 1865. The oldest son, Henry W. T., who had been shipped off to New York by his mother, while she stayed in Germany with his brothers, had become resentful when, a few years later, Fred landed in New York, somehow reminding him of the childhood he never had. His resentment expressed itself in abusive language and an insulting manner, and his uncle Theodor predicted that "this young man will with his haughtiness hurt us all." He was therefore passed over, and it was Charles who was given the desk next to William at Steinway Hall[2] and was made the third member of the board of trustees, alongside William and Theodor. It was Charles

Steinway family and friends playing croquet on the lawn of the mansion in Astoria, c. 1888. *Left to right:* Julia Ziegler Schmidt, Henry Cassebeer, George Steinway, Charles Steinway, F. A. O. Schwartz, Marie Steinway (wife of Charles), Ida Schwartz (daughter of F. A. O.), Fred Steinway, and Henry W. T. Steinway.

whom William sent to London when it was discovered that William Maxwell, partner and manager of Steinway's London showroom, had misused funds for nine years and had never severed his ties with Blüthner. By April 1891 the distribution of Steinway shares told the whole story: William held 6,000 shares, with Charles H. and Fred the next two largest shareholders, with 1,350 each, and Henry trailing behind with 1,000.[3]

Charles had a love of music—an important passion for the president of a piano company. He was also a pianist and a composer. One office employee recalled that "after regular business hours it was [Charles's] habit to go into the upright room just back of his desk" and play some of his pieces. Steinway & Sons needed a music man at the helm.[4]

The problem was that Henry W. T. believed that the presidency of Steinway & Sons was his birthright as oldest male grandchild of the founder and bearer of his name. A mere three months after Charlie assumed his desk next to William at Steinway Hall, William reported that he had "quite a talk with Henry Steinway who has lately been very rough in his manner." Later Henry bitterly declared: "I am the eldest brother and he [Charlie] was the vice-president." As such, he felt that he shouldn't have to obey anybody, certainly not "boss William."[5]

This attitude was particularly difficult for William, because Henry lived on the third floor of Steinway Hall, right above William's office, so William saw him frequently, "every few days up to 1888, when my office was placed on the other side of the building," he recalled. Henry's sleeping in annoyed William, who took him to task on it. But by spring of 1885, Henry, about to turn thirty, was starting to fight the strong arm of William and was refusing to "abide by the will of the majority."

Toward the end of the summer of 1887, according to William, his nephew "bitterly denounced Hamburg & London business" and Uncle Theodor. Henry claimed that the Hamburg plant, privately owned by his uncles, was profiting at the expense of the London showroom. Theodor was furious, because he had been close to Henry, had trained him to manage the factory and buy lumber, and was now being accused of dishonesty. Theodor also believed that the other nephews secretly agreed with Henry. The problem with simply buying him out, Theodor wrote to William, was that "the brat would be capable of making pianos under the name of Henry Steinway or having them made, and this would be even more of a disaster for [the

Fred, Henry W. T., and George Steinway and Constantin Schmidt on the front porch of the Steinway mansion.

family]." So Theodor advised William to appease Henry under the banner of "all's well that ends well. [They] must see to it that the Steinways do not separate, otherwise farewell to prosperity."⁶

Things came to a head when Henry, as factory superintendent, was asked to keep a tally of costs in the factory and refused. The board of trustees then passed a resolution that everyone must do his job and listen to William. A month later the board gave Fred the job of obtaining "any and all figures . . . pertaining to the calculation of the cost of any and all parts of pianoforte manufacturing." He was to get two copies from Henry, one to remain in the 53rd Street factory, the other to be put in a vault in Steinway Hall.

Henry then dropped the other shoe and informed William that not only was he not keeping the records he had been asked to keep but that "he had destroyed the said material." When William asked him why he was acting contrary to the instructions of the board of trustees and the president, Henry claimed that the data were of no value. William and the board of trustees reprimanded him and ordered him to "make up all detailed data and tabular statements" relating to the cost of manufacturing pianos. They even provided him with help to make the calculations.

Henry then started sending the company letters filled with "insinuations against William Steinway personally," against the board of trustees, and even against his dead Uncle Theodor. William showed these abusive messages to the trustees, who encouraged him to write a letter to his irate nephew explaining "that unless he behaved himself properly hereafter he would have to be discharged." It didn't work.

At the end of 1891 William brought Henry before the board of trustees for a showdown. During the meeting, William had to "call to order & reprimand Mr. Henry W. T. Steinway for making offhand and insulting remarks and to notify him that he would be ejected from the premises if he did not behave like a gentleman." What became clear was that Henry not only had no intention of producing the cost analysis sheets but that he was preventing others from doing so either. William warned him that if he continued to be "grossly disobedient" and rude, he would have to resign as superintendent of the factory. Only if he behaved and apologized for maligning members of the board could he work at Steinway & Sons. Henry declared that "he would not take back a single word of what he had said or written." William then told him that if he didn't resign by New Year's Day, he would fire him. On New Year's Eve Henry W. T. resigned, the first family member to be forced out of the company.⁷

He asked to keep his desk at Steinway Hall and his horses at the stables out in Queens, but Charles Tretbar, on William's orders, told him to pack his desk and his horses and get out. He gave him a box for his mail at Steinway

Hall and permission to come by periodically to pick it up—for the time being. Tretbar had worked for Steinway & Sons since 1865 and was one of William's closest confidants. By 1892 he had become treasurer to the board of directors and was in charge of what was called Steinway's "Artist Bureau," later renamed "Concert & Artists" department.[8]

After his resignation, Henry and his accountant ensconced themselves at Steinway Hall to examine the books and records of Steinway & Sons in preparation for three major lawsuits against William and the company. A month later William tossed Henry out of Steinway Hall.[9] But knowing that the books were being scrutinized and that Henry and his accountant would be back with a court order, William and his nephews started to clean house. Charles and Fred agreed that William's investments were wasting "the profits of our business." They knew that their older brother Henry was "rubbing his hands full of pleasure that we three donkeys were led quietly" while these losses were being inflicted by William. They resolved to start charging William for the upkeep of his summer home, the old Pike mansion in Queens. They also decided to charge Henry rent for his fully furnished, five-room apartment on the third floor of Steinway Hall, where he had lived rent-free since 1877. Fred persuaded the board of trustees to resolve to take "no important step in either the manufacturing or selling department of this business without consultation with other trustees and executive officers." The board also instigated an annual meeting of the stockholders of Steinway & Sons. Although the Steinways had been having a meeting of this type every April since 1889, it was only now that they gave it an official heading in the minutes.[10]

In the summer of 1892 Henry initiated three lawsuits against the family and made sure that they were well publicized in the New York press. The first maintained that Steinway & Sons in New York was selling goods to Steinway's Pianofabrik in Hamburg, which was owned separately by William and Theodor, at far below cost and that the Pianofabrik was then selling finished pianos back to Steinway & Sons in London "at a very large profit." The lawsuit asserted that the low price had been fixed by the brothers to put money in their pockets at the company's expense. The company at that point consisted of William and Theodor as the two major shareholders and Charles, Fred, and Henry W. T., as minor shareholders. Moreover, the Hamburg factory, although not part of Steinway & Sons, with no profits accruing to Steinway stockholders, was treated as if it were a branch, with free use of the Steinway trademark and patents.[11]

The second suit, started a year later, attacked the trust established in accordance with C. F. Theodor's will. When Theodor died in 1889, he had no children to inherit his fortune. Henry claimed that it was illegal for the trustees (his uncles and aunts) and their children to own the same stock at the same time. He called for the will to be voided, on the grounds that it passed through two living persons. The defense was that the trustees were only holding the stock.[12]

The third suit, also filed in 1893, declared that William had wasted money, on a land business in Astoria, "maintaining bath, park, kindergarten, library and a teacher of German and music at the public school"; on a banking business "receiving deposits, loaning money and discounting notes"; on the construction of an electric generating facility for his trolley line; and on contributions to charities, artists, musical organizations, and political parties. All these charges were true, and the details exposed the way in which William used Steinway & Sons to bankroll his private businesses, philanthropy, and personal subsidies.

William had bought property in Queens, most of it along the routes of his railway lines, had levelled the land, laid out lots, cut roads, and constructed houses that he either sold or rented. Though he did all this privately to begin with, in 1870 it became a Steinway & Sons business, one that constantly lost money. Purchases of land, expenditure on maintenance of the houses, and sales were kept in the books alongside lumber purchases, payroll, and factory expenses. Steinway & Sons was as much into William's real estate business as it was in the piano business. The only part of the former that consistently made money was North Beach.

Henry also charged that William's involvement in politics was at Steinway & Sons' expense. William was a delegate at the 1888 Democratic National Convention which gave his longtime friend President Grover Cleveland the nomination. William had been corresponding with Cleveland since 1856. Cleveland was then a young lawyer in Buffalo. William had given the forty-nine-year-old president a piano when he married his twenty-two-year-old ward, Frances Folsom, in 1886.

The relationship with Cleveland entailed a mix of business and pleasure. All William's contributions to Cleveland's reelection campaign in 1888 had been subsumed by Steinway & Sons under publicity expenses. For William, the link between politics and pianos was as much a matter of course as singing in the Liederkranz choir. He enjoyed having dinner at the White House and smoking a cigar with the president.[13]

As a German-American whose father and older brother had always been more comfortable in their native tongue, William believed that hobnobbing with Grover Cleveland was a chance to chisel the Steinway name into the American grain. At the same time he treasured his German heritage and supported almost everything German in America. He was close friends with Carl Schurz, one of the fathers of the Republican Party and Secretary of the

Interior under President Hayes; with Hugo Wesendonck, founder and president of the Germania Life Insurance Company (now the Guardian Life Insurance Company); and with Oswald Ottendofer, editor and owner of the *New York Staats-Zeitung,* the leading German-language newspaper in the United States. When the *History of German-Americans of New York from 1848 to the Present* was published in 1891, it was dedicated to William Steinway. William raised more than $100,000 for the German hospital in New York (now Lenox Hill Hospital), supported the *Rechtsschutzverein* (Legal Protection Association) which helped provide German laborers with legal advice and lobbied for popular German-American causes like opening the beer gardens on Sundays.

While Henry had nothing against philanthropy, he didn't want Steinway & Sons footing the bill. He was a shareholder, and he wanted all the money to go toward manufacturing pianos. William, by contrast, saw his benevolence as boosting the Steinway name in the German community both here and abroad, and, after all, it was a community known to love music and buy pianos.[14]

Henry maintained that Steinway & Sons also subsidized William's trolley lines. From 1883 to 1885 William purchased every trolley line in western Queens and then consolidated them into the Steinway Railway Company. His rail interest brought him into contact with Patrick Gleason, the notorious mayor of Long Island City known for renting public school buildings from himself, buying water for the city from a company he owned, and raising taxes on his enemies. William was questioned by Henry's lawyer about lending money to Gleason. William claimed that his loans to Gleason were all part of his business dealings when he was buying Gleason's trolley line.[15]

Part of William's rail line taking passengers to North Beach ran on Steinway & Sons' property. William headed the company, the rail interests, and the amusement park. He was also New York's first Commissioner of Rapid Transit. William's commission explored the idea of an underground mass transit system. In 1891 the "Steinway Commission," as it was called, issued a blueprint for the first New York City subway. The plan was to make Union Square the hub, making it easy for passengers to get to Steinway Hall on East 14th Street. But there were no realistic bids, and the financial depression precipitated by the stock market crash of 1893 put an end to the idea of private financing for a New York subway system. Three years later, when a new rapid transit board was paralyzed by arguments over whether to build a subway or an elevated line, it was William Steinway who came up with a compromise, sketching out what was to be part of the subway network that New Yorkers live with to this day.

William's involvement in New York transit undoubtedly facilitated the signing of consent forms for the rail line to cross private property. The overlap between William's private businesses and Steinway & Sons was always to William's advantage, because he could get services at cost from the company for his own profit. For example, in 1892, after electrifying his Steinway & Hunter's Point Railroad Company, he used steam power from the Queens factory, paid for at cost, to run the dynamos. This was fine when the business was just William and his brothers, but now Henry was questioning these procedures.[16]

Steinway & Sons' lawyers did not deny these charges. They were all true and well documented in the board of trustees' minutes. But they pointed out that Henry was not only a member of the board but also superintendent, in charge of the New York and Queens factories from 1877 to 1891, when all these decisions were being made. Why didn't he oppose them then? He was also in charge of shipments to Hamburg and fixed prices and determined costs. The Hamburg factory went into operation in 1880. Why did he wait twelve years, until 1892, to take issue with these practices?

Also impressive during the hearings was William's memory of details, meetings on specific dates and with whom, and conversations with his nephew. The *New York Times* reported that "Mr. Steinway showed the most wonderful memory for every event connected with his business during the past thirty-five years. He not only remembered the year and date, but the day and in some instances could even tell the hour of certain events. Judge Beekman himself was astonished, and commented on the matter. Mr. Steinway smiled, saying: 'Yes, they used to call me the walking dictionary.'" What William never told Judge Beekman was that he kept a diary, though he did admit this a year later, during a Court of Appeals trial.

In the end, Henry lost all these suits against his family, but he kept the battle going with demanding letters and court appeals well into the twentieth century.[17] Moreover, though he lost in court, he succeeded in bringing about profound changes in the way Steinway & Sons did business. In 1893 the company closed the "Accommodation" account used by William as a private bank account to lend money for personal investments to companies like the Astoria Veneer Mills, East River Gas & Light, and the Astoria Silk Works. The use of company stables for privately owned horses and company housing for family homes came to an end. Records of family and business expenses were now kept separately. All this reflected the transition of the company from a tightly controlled family business to a far larger, more complex entity which required different standards of accountability.[18]

Henry W. T.'s full-time job became stalking Steinway & Sons. He lived on his Steinway stock and enjoyed the rest of his life singing at Lierderkranz, socializing at the German Society, traveling the world collecting specimens of wood, and fishing for black bass at Henderson Harbor, New York, with his buddies. Henry's separation from the family was so absolute that the next generation of Steinways, those born after 1910, didn't even know he existed until he died in 1939.[19]

NINE

Paderewski: Superstar
and Super Salesman

Wparagraph continues... I T H   H E N R Y   W.   T.
watching every dime that William spent, Steinway programs and policy
became very discreet. The company was even reluctant to bring Ignace
Paderewski to America. Daniel Mayer, concert manager and also director of
the artist department of the Erard Piano Company, had discovered Paderewski and brought him to London in May 1890. Paderewski, thirty years old,
had given three concerts in four weeks. According to Marks Levine, an
associate of Mayer's, "the receipts for the first concert were just under
90 pounds; the receipts for the third concert were 900 pounds!" William
Steinway was in England at the time, and Mayer invited him to hear Paderewski at one of the Philharmonic concerts. A few weeks after the concert,
Mayer claimed that Steinway said: "I must bring Paderewski next year to
America. You can rely upon my making this arrangement." All that William
wrote in his diary was "agent Mayer wants us to take up pianist I. J. Paderewski."

Eight months later, in March 1891, William cabled Mayer: "Deeply regret cannot take Paderewski this year. Hope to make arrangement for the
Chicago Exhibition Year [1893]." Within ten days Mayer was at Steinway
Hall demanding that William keep his promise to bring Paderewski to
America. If not, Mayer would arrange Paderewski's tour under other
auspices—Erard. But Steinway was already committed to Rafael Joseffy's
country-wide tour for the 1891–92 season, and bringing Paderewski over at
the same time would be competition for Joseffy, the popular Hungarian-
American artist. It would also be expensive for Steinway to manage two

national tours. He just couldn't do it, he told Mayer. At that point Mayer left for a brief trip to Niagara Falls, but by the end of March he was back at Steinway Hall pressing for a Paderewski tour. William finally gave in and told Mayer, "I do not want you to feel that I have broken a promise to you and I have therefore persuaded my partners to make the contract. Let's write it out." At the Steinway & Sons board of directors meeting on 25 March all but one voted in favor. Only Fred Steinway thought that Paderewski would be a waste of money.[1]

Steinway & Sons guaranteed Paderewski £6,000 ($30,000) income and "all expenses for travel and hotel accommodation, including the two ocean crossings (paid)." If he earned more, it would be all his. The company also undertook to provide someone to prepare the piano in accord with the "wishes of Mr. Paderewski, as much as possible." All Steinway wanted in return was the exclusive link to his name and a "testimony about their grand pianos at the termination of the tournee."

Paderewski would be managed by Steinway's Concert & Artists man Charles Tretbar. It was Tretbar who arranged the eighty concerts and recitals starting in November and ending in April, with no more than five performances a week. Paderewski remembered his first meeting with Tretbar as discouraging. His ship sailed into New York harbor on a bitterly cold, rainy November night. Tretbar met him at the dock and immediately confessed that he didn't expect much from him or his tour, since American audiences had already heard the greatest virtuosi, Rubinstein, von Bulow, and so on, and were more interested in singing and even violin playing than piano music. So he warned the young redhead from Poland that he should not expect extraordinary houses, even if he, Tretbar, had done his best for him.

To minimize expenses, Tretbar had arranged for Paderewski to stay in a second-rate hotel. The Union Square Hotel was around the corner from Steinway Hall, a favorite lunch spot for piano men, and a regular haunt of William's. But Paderewski was appalled by the "noisy commercial travelers," the insects, and the mice. The next day he played for William, who recorded in his diary: "Paderewski tries our Grands, he is an immense player." Paderewski also let it be known, through his secretary, that he would not stay in that hotel another hour.

He was immediately moved to the Windsor Hotel on Fifth Avenue and 46th Street, "a very old-fashioned but comfortable hotel with good food," he later reported. The Windsor was one of the most comfortable, attractive hotels in the city. According to *King's Handbook of New York,* the Windsor attracted distinguished foreign visitors, prominent railroad officials, manufacturers, and families coming to town for the opera or the social season. The cheapest room was $5 a night, compared to $1.50 at the Union Square.

Paderewski playing a Steinway in 1896. Drawing from *Town Topics*, 30 January 1896. This copy was inscribed by Paderewski.

Paderewski also enjoyed the billiard table there, and in time people came to watch him play pool. He claimed that one of his silent admirers was the future president, William McKinley.

But there was a problem in that the permanent elderly residents of the Windsor complained about Paderewski practicing at night, so he was forced to go to Steinway Hall in the evenings if he wished to practice. There, as he later described it, he would play through the night with only two flickering candles for light and an audience consisting of the night watchman and his personal secretary, both fast asleep.

After settling into a practice routine, Paderewski started to look more closely at his commitments for the first week of the tour, in New York. He discovered that Tretbar had arranged for him to play six piano concertos, two of which he barely knew. He was also scheduled to play six recitals in the following two weeks, which meant a concert almost every other day with a different program each time. He was stunned. Filled with disbelief and horror, he told Tretbar: "Why, in Europe, I might not have an opportunity of playing six concertos in one season. But in New York, I am expected to play six concertos in one week!" Paderewski later divulged that Tretbar then admitted that he was trying to sabotage the tour by exhausting the maestro because he was afraid that Paderewski would be a bigger success than "a particular friend . . . whom he adored." Paderewski wanted to complain to William, whom he knew was the ultimate authority, but Tretbar convinced him that Mr. Steinway was very ill with rheumatism. It was not true. William had been sick for three weeks in October, but by the time Paderewski arrived on 11 November he was in good health, if "excessively busy."[2]

Steinway Hall had closed for concerts in 1890, in anticipation of the opening of Carnegie Hall a year later. It was at Carnegie, on 17 November 1891, that Paderewski played his first concert in New York, with Walter Damrosch conducting. Walter was the second son of the distinguished conductor Leopold Damrosch. After his father died, young Damrosch completed his father's 1884–85 season. But even with a Damrosch at his side, the audience for Paderewski's debut was small. Paderewski, disappointed by the turnout, recalled in his *Memoirs* that his opening "was not a phenomenal success." William Steinway disagreed, and so did the small audience, who went wild. William scribbled in his diary: "Paderewski's first concert at Music Hall, grand success, he is a most wonderful player."

It wasn't until his third concert, when he played the Rubinstein concerto, that Paderewski noted that "the reception was really remarkable, tremendous." He proclaimed that the third concert was "the real beginning of my career in America." The profit was a record-breaking $3,000, but very little of it went into Paderewski's pocket. Tretbar, concerned that Steinway & Sons would not make the guaranteed $30,000, had gone to local agents and sold Paderewski recitals for as little as $200 a night. The result was that Paderewski played to packed halls in New York, Philadelphia, Chicago, and smaller cities for $200 and $500 a night, while the box office cleared $3,000 each time. Tretbar stayed in New York City but sent C. T. Fryer, a charming Englishman, to travel with Paderewski, attend every concert, and make sure that there was a Steinway piano, in tune, at every stop. As Paderewski recalled, "I was completely in the hands of Mr. Tretbar. He arranged everything, but . . . [Fryer] did the work." On the road, Paderewski's self-imposed schedule was a grueling seventeen hours of playing or practicing, one hour for meals, and six for sleep.

As friends published poems about him and eminent pianists applauded his playing, his popularity soared to such an extent that even his concerts in small cities like Portland, Maine, were sold out. Audiences were refusing to leave the concert hall unless he played at least an hour of encores. According to Harold C. Schonberg, "he exuded mystery and, his admirers thought, genius. He was everybody's dream of what a pianist should look like, and he cultivated the image." It was Paderewski's personality and flaming red hair that captured American audiences as much as his music. To this day, critics argue as to whether he was more style than substance; but he became a legend, even though most Americans could never pronounce his name—Paderevski, not Paderooski—and had never been attracted to classical piano music before he appeared on the scene. Schonberg described "his hold over the public, his noble tone, his almost palpable magnetism, poetry, glamour and mystery," as pianism personified. It was wonderful for the ego, but after shaking hands with thousands of people after each performance, Paderewski's right hand would swell to twice its normal size, causing him much pain.

There was another reason too for the pain in his right hand and arm. Although never publicized at the time, Paderewski claimed that the Steinway piano in 1891 "had a certain peculiarity which was rather dangerous for concert players. Their action at that time was extremely heavy and fatiguing." He complained and was promised that it would be fixed. But it didn't happen right away. Paderewski explained that "it was not changed because the workmen refused to accept [my] criticism. . . .They were convinced that what they were doing must be accepted as perfection. . . .They respected [my] criticism and ignored it." He insisted that to produce a very large sound on a Steinway was a terrific strain for any artist and continued to complain about the action throughout the tour. Finally, in March 1892, Paderewski's grand action was completely overhauled. Paderewski recalled the incident as a great victory.

But one cold night, after Steinway had changed the action on his piano, Paderewski arrived in Rochester, New York, and went directly to the concert hall from the train. He walked onto the stage, sat down, and struck a few chords. Suddenly a terrific pain shot through his arm. It felt as if he had broken a bone. He was in agony and wanted to run off the stage. But, arm stiff and pulsating with pain, he continued to play Beethoven's *Appassionata*. After the concert that night he went to a physician, who told him that he had "strained some tendons" in his arm and seriously injured his finger and that the only cure was rest. But Paderewski had concerts scheduled every day, sometimes afternoon and evening. He could not rest.

In every town he visited, he had to find a physician to treat his finger just before a concert or it wouldn't move. He was in constant pain. Every physician warned him that he was ruining his hand and arm for life. But he couldn't stop, and by now the tour was almost over. He became accustomed to the pain and taught himself to play with only four fingers of his right hand. He finished the tour, irreversibly injuring his arm and the ring finger of his right hand, and forever blamed the Steinway piano and Tretbar's tour plan for his suffering. He later discovered that the piano in Rochester had been shipped back to the factory for repairs prior to his arrival, and that one of the regulators, not knowing that this was Paderewski's special piano, had restored the action to its original stiffness. He never totally recovered the use of his fourth finger, and "for all we know," Harold Schonberg intimates, "he was never again the pianist who came to America in 1891."

On Paderewski's return to New York, William, perhaps aware of the tragic consequences of the punishing tour and certainly wanting more mileage out of this superstar, gave Paderewski an extra $4,000 and offered him more concerts. The additional concerts would be clear profit for Paderewski. He agreed, even though he was riddled with pain and convinced that he would probably never play again. He regularly used hot water, massages, and electricity to nurse his dead fourth finger back to life. He played on in agony and made more money in those twenty-seven extra concerts than in all the preceding eighty. All in all, he had performed 107 concerts in 117 days. He left with $95,000, without praising either the Steinway piano or the Steinway company. He later apologized for his hasty departure and for forgetting to endorse the piano. But, on his return to Europe, he played not a Steinway but an Erard piano.³

Nevertheless, William signed him up for a second season, this time sixty concerts, not eighty. Paderewski postponed the starting date to December to give his arm and finger more time to recuperate. William explained the delay to his board as caused by "inflammatory rheumatism." With rest and massages, his arm healed, but the finger remained weak. That Christmas, Steinway & Sons bought Paderewski a solid silver punch bowl and ladle from Tiffany & Company. The Steinway trustees had just awarded each other an extra $5,000 in salary from excess profits in 1892, much of it generated by Paderewski. The least they could do was give him a $550 punch bowl.

Paderewski's second tour was a phenomenal success, both for the artist and for Steinway & Sons. It included a posh private railway car with a bedroom, kitchen, dining room, and salon with a Steinway piano. Paderewski was accompanied by his secretary, a tour manager, his valet, a piano technician, a chef, and two porters. Later he would add a masseur and a private physician. The concerts were spread out and were arranged according to railroad schedules. He was so popular, so charismatic, so worshipped, that crowds, mostly women, would gather at railroad crossings just to get a glimpse of his profile and line the streets from his hotel to the hall where he was playing. At his concerts his business manager would give fifty free tickets to young students who promised to rush the stage at the end of the performance in a mad desire to get closer to Paderewski.

This time he found his Steinway piano "in marvelous condition." It had been prepared with "care and affection" just for him. Paderewski "had nothing to say, but to play and praise the instrument. They were beautiful. . . . They are the greatest pianos in the world." But his finger plagued him throughout the tour. It became infected, and he had to have surgery. But he returned to playing soon after the operation, thereby opening the wound. The consequence was that "at the end of every concert the keyboard was covered with blood." He later blamed his bloodshed on "necessity and ambition and, of course, the all-conquering disregard of youth."

Toward the end of the tour he was invited to Chicago to play at the World's Fair of 1893. This was the Columbian Exposition, celebrating (slightly belatedly) the four-hundredth anniversary of Christopher Columbus's arrival in 1492. When Paderewski got there, everyone was preparing for the opening. President Grover Cleveland opened the fair on 1 May in front of at least half a million people who had paid fifty cents each to get onto the grounds.

Paderewski had a problem, however. He was committed to playing a Steinway. But Steinway & Sons, fearing that the judging in Chicago would be rigged in favor of Chicago manufacturers, had at the last moment withdrawn from the exhibition. In fact, all New York piano manufacturers and most piano makers from the eastern United States had pulled out. What they objected to specifically was that, instead of a panel of judges from all over the world, as was usual at fairs, the Chicago fair had one judge: Florenz Ziegfield, head of Chicago Musical College and father of the impresario. Easterners doubted that a Chicagoan who was head of a college that had W. W. Kimball, the largest piano maker in Chicago, on its board would be fair. In response, the Chicago manufacturers said that if easterners didn't exhibit, their pianos could not be played at any of the fair's concerts. But at the last minute the music council declared that the Music Hall, where Paderewski was to play, was a separate institution and thus not connected to the fair, so he could play there on a Steinway. The competition was outraged when they heard that Paderewski was being allowed to play, and the newspapers re-ported that Paderewski had sold out to Steinway.[4]

William was understandably delighted that "Paderewski played at the Chicago Fair on a Steinway Grand in spite of all opposition." At the time, he had very little else to make him happy. His second wife, Elizabeth, had just died of Bright's disease at the age of forty, and in June the nation's economy went into a tailspin when the stock market crashed, taking Steinway & Sons with it. The problem was that the railroad companies had borrowed heavily to lay more tracks and build new stations and bridges. Manufacturers had also overextended themselves during the 1880s and into the 1890s, and profits were not covering the cost of expansion. Companies were trying to automate to cut payrolls and increase profit, but it wasn't working. They always ended up in more debt because of the cost of the machines, and the nation ended up with rising unemployment. In New York City some twenty thousand people were homeless and roamed the streets, picking through garbage and sleeping in hallways.

Steinway & Sons' profits dropped more than 30 percent. On 28 June William noted in his diary: "financial outlook simply dreadful." The next day he recorded: "terrible panic downtown," and again a month later: "dreadful panic on Wall Street." By August he was describing the financial situation as "truly alarming" and the piano business as "at a standstill." In 1893 the number of pianos shipped (including Hamburg) dropped from more than three thousand to less than twenty-five hundred. Expecting to come out of this crisis, Steinway increased production. But nobody was paying their bills. To help the larger dealers stay in business, Steinway ex-tended credit to them. To cover its own expenses, Charles H. Steinway, heir to William's tottering throne, convinced the board to approve "a mortgage of $150,000 at 5% per annum for one year from the Farmers Loan and Trust Company on our Steinway Hall property." By August they were on the doorstep of the New York City United States Trust Company for an addi-tional $125,000, this time putting up the 53rd Street factory. Sales picked up in September, and helped by the European operations, mostly Hamburg, Steinway limped along until the end of 1893.[5]

But new alliances were forming in Europe which foreshadowed future problems for Steinway. The relationship between France and Germany was deteriorating. France was becoming increasingly allied with Russia. The two had agreed to come to each other's aid in the event of an attack by Germany, Italy, or Austria-Hungary. These were the alliances that put Europe on the road to World War I. By 1894 the growing friction between Germany and France had persuaded Steinway & Sons to switch jurisdiction over their pianos in France from Hamburg to London. But such simple solutions to the problems arising from growing tensions in Europe would become increasingly difficult to find.

In the midst of the worst depression yet seen and a tottering world order, Steinway & Sons suffered a further blow. During the early morning hours of 30 November 1896 William Steinway died, at the age of sixty-one. He had been suffering from typhoid fever for weeks. On the evening before his death he had looked at the assembled family and said: "Must I really die?" He had then sunk into hallucinations brought on by injections of strychnine, used as a tonic to stimulate the nervous system.[6]

Fred wrote to his mother that a man like William Steinway "comes only once a century to a family." *The New York Times* ran a long front-page obituary. An avalanche of letters poured into Steinway Hall. Mayor Strong ordered that flags on all city buildings be placed at half-mast. A simple Unitarian service was held privately at William's home on Gramercy Park.

The Liederkranz Hall was draped in black in preparation for the thousands of invited guests who would come to view William's body. At the head of his casket was an enormous floral lyre made of violets. Palms, wreaths, hyacinths, cut roses, and an arrangement in the form of a grand piano made of German ivy and white roses, with a keyboard of violets and white carnations, filled the concert room as background for the public funeral. Just inside the entrance to the Liederkranz Hall was a life-size portrait of William and below it, written with violets, the inscription "Our President." It would take nearly an hour for just the workers from Steinway & Sons to file past and look at their employer's face for the last time. Outside, the police kept the uninvited crowd away from the hall.

Inside, Carl Schurz sobbed uncontrollably as he delivered the funeral oration for the man he proclaimed to have loved dearly. Then the doors to the hall were thrown open, and Steinway & Sons' piano workers marched in a column eight deep, escorting the casket from 58th Street to the 23rd Street ferry. More than a hundred carriages, filled with mourners, followed the hearse to Brooklyn and then on to a hill at Greenwood Cemetery where the Liederkranz male chorus sang as William's body was placed in the Steinway mausoleum. New York and the music world mourned the loss of one of the greatest impresarios.[7]

After William's death the company slid further into a financial slump, with 1896 the worst year yet. Adding to their troubles, an inventory of William's estate shortly after his death revealed almost half a million dollars invested in doubtful or worthless enterprises such as the Astoria Homestead Company, the Irving Place Theatre, and the Daimler Motor Company. Henry W. T. Steinway was right: William's other businesses had been a drain on the resources of Steinway & Sons. When piano making was flourishing, very few noticed or cared; but during a depression the strain of these other investments was indisputable.

William had been a speculator, a risk-taker, a typical late-nineteenth-century entrepreneur. But he was often involved in ventures he knew nothing about and consequently lost money. He invested in Astoria Silk Works without any knowledge of silk making. He financed a trolley business without ever having run a trolley line. He bought real estate without any background in land development. And he died at the worst possible moment for an unsuccessful speculator, when the economy was in decline. Had he lived, he could possibly have carried the investments into the next upswing of the piano business, because of the trust placed in him. But by 1897 William's estate was in desperate financial straits, which in turn meant trouble for the company, since William owned most of the company stock, more than 8,000 shares.

Adding to the problem was the fact that the German piano company Grotrian had been permitted by decree of the Imperial Court to use the name Steinweg. Grotrian had been trying to palm their pianos off as Steinways ever since 1867, when, following the Paris fair, the name had become valuable currency in Europe. Now they could compete legally with Steinway using the name Steinweg.

The cousins—Charles, Fred, and Henry Ziegler—decided that the only way to raise much-needed cash and get the company going again was to sell Steinway & Sons to an English syndicate for $6 million. This was not a new idea in corporate finance. British investors had been making multi-million-dollar purchases of American flour, grain, steel, and cotton companies since the late 1880s. Charlie went to London during the summer of 1897 to make the sale. As he wrote to his brother Fred and cousin Henry, we "ourselves know the main reason why we wanted to sell the William Steinway Estate shares, but of course I could not even breathe a word of this to the people over here and hence had to keep that small secret to myself." They prepared all the papers and put the stock up for sale. Everyone assured Charles that it would be oversubscribed. But they raised no more than $500,000. Charlie's explanation was that the rich were away on vacation at the time.

But the real reasons were different. Neither Charles nor Fred nor Henry Ziegler commanded the trust that William had commanded. Charles, facing the "calamity of the collapse of the estate and consequent scandal on the name Steinway to come," wondered "once in a while why I don't collapse and go crazy. . . . I am completely knocked out." But the only thing he could do was "put on a brave face, keep a confident demeanor and wait."[8]

TEN

From Near Bankruptcy to
Fabulous Wealth

THE NEPHEWS NOW
ruled what was left of Steinway & Sons. Charles became president, his
brother Fred, vice-president, and their cousin Henry Ziegler was in charge
of all experimentation.

Charles was financially conservative, artistically creative, and socially
flamboyant. He was the one who had insisted that they put the dealers on a
cash basis after Smith & Nixon in Cincinnati went bankrupt and almost took
Steinway with them. He enjoyed composing waltzes, playing the piano after
business hours at Steinway Hall, winning at billiards, and pursuing beautiful
women. As one relative remembered, "Charlie had a girlfriend [Mary Claire
Osgood]. Charlie's wife had a boyfriend [Captain Edward C. Lefebvre]. . . .
Charlie would make annual trips to Europe with his wife Marie. Her boyfriend would show up over there, and his girlfriend would show up too.
They'd all go to Monte Carlo to gamble. And they lived high, wide and
handsome."[1]

Fred became head of the factory. He was even more financially prudent
than Charlie. He was the one who had voted against the Paderewski contract
and in most board meetings was the lone vote against dividends and extra
pay for themselves.[2]

Henry Ziegler, Doretta's son, had worked with Uncle Theodor on scale
design in the department of inventions and construction. It was Ziegler who
had introduced the 7⅓-octave "B" grand by adding three extra treble notes
to the normal 7-octave piano, thereby giving the keyboard the 88 keys and
7⅓ octaves that it has today.[3]

Charles H. Steinway.

Charlie, Fred, and Henry were together all the time; daily conversations replaced letters, and knowing looks supplanted memos with the result that most of their discussions went unrecorded. They continued to be wary of their troublesome brother, Henry W. T., and the published record became more formal. The headline above the monthly minutes: "Meeting of the Board of Directors of the Corporation of Steinway & Sons" was now in gothic lettering, and in a few years the minutes would be typed rather than handwritten. Moreover, the content became cryptic, limited to financial reports and phrases like "various important matters were discussed."

At the end of 1897 both the nation and Steinway & Sons started to pull out of the depression. The impetus for the recovery was the rebuilding of the nation's cities and the setting up of new industries, chemical and electrical, based on laboratory research done during the 1890s. New discoveries of gold and good harvests also spurred the economy. A boom in piano purchases was stirred by the player piano, motion pictures, and captivation with ragtime.

Ragtime, a distinctively American mix of banjo and folk tunes, came out of the African-American experience on southern plantations and was culti-vated by African-American musicians in the city's saloons, brothels, and gambling houses. At first most composers condemned the new tunes as what Edward MacDowell labeled "nigger-whorehouse music." According to Eubie Blake, his mother, a very religious woman, "hated ragtime like all the high-class Negroes. . . . When I played it at home," Blake confessed, "my mother would yell, 'Take that ragtime out of my house. As long as I'm here, you don't play ragtime in this house!' I had to go somewhere else to practice. She knew where it came from." But by 1910 the prejudice was gone, and Scott Joplin's "Maple Leaf Rag" would be the first piece of sheet music to sell a million copies. White composers started to adopt ragtime as if they had invented it. Ragtime was piano music, and for piano manufacturers like Steinway & Sons that meant sales. Ragtime did for the piano what rock'n'roll would later do for the guitar.

Another new piano market was provided by the small movie houses springing up across the country to show silent films. They all bought pianos. Piano music was used to add suspense to the chase, terror to the lady strapped to a log approaching the buzz saw, anxiety as the oncoming train seemed headed for collision with the broken-down milk wagon, and sizzle to the glance of a leading lady from an otherwise silent screen. Lyon & Healy, a Steinway dealer in Chicago, offered a school for aspiring silent movie pianists.[4]

This expanding market showed up in Steinway's new annual profit and loss and balance sheets. In only three years, between 1896 and 1899, Steinway went from near bankruptcy to $420,000 profit. During the next three years profits soared even further, reaching an all-time record of more than half a million dollars each year. In 1900 Steinway & Sons made so much money that the directors voted to increase their own salaries by a third, from $12,000 to $16,000. Compared to what the average working-class family in New York City earned—between $600 and $700 a year—this was a lot of money. Average rent for a three-room apartment on the Lower East Side, in a high-rent district, was $13.50 per month; a good corduroy coat from Sears, Roebuck sold for $2.85; a toothbrush was less than a dime; a complete 100-piece dinner set was $19.95; and a tombstone cost $6.99, though to have your name and dates of birth and death etched in the stone cost 6 cents a letter extra.[5]

To increase production, Charlie built a second factory in Queens, a few miles from the original buildings. The original Queens factory, on Riker Avenue, was on Bowery Bay; and the dampness from the bay prolonged the drying time of wood, varnish, and glue. Not only did Steinway need more room; it also needed a factory on higher, drier ground. In 1901, for about $100,000, Steinway bought a new factory on Ditmars Boulevard which provided both. It was a three-story, **U**-shaped brick building of about 125,000 square feet. "Ditmars," as the new factory came to be known, was less than a

Steinway's newly built Ditmars factory, 1902. Another three stories were added in 1911.

mile up the road from the original factory and furnished the perfect site for final assembly, finishing the case, and regulating the keys and actions coming from "Riker," the new name for the original Queens factory site.

One Steinway worker recalled that piano parts were "trucked in a big van, drawn by a pair of magnificent brown horses, to the Ditmars Avenue plant, where [the piano] was put together and finished." The horses also came in handy during snowstorms, when they would be hitched up "to a huge V-shaped contraption of heavy planking, and [driven] through every street" in Steinway Village to clear the snow. Charlie also opened a showroom at the new Windsor Arcade on Fifth Avenue at 46th Street, site of the old Windsor Hotel where Paderewski had stayed. Like other piano manufacturers in New York City, Steinway & Sons was moving uptown.

The new showroom and factory were financed by the tremendous profits that the company was making. Steinway & Sons was rolling in money, so much so that they started burying cash, $70,000 to $250,000 a year, in accounts called "Undivided Profit" and "Sinking Fund." Even William's estate started to be remunerative, as Steinway stock soared and a plot of Astoria Homestead Company land was sold to a syndicate of Western bankers for $300,000. From a debt of half a million dollars, it went to more than $1.5 million in assets. The sale of William's Steinway stock (8,023 shares) and his land, worth much more since 1896, bailed out the estate.[6]

Plate rubbers in the Steinway foundry, 1908.

Foundry workers, 1908.

Action makers, 1908.

Upright bellymen (soundboard makers), 1908.

Proud at having saved a bankrupt company, Charlie decided to promote the Steinway as the national piano and the company as the first piano manufacturer in the world to have produced a hundred thousand instruments. The one-hundred-thousandth Steinway was built in 1902, by the "Art Piano-case Department," for President Theodore Roosevelt, to go in the East Room of the White House. To match the decor of the recently renovated White House, the entire piano, including the bench, was gilded with gold leaf, and on the lid was a painting entitled "America Receiving the Nine Muses," depicting ten women in pink, mauve, and gray centennial revival-style ball gowns against a vivid green background. Steinway carver Juan Ayuso even chiseled American bald eagles into the piano's three legs. Its value was estimated as $7,500—extremely high considering that the most expensive concert "D" grand sold for $1,600 net. This piano was given to the nation in 1903.[7]

Charlie continued to support worldwide dealerships and to supply Steinway artists with pianos, tuners, and cash. He even published a booklet, "The Portraits of Musical Celebrities," that included testimonials from the more famous artists and the names of all Steinway artists. In exchange, artists like Moritz Rosenthal, Teresa Carreño, and Leopold Godowski agreed to use Steinway pianos exclusively and to have the name "Steinway & Sons" inserted in their programs and circulars. Charles also insisted that the following statement be included: "These artists use the Steinway pianos exclusively for the said season with no money consideration being paid by either of the parties to this contract." It wasn't true. Carreño was paid $50 per concert, although the money was labeled "for advertising," and Godowski was paid $300 per concert, also "for advertising." Instead of just giving Carreño $50 or Godowski $300 per concert, Charlie bought tickets or advertising worth that amount for each public concert. He could then say, if questioned, that he did not give the artist money. He was just buying tickets or paying for advertising.[8]

Charlie was perfectly willing to support artists financially, albeit in this devious way, but did not have much patience if they questioned the quality of his pianos. Even the great Paderewski encountered the limits of Charlie's tolerance. In December 1904, when Paderewski was in San Francisco on tour and was being courted by Steinway dealer Sherman, Clay & Company, he was annoyed when his favorite tuner did not arrive with the five Steinway concert grands shipped especially for him. He refused all five pianos and sent a telegram to New York claiming that the instruments were "unplayable." Perhaps he was remembering his first experience with the Steinway piano; possibly the actions were too tight. Charlie wired back: "Have ordered pianos returned to New York. Withdraw our piano service."

Paderewski threatened to go to another manufacturer. That's when Leander S. Sherman, a good friend of Paderewski and partner in Sherman, Clay & Company, entered the fray. He wrote to Steinway that "for Paderewski to start with the Steinway and either give it up or have it taken from him would furnish every rival salesman in the country with 'Knocking Material' for years to come." He provided Paderewski with a local tuner. This calmed the waters. He then wired Steinway that Paderewski really did "not wish to change manufacturers unless you force him to do so." Sherman proposed sending two more grands and Paderewski's favorite tuner for a few days, all in the spirit of diplomacy. He cabled Steinway that "Ignace thought your instructions to withdraw pianos unnecessarily severe." He redefined "unplayable" to mean that the pianos were "only unsatisfactory to himself." Sherman then suggested that Steinway wire back an apology over the misunderstanding of the word "unplayable." Sherman subsequently wrote: "I have come to the conclusion that personally I never would hold Mr. Paderewski responsible for what he may do or say, I would excuse everything. The man leads an unnatural life. He is awake when he should be asleep, and he sleeps when he should be awake. If you and I had been petted and pampered as much as he has, we would probably be queer too."

Sherman's mediation was successful. The misunderstanding was cleared up—for a while—and Steinway sent Paderewski's favorite tuner to meet him in Portland, Oregon, with new hammers. Paderewski, in turn, apologized for hurting Charlie's feelings. He was courteous and played the gentleman in continuing the tour with a Steinway, but, according to Ernest Urchs, who was with him in Seattle in January 1905, it "will take some time to heal his wounded feelings."

After April 1905, Paderewski recalled in his *Memoirs,* he did not play any more that year. The following year brought further disagreement with Charlie. Paderewski again asked for "different instruments," claiming that the ones shipped were not satisfactory to him. Charles wired back: "Your telegram is so offensive that I have instructed our representatives everywhere to withdraw all our pianos from you from now on." It was a complete break with the most popular pianist of the day. Neither one backed off or apologized. Charles was making so much money and Steinway & Sons was doing so well that he really didn't need Paderewski. For his part, Paderewski claimed that he was making an artistic decision that Steinway pianos were just not good for him. On his next two concert tours he played a Weber piano.[9]

One reason why Charlie was less dependent on Paderewski in 1906 than Uncle William had been earlier was because Steinway & Sons' profits were now less dependent on piano sales in the United States. Half the $400,000 they made that year came from elsewhere: from Hamburg ($70,000), London ($32,000), the sale of Long Island real estate ($69,000), and piano rental ($32,000). Instead of looking to Paderewski to boost trade in North America, Charlie sent Ernest Urchs, who assumed some of Tretbar's work and became the "general wholesale representative and manager of the artists' department for Steinway & Sons," and a newcomer to the company, William R. Steinway, William's eldest son, with his second wife, on the road.

Urchs initiated William R., then in his twenties, into the world of sales trips. On their ten-week jaunt they visited dealers in fifty cities throughout the country. Urchs reported that, despite a "wave of conservatism" brought on by the depression of 1907, the volume of business done during the trip surpassed that of any other year. Dealers were doing a brisk trade, especially in medium-grade pianos. Surprisingly, the cheaper makes were not selling. But with loss of faith in the banks, people may have felt that putting their money into a good Steinway was safer, like putting it under the mattress. It would always be there.[10]

William R. Steinway, known as Billie, was being groomed to take over the helm. He had graduated from St. Paul's, an Episcopal school on Long Island, and had then gone to work at Steinway & Sons. As one family member recalled, "he was not very hot on the manufacturing, on the manual end of the business." Nor was he known for his punctuality; when his father died, he arrived at the house too late to say good-bye to him. Billie, like his Uncle Charlie, "was a bon vivant; he loved a good drink, a good dinner, a good cigar, and a funny story."—Moreover, he and Charlie liked each other. It was apparent that Charlie expected him to take over Steinway & Sons.

During the opening years of the twentieth century, 500,000 of the 650,000 pianos produced in the world were manufactured in two countries, the United States and Germany. With an eye to the flourishing European market, Charlie Steinway decided to have a family member in charge of its overseas operations. In 1909 he placed Billie on the Steinway board of trustees, shipped him off to manage the new Berlin showroom, and crowned him European general manager of Steinway & Sons.

There was only one problem: Billie did not want to live in Germany. To keep his young nephew in Berlin, Charlie procured a spirited peasant girl, Marie Kiesler, from a small town in Pomerania. A millinery worker by day, a streetwalker by night, Marie, or Mariechen as she was known, did more than detain and delight twenty-eight-year-old Billie. They fell in love.

In 1909 Charlie had to reckon with the fact that the market for pianos was moving more and more towards the player piano. He had to decide whether Steinway & Sons would add a player piano to its catalog. Steinway was a prestige concert grand house. Even uprights had been resisted to the point that the factory was never regeared to make them. Those bottom-line instruments just had to be fitted into a factory designed to make grands.

Ironically, Steinway, so heavily invested in concerts and artists, now had to decide whether or not to make pianos that played without a pianist. For a company that based its sales campaigns on the fact that since the leading pianists in the world use a Steinway, "you should too," this was a thorny issue. But, as national piano sales went more and more to player pianos, Charles could not stand on the sidelines any longer.

He opted to get into the player market, but only halfway. In 1909 Steinway & Sons signed a twenty-five-year agreement with the Aeolian Company, whereby Steinway would build at least six hundred new pianos per year set up for the incorporation of player equipment exclusively from the Aeolian Company. They would charge Aeolian "approximately fifty dollars per piano in excess of their regular wholesale prices." Aeolian agreed to pay cash for these special pianos, which would be sold exclusively by Steinway and Aeolian dealers. Aeolian sold players in the United States under the label "Duo-Art," the two arts: the art of piano maker and the art of the reproducer. Aeolian agreed to promote its "Steinway Pianola" over its "Weber Pianola," to withdraw from the concert field, and to "exploit the Weber Piano in public only through such minor pianists as Steinway & Sons may permit."[11]

Business improved, and profits climbed to $400,000, with gross profit on sales surpassing that of most years since 1900. The following year, 1910, Steinway put close to $200,000 into its "Sinking Fund," another $360,000 into "Undivided Profit," and still had $450,000 left in net profit. Arthur Loesser, in his thoughtful study *Men, Women, and Pianos,* estimated that on every working day of 1910 twelve hundred people bought a new piano. National advertising encouraged people to admire the rich, and owning a piano made them feel like they had a small part in that affluent life. Furthermore, music education became more widespread in the public schools, as did public performances. The player, the upright, and the rise of cheap, inferior pianos also attracted new customers to the music stores.

Steinway & Sons sold more than six thousand pianos in 1911, more than twice the number it had sold twelve years earlier. This was low, compared with the newly formed American Piano Company, which was producing fifteen thousand pianos a year, and the larger Midwest firms, W. W. Kimball in Chicago and Wurlitzer in Cincinnati. But these other companies were producing low-end, cheap, "commercial" pianos, mostly uprights, on an assembly line, so were not making inroads into Steinway & Sons' market. Steinway's real competition was no longer Weber, which had declined in the

Steinway and Weber player piano of the 1920s.

1890s and become a subsidiary of Aeolian, or Chickering, which had fallen long ago and in 1908 had been gobbled up, along with Knabe, by the American Piano Company. Steinway & Sons' major competitor in 1912 was Mason & Hamlin, an old Boston organ house that had turned to making a few hundred high-quality grands a year and had merged with the Cable Company of Chicago, which pumped in the necessary capital.[12]

Fred Steinway and Henry Ziegler praised Charles and rewarded him well (a $5,000 bonus beyond his $25,000 salary) for these lucrative years, the successful deal with Aeolian, and the recent profitable sale, on 20 May 1909, of the 53rd Street Manhattan factory for $650,000. It was one of the most important real estate deals of the time, because it started the transformation of Park Avenue from an industrial area to the high-priced residential street it would be for the rest of the century. The New York Central Railroad track was lowered and covered; the line was electrified; and the street above it made it easier to cross the tracks when compared to the footbridges that linked the crosstown streets before. With the lowering of the rail line, Park Avenue was no longer cut off from Fifth Avenue by an ugly railroad with smoke-belching steam locomotives passing by regularly. Park Avenue was about to become one of the most expensive places in the world, and Charles Steinway had signaled that transformation. The profit enabled him to pay off the 1893 mortgage on the factory and build three new stories on the Ditmars factory in 1911.

Between 1911 and 1914 both the world and the United States economy declined once again, but Steinway profits now seemed recession-proof. Hamburg (independent of the New York factory in terms of parts and plates since 1907, when increased tariffs on metal plates made their importation prohibitively expensive) and the London showroom were contributing a crucial amount to the profit. Hamburg brought in $166,000 net profit in 1911 and $200,000 the following year. New York sales were helped by Henry Ziegler's new, small 5-foot, 6-inch "M" grand. It was in the Steinway tradition to offer a less expensive, high-quality instrument—witness the small Parlor Grand, the 6-foot model A, introduced in 1878. Over the years the company had been tempted to offer a second, lower-quality line for people who could not afford the regular line but in the end decided to stay with the one-grade policy, so enabling it to advertise that "all Steinways are the best." The M was part of that policy. This baby grand was a great success. Priced at just $750, nine hundred were sold in 1912. Indeed, the M became the company's bread-and-butter model for the rest of the century.

With the new M, the contract with Aeolian, and a healthy market in Europe, Steinway & Sons made half a million dollars net profit in 1911, and even more the following year. The combined Hamburg and London profits were now regularly logging in as almost half the net profit. Charles, ecstatic, reported to the shareholders that even though there were "general unsettled business conditions maintaining all over the world during 1912 our company's progress and prosperity has not been affected thereby." He had taken a company on the verge of bankruptcy, about to be sold, and had made it more lucrative than ever before.[13]

Then, the summer of 1914, war broke out in Europe. Charles gravely explained to his board of directors that, because of the war, business was suffering greatly in Europe, and that, because the Hamburg factory was all but closed, the German operation was losing money. Hamburg went from profits ranging from $160,000 to $200,000 per year to losses of $5,000 in 1914 and $38,000 in 1915.

Another outcome of the war was that women entered the factory in significant numbers. They worked mostly in the action department, replacing young men who had gone off to war. They were paid hourly wages, while most of the men in the factory were paid piecework. Under Charles's management, women assumed a larger role in the company. Perhaps because his father died when he was eight years old, making him more dependent on

Steinway's "bread and butter" piano, the model M, introduced in 1912.

his mother than he would otherwise have been, Charles had confidence in the staying power of women. No longer confined to the action department or clerical jobs, women like Henrietta Frederica Kammerer found their way into management. Kammerer was hired in 1896 and for ten years assisted Tretbar in the Concert & Artist department. Starting as Tretbar's secretary, she eventually directed the work of the entire department.[14]

The losses in Hamburg and the effect of unstable conditions throughout Europe and in the United States eventually showed up on the balance sheets of Steinway & Sons. The war not only devastated Hamburg profits, but also cut London profits in half. For the company as a whole, net profit for the year dropped from half a million dollars to $240,000 in 1914. This took such a toll on Charles that he was confined to bed and out of commission until

1916. Although Steinway & Sons continued to lose money in Europe, it managed to recover in the United States, where the war brought prosperity. The year 1916 was a banner year for Steinway & Sons in the United States, with gross profit from sales topping $1.1 million. Americans meant every word when they sang Irving Berlin's "I Love a Piano" (1915). Steinway produced 6,561 pianos that year, the most pianos in their history. The net profit was $360,000 even after they had salted away $200,000 in various reserve accounts. This enormous profit continued into the following years.[15]

In January 1917 Charles informed his board of directors that "on account of stoppage of private messages between the United States and Europe the corporation has received no reports from the Hamburg and London branches." The next month they established radio contact. But on 2 April 1917, in response to German submarines sinking unarmed American merchant ships, the United States entered the war. For the first—but not the last—time, Steinway & Sons found itself on both sides of the battle, its factories contributing to the war effort in both the United States and Germany. All information from Hamburg was cut off.

At the outbreak of World War I, Billie refused to leave Mariechen. He lived with her in Berlin throughout the war, as an enemy alien. He wrote to his brother Theodore that business in Hamburg was "fairly bright and steady" and that the factory was "always almost a couple of months' orders behind." As an alien in enemy territory, Billie had to sign in at a government office every day and watch a clerk fill out forms. He had some rubber stamps made to speed up the process and to ingratiate himself with the clerk. According to American military intelligence reports, they discovered that Billie, living in Berlin, had proposed to Charles, in New York, that "an attempt be made to correspond through" the Steinway agent A. Belmont in Norway or through the Spanish embassies in Berlin and Washington. The Norwegian agents for Steinway & Sons were still in correspondence with New York and were also "obtaining supplies from the Hamburg and Berlin houses." All this made Charles suspect. He and his wife were put under surveillance, with copies of all reports going to the bomb squad of the New York Police Department. The report on Charles said that he was not a risk and "would give what ever aid he could to this country, as he believes the United States are fighting for a cause that is just."[16]

In 1919 Charlie Steinway was one of thousands of New Yorkers who died of flu. It was the worst epidemic of any kind in New York City since the cholera epidemics of the nineteenth century. Charlie, sixty-eight years old, died alone in the Sherman Square Hotel on the Upper West Side of Manhattan.

According to one account, he was worth $5 million. He had just purchased a factory in London to start manufacturing pianos there. He had more than doubled the assets of Steinway & Sons from $3 million to $6 million. He had more than tripled the number of pianos sold since William died. He had put all the dealers on a cash basis, refusing their notes after many of them went out of business in the summer of 1893, modernized the bookkeeping to monthly statements, established national advertising, opened a retail store in Berlin with a Concert & Artist department, started a branch store in Cincinnati, and put Steinway & Sons in the player-piano business without jeopardizing its reputation. In a word, he had saved Steinway & Sons.

After the war Billie notified the family that he planned to marry Mariechen. He didn't expect any objections. After all, Mariechen and Charlie had been great friends before the war. But Charlie was dead, and his more conservative younger brother, Fred, now headed Steinway & Sons. Fred and his willful wife, Julia, insisted on social etiquette. The message back to Billie was "Get rid of that girl"; there was no room in the house of Steinway for an erstwhile streetwalker. Julia D. Steinway was not about to give up her throne to Mariechen Kiesler. Billie was instructed that if he wanted to be the next president of Steinway & Sons, he should "come back to New York and marry a nice American girl."

Fred and Julia then authorized Theodore Ehrlich, who had been sent to Hamburg in 1909 to end a strike and straighten out the books, to pay Mariechen off. The deal, according to family legend, was a million dollars if Mariechen would leave Billie and go back to Pomerania. She must have agreed. But Billie followed her back to her village, Stalluponea, and on 14 October 1921 they were married. Fred declared, "Well, that's it. You'll never be president of Steinway." Billie fired back, "The hell with it."[17]

ELEVEN

The "Instrument of the Immortals" Goes National

I
N 1919 FRED STEINWAY had more important matters to deal with than the love life of his nephew. He was head of the most prestigious piano house in the world, and postwar America was entering the "great age of piano ownership." President Calvin Coolidge once said that he never "imagined a model New England home without the family Bible on the table and the family piano in the corner." In their study *Middletown*, Robert and Helen Lynd estimated that by 1928 more than half America's city dwellers had pianos in their homes.[1]

A national survey revealed that one out of every four children above third grade was taking private piano lessons. Many states required "piano" as a subject in school. Choral societies, orchestras, music contests, and piano classes spread throughout the country in the overheated auditoriums of settlement houses, schools, and churches. By 1929 Americans were spending $900 million on music education.[2]

Topping the ledgers in piano sales were player pianos. The "player" was easy to use and accessible to everyone. But, more important, it was a machine at a time when Americans were in love with machines. Like the phonograph, toaster, and washing machine, the player piano was popular because it could go on being used. By 1923 some 56 percent of the 360,000 pianos produced in America were players. It was the perfect instrument for a society demanding immediate, repeatable, effortless gratification.[3]

Competition among player piano manufacturers was keen. The leaders were Aeolian, Welte & Söhne, and the American Piano Company (better known as Ampico). In New York the American Piano Company converted five entire floors of its building on West 57th Street, one block from Steinway Hall, into a laboratory for the study of player pianos. The goal was to make a player piano that would sound as if Paderewski was at the keyboard. But the results were debatable. Every piano company claimed that its player reproduced the nuances of celebrated artists. The American Piano Company, Welte & Söhne, and Aeolian all sold their players with testimonials that all the prominent concert artists, including Paderewski, were precisely reproduced on their instrument.[4]

This demand for pianos, both player and straight, presented a fundamental challenge to Fred Steinway, the new president of Steinway & Sons: could he increase production without sacrificing quality? It was one thing to make an exceptional piano for Paderewski; quite another to make the other eight thousand quality instruments required that year.[5]

Fred Steinway looked to Henry Ziegler, his vice-president, and Ziegler's nephew Theodore Cassebeer, the factory manager, to come up with a solution. As one family member later recalled, "These three guys lived in each other's pockets," and never stopped talking about pianos. To resolve the "quantity versus quality" dilemma, they had to find a completely new way to make a Steinway.

It was fortunate that the most practical president in the company's history, Fred Steinway, presided over its most turbulent era. Unlike his older brother and predecessor, he was an "ultra-save man" who disliked bank loans, even during the slow summer months when the company was short of cash. Fred also refused to "splurge in subvention to the artists" until he was sure that endorsement by artists paid off for Steinway. When he woke up to the fact that great artists playing Steinway instruments before New York fine audiences had a great deal to do with the flourishing retail trade, he admitted to Henry Ziegler that he had been wrong "to judge harshly of the money spent by us on them [the artists], it seems to be paying for itself."[6]

Fred Steinway was raised by his mother in Brunswick. He was only five years old when his father, Charles, died and his mother, thirty-one at the time, moved her family from New York to Brunswick. The two older boys were shipped back to America when they turned fourteen and enrolled in the Mount Pleasant Academy in Ossining, New York—but not Fred. In a letter to her brother-in-law, William, she made it clear that she would "not permit Fred to return to America."[7]

But when Albert Steinway also died of typhoid fever, on 14 May 1877, this left only William and Theodore to run Steinway & Sons. Henry W. T., Sophie's eldest son, only twenty-one at the time, became de facto head of the piano factory. Sophie's other son, Charlie, was taken to Steinway Hall to assist William. Now they needed Fred, too. He had fulfilled his late father's

Fred Steinway.

wish and passed the *Abitur,* his state high school exams. Furthermore, Sophie had remarried and was thus less in need of Fred's companionship. According to William, Fred was ready to take his place with his brothers, and in fall 1878 Sophie let him go to America.[8]

Because he had spent most of his childhood in Germany, Fred was more German than his brothers, and always cautious and genteel. Henry Z. Steinway, his cousin once removed, recollected that no one at the factory "could imagine him with his coat off."[9] Moreover, unlike his brothers, Fred had not apprenticed at Steinway & Sons during his youth. He had never worked, as they had, in each department of the company learning to make pianos. He arrived in New York, aged eighteen, too old to go through the usual three- to four-year apprenticeship which commonly began at fourteen. Instead, William enrolled Fred in the Columbia School of Mines (Engineering School) for a few years and put him in the factory to assist his older brother Henry.

In 1919, when Charlie died, Fred became president and Henry Ziegler vice-president. Titles notwithstanding, they managed the company as partners.[10] By 1920 they had been working together for forty years. Ziegler had started work in the piano factory in 1880, two years after Fred arrived from Germany. They became the best of friends.

In his diary Fred recorded that he spent most "evenings at Ziegler's . . . after supper [they either] played billiards . . . [or] cards." Sometimes they just chatted over a bottle of champagne. Fred was all for a genteel life-style. Once, in a letter to Ziegler, he apologized for being "rather slow in completing this work . . . [and blamed] nothing else but pure cussed laziness on my part." A typical day included an extended lunch at Lüchow's, where he would remain until four, drinking two beers and one whiskey and Chartreuse mixed, then home and on to the opera.[11]

By contrast, Ziegler was obsessed with work. His goal in life was to improve damper felts, varnish, hammer heads, strings, and plates.[12] He was constantly on the lookout for new ideas and was always checking out the competition. A typical Ziegler letter started out: "Dear Boys [Fred and Charlie]," and went on to expound on, say, the Bechstein grand that he

> had a splendid opportunity to study . . . at our dealer Wolf here in Wiesbaden. He gave me the key for ware rooms . . . and I wallowed. Bechstein Upright was *very good*—his grand *very bad*—and very costly construction at that. . . . I heard a fine concert last night . . . [Maria Teresa] Carreño [the Venezuelan pianist] tried her best to knock the tar out of the Bechstein—but she couldn't—there was nothing but Iron. . . . I assure you, the Bechstein is the bummest, stiffest-toned thing I ever heard. . . . Nevertheless Carreño had an immense success—which shows that the public does not care a rap about the piano.[13]

Fred's own brothers were not available in the way Ziegler was; Henry was unapproachable, and Charlie was too rowdy. Hence Ziegler became the substitute older brother to whom Fred could turn. They were good for each other. Fred learned about hard work from Ziegler, and Ziegler learned about leisure from Fred. When they were apart, Fred lamented: "Now you are far away in France . . . and I am cast upon the desert of a homeless life . . . . I shall spend Xmas with Cassebeers and shall think of you and miss you all the more." With affection, Fred called Ziegler "Popsie" because he was the first of their generation to have children. For his part, Ziegler named his only son Fred.[14]

This was who Fred Steinway banked on in the 1920s to protect the quality of Steinway pianos while stimulating production to double its previous rate. They paid themselves handsomely to do the job. By 1925 Fred as president and Ziegler as vice-president were making well over $30,000 a year and owned some half a million dollars each in Steinway stock.[15]

During the twenties a chauffeured car brought Ziegler from his house in Hewlett, Long Island, to the piano factory in Queens. Sitting in the back seat wearing a wing collar, sporting a full dark mustache, topped off by a bowler hat, Ziegler was dressed for the part. Joe Marschek, office manager in the 1920s, recalled instructing a new cost clerk, Frank Walsh, that "when Mr. Ziegler comes in in the morning . . . you jump up and take off Mr. Ziegler's

Henry and Addie
Ziegler at the Steinway
mansion, c. 1890.

coat and hang it in the closet." Walsh refused, telling Mr. Marschek that he
was hired as a cost clerk not a coat clerk.[16]

Ziegler's department, "Construction and Invention," was on the top
floor of the Ditmars factory. This piano laboratory, the "pattern room" as it

was called, was full of clutter, but also sunshine, thanks to windows along one entire side. Perched at the top of the factory, with a freight elevator at each end, Ziegler could have pianos delivered to him for examination from any department in the factory at anytime. Often he asked for a model A or a model D grand to tinker with. Surrounded by grands, uprights, experimental harps, new actions, and blueprints, Henry Ziegler worked to improve the modern Steinway piano.[17]

He always took his new ideas to Fred. During the twenties they met every afternoon at Steinway Hall to talk business. It was in the fall of 1922, during one of these daily exchanges, that they first came up with the ideas that would solve their production problems. At the next Steinway & Sons board of trustees meeting they announced a new-style 6-foot baby grand to be designated model "L." The factory in Queens was to be retooled to produce L's in both mahogany and ebony.[18] Their second recommendation was that the company begin manufacturing the M in ebony. They had been making Ms in mahogany for the past ten years but ebony would be less expensive.

The L and the M were both small and quick to assemble; the M was 5 feet, 7 inches, in length, and the L 3½ inches longer—two small grands with big voices. When made as cases for Aeolian, six inches was added to both of them to allow room for the player mechanism. The factory geared up to make thousands of these new models a year, both as regular pianos and as player pianos. Henry Z. Steinway recalled that the L and M were the "bread and butter production-line pianos that went out by the quintillion."[19]

Fortunately, their cousin Theodore (Teddy) Cassebeer had the necessary time, skill, and commitment when Fred and Ziegler asked him to produce a "quintillion" small Steinways a year. His first move was to overhaul the procedure for shaping the rim.

In 1878 Theodor had patented a new rim-bending process, using iron presses and screw clamp-bars to shape sixteen layers of straight-grained thin wood veneers to the curved rim of the grand case. After the layers were glued together, a team of men, in what looked like an attempt to tame an 18–25-foot ham and cheese hero, picked up the cumbersome sandwich and with muscle and clamps bent it around an immense iron press into the flowing curves of the grand. While in the press the wood was eased into its new shape by steam. To produce the long strips of veneer, Steinway had to build its own veneer mill. According to Steinway's catalog, no other sawmill existed in which veneers longer than 16 feet could be produced. Bending wood was not a new idea; Americans had been doing it since 1818. Woodworkers knew that a curved wooden object was stronger than one cut to shape. They also knew that if a piece of wood was held by a form, in a curved position along its

Steinway's rim-bending machine, with workers clamping the rim so that it will hold its shape. Photo taken in 1934 by Margaret Bourke-White, *Fortune,* © Time Inc.; reproduced with permission.

entire length, it would maintain its new shape. This had worked for plow handles, wheel rims, and sleighs. Why not for piano cases? There was a surge in patents for wood-bending machines, and Theodor was part of that rush to the register's office.[20]

In the 1920s, Steinway was still building two rims: an inner rim and an outer rim and then gluing the two together. John Steinway recalled Cassebeer figuring that it would be feasible to "bend the maple rim all in one shot," thus doing it faster and producing a more solid construction.[21] He drew up plans and persuaded Fred to invest in new presses. Within months, rims started rolling off the presses at twice the speed.

There was only one problem: while drying in the kilns, most of them cracked. Cassebeer couldn't figure it out. He sent for Frank Lehecka, a Bohemian piano maker at Steinway whose father had worked for Steinway in the 1890s and who was considered a "valuable man" by Fred and Ziegler.[22] Frank liked to pin people to the wall and tell them long, boring stories about how to make better pianos. Other workers would walk by, watching Frank's captive audience suffer from his tales, his bad breath, and his spitting.

But no one knew wood better than Frank; so everyone submitted to this ordeal.

Looking at the cracked rims, Frank told Cassebeer to stop using poplar as the core wood with maple as the outside wood. He explained that "in bending rims the poplar will absorb at least twice as much moisture from the glue than maple. Therefore [the poplar] expands more, and then, while in dry kiln [the poplar] wants to shrink to its original width. The maple [expands and then] shrinks very little, so, something has to crack!" The solution was easy: to use maple for all the layers. Cassebeer did just that, and it worked. At last Steinway was able to produce rims in half the time—without cracks.[23]

Cassebeer's next move was to develop new presses, gadgets, and tools to improve veneering techniques. With the encouragement and approval of Fred and Ziegler, he was gradually changing the way a Steinway was constructed. Then he started to experiment with a new finishing material—lacquer.

DuPont had developed a lacquer spray (nitrocellulose) after World War I as a fast-drying coat for automobiles on the assembly line. What Steinway needed, however, was a lacquer spray for wood, not metal. With varnish, the coating process could last two to three months, depending on the weather. With lacquer spray the whole job could be done in two to three days.

Murphy Varnish Company in Newark, N.J., was commissioned under DuPont to develop a lacquer for pianos. Together with Cassebeer, they developed a special formula for Steinway, Murphy Varnish no. 11, labeled "TC Lacquer" (for Teddy Cassebeer). This new, fast-drying formula transformed piano making at Steinway & Sons. What once took months now took days.[24]

All that remained was to find a way to make the rest of the piano as quickly as they could now assemble rims and spray on lacquer. Teddy told Fred and Ziegler that, to accelerate production further, he needed the help of his cousin Paul Bilhuber. This was agreed, and Cassebeer, with guidance from Ziegler, trained Bilhuber in piano design and construction. They also enrolled him in a few physics, engineering, and metallurgy courses at Columbia College. Bilhuber used his talent for sketching, learned from his mother, to figure out the production problem. He started by walking around the factory, making sketches of piano-making procedures. Then he sat down at his drawing board to design machines and procedures that would enable the same number of workers to produce more pianos in less time. Next he reviewed the drawings with Stanley Weber, an old German machinist at Steinway & Sons, and Weber assembled prototypes.[25]

Ultimately, Bilhuber's "contribution was not an invention but the breaking up of operations." For example, in case making, what had been a two- to three-day task became a job requiring a skilled worker for one day, with unskilled workers finishing up the work on a second day. Bilhuber trained unskilled workers to do specific procedures on the case, with the result that the same number of skilled workers, plus more inexpensive unskilled workers, could turn out more pianos.[26]

He was also able to persuade Steinway piano workers to use machines for defined tasks. He explained to them that they would make more money by producing more pieces and that the work would be easier, since it would entail fewer clamps and tools. They complied out of respect for him. He spoke German fluently—which went down well with the foremen, all of whom were German—and he was an expert woodworker. Furthermore, he had an enthusiasm for new ideas that was infectious. When Charles Ruperich, an old-timer at Steinway & Sons, retired in 1926, he willed his workbench and tools to Bilhuber, as a gesture of appreciation.[27]

The production increase was tremendous; it almost doubled.[28] Between the Bilhuber machines and the Cassebeer inventions, more workers were

Paul Bilhuber (*wearing a suit*) and Stanley Weber (*in machinist's hat*) reviewing Bilhuber's equipment modification.

delivering many more pianos. By 1925 there were 2,300 piano workers at Steinway & Sons, up from 1,500 workers two years earlier. In 1926 they shipped 6,294 pianos from the Queens factory, an unprecedented number, unequalled to this day. Net profit increased almost 500 percent in five years, from $300,000 in 1921 to $1,425,000 in 1926. In addition, profit per piano tripled, from $75 in 1921 to $225 in 1926—all without any increase either in the price of a Steinway or in the average pay for the piano workers, which stayed around $30 to $40 a week. Part of the increase in profit from 1921 to 1926 came from the shift from wholesale to more retail sales, thereby cutting out the dealers. The New York retail price was about the same in 1920 and 1926, ranging from $875 for a V mahogany upright to $2,700 for a D ebony concert grand.[29]

In 1926, awash in all this cash, Fred constructed a million-dollar factory in Queens, next door to the Ditmars Avenue works, and filled it with Bilhuber and Cassebeer machinery. The new two-story factory was given a foundation that would allow for four more floors at some future date. Fred intended to add these floors and equip them with more machines and workers. For Fred Steinway and his family, making pianos was like printing money. The demand seemed interminable; in 1925 total sales amounted to nearly $8 million.[30]

Nor were pianos the only commodity making the Steinway family wealthy. They made a fortune selling land in Queens: the land that William had purchased fifty years earlier. Profits on land sales from 1921 to 1927 netted them $750,000, more than twice the total of the profits on all Steinway pianos sold in Europe during the same period.[31]

This profit stemmed from a real estate boom in New York City. After World War I there was a housing shortage for the five and a half million residents of New York, and the population was rising all the time. Millions of immigrants had arrived during the past thirty years; now their children were marrying and starting families and looking for homes of their own. Postwar prosperity had provided these families with the money to move, but housing construction had slowed down during the years leading up to the war, so competition for housing was fierce. To alleviate the housing problem, the city passed legislation eliminating property taxes on all new houses for the next ten years, starting in 1920. The result was a scramble for land in the outer boroughs. By 1930 the population of Queens had doubled to a million people. Part of the lure of Queens, especially Steinway Village, for young couples was that, with the opening of the Queensborough Bridge in 1909 and the extension of the IRT line to Ditmars Avenue (within a mile of the Steinway factory) in 1919, travel to and from parents and jobs in Manhattan was easy.

Steinway & Sons had not only land in Queens but also enough capital to offer mortgages to finance both its purchase and home construction. Many of their customers were Steinway piano workers and their families. Theodore E. Steinway, William's youngest son, encouraged building loans and mortgages to "our men," because he believed that "it inured to our benefit to have our men well housed and near our plant." In 1925, the high point in this land rush, Steinway & Sons made a net profit of $325,000 in real estate.[32]

Money was flooding into Steinway's coffers, millions a year. Fred used some of this wealth for two investments that would enhance Steinway's visibility. The first was the promotion of a distinctive national image for the company; the second a showplace worthy of that unique image—a new Steinway Hall.

Under William, there had been advertising at Steinway & Sons, but no advertising *plan*. William would scribble an advertisement and would then send his office boy Darcy to the papers with copy for the morning news. But in 1900 N. W. Ayer & Son convinced Charlie that people who were not interested in music or pianos could be persuaded to buy Steinways. Charlie signed on immediately. Within a year sales went up. For the first time Steinway & Sons was on contract with an advertising agency that did layouts with professional writers and artists.[33]

Under Fred, Ayer came up with a lavish national campaign. Raymond Rubicam, the young copywriter later to found the advertising firm of Young & Rubicam, assigned to the Steinway account, later recalled:

I learned that the [Steinway] had been used by practically all the greatest pianists and almost all of the great composers since Wagner. But when I found the [advertisements] in the proof book I discovered that they consisted of lovely ladies sitting at pianos in lovely drawing rooms and that the text [without headlines] told little of the great Steinway story. Without effort, the phrase formed in my mind, "The Instrument of the Immortals."

He then discovered that Steinway had a collection of oil paintings of the great celebrities who had played its pianos and that it had published a booklet entitled "The Portraits of Musical Celebrities," which was handed to potential customers at Steinway Hall, as "point-of-sale" literature. But, according to Rubicam, Ayer had been forbidden to use the paintings or the booklet in national advertising. Fred's reluctance, like his predecessors', stemmed from a fear that excessive advertising would damage the family name and put Steinway pianos on a par with patent medicines.[34] Nor was he convinced that investment in advertising would result in more sales. He remained the practical businessman who wanted to see sales go up before he shelled out more money. So Rubicam was denied access to the Steinway oil paintings.

Instead, he dressed up a model "to look like an 'immortal' of the Franz Liszt type," and posed the model "with a strong beam of light from above illuminating him and his piano." The "misty focus" and a well-placed beam of light to induce a reverential attitude in the reader was not a new idea; it was part of national advertising and had been used by Steinway since 1916. Nor was the link to great artists anything new. The promotional connection between artists and the piano had been there all along. What was new was Rubicam's addition of the phrase "The Instrument of the Immortals" and his promotion of the Steinway connection to celebrated artists to the exclusion of other themes like "families and sweethearts gathered around a Steinway piano."[35]

A few days after his new ad began to run, Rubicam remembered the treasurer of Steinway calling him. He was surprised to discover that the treasurer was in charge of advertising, but at Steinway & Sons that was how it was done. Friedrich Reidemeister was both supervisor of advertising and chief financial officer. He sat across the desk from Fred at Steinway Hall, and, as Henry Z. Steinway recalls, "the two were buddies from way, way back, since (Fred) first came to America." Reidemeister was Fred's most trusted ally at Steinway Hall. That day he told Rubicam "that for the first time in 20 years of advertising [Steinway] had actually received a considerable number of voluntary and wholly favorable comments on an ad." He went on to report that Fred and his associates had "changed their minds: Ayer could use the oil paintings of great pianists along with the phrase, 'The Instrument of the Immortals,' as the central idea in a series of advertisements."[36]

A set of four-color double-page advertisements were launched in the *Saturday Evening Post*, with commissioned paintings of famous musicians by renowned painters: N. C. Wyeth, Harvey Dunn, and Rockwell Kent. Like so many other companies, Steinway had gone lavish and national in its advertising and was using the work of prestigious artists printed in color to contribute to the allure of their advertising page.[37]

In effect, what Fred was doing was giving Rubicam license to create a distinct national image. Whereas in the past Steinway & Sons had sold technology, patents, the instrument, and artists, they were now selling emotion and prestige. The new advertising emphasized that "if Paderewski, Rachmaninoff or Hofmann came to your house you would have an instrument worthy of their touch." The recognizable name guaranteeing the quality of the product was becoming more popular on the advertising pages of the 1920s magazines.[38]

Steinway emphasized elegance and distinction. Not only was a Steinway

A Steinway & Sons advertisement of the 1920s, which includes a reproduction of a painting of Sergei Rachmaninoff by Charles E. Chambers.

piano "The Instrument of the Immortals," it was also an exquisite piece of furniture, one to be enjoyed for its aesthetic cachet. The message was that a Steinway guaranteed culture for a family.[39] Like other firms in the 1920s, Steinway was also selling a psychic by-product by claiming that its piano was a solution to the anxieties arising from living in an increasingly impersonal setting. A Steinway piano epitomized skill and craftsmanship in a world of shallow reproductions, art in an age of mass production. It was the original, the genuine item in a time of fraud, a witness to traditional values for people discontented with the tempo of change in the 1920s.

Fred now turned his attention to building a new Steinway Hall to house his exalted piano. Planning for a new, less extravagant Steinway Hall on West 57th Street had actually begun in 1916. Fred and Charlie had decided to buy land for a twelve-story building to replicate the original hall uptown "in the shopping district . . . [where] high class business" would be conducted. Fourteenth Street had been abandoned as New York's cultural center. They had purchased five private homes: three on West 57th Street, two on West 58th. The deeds to all five houses were to be delivered to Steinway & Sons on 1 August 1916.[40] Preliminary plans for the new building were already drawn.

But, on 25 July the Board of Estimates and Apportionment of the City of New York adopted a "Building Zone Resolution." It was the first comprehensive zoning legislation in the nation, and there has been nothing more important in shaping New York City either before or since. Prior to this, factories could be set up anywhere, regardless of how much damage they might do to residential districts. A building could be as tall and as wide as the foundation permitted, with no concern that it might eclipse the building next door or create cavernous city streets. One purpose of the 1916 zoning resolution was to control building heights and size—buildings like the planned twelve-story Steinway Hall.[41]

Unfortunately for the Steinway family, the block that included the site for the new Steinway Hall was designated residential, with "no business buildings allowed." This appeared to guarantee that Steinway Hall would never be constructed on that site.[42] So Steinway & Sons immediately rescinded all agreements to purchase the houses on West 58th and 57th Streets. Hermann Biggs, who with his wife owned the three houses on West 57th, fired back a letter to Messrs. Steinway & Sons complaining that he had emptied two of his houses of all their tenants, moved his family from the third house, and just signed a five-year lease on a new home. Biggs pointed out that "ample public notice was given by the City of its proposed action." In fact, Biggs wrote, "I have . . . performed all my obligations under the contract. I expect you to perform yours."[43]

The outcome was a four-year court battle resulting in a test case on "incumbrance" as a consequence of zoning regulations. Steinway & Sons lost and were directed by the Court of Appeals in Albany to take title to the land on West 57th and 58th and pay all costs and interest to Biggs.[44] By the time the case was settled, in 1920, the City of New York had amended its zoning law so as to free 58th Street for business purposes. But Fred waited three years before starting construction on Steinway Hall. The previous year had been disastrous for Steinway & Sons, since the piano workers had been out on strike for most of the year.[45] He needed time to build up the company's cash reserves before approving investment in a new Steinway Hall.

On 14 November 1923, eight years after the initial plan had been drawn up, Steinway & Sons' board of trustees resolved to build the new Steinway Hall on West 57th Street according to the plans of architects Warren & Wetmore. This was to be far more than a replica of the original hall; it was to be more like a palace. The estimated cost was $3 million. The new hall (which is still the Steinway showroom) would be a museum where fine art and grand pianos would be on display. The original Steinway Hall on East 14th Street was sold for roughly half a million dollars to Samuel Klein, who razed most of the old hall to build his department store.[46]

Fred Steinway had selected one of the most prestigious architectural firms in America to create the new "House of Steinway." Warren & Wetmore had designed the New York Yacht Club, the gate-house at Greenwood Cemetery in Brooklyn, and Grand Central Terminal; Steinway Hall would be in the same beaux arts tradition.[47]

On the facade of the building, roughly two floors up from the street, W. L. Hopkins, the architect in charge, placed "a band of ornaments in the form of garlands in which were enclosed eight medallion portraits: Brahms, Bach, Haydn, Mozart, Schubert, Chopin, Liszt and Grieg," so establishing the theme for the new "House of Steinway."[48] A formal showcase was created in the front of the building by cutting a 15- by 10-foot window into the facade at street level. Inside, burgundy draperies were drawn apart to reveal a large, domed reception hall. Outside, the window was framed with marble columns on both sides, and above it was a sculpture in highly polished golden-vein marble showing "Apollo, the Greek God of Music and the Muse of Music placing a laurel wreath upon his head."[49] Passersby would stop to admire the unusual setting and to gaze through the window. Some would be drawn into the hall to buy a piano; others were enticed into the building as a place of interest in its own right.

The eye-catcher was the main reception room, a large rotunda, octagonal in shape, 40 feet in diameter, with a domed ceiling 35 feet up, decorated with hand-painted allegorical scenes. Lions, elephants, goddesses, and nymphs

floated overhead, depicting the influence of music on human relations. Hanging from the center of these paintings was a nineteenth-century Viennese crystal chandelier with two tiers of lights, giving the impression of a brilliant star falling from the scene above.[50]

Original artwork was commissioned to hang on the walls: a Rockwell Kent representation of Wagner's "Entrance of the Gods into Valhalla" decorated the east wall; paintings by N. C. Wyeth and F. Luis Mora (President Harding's portrait artist) hung nearby. Setting off the paintings were fluted white columns alternating with green pilasters of highly polished marble from the island of Tinos in the Greek archipelago. The floor was made of yellow Kasota stone with small squares of Alps green marble and was partially covered by an exquisite rug specifically designed and woven for Steinway & Sons in Czechoslovakia.[51] There were no pianos in the reception area.

But, should you wish to look at pianos, salesmen, perched at kidney-shaped desks (replicas of pieces of decorative art in the British Museum), were ready to escort you through a set of large Bresce Verte Italian marble pillars to one of the piano selection rooms situated along green and gold corridors on the first and second floors.[52] Each selection room was distinctive. They were like stage sets, with drapes over false windows, artificial skylights, comfortable chairs, and serene paintings. One "display salon," as they were called, replicated a music room in an upper-class apartment, "with fireplace and suitable furnishings designed primarily to show how the small grand piano fits into the decorative scheme of the average home." Another, named the "Directoire Room," sported panels of French wallpaper printed by hand from contemporary blocks. The room was finished in rose, white, and gold, with antique lighting fixtures imported from France. The ceilings and interior walls of the eleven selection rooms were insulated with "Flaxlinum" to enrich the acoustics. "The floors were covered with deep-pile Chinese rugs. . . . All of the doors were fitted with rubber insets on the edges in order to make the display salons practically soundproof."[53]

These rooms provided the perfect place to try out pianos. Steinway did not sell from samples. If you liked it, it was yours. To close a sale, the customer was always ushered back to the rotunda reception area to discuss closing terms and delivery.

Artists were treated differently. They were escorted to a large room in the basement designed for the testing of concert grands. That is where Hofmann, Paderewski, Rachmaninoff, and other Steinway artists selected the pianos they would play at Carnegie Hall, on tour, or in the new Steinway concert hall upstairs on the third floor. The walls of this small, intimate hall

Steinway Hall on West 57th Street, c. 1925.

Main reception room of Steinway Hall, as seen from the showroom entrance.

were decorated with five early eighteenth-century Dutch paintings: one of an old castle, the other four, 10 by 12 feet each, of the four seasons. The 240 chairs for the audience, designed exclusively for Steinway, with its lyre trademark as a backrest, were imported from Austria. Behind the concert hall were the executive offices of Steinway & Sons. In a back room sat Fred, far from the visiting artists, who were either complaining or looking for favors.[54]

Of the sixteen stories, the first four were used by Steinway & Sons, the next eleven were rented,[55] and the top floor, planned as an apartment for Fred and Julia, although they never actually lived there, was a penthouse. It had the only kitchen in the building, as well as two bathrooms each fitted with medicine cabinets, razor strap hooks, platform scales, douche bag hooks, a shower, and a bath tub. There was an office for Fred, a dressing room for Julia, and, as Henry Z. Steinway remembered it, "a rather large, handsome room, very Beaux Art, where you could throw one hell of a fine party for 100 people." The floors were all oak herringbone. On the roof garden overlooking the city the urns on the parapet walls were made of cast stone to match the color and texture of the limestone facade.[56] Here, from the top of the new Steinway Hall, Fred and Julia would literally reign over the "House of Steinway."

When it opened in October 1925, *Music Trades* magazine described the building as the "Steinway Shrine." During the inaugural festivities the multitude of veiled statues presented to Fred by leading artists and music dealers prompted Rubin Goldmark, head of the composition department of the Juilliard School, to comment that he "thought we might be in for some secret manifestation of the Ku Klux Klan which would have been strangely in contrast to the idea of Steinway & Sons."[57]

After the formal presentations, Fred led the invited group of artists, critics, and Steinway dealers, 160 in all, across the street to the Lotos Club for dinner and more speeches about the "spirit and tradition of Steinway & Sons." To publicize the opening of the hall, Steinway & Sons and the Radio Corporation of America sponsored a series of concerts conducted by Walter Damrosch and recitals by Josef Hofmann, all of which were broadcast.[58]

Fred constructed Steinway Hall to be the showcase and salesroom for the "The Instrument of the Immortals." But it was more than just a place where people purchased pianos. It was monument to past achievements, celebrat-

Piano showroom at Steinway Hall, c. 1925.

ing all that Steinway had achieved since 1853. Fred was honoring what he could put his hands on, what he could put in the bank. He saw Steinway's achievements in 1925 in terms of fame and fortune. But now he had to do something about revitalizing his aging and retiring staff. He had to bring Steinway management into the twentieth century.

TWELVE

A Marriage of Music and Commerce

F RED STEINWAY WAS
sixty-five years old at the time of the opening of the new Steinway Hall, and
his man in charge of sales, Nahum Stetson, was about to turn seventy.
Steinway & Sons clearly needed some young blood, at various levels.

Stetson was born in 1856 into a wealthy New England family that owned
extensive iron works with main offices in Bridgewater, Connecticut. He had
been secretary to the Bureau of Machinery at the centennial exposition in
Philadelphia in 1876, which was where Albert Steinway met him and hired
him as a salesman. A huge man with an overpowering presence and spirited
mustache, Stetson rose quickly in the ranks. Within seven years he was
placed in charge of sales and marketing, and William Steinway was referring
to him as "Manager of the Warerooms." Stetson hired a talented and committed sales force to work at Steinway Hall and to travel across the country
selling pianos; he also established a national network of agents. He was
elected to the Steinway & Sons board of directors and made corporate secretary in 1892,[1] and it was he who arranged for the one-hundred-
thousandth Steinway piano manufactured in New York to be placed in the
East Room of Teddy Roosevelt's White House. But, Henry Z. Steinway
recalled, as Stetson "grew old in service the real power in selling moved to his
assistant Ernest Urchs."[2] Stetson was the grand old man of Steinway's past,
but he was aging, overweight, and ailing. With Stetson's blessing, Fred promoted Ernest Urchs to head Steinway's sales force.

Born Charles Ernest Urchs, he was a native New Yorker. His father,
Francis C. Urchs, started out as a merchant in Cologne, Germany, but

Nahum Stetson at his desk in
Steinway Hall on 14th Street in
the 1890s. His dealer files are
at his elbow.

became a singer in New York. His place on Hester Street was known to
many vocalists in New York. In the early 1860s William Steinway often sang
with Francis Urchs. Ernest had inherited his father's talent for music as well
as for business. This mix of merchant and musician defined Ernest Urchs for
the rest of his life. Toward the end of Urchs's career with Steinway & Sons,
an insightful reporter described him as an "ambassador from the business
world to the musical world. . . . The only man I know, or ever heard of,
who combines two qualifications that ordinarily are not combined in one
person—music and business."[3]

Although a talented pianist, Urchs started in the piano trade as a retail
salesman for Chickering & Sons in New York. When Frank Chickering died
in 1891, the company fell on hard times, and several good men left and were
hired by Nahum Stetson. Ernest Urchs was one of them. He began in retail
sales, playing and selling pianos on the floor of Steinway Hall, and was
quickly promoted to traveling salesman for the wholesale department under
Stetson.[4]

In 1896 one of Steinway & Sons' key dealers in the Midwest, Smith &
Nixon in Cincinnati, was on the verge of collapse due to financial difficulties.
William's solution was to take their inventory and establish his own music
store, as he had with other dealers who had gone under. Urchs volunteered

Ernest Urchs, 1917.

to direct William's new Cincinnati store. They called it Ernest Urchs &
Company, "sole representative for the celebrated Steinway piano."[5]

But when William died, the cash at Steinway & Sons dried up, and within
four years Ernest Urchs & Company was liquidated. Fred, annoyed, noted
in his diary that Urchs had a "crazy idea about his own value" and "should
change his demeanor."[6] He offered him his former salary of $3,000, to which
Urchs responded that a rival concern had offered him twice that amount. In
the end, he accepted the lower, traveling salesman's salary of $55 per week
but was back a few months later battling for more.

Ernest Urchs was a powerhouse in a tie and a Prince Albert jacket. He
enjoyed good cigars, music, and challenges. Short and stocky, Urchs blasted
his way through life, seizing opportunities with the endless energy of a
young bulldog. Byron H. Collins, who started in retail sales at Steinway Hall
in 1905, remembered that "if one agreed with [Urchs] and subtly flattered
him all was well, but if one differed with him he never forgave [you]." At
times his success made him a bit imperious. One of his associates remembered that Urchs would sometimes telegraph a dealer: "I am passing through

Toledo on the 6:43 train. If you have some orders bring them down and I'll be glad to receive them." He was not getting off the train for a small-town dealer. Some of the smaller dealers told Collins that they thought Urchs devoted too much time and attention to the larger dealers, by-passing the little fellows who needed help and encouragement. But Urchs could get away with that in the booming twenties.[7]

With influential, prestigious people Urchs was always accommodating and thoughtful. He had been this way since grammar school. L. J. Burchard, his teacher in Grammar School 35, "found him capable, attentive, and anxious to please."[8] It was the "anxious to please" aspect of his personality that made him so successful at Steinway & Sons.

He was perpetually sending notes and small gifts to artists, music critics, major dealers, and Steinway family members. They all adored him for the attention he paid them. One Steinway youngster wrote back to him: "Dear Mr. Urchs, I am reading your book now. Jules Verne is my favorite author, and I have read 'The Mysterious Island' also written by him, sincerely yours, Theo D. Steinway." The books, the silver spoons, the marionettes were all purchased out of his own pocket. No one ever knew how hard he worked. Or that he worked all the time.[9]

By 1925 Urchs was managing what were once two distinct, large departments at Steinway & Sons. Twenty years earlier, when Charles Tretbar retired, Urchs had seized control of his Concert & Artists department. During the early 1920s Fred had transferred Stetson's wholesale department to Ernest Urchs, who then had both Stetson's and Tretbar's old posts. No non-Steinway family member since the days when Charles Tretbar was William's number two man had amassed so much power at Steinway & Sons.[10]

But the skill required to seize a powerful position is different from that required to retain it. Urchs had both. He recognized that to retain control he had to keep the "immortals" pleased and playing Steinway pianos. The most important Steinway artist during the 1920s was Paderewski. Urchs decided that Paderewski's happiness was his highest priority. As one of Urchs's assistants noted:

Mr. Ernest Urchs worshipped Paderewski (who was the godfather of Urchs's daughter, Otinita) and whenever Paderewski made a tour in the United States Mr. Urchs would not only attend any and all of his concerts in New York but he would go to Newark, Boston, Philadelphia, Baltimore, Washington and even Chicago to hear him. . . . The day Paderewski arrived in New York from Europe was a holiday for Mr. Urchs. All business practically stopped as far as he was concerned and all his time was devoted to Paderewski. . . . Mr. Urchs was so partial to Paderewski that some other great Steinway pianists, notably Josef Hofmann, deeply resented this attitude of Mr. Urchs and preferred to transact their business with Steinway & Sons with somebody else of the firm.[11]

When Urchs was in Europe, he always visited Paderewski at his estate near Morges, on Lake Geneva, in Switzerland. He managed all Paderewski's American investments and looked after his ranch on the Pacific coast. Paderewski's United States tours were sketched out and controlled by Urchs—tours that brought in over half a million dollars. To Urchs, Paderewski was the world's greatest pianist.[12] The only problem was that Paderewski wasn't immortal. Urchs had to scout for young Paderewskis. He watched young pianists like a baseball manager keeps his eye on farm teams. Part of his job was to look over the new crop of pianists on both sides of the Atlantic and pick the stars.

Urchs knew talent when he saw it, and he knew what talent would capture the concert world. He surveyed the musical landscape in search of artists who would take Steinway & Sons into the twentieth century. One unknown pianist who caught his attention in 1925 was a young Russian Jewish refugee, Vladimir Horowitz. Urchs believed that Horowitz had the potential to join the ranks of Paderewski, Hofmann, and Rachmaninoff. Now all he had to do was orchestrate the birth of this new "immortal."

His chance was 2 January 1926, Horowitz's debut in Berlin. He counted on Rudolf Vetter, the charming manager of the Concerts & Artist department at Steinway's Berlin house, and Paul Schmidt, Fred Steinway's assistant and nephew in Hamburg, to attract the young Russian pianist to Steinway & Sons. Many other piano companies were seeking Horowitz's endorsement prior to his Berlin debut. Horowitz recalled that he "didn't know what piano to play and nobody told me. Some said 'Go to Weber' and others something else. So I visited Blüthner, Bechstein, Bösendorfer and Steinway." According to Horowitz, Paul Schmidt "proved persuasive in demonstrating the unique qualities of the Steinway grand—the clarity and brilliance of its treble and the sonorous, virile bass," which was far superior to the Blüthners he had performed on in Russia. Schmidt also underscored the Steinway's ability to project in a concert hall. Horowitz decided, "That's my piano" and never played anything but a Steinway, anywhere, ever again.[13] In exchange for his loyalty, Urchs provided Horowitz with a piano and a tuner whenever he played.

His debut in Berlin was a disappointment, however. The house was half empty, and none of the music critics attended. Those who did attend were mostly from the Russian Jewish community. A second performance was scheduled for two days later. This time the audience was a respectable size and enthusiastic, but it was not the performance that would launch his career.[14]

The next month he played two recitals in the ballroom of the stately Atlantic Hotel in Hamburg. He was still an unknown pianist, but though the recital hall was half empty, the reviews were favorable. Horowitz remembered it as "a good artistic success but, as usual, no money."

The following afternoon, as Horowitz and his manager, Alexander Merovitch, returned from a walk at the city's zoo, they found the manager of the Hamburg Philharmonic anxiously waiting for them in their hotel lobby. He had been searching for Horowitz all day. A pianist had fainted at a dress rehearsal, and he wanted Horowitz at the hall in forty-five minutes' time as a substitute. "It's the chance of your life!" cried Merovitch. "All right," Horowitz announced, "Tchaikovsky Concerto!" He shaved, dressed, and, with no practice, headed off for the opportunity of a lifetime, a performance with the Hamburg Philharmonic to a packed house.

The conductor, Eugen Pabst, didn't know Horowitz. When they met during the intermission, minutes before Horowitz was to perform, Pabst advised Horowitz: "Just watch my stick, you, and nothing too terrible can happen." The audience was not expecting much from this substitute soloist, but with Horowitz's first chords, Pabst and the audience stared at the piano in amazement. Mystified, Pabst left the podium to stand by the piano so that he could watch the incredible hands of Vladimir Horowitz. He conducted from there, and both he and the audience were stunned by this pale, twenty-three-year-old Russian.

Even before the performance had ended, the audience were on their feet in riotous applause. Pabst rushed over to Horowitz and embraced him. One critic declared: "Not since Hamburg discovered Caruso has there been anything like it." "That was my big break," Horowitz said years later. "Who knows? If it were not for that concert, maybe my career would have never amounted to much. If one plays well it is not always enough. But in Hamburg they loved me right away!"[15]

Urchs banked on Arthur Judson, a good friend of the Steinway family and a tenant at Steinway Hall[16] to bring Horowitz to American concert halls. Judson was "a huge man, with a massive head, a rectangular, ruddy face, and great hands that had the strength of a lumberjack and the sensitivity of a violinist." He was one of the most prominent concert managers in America. He handled two important orchestras: the Philadelphia Orchestra and the New York Philharmonic. Judson had launched the careers of such artists as Jascha Heifetz, Rudolf Serkin, and Eugene Ormandy. He was also a pioneer in radio broadcasting and in 1926 founded CBS. He thus controlled a large share of the American music market.[17]

Like Urchs, Judson was both a musician and a businessman. He saw himself as a "salesman of fine music." With his backing, an unknown artist could become well known in less than a year. In the spring of 1926 Arthur Judson was in Paris to sign up the Spanish pianist Jose Iturbi for an American debut. While there, he heard from Henry Prunières, French musicologist and critic, about this new wizard at the keyboard, Vladimir Horowitz. Judson also knew from Urchs about Steinway's interest in Horowitz. Furthermore, Merovitch was pushing Judson to audition Horowitz, in hopes of an American tour. Judson agreed to hear Horowitz in recital at the Opéra. He was overwhelmed and ended up returning to America with an exclusive contract to manage Horowitz and no contract with Iturbi. He scheduled Horowitz to arrive in America on 9 January 1928 for a thirty-concert tour.[18]

During the summer of 1927 Urchs went to Europe to hear Horowitz play with the Hamburg Philharmonic under the baton of Karl Muck. He wanted to hear for himself this young artist, who was then celebrating his twenty-fourth birthday.[19]

The critics reported that Horowitz was now Hamburg's favorite pianist. Reviewers prized his technical brilliance but criticized him for allowing his technique to be "more dominant than [his] poetical ideas." Urchs disagreed. Later he wrote: "*Horowitz*—a splendid musician with poetry in his soul, a stupendous technician." *Piano Trade* reported that "Mr. Urchs, who probably knows more about more contemporary pianists than any other living man, said 'watch Horowitz'."[20]

Horowitz sailed for New York on Christmas Eve of 1927 aboard the S.S. *Hamburg.* As Horowitz crossed the Atlantic, Urchs and Judson were working to make him a celebrity. Judson's public relations people billed Horowitz as "a superhuman combination of Rubinstein, Rosenthal, Paderewski, Busoni, Rachmaninoff, and Hofmann."[21] Urchs persuaded Fred to pay for an expensive advertising campaign to promote Horowitz as a Steinway artist. He then ran full-page advertisements in the Sunday edition of the *New York Times,* in what was known as the "Rotogravure Section." Half the page was taken up with a picture of Horowitz, bow tie and hair slicked back, looking handsome and dapper. Next to his photograph was an announcement of his appearance as "soloist with the New York Philharmonic Orchestra in Carnegie Hall on January 12th, 13th and 15th." The other half of the page consisted of a paragraph urging the purchase of a Steinway piano, "The Instrument of the Immortals," and an endorsement by Horowitz.

It was a gamble, based on the assumption that because Horowitz played a Steinway, more people would want to buy one—in short, that the money spent on Horowitz would come back in piano sales. Years later one of Urchs's assistants explained the strategy this way:

"Of course," the local managers would say to themselves, . . . "the renowned Arthur Judson, will tell us that Horowitz is sensational but, you know, with all due respect to Arthur Judson, as a manager he will naturally say this about his artist. . . . But Steinway & Sons devotes a whole page in *The New York Times*. . . ! Steinway & Sons! They wouldn't do it unless he really was exceptional! This unknown pianist by the name of Vladimir Horowitz must be good! He must be very good! He must be exceptionally good!"[22]

To determine just how good Horowitz was, all the luminaries of the music world showed up at Carnegie Hall on 12 January; Josef Lhevinne, Mischa Levitzki, Moritz Rosenthal—"a convention of East European Jews, with an honorary membership for Rachmaninoff," as Merovitch sarcastically described the audience. In addition to these artists, scattered throughout a packed Carnegie Hall, sat Ernest Urchs, Fred Steinway, Arthur Judson, recording executives from RCA Victor, and every major music critic from the daily press. "Everyone is here!" cried Horowitz. And he was right.[23]

But in view of his obscurity in the broader American music world, the program for the eighty-sixth season of the Philharmonic Society of New York highlighted the "first appearance in America" of Sir Thomas Beecham, the guest conductor at Carnegie Hall that evening, not Vladimir Horowitz, who was noted in small print, thus: "Assisting Artist: Vladimir Horowitz, Pianist (First Appearance in America)" playing the Tchaikovsky Piano Concerto No. 1 in B-flat Minor, Op. 23.[24] But when Horowitz appeared on stage, he electrified the hall. The only obstacle was Beecham, who, while directing an orchestra, often danced and gyrated to the music.[25] During his debut with Horowitz, agitation escalated when Beecham's suspenders snapped early in the performance, leaving him literally holding on to his pants! He was unquestionably entertaining, "but as a conductor," noted Ernest Urchs, "not more than a first class amateur,"[26] and as an accompanist for Horowitz, "the worst fizzle I have ever beheld."

Horowitz sat at the keyboard shocked that Beecham was ignoring his faster tempo, an expected courtesy to the soloist. The concert degenerated into a tug-of-war between the two men. According to Urchs, "It was so painful that the audience sensed it—I fidgeted in my seat. In the last movement towards the end Horowitz took the bit in his teeth and Beecham had to follow." Years later Horowitz recalled that hellish opening night: "I knew my career was at stake, and at the moment we were no longer together at all. I thought, you go your way and I'll go mine. Maybe in the restaurant after the concert we'll meet again, but not during the performance."[27]

That night Horowitz was defeated. Urchs, upset for Horowitz and concerned about what this setback might mean for Steinway & Sons' sales, noted that "it was a most unfortunate event for Horowitz. He was so crushed in spirit after the performance that he could not talk and declined to go to a reception given in his honor."[28]

The reviews applauded Beecham, and Olin Downes, writing in the *New York Times*, complimented Horowitz on his "amazing technique, amazing strength, irresistible youth, and temperament." But he had many reservations about the performance. His verdict overall was that "very possibly Mr. Horowitz is a great musician as well as virtuoso. . . . But he has that to prove."[29]

On 20 February 1928, in Carnegie Hall, Horowitz had his chance to set the record straight. The program revealed his understanding of what was at stake: "from Liszt . . . not an etude or rhapsody, but the B minor sonata, a sovereign test of the powers of any pianist." Urchs, watching the numbers as well as the program, as always, recorded that it was a "good house, over $1400 in box office sales."[30] That night Horowitz demonstrated that he was not only a dazzling technician but also an artist and someone to be reckoned with. In his *New York Times* column Olin Downes declared that Horowitz promised "to become as he ripens one of the greatest figures among the pianists of the day."[31]

Urchs was delighted that the "best critics" now realized that Horowitz was an excellent musician as well as a marvelous technician. This would now translate into influential endorsements and increased Steinway sales. Urchs looked forward to Horowitz's return in October.[32] His plan had worked.

He never did hear Horowitz in October, however. He died suddenly that summer of a heart attack, on the job at Steinway Hall. He was about to celebrate his sixty-fifth birthday. His death certificate listed his occupation as "merchant," but that Sunday the Philharmonic Symphony Orchestra recognized the musician in Ernest Urchs when it replaced the fourth number of its concert program, Bach's air for strings, with the funeral march from Wagner's *Götterdämmerung*, "in memory of Ernest Urchs, the artist."[33]

Steinway & Sons was growing too rapidly for Urchs's job to be managed by one person anymore. Moreover, his replacements, no matter how many, were not going to be German. There was a lingering anti-German feeling in America, going back to World War I. Until then there had been a national conviction that Germans were a positive influence in the country; but during and after the war there was a widespread feeling that all vestiges of German culture should be eliminated from American life. Officials banned "pro-German" books from public schools; Iowa prohibited the use of any language but English in public places; Pittsburgh banned Beethoven's music; sauerkraut was renamed "liberty cabbage"; German towns, businesses, and individuals changed their names; and, in Illinois a German-American miner was wrapped in a flag and lynched.[34]

The "Red scare," the anti-Bolshevik fever that gripped the nation after the war, was thoroughly interwoven with anti-German emotion. Thus "New York State's famous Red-hunter, Clayton R. Lusk, proclaimed that paid agents of the German Junkers had started the radical movement in America as part of their plan of world conquest."[35]

This anti-German hysteria had led Urchs, along with Fred Steinway and Henry Ziegler, to seek to make Steinway & Sons less German. Although by 1920 the focus of American bigotry was shifting from Germans back to Catholics, Jews, and African-Americans, they decided that new, non-German blood was needed. Young assistants were hired who were easily identified with the Allied or anti-Bolshevik forces, and by 1928 no one on the sales force at Steinway Hall had a German accent.

Urchs groomed an anti-Bolshevik Russian refugee, Alexander Greiner, to succeed him as head of the Concert & Artists department. Sascha Greiner had been born in Riga, the capital city of Latvia.[36] His family was German-Latvian, the perfect background for the shift in image that Steinway & Sons needed now that the country had turned anti-German. Moreover, Urchs needed an assistant to attend to Horowitz, and no one at Steinway Hall spoke Russian. So Greiner's Latvian heritage was to his advantage. He was immediately assigned to entertain Horowitz and ensure his loyalty to Steinway & Sons. For the next thirty years Horowitz was to remain his responsibility.

In January 1928, when Horowitz stepped off the boat in New York, Greiner was there to welcome him and introduce him to the American music world. Horowitz was particularly anxious to meet Rachmaninoff, whom he referred to as "the Musical God of my youth." Greiner arranged for the two artists to meet in the basement of Steinway Hall. There they played Rachmaninoff's Third Concerto. Overwhelmed, Rachmaninoff recounted that "he had listened open-mouthed as Horowitz pounced with the fury and voraciousness of a tiger. He swallowed it whole." The work later became Horowitz's trademark. Horowitz always insisted that "Rachmaninoff gave this Concerto to me."[37]

From the day Horowitz arrived in New York, Sascha Greiner courted and coddled him. At Sascha's house they would join other Russian refugees to drink vodka, eat blinis (a Russian pancake served during Lent), and play cards. Sascha's favorite card game was "Preference." Only the old-timers among the Russians knew how to play it. Sascha liked it because "no one gets angry if one player makes a mistake," and Sascha was not a good card player. This made him a particularly attractive fourth for Preference. He

Alexander Greiner (*with the bow tie*) toward the end of his career, in 1955, with Oscar Levant (*seated*), Vladimir Horowitz (*at the keyboard*), and John Steinway (*standing*).

was sure to make mistakes, guaranteeing profits for everyone else around the table.[38] As Sascha pictured it, a mistake in bridge angered your partner, a mistake in poker profited only one other person, but a mistake in Preference made everybody around the table happy. And it was Sascha's job to make others, especially Horowitz, happy.

Greiner had been on the job two years when Ernest Urchs died. He was then promoted to head of the Concert & Artists department. He had impressed everybody at Steinway Hall. He had the personality to charm the artists and had learned from Urchs to pay attention to the details: to greet famous artists with a bouquet of roses at the pier when they arrived from Europe; to escort them graciously to their hotel room, a suite large enough to house a Steinway concert grand; and to store a bottle of vodka in his desk at Steinway Hall, for the artist's pleasure during an extended tête-à-tête.[39]

Greiner accorded all the people he worked with this graciousness: Anna the switchboard operator at Steinway Hall, as well as Horowitz. Three postcards he sent to Alice Jordan, his secretary, many years later revealed that he had learned Urchs's lessons well—the value of gracious notes and thoughtful gifts. Greiner, in Rome at the time, mailed these picture postcards to Steinway Hall with a note telling Alice that "these holy pictures were blessed by the Holy Father, who appeared in person at 12:10 P.M. today to bless the people. Please [keep one for yourself,] give one to Anna and the third to . . . the bartender at the Barbizon, Antonio Capiello, for his bambino."[40] Greiner was always sending notes of this kind through the mail or as interoffice memos, with the result that artists who called for Mr. Greiner received a warmhearted "He'll be right with you" from Anna at the switchboard, and when Sascha walked into the Barbizon Hotel across the street from Steinway Hall, Antonio made sure that Sascha's table was available and that the drinks had a little extra kick in them. Around the table Greiner would regale his guests for hours with marvelous anecdotes about Steinway artists. Most of his tales had to do with a Steinway piano or a Steinway artist. Fritz Steinway (a grandson of William's) once pointed out that Greiner never forgot that it was his business "to promote and sell pianos."[41]

One of the best-kept secrets, both at the lunch table and at Steinway Hall, was that Greiner was among those who regarded Paderewski's popularity as overrated. In fact Greiner's "Memoirs" were suppressed for thirty-three years, in part, because of his castigations of the honored Steinway artist.[42]

In them Greiner claimed: "I have never even heard Paderewski play well, not to say beautifully. His left hand was never together with his right perhaps in keeping with the Biblical dictum that the right hand should not know what the left was doing. His technique was labored, it was not natural as with the great keyboard masters: Josef Hofmann, Busoni, Rachmaninoff, Godowsky. I never did understand Paderewski's success as a pianist."[43] Whereas Greiner's "Memoirs" expose a deep-seated contempt for Paderewski, they document a profound and lasting love for Josef Hofmann, the other preeminent Steinway artist during the 1920s.

He proclaimed: "when Hofmann felt like playing, when he was 'in the vein,' it was incredible. The piano sang and thundered. Runs were really what the French call 'perlé,' they were like a string of glittering diamonds. I have heard Hofmann play Schumann's great Phantasy and I never want to hear it played by anyone again. And the way Hofmann played Chopin! Inimitable! No wonder the great Rachmaninoff considered Hofmann the King of pianists."[44]

Greiner insisted that Steinway & Sons serve "the King." He persuaded the company to manufacture a special piano for Hofmann with white keys that were slightly narrower than the standard width, thereby making it easier for his small hands to move about the keyboard. The overall length of the Hofmann narrower keyboard was seven-eighths of an inch shorter than the standard 48 inches. In addition, the Hofmann piano's fall-board (the part of the piano that closes to cover the keyboard, which usually had the name "Steinway & Sons" at its center) was always highly polished, with "Steinway & Sons" moved to the left-hand corner. Greiner remembered it as like a mirror which reflected Hofmann's hands when he played. When he asked Hofmann why he liked the fall-board so highly polished and the name off center, he said: "I like to watch my hands when I play. It amuses me." The name in the center, by contrast, distracted him.[45]

Hofmann's home in New York was Greiner's office at Steinway Hall. Typically, when Hofmann arrived in New York, he went directly to Steinway Hall. There he deposited his bags and relaxed with his friend. Their discussions were always more about women and personal problems than pianos. Hofmann, married to an older woman, was always in some predicament with a new, young girlfriend.

Throughout the years, no matter how close they became, Greiner always referred to the maestro as Mr. Hofmann. Hofmann called Greiner "Sascha" and wanted Sascha to call him "Josef." But Sascha refused. As he explained, it was "not because of any exaggerated modesty, but because Hofmann was so far above me in talent and accomplishment, even age, that I just could not do it. I could not overcome my European upbringing and tradition." He once told Hofmann that he had one wish before he died: to hear him play all twenty-four Chopin études.[46]

But it was not only the artists who appreciated Greiner's "European upbringing and tradition." Fred's wife, Julia, who also worked with Steinway artists, also valued it immensely. Julia was duchess of Steinway Hall and, like Urchs and Greiner, was engaged in trying to play down the German connection and promote Steinway & Sons as the finest American piano company. Julia's strategy was to establish herself as the center of the New York music world and take the Steinway name with her.

Her marriage to Fred had been a genealogist's nightmare. Julia was the daughter of his cousin Louisa Cassebeer; this made Fred her uncle once removed as well as her husband. It also made Julia her own mother's cousin. Quite confusing, but not unusual for wealthy families at that time, who used marriage to consolidate their wealth. The rationale of those supporting such inbreeding was that it kept the fortune in the family. But it was not universally accepted to marry so close a relative. While planning the marriage of Fred and Julia, "kissing cousins" became a hotly debated issue around the Cassebeer and Ziegler dinner table.[47]

The union was promoted by Julia's grandmother Doretta Steinway Ziegler, daughter of the founder and chief potentate of Steinway & Sons. Doretta set about arranging prosperity and prominence for her eldest grandchild. Doretta's daughter, Louisa, had married an ineffectual but amiable man, Henry A. Cassebeer. During the 1880s William Steinway had tried to help Henry by appointing him head of the Steinway trolley lines and a trustee of North Beach amusement park on Bowery Bay in Queens. Henry mismanaged both assignments, and his incompetence cost Steinway thousands of dollars. In his diary William described himself as "aghast at the way in which Cassebeer has mismanaged my RR and run it most fearfully into debt."[48]

The Cassebeers were the poor cousins in the Steinway clan. Moreover, Julia, the short, fat, dumpy, outspoken eldest child was still single at twenty-five. And there was Fred Steinway, Doretta's nephew, a bachelor approaching forty, with no experience of women and worth a fortune. His evenings were usually spent at the billiard table or in the Steinway box at the concert hall with Friedrich Reidemeister, Henry Ziegler, or Teddy Cassebeer. Doretta, through her son Henry Ziegler, Fred's surrogate father, and her daughter Julia Schmidt Cassebeer (Henry Cassebeer's second wife and young Julia's stepmother), arranged to bring Fred and Julia together.

Their nine-year courtship tested Fred's affection to the utmost. Julia was not easy to love. She was often aloof and usually pushy. In one letter to his self-assured sweetheart, whom Fred lovingly called "My dear Julchen," he lamented that his thoughts "very often wander with longing to a dear jolly good girl far away. . . . Let me know when you expect to get back, so I can begin to count the days." Julia's return letter was apparently short and detached, and Fred fired off a reproachful note threatening to refer to her as Miss Cassebeer instead of "My dear Julchen . . . because you wrote to me that Sunday letter in such a distant manner."[49]

After nine years of Julia's imperiousness, the love Fred once had for her had all but evaporated. Even on the night he proposed, Julia gave him a hard time. Her acceptance was conditional on Fred losing weight, and she put him on a two-week trial diet. He wrote in his diary that he had "very little sleep that night."[50] He had proposed more out of obligation to Henry and Addie Ziegler than affection for Julia.

She agreed to marry him. But it was clear to the family and to Julia that what little romance there may ever have been was gone. Nothing made it more obvious than Fred's inattention during their engagement party, when he danced with others but never with Julia. As Fred reported in his diary, the family enjoyed "very fine eating" and "afterwards a little dance at the 'Verlobung' [engagement] dinner" held at Henry and Addie Ziegler's. He danced

Fred and Julia Steinway at North Beach
Amusement Park.

"twice with [his cousin] Hettie, not with Julia." There was a "great kick about it the next day." They spent the evening at Julia's parents' home. But "before going home he had a fight with Julchen about not dancing with her."[51]

When their wedding day arrived, it was not anything special for Fred, and he worked at the factory until an hour and a half before the ceremony. Although he was up all that night, his diary entries about the event are quite terse. He noted that Julchen forgot her bridal bouquet after the ceremony and did not have it with her at the reception, which was held in the North Room at the Waldorf. This was a quiet dinner for fifty people, which ended at 11 P.M. They then went back to his place. Julchen slept in Friedrich's room, and Fred packed until 1:30 A.M. He was very nervous and stayed awake all night.[52]

The marriage was not consummated that night or either of the next two. Fred wrote cryptically in his diary "not yet." Finally, three days after their wedding, he scribbled "first time." They were in Washington, D.C., first stop on a two-month honeymoon. After their moment of connubial bliss, probably the "first time" for both of them, they traveled by trolley to Arlington Heights National Cemetery to visit Sheridan's grave.[53]

There were two more entries in Fred's diary about their sex life. He noted a "second time" and "third time that night."[54] There was no further record of sexual intimacy, and Fred's record of their travels reads more like a business trip than a honeymoon. At every stop they visited a Steinway dealer.

For her part, Julia was not looking for tenderness or passion; all she wanted was cash and a crown. Fred was more than forthcoming. A month before their marriage in the spring of 1899 he drew $300 from Steinway & Sons for Julchen's trousseau expenses. The following week he "gave Julchen a check of $250 to deposit in her bank," and two days later they were at Marcus jewelers spending $150 on china. That summer, after they returned from their honeymoon touring the American West, Fred "transferred two hundred and fifty shares of Steinway & Sons to Julia."[55] Steinway shares at the time were worth $200 each, so Julia's wedding present amounted to $50,000. For Julia, it was all working out according to plan; the Cassebeer family was now wealthy.

This was just the start of Fred's generosity. He also financed the renovation of his brownstone at 15 East 53rd Street, hiring the elegant New York furniture house Pottier, Stymus & Company to design the interior and manufacture the cabinets. This celebrated firm had manufactured furniture for Fred during his bachelor days and had also produced many fancy piano cases for Steinway & Sons. Pottier, Stymus & Company listed among their clients Henry M. Flager, William Rockefeller, and Astor's Hotel Waldorf. William Stymus, Jr., president of the company, gave Fred's house special attention. There would be no stock items; each cabinet, table, and chair would be a work of art. The brownstone on East 53rd Street was transformed into a palace.[56]

Their new home was also designed with a view to the family that Julia was counting on. But Julia would never bear children. Fred's diary is filled with reports of Julia being sick, frequently during the first week of the month, an obvious indication of menstrual cramps. They tried everything, from castor oils to blackberry brandy, to cure Julia. Nothing worked. Finally, at the end of the year, Dr. Krug diagnosed Julia's pain as caused by her womb being bent forward. The only way to correct this would be to operate, then follow up with monthly treatments. Fred nervously scrawled in his diary that the operation was "not dangerous."[57]

His description of the operation, which took place two days after Christmas in Julia's mother's house, reads more like an account of medieval torture than the practice of gynecology. Julia was given laughing gas and was strapped to a saddle to spread her legs. Her hands were also strapped. Two nurses assisted Dr. Theodore J. Annelt and Dr. Krug during the surgery. According to Fred's fitful account, it was brutal. Julia's uterus was "tough and contracted." The doctors "had to force a passage through the 'multer' [cavity]." Throughout the late afternoon Julia was tied to the table with her legs forced apart as four strangers pried and cut at her most private parts. For Julia the invasion of her privacy was as painful as the mutilation of her body. The next day she was in bed with a high fever. Dr. Krug visited and "took cotton rolls out of her womb." She spent the next ten weeks in bed.[58]

The scars would last a lifetime, and the thing she coveted most—a family—she would never have. But she resolved to get one another way. Her sights were set on her brother Edwin's child, Florence.

When Florence was ten, Edwin, who had no money, asked Julia for money to pay for Florence's education. But Julia didn't trust him. She presumed that the so-called education money would be spent on booze and women, and that very little would go to Florence's education. So she proposed a deal that had been on her mind for years. She would adopt Edwin's daughter, change her last name from Cassebeer to Steinway, and raise Florence as her own. Reflecting on this odd arrangement, Henry Z. Steinway suspected that "Edwin was happy to have his powerful and wealthy sister Julia raise Florence. And apparently Harriet, Edwin's wife, didn't care."

Fred stayed out of it. As he saw it, this was Julia's business, not his. His one concern was that if Julia predeceased him, it would be his responsibility to raise Florence. Only after it was agreed that in the event of Julia's premature death Florence would go back to her parents did he go along with the plan. Florence would be Julia's daughter, not Fred's. Betty Steinway Chapin, reflecting on family matters, acknowledged that "Uncle Fred had no interest in Florence."[59]

Betty emphasized that "Julia had high hopes for this wonderful, social queen that [Florence] was going to be." Her goal for her attractive daughter was that, like her new mother, she would marry well. Florence went to all the right dances to meet all the right boys. Betty portrayed Florence "flitting in and out and going to this party and going to that party, having a wonderful time . . . not overburdened with brains." She wore her hair short, her skirts tight, and left her bra off. Like most women her age, Florence experimented with smoking, drinking, and petting. She was a flapper. Betty depicted her as exceptionally pretty and truly wild: "Gatsby wild . . . the epitome of the twenties."[60]

During the 1920s she lived first in the Dakota apartment house on Central Park West and 72nd Street and later at 420 Park Avenue, perfect settings for the Gatsby life-style that Julia encouraged. Julia hosted parties there for the Steinway family and the music world. Betty remembered that Julia "used her house all the time, and loved being Mrs. Steinway. Adored it." She was also "the queen bee of the New York Philharmonic, . . . one of the few on that board who knew anything about music."[61]

If you were not part of Julia Steinway's circle, you were not part of New York's smart set. Betty recalled her parents, Theodore and Ruth Steinway, coming home from one of Julia's elegant parties and discussing the sophisticated crowd, the rich food, and the delicious wines.[62] Julia D., as she called herself, had a team of maids, cooks, and butlers trained to cater to this lavish life-style. Her dinners were always formal, black-tie affairs. Guests were rushed through cocktails and quickly seated for a marvelous four-course dinner with superb wine. She was adept at knowing who liked who and who was in town. Through Urchs, she always knew whether an artist was in New York or on the road. When he was in town, Fritz Kreisler, the renowned violinist and an extremely sophisticated world traveler, was a regular guest at Julia's. One family member still loves to tell about a dinner when "Rachmaninoff, the great pianist, sang Russian ballads accompanied by John McCormack on the piano." John McCormack, who had begun his career as an opera singer but was then touring as a concert tenor, was very popular and would always sell out a house when he came to New York. It was said that every young Irish girl had to be given the night off when he sang in New York. He was ideally suited to Julia's salon: well dressed, well behaved, and famous.[63]

Greiner's favorite Julia dinner party story was when the Rachmaninoffs, the Fritz Kreislers, Vladimir Horowitz, and George Gershwin were among the guests. After dinner, as Greiner recalled the evening, George Gershwin was asked to play the piano. But,

> if anybody asked Gershwin to play one of his recent compositions on the piano it became something of a calamity. You couldn't drag George from the piano! Gershwin played and played and Rachmaninoff was visibly bored and annoyed. Horowitz had written a fox-trot, a rather charming and effective piece (especially when he himself played it), which he had on one occasion played for Rachmaninoff. While Gershwin continued playing Rachmaninoff turned to Horowitz and said:—Now go to the piano and play your fox-trot which is much better than anything Gershwin ever wrote!—Horowitz politely, but firmly, refused.[64]

Julia became so powerful in the music world that pianists sought out her friendship to advance their careers. If Julia liked an artist, she could mention them at the right time to the right person. When you are "plugged in," commented Henry Steinway on Julia's connections, "there are things you can do."[65] Among those whose careers Julia promoted was the pianist Myra Hess, who became a close friend.

Betty Steinway Chapin contended that if Julia had been a man, the history of Steinway & Sons this century would have been completely different. But at Steinway & Sons there was no room for women at the top. Not since Doretta, Julia's grandmother, had a Steinway woman even tried to participate in the piano business. Nevertheless, Julia had a powerful influence during the 1920s. Urchs and Greiner were merely employees, whereas Julia was the real thing—a Steinway. She joined Ziegler and Reidemeister as part of Fred's inner circle and definitely played a role in Fred's decision to make Ernest Urchs head of the Concert & Artists department.

Essential ingredients in Fred and Julia's social life were their vacations abroad and in New Hampshire's White Mountains.[66] But the summer of 1927 was different. Florence was fourteen and, according to Julia, needed to meet the more sophisticated old money crowd. Julia moved the family to Kimball House in Northeast Harbor, Maine. She had heard about this tony Maine village from two close friends, Walter Damrosch and Fritz Kreisler, who both spent their summers in nearby Seal Harbor.

Northeast Harbor, established by Charles W. Eliot, president of Harvard College, attracted educators and intellectuals from Boston and New York. It was not as trendy as the neighboring village on Mount Desert Island, Bar Harbor, but it was a perfect place for Florence to meet the right men. It was also the ideal spot for Julia and Fred. Julia's musician friends were only three miles away in Seal Harbor, and for Fred's enjoyment the Northeast Harbor Golf Club was at hand.[67]

Kimball House was a classic New England hotel, with about eighty rooms in the main building and several three-story cottages scattered about the grounds.[68] "Pyne" cottage, where the Steinways stayed, had a family sitting room on the first floor, complete with a Steinway piano. On the second floor were four bedrooms and two baths for the family, and on the third floor three bedrooms for the staff. The Steinways paid $1,200 for the season, with all their meals taken in the hotel or delivered to the cottage.[69]

That summer was surprisingly hot, even for coastal Maine. By 16 July thermometers were registering record-breaking temperatures. Fred came back to the cottage that Saturday, exhausted from the heat, and decided to nap before dinner to help him stay awake during the Bridge game scheduled for later that night. Fred enjoyed the game and stayed late at the party.[70] Early next morning Julia was stirred by Fred grasping at his chest. She called for help, but it was too late. Fred Steinway died that Sunday morning of a heart attack.

Without any ceremony, Fred was brought back to New York and laid to rest in the family mausoleum in Brooklyn's Greenwood Cemetery. There wasn't even a testimonial in the company newsletter that month, nor in the end-of-the-year issue, presumably because Steinway & Sons feared that news of Fred's death might breed apprehension about the future quality of

Steinway management in 1925. *Seated, from left:* Henry Ziegler, Fred Steinway, Billie Steinway. *Standing, from left:* Theodore Cassebeer, Charles F. M. Steinway, Fritz Vietor, Paul Schmidt, and Theodore E. Steinway.

its pianos. To provide a smooth but swift transition, Julia and her uncle, Henry Ziegler, nominated Theodore E. Steinway, William Steinway's youngest son, to succeed Fred. Within a week of Fred's death the board of directors met and ratified that choice.[71]

There was only one problem: Theodore didn't want the job. Theodore, then forty-four, dreamed of a life filled with concerts, literature, stamp collecting, amateur acting, and tinkering; not commerce, litigation, sales decisions, and fiscal concerns. He was an intellectual, not an industrialist. He enjoyed working with Ziegler in the factory and planned to experiment with pianos in his cousin's workshop for a few more years and then retire.

Dismayed, he appealed to his mentor, close friend, and cousin, Henry Ziegler, to assume this burden and become the next president. Ziegler, then seventy, regretting that there was no other choice, answered: "Theodore, it's got to be a Steinway, and you're the Steinway."[72]

THIRTEEN

A Reluctant Leader

I T FELL TO THEODORE E.
Steinway, who never wanted to be president, to lead Steinway & Sons
through the most dreadful depression in American history. Theodore often
remarked that "Frederich Steinway went out on the path of glory and I came
in on the path of destruction."[1]

Until 1927 Theodore had successfully dodged the Steinway family piano
business. His older brother Billie had distracted the family; he was the
adored one, the "little Prince." Their father William's diary is filled with
notes on "Baby Billie's" size, weight, and infant vocabulary, but there is very
little about Theodore or his baby sister Maude. Betty Steinway Chapin,
Theodore's daughter, remembered that "Billie was the one who everybody
had high hopes for. . . . Billie was brilliant, sociable, charming, successful."
Billie was the designated heir to the Steinway throne; the only question was:
"What are we going to do with Theodore?"[2]

Theodore had always been glad to play second fiddle to Billie. According
to his son Henry, he was "scared to death of the old man" and delighted to be
out of his father's line of sight, which left him free to pursue his own life,
independent of family expectations.[3]

Theodore was shy and delicate. As a boy, he "stammered somewhat" and
was labeled "sensitive and somewhat withdrawn" by a family who felt it
necessary to apologize for such characteristics. His mother had died of
Bright's disease when he was nine, and the stuttering had then become more
pronounced. His father sent him off to boarding school, only to find that he
grew worse, as a result of the boys making fun of him. According to his older

half-sister, Paula, who filled in for his mother, Theodore was "quite a bright little fellow though quite wild." She noticed that he did not stutter as much with people who took the time to listen to him. But he did not make friends easily and appeared aloof on first encounter. Only his buddies ever recognized that beneath the startled deer appearance was a warmhearted little fellow.[4]

His father died a month after his thirteenth birthday. Billie, Theodore, and Maude were then raised by Paula, who was married with two young children of her own. Paula was the daughter of William's first wife, Regina, who was sent off to France when Paula was ten, disgraced by divorce proceedings that revealed innumerable love affairs and an illegitimate child. Now the daughter of that marriage "inherited" the children from the second marriage and, along with it, the obligation to raise the future leaders of Steinway & Sons. In Paula's household on West 74th Street everything was *auf Deutsche:* Rhine wine, Wagnerian operas, *Strumpfel Peter* fairy tales for the children to read, and a slender stick, almost as long as the family dinner table, to remind the children to keep their backs straight and to watch their manners. Paula did not raise the children of her father's second marriage by herself. Cousins Charlie Steinway, Fred Steinway, and Henry Ziegler controlled the purse strings from William's estate and were in on all decisions about the children's future. Theodore was whisked off to the cathedral school of St. Paul's, in Garden City on Long Island; but by the time he was ready to go to college, his father's estate was a mess. Henry Steinway judged it "was about as unliquid as it was possible to be . . . lots of loans and mortgages, everything but cash." Theodore's dream of going to Yale after boarding school was crushed.[5]

Instead of Bulldog and Eli, it was soundboards and strings for Theodore. But deep down inside he knew that, if they had tried, the Steinways could have scraped together the money for four years at Yale. Decades later, their decision still gnawing at him, he told his son Henry that "the family, which included Fred and my older half sister, Paula, and others, decided no, I should go to work, that I was too flighty, and that my head was always in the clouds."[6] They believed that the best remedy for a head in the clouds was feet in the factory, and in September 1900 he started his three-year apprenticeship at Steinway & Sons. The Steinway family had decided "what to do with Theodore."

Theodore worked in several different departments at the 53rd Street factory, so as to learn all facets of piano making. Many of his teachers remembered him as a thorough mechanic. During this time he looked for both a sanctuary within the factory and a buffer to protect him from the family. He discovered the perfect hiding place in Henry Ziegler's department of construction and inventions. In Henry Ziegler, Theodore found the concerned, gentle parent he never had. He eagerly sought a place as one of Ziegler's boys, alongside Fred Steinway and Teddy Cassebeer.[7]

It was not long before Ziegler was calling Theodore "Toot" and signing short endearing notes to him "Popsie." Some years later, when his second son was born, Theodore wrote to his "Dear Uncle" Ziegler announcing that he and his wife had decided to name the child Henry Ziegler Steinway as a tribute to the "deep personal regard and affection" he felt for him.[8] Theodore and Ruth had two more sons after that, four in all, but not one of them was named after Theodore's father, William.

Theodore's passions were acting, reading, collecting stamps, and listening to music. He was not a factory man; nor was he obsessed with building a better soundboard or improving the Steinway action. Although he enjoyed tinkering with pianos, because he liked to work with hand tools, his real interests lay outside the factory, and he looked forward to retiring at the age of fifty to pursue his hobbies full-time. Ziegler understood this about Theodore and gave him the freedom to investigate the world beyond Steinway & Sons. He encouraged Theodore's intellectual pursuits, particularly his love of music.

Theodore was often at the theater or at concerts, and a lot of his time was spent racing around town with his friends, other wealthy New York bachelors —all this financed by the soaring profits of Steinway & Sons during their pre-1914 golden era. Theodore cut quite a dapper figure with the New York smart set, black hair combed straight back, full mustache trimmed short, and a tight athletic body. He even lost his stammer, and by the time he turned twenty-one he had become an eloquent speaker and actor. His "love for plays and players," he remembered later, "led me inevitably into the temptation of acting myself." In 1906 he joined the "Players" club and the Amateur Comedy Club. At the Players, he wrote, "I met the choice and master spirits of the age in the theatre . . . Otis Skinner, Charles Coburn, Howard Lindsay, and oh, so many more." He also became friends with Players club member John Barrymore, whom Theodore referred to as "that divine madman,"and even started to wear his hat like Barrymore. According to Betty Steinway Chapin, the old pictures of her father and John Barrymore reveal a striking likeness.[9]

In an "Address to the Players" thirty-five years later, Theodore confessed to his friends that "from the moment my mother named me, I was destined to become a Player." He revealed, for the first time, the confidential history of his middle name Edwin; it was in memory of Edwin Booth, founder of the Players. His parents were great admirers of Mr. Booth, and his father's diary was filled with references to him, such as "saw Booth the magnificent last night. . . A majestic performance of 'Iago' by Mr. Booth. . . Booth grows greater every day." My parents "wanted some part of this great man's memory to go with our family," he explained; and so they named him Theodore Edwin Steinway, Theodore for his uncle, Edwin for Mr. Booth.[10]

At the Amateur Comedy Club, Theodore played many parts in many plays, but there was one performance he would never forget, their 1909 Christmas production of "The Student Prince." The rehearsals were held in the basement of Carnegie Hall, then called the Carnegie Lyceum auditorium. For this play the Amateur Comedy Club was joined by the recently formed women's acting company "The Snarks." Ruth Gardner Davis had helped found "The Snarks" and was in the show. Ruth was from an old Yankee family, recently established in the New York banking house of Blake Brothers. Although from a completely different background, she immediately identified with Theodore's need to stay clear of his family.[11] In Ruth, Theodore found his emancipation from the Steinways. In Theodore, Ruth discovered her "Student Prince."

Theodore came into Ruth's life like a revelation. Decades later, at the age of eighty-eight, Ruth remembered very well when she met him. "He was so different from anybody I'd ever known." She fancied Theodore and his "theatrical crowd" much more than her own "social crowd." Theodore "was certainly more sophisticated, and more worldly," according to their daughter Betty, "than the rest of the young boys who were sort of Harvard undergraduate types, running in and out of the (Davis) house."[12]

Theodore came with unfamiliar ways. He was the son of a German immigrant and manufacturer in a world of Yankee bankers. The Harvard types were who Ruth's mother, Anna Elizabeth Shippen Davis, called "Gar" by her family, expected her daughter to invite to their summer cottage on Long Pond. Theodore was too exotic, too different, which was what Ruth found so attractive about him.[13]

Theodore was discovering the world of an old New England family, and Ruth was getting a taste of a world a lot more interesting than her own. As their daughter Betty neatly summed it up several decades later, "I think you've got a quid pro quo there."[14]

They went together for three years and then got married on a Saturday afternoon in April 1913 in New York City; Theodore was thirty and Ruth was twenty-four. The wedding was written up in the newspapers as one of the largest "and most fashionable of the early spring weddings . . . hundreds of society people being present." Ruth "wore a gown of white satin trimmed with duchess and rose point lace and a veil of old lace held in place in cap effect by two diamond ornaments which were the gift of the bridegroom." Theodore's brother Billie came from Hamburg to be his best man. Ruth picked her younger sister Sybil to be her maid of honor.[15] After the wedding there was a reception at the Davis house on Madison Avenue, and two weeks later the newlyweds sailed for Europe.

Their honeymoon included "some time in and around Naples visiting Capri and Sorrento and taking the beautiful Amalfi drive." Then they headed north to Rome and Florence, where they were entertained at the home of Albert Spalding, the violinist, then Milan, Switzerland, Venice, and Munich. Their three-month voyage ended in Hamburg, where they met Billie, toured the Steinway factory, and flew 450 feet above Hamburg in a Zeppelin.[16]

Theodore adored Ruth. Like Billie, he used his marriage to free him from the Steinway family tradition. Their sister Maude also rejected her Steinway heritage, albeit in a different way, by joining and supporting various spiritualist cult groups. All William's children from his second marriage rebelled— not unusual for the native-born generation of immigrant parents. Theodore "had a strange thing," his son Henry noticed, "he didn't like the German family customs." For instance, "his birthday was never celebrated in the house, and if you know Germans, . . . birthdays, anniversaries, all those things are very important. So we were raised in an extremely Yankee way. . . . I never heard German at home . . . there were no Christmas cookies and Kaffeeklatsches." When Henry apprenticed at Steinway & Sons in the late 1930s, he had to attend the Berlitz School to learn German so that he could talk to the piano makers at the Hamburg factory. During an interview about the family, Betty responded to a question about whether she was raised in the Davis tradition with one word: "Totally."[17] Theodore and Ruth redefined for themselves and their children what it meant to be a Steinway.

A few years after they were married, Gar, at a Long Pond Sunday dinner, announced "that any son-in-law who would build a summer home" in Long Pond would be given the land. Theodore wrote in his memoirs that at that moment "my wife gave me the eye and I gave it back so after dinner I went to the wood shed and got an ax and four stakes and said to Gar 'we are ready to stake your generous gift!'" Ruth staked out the plot of land. The property included a tiny cabin, which had once been her childhood retreat. Their new house on Long Pond cost $7,200 to build and furnish. They moved in that spring. "For a time," Theodore noted, "we called the house 'Camp Stamp' as I sold my British India and British Africa colonies (stamp collection) to provide the necessary cash."[18]

To say that Theodore loved Long Pond would be an understatement. "It was the ultimate refuge," his son Henry wrote, "a complete turn away from the Germanic family life with which he was raised, and which he hated." During the summer he played baseball with the Long Pond home team, the

"Ponds," against "Chiltonville." He also kept all the records for the Chetolah Yacht Club, which met at his dock, and even maintained the buoys. In the evenings he captivated the group at parlor games such as charades; no one who spent a weekend at Long Pond ever forgot Theodore's imitation of a hippopotamus. Every weekend during the summer he traveled back and forth from New York with the rest of the men on the Fall River boat, passing the Steinway mansion as they sailed from the East River into Bowery Bay.[19]

Theodore did retain his Steinway craftsmanship, however. Steinways were builders, and Theodore had that in his genes. There was nothing he enjoyed more than laying a new brick walk around the Long Pond house or giving the house trim its yearly coat of green. Betty remembered an "enormous cellar where my father spent enormous amounts of time making chairs and tables and fixing things." Most of the wood came from Steinway & Sons. The porch chairs and the wood paneling for the house, as Theodore reported in his memoirs, were from "an enormous load of North Carolina mountain cypress, . . . bought by [uncle] C. F. Theodor Steinway in 1862 for soundboards."[20]

In the city Ruth and Theodore lived an affluent life. It was not "big wealth," according to their son Henry, "but by then [Theodore] had an income from the estate of his father of probably $35,000 a year . . . and you could live damn well on that." A cup of coffee cost a dime in those days, a pack of cigarettes a quarter, a man's silk shirt less than $2 and a seven-room apartment with three bathrooms on a high floor in a good neighborhood rented for less than $200 per month. Ruth and Theodore's first home, 375 Park Avenue, was a beautiful, plush New York apartment built on the exact location of the old Steinway factory.[21] Theodore wanted to live there because the 53rd Street factory was once supervised by his favorite uncles, Fred Steinway and Henry Ziegler, which made it hallowed ground. It was the romantic in him that took delight in raising his family on the site where Fred and Ziegler worked as young men and where they taught Theodore his trade. It had connections with parts of his past that he cherished, parts that served as stage props for the new Steinway script he was writing.

Theodore's love for music had been instilled by Henry Hadley, the eminent American composer and conductor and the director of music at St. Paul's School from 1895 to 1902. Henry Steinway recalled that his father spent whole evenings "reading through piano transcriptions of Wagner operas, and in a soft voice, for himself alone, sang all the parts and described the stage action." Betty also remembered, with some pain, her father's passion for Wagner: "every time the Met did Meistersinger we had to go," Betty recounted. "I went with him once, and I ended up really fairly black and blue in the ribs, because I sat next to him," and periodically he would poke her,

In Ernest Urchs's office at Steinway Hall in 1925. On the left are Ruth, Theodore, and young Henry Z. Steinway. Standing on the right is the pianist Ernest Hutcheson, with his wife seated below him and Teed Steinway next to him. In the middle is Urchs, and seated on the floor is Roman de Majewski.

saying, "They've cut out six bars there. . . . He knew his Wagner, . . . and you mustn't tamper with the great old man's works, so he felt."[22]

His passion for Wagner became a valuable diversion from the harsh realities he was up against in the late 1920s, when the United States economy and the piano business in particular went into free fall. Theodore's response, according to his son Henry, was "to keep the flag flying at all costs to himself and his associates, . . . with no thought of liquidation, sale, or just plain closing down until better times."[23]

Steinway & Sons had had some lean times since the beginning of the twentieth century but had always made a profit; before and after World War I, Steinway & Sons' income was usually about half a million dollars a year. In 1923 earnings doubled, soaring to a million dollars and staying above a million for the next three years.[24] Steinway & Sons had never made this much money before; nor would it ever again.

Piano sales and Steinway profits started to drop in 1927. Consumers had been moving rapidly toward ready-made music transmitted by radio and phonograph and away from the piano. The depression changed this bad situation into a disaster. After 1929, nationwide piano shipments dropped by 90 percent. It was not long before sales at Steinway & Sons plummeted as well. Whereas in 1929 they had sold more than five million dollars' worth of new pianos, in 1932 sales had collapsed to under a million dollars' worth. Steinway & Sons lost well over a million dollars that year.[25]

But even if there had not been a depression, piano sales would still have collapsed. Pianos had lost their panache by 1929. The gauge of respectability and social standing in America had shifted to other possessions.[26] Americans had deserted the piano. They were more interested in listening to music than making it, to being consumers of amusement rather than producers of it.[27] Most people preferred to go to the movies, put a few records on the phonograph, or listen to the radio than play the piano. Amos 'n' Andy over the airwaves or Fredric March on the big silver screen in *Dr. Jekyll and Mr. Hyde* was effortless and easier than learning to play a Mozart sonata.

In 1920 there were only five thousand radios in the United States, most of them in the hands of electronic tinkerers; by 1933 two-thirds of American homes had at least one radio. Across the country people listened to the music of Paul Whiteman live from New York on the radio. Radio manufacturing expanded so much that the National Lumber Manufacturers Association reported that although lumber sales to piano companies were down 60 percent, the loss was absorbed several times over by the demand for wood for radios.[28]

During the 1930s a hundred million people, more than three-quarters of the nation, went to the movies each week. They no longer gathered around the piano at home to sing. Moreover, the advent of "talkies" in 1926 meant the end of the piano in the movie house, once crucial for the silent film. And during the intermission, "machine music" replaced live orchestras, once common in movie theaters.[29]

In 1914 Americans spent $56,000,000 on pianos, more than twice what they spent on phonograph records; but five years later, records captured the lead with $158,000,000 in sales. Although Thomas A. Edison had invented the phonograph in 1877, it was not until 1915 that it started to compete with the piano. The Victor Talking Machine Company of Camden, New Jersey, brought out a practical, popular series of phonographs under the trademark Victrola. By 1929 the phonograph—or what many people called "the Victrola"—was the main source of music in most American homes.[30]

Greiner blamed the automobile for the shift. Families "were roaming the roads in their motor cars," he said, rather than sitting in their living rooms playing the piano. Moreover, in a consumer society it was important to flaunt your possessions. A drive through the neighborhood in an automobile was a more obvious display of wealth than sitting in your living room playing the piano, even if you did what many people did and placed your piano in the window. More people would see you. Greiner was right. The car became a middle-class obsession and competed in the family budget with any plans to purchase a piano. In 1930 a Model A Ford cost $435, while the cheapest Steinway upright was $875. Few families could afford both, and most opted for the car. In spring of 1927 the fifteen-millionth Model T rolled off the assembly line in Detroit. By 1929 more than twenty million of America's thirty million families owned an automobile.[31]

All these modern conveniences—the radio, movies, the phonograph, and the automobile—captured dollars that once went toward the down payment on a piano. In 1923 the player piano accounted for more than half the pianos shipped in America; ten years later there were no factory shipments of players at all. The radio, more than all the others, was directly responsible for the downfall of the player piano. For many people the player piano was not a musical instrument but a reproducing device, and when a novel, more versatile, and less expensive device came along, they didn't think twice before making the switch. Why pay $4,000 for a player piano when you could buy a radio for $90?[32]

Steinway & Sons had never made players directly but since 1909 had supplied Aeolian with about 10,000 pianos under the terms of their contract. During the 1920s Steinway had shipped an average of 500 pianos a year to Aeolian. But by 1933 player sales had dropped so drastically that Aeolian was stuck with more than 240 players in stock. To terminate the contract, Theodore agreed to take all the players back. Steinway & Sons made them back into normal pianos and added them to the 2,000 pianos they already had in their inventory.[33]

Nor was this desperate situation limited to player pianos. Steinway & Sons had shipped more than six thousand regular pianos in 1926; six years later only nine hundred pianos left the showroom. Steinway & Sons endured other losses too. Rental income from Steinway Hall plummeted by more than $100,000; the piano rental business dwindled from more than $64,000 in 1929 to less than $24,000 in 1933; and the sale of secondhand pianos fell off by more than $90,000.[34] Theodore, all alone at the top of the company, was stuck with the task of trying to staunch the wound of his hemorrhaging giant.

He had already saved some cash by closing the Steinway-owned music stores in Cincinnati, Columbus, Charleston, and Huntington, West Virginia. These outlets had been losing money since 1924. Fortuitously, as Theodore's son John maintained, Steinway & Sons was out of the last of the stores, Cincinnati, by the summer of 1929, "just a couple of months before the crash and the ensuing depression." According to John, his father "was either extremely smart or very lucky" to have made the decision to close those stores. "We were into expensive real estate or expensive leases . . . which could have been a hell of a thing, with the depression on. . . . So we were damned lucky" to get $160,000 for the Cincinnati lease.[35]

Theodore also cut the $150,000 worth of perks given to Steinway artists every year and by 1932 had sliced that budget in half. Steinway & Sons would no longer cover the cost of shipping grand pianos to local concert halls across the country, nor would it pay a subsidy per concert or travel expenses for a tuner to accompany the "immortal" artists. But for a few years, at least, the subsidies for Paderewski and Hofmann continued. Paderewski, enormously wealthy and generous, refused his $8,000 subsidy for the 1930–31 season because Steinway's business was so depressed. Mischa Levitzki, the up-and-coming Russian pianist, was not paid a subsidy but was provided an ample, unique credit line at Steinway & Sons. He borrowed between $10,000 and $30,000 a year until 1935, a huge amount for penniless times. Perks for Vladimir Horowitz, Ignaz Friedman, Ossip Gabrilowitsch, and Alfred Cortot were also maintained for a while. When they were on tour, Steinway & Sons footed half the bill for shipping their pianos to the local concert hall plus the tuner's salary.[36]

Most Steinway artists, except for Paderewski and Hofmann, "found it possible to get along without an accompanying tuner. . . . They also found it quite unnecessary to have a piano for practicing in the hotel in every city where they played—since they [now] had to pay for this luxury!"[37] reported Greiner. He had always maintained that the "furnishing of hotel pianos, ostensibly for practice purposes, was an unbelievable waste." He delighted in telling the story about the grand

furnished by the Steinway dealer in Buenos Aires, Argentina, for Alexander Brailowsky, a great favourite in South America, at his hotel suite. When Brailowsky had finished his concerts in Buenos Aires and the hotel piano returned to the dealer, a long spot, spoiling the polish of the piano, was found on the top of the Steinway grand. It turned out that when Brailowsky found that the creases of his trousers of his full dress were badly out of shape he had the tailor press the pants right on top of the piano in his hotel room! When this story, true or fiction, was told to Theodore E. Steinway, President of Steinway & Sons, he suggested that I write Brailowsky and ask him to give us a testimonial reading: "The Steinway is the finest piano on which to press my pants."[38]

Eventually Steinway & Sons just supplied the piano, and the artist paid all the other costs. Greiner remembered those years of cutting services to the artists as "quite an 'operation.' It was like pulling teeth," he recounted, and "not all the teeth at once but one by one."[39]

Greiner worried that he would lose artists to other piano companies, because "money talks."[40] He spent countless hours easing pianists into the new arrangements and listening politely to their arguments about why they should be made an exception and should not be charged for concert service. The "great ones"—Paderewski, Hofmann, and Rachmaninoff—were visited by Theodore as the head of the house.[41] Greiner described these appointments as difficult for Mr. Steinway. When Theodore visited Rachmaninoff to explain the new terms, Greiner went with him:

Rachmaninoff listened quietly and when Mr. Steinway had finished Rachmaninoff said that he fully understood and that he very much appreciated that Mr. Steinway had personally called on him. A few days later at Rachmaninoff's home he asked me: will Horowitz also pay for concert service? Mr. Rachmaninoff, I replied smiling, you really don't think that Steinway & Sons will do for Horowitz what they are not doing for you, Hofmann, or Paderewski? Of course, of course, I understand and believe you, but I just wondered.[42]

Greiner contended that not a single artist left Steinway & Sons at that time because of the change in policy.[43]

The drastic cuts in artists' perks and the sale of all the Midwest stores helped, but Steinway & Sons remained in the red. Theodore then gambled and invested more than $400,000 in a new national advertising campaign, whose theme was a concern for the passing on of values from parents to children. Anton Bruehl's photographs of precious progeny playing the piano replaced pictures of the "immortals," and the copy under the half-page photograph contended that a Steinway piano builds character, encourages virtues, and breeds popularity.[44]

"The world has changed rapidly," read the new full-page Steinway & Sons' ad; "it is now filled with airplanes, fast motorcars, and new theories of human relationships; the old world of swimming holes and horses is vanished. But there remain some unchanging fundamental things that serve to connect all generations, all men." Music could link the past with the present, and for generations Steinway & Sons had provided the musical instrument that could develop a sustained relationship between parents and children. "Now more than ever," the Steinway advertisement claimed, children "must have plenty of just the right thing to do." Make music part of your children's life, and you "imprint upon their dawning little personalities that rare glamour that makes the whole world come smiling."

It might be expensive to substitute a Steinway for a toy, the advertisement went on to say; "but a first-rate environment will definitely help to produce a first-rate person." In a world in which the economy was unraveling and family relationships were being redefined by unemployed fathers and working mothers, parents needed to be assured that they could assemble a shield for their children.[45]

The new advertising campaign proved to be no quick fix. Sales in 1931 were under $2 million, down from $5 million in 1929. As a result of mounting debt and increasing inventory, Theodore was driven to eliminate dividends on Steinway & Sons stock, suspend the Christmas bonus, cut salaries, including his own, and fire piano makers.[46]

The company was losing $2,000 a day in 1931, more money than most piano makers earned in a year. Theodore took hundreds of Steinway workers off the payroll, reinstating some on a per diem basis to manufacture a piano or two or to do a repair job. In 1929 the payroll had been over $700,000; by 1933 it was less than $300,000. A firm that once employed more than two thousand people was down to six hundred, most of whom worked part-time. Jess Manyoky, a tone regulator, had worked on five or six pianos a week in 1929; but this dropped precipitously to two instruments a week during the first six months of 1931 and then two pianos every other week that summer. His annual income (based on $10 per piano regulated) of $2,424 in 1929 dwindled to $670 in 1931.[47]

During the summer of 1931 the National City Bank called in about a million dollars in loans to Steinway & Sons. Theodore did not have the money to pay. He panicked. He went from the Chemical Bank to New York Trust and then to Chase Bank, borrowing heavily to bail out the firm. "And in those days," Theodore's son Henry recounted, "for commercial loans, they like to have them cleaned up every three or four months . . . and they knew perfectly well that we were going to the next bank (to repay the first bank), Chase would be cleaned up with a check from Chemical, and so on we went around the daisy chain."[48]

This money chase triggered an announcement that the factory would close in September. The banks insisted that Steinway & Sons sell off its inventory before manufacturing any more pianos. In addition, according to Henry Steinway, Teddy Cassebeer "was realistic enough and practical enough to say, 'It's just got to stop [Theodore] you're just wasting the stockholder's substance.' . . . Look, we're just pissing away what is basically their money, which is what it was."[49]

Although never even mentioned in the Steinway & Sons board of directors minutes during 1931, Theodore fired more than a thousand workers that year. It is apparent from payroll and employment records that between 1931 and 1936 the factory was run by a skeleton crew of foremen, office workers, and hundreds of part-time piano makers.[50]

Jess Manyoky regulated only ten pianos between September 1931 and March 1932. In 1932 he worked on just fourteen pianos, and, according to his work log, 1933 was not much better: from January to October he worked on two pianos. For piano makers who had spent their whole working lives at Steinway, being offered such meager part-time work was perceived as a double cross. Charlie Vavra, one of the payroll clerks, known among his friends as the Czechoslovak comedian, told Henry Steinway a story about Paul Eichenbrenner that illustrated how old-timers at the factory felt. Eichenbrenner had worked continuously at Steinway & Sons since 1908, and his father, Ernest, had been there since 1870. According to Charlie, Paul came in to pick up his paycheck in September 1931, only to be told that after twenty-three years at Steinway & Sons he was to be laid off for a while due to the lack of orders. Eichenbrenner turned to Charlie, protesting that "if this wasn't going to be steady work you should have told me and I never would have taken the job."[51]

The factory remained officially closed for two years, although numerous piano makers were brought back on an "as needed" basis to work on one or two pianos. Theodore was exhausted and was amenable to Steinway & Sons limping along with a part-time work crew until the economy recovered. It was probably Cassebeer who decided toward the end of 1933 that Steinway & Sons had enough potential business to reopen the factory a few days each week. Theodore and the banks went along with his decision.

During the next three years people were rehired as production increased. Jess Manyoky started full-time again on 18 October 1933. His pay per piano dropped to $7.30, but over the next ten weeks he worked on forty-four pianos, more than doubling his income of the previous year. But Manyoky's story is somewhat misleading. Steinway & Sons did not double its payroll in 1933; for the next two years it remained constant at roughly $300,000. What did change, and what Manyoky's story illustrates, was the constitution of the work force; part-time workers were eliminated in favor of a smaller full-time crew. It was not until 1936 that there was an increase in the payroll at Steinway & Sons.[52]

When Theodore proclaimed the factory reopened, on 7 August 1933, it was a moment of hope for the few who had been hired and for the Steinway family, especially for Fritz Vietor, who had been pressuring Theodore to try again. It was an attempt to put the spirit back into Steinway & Sons. Unfortunately, 1934 turned out to be the worst sales year in Steinway's history. Even adding $50,000 to the advertising budget and hosting the first national piano-playing contest in New York at Steinway Hall didn't help. The net loss that year was $390,000. It would be another two years before Steinway & Sons' sales increased.[53]

In 1935 the national piano market started to recover. Roosevelt's New Deal legislation was pumping the nation's economy and stimulating its musical appetite. Subsidized by government funds, adult piano classes at public libraries, local YMCA's and YWCA's, and over the radio were becoming extremely popular. Group instruction techniques were devised using paper keyboards for those who could not afford to buy pianos. At the same time, Ignace Paderewski and Leopold Stokowski were observing increases in attendance at their concerts, and many musicians in the orchestra were receiving stipends from New Deal programs. Attesting to a revived interest in live music, New York's mayor, Fiorello H. LaGuardia, and the nation's First Lady, Eleanor Roosevelt, were the distinguished guests at the Music Educators' National Conference, which hosted a performance of choral and symphony music by 3,500 school children, to whom more than 18,000 people listened. The number of pianos shipped began to increase, and music trade associations reported a developing thirst for live music in the United States, a sign of hope for Steinway & Sons and the other thirty-five American piano makers still in business.[54]

The Federal Music Project, an arts program of the Works Progress Administration (WPA), played an essential role in this musical awakening of America. Free piano lessons and concerts were financed by the Federal Music Project, an agency that employed 18,000 people and spent more money than any other WPA cultural program. The WPA was the major distributor of government funds to the unemployed and an important stimulant of the economy. In 1935 the largest single government appropriation in the nation's history, five billion dollars for work relief programs, went to the WPA.[55]

The 1930s was also the beginning of the big band era, a time when lovers swooned to Glenn Miller's "String of Pearls" or swayed to the mesmerizing tunes of jazz wizards William "Count" Basie and Edward "Duke" Ellington. A new type of music was evolving, pioneered by Louis Armstrong, Fletcher Henderson, Bix Beiderbecke, and others. "Swing," as they called it, sounded like the hottest jazz jam session ever. A hit more with the crowd than with traditional music critics, swing struck more conservative ears as "an unregenerated racket." Devotees, on the other hand, compared its inventiveness to van Gogh's distortions of photographic realism.[56]

Although swing had been around for twenty years or more, played primarily by African-American musicians in small jazz clubs in the Deep South, it was Benny Goodman who brought this new form of jazz to national attention, during the late 1930s. In the Goodman band Gene Krupa supplied the pulse on the drums for their unique rendering of "Body and Soul," Teddy Wilson's inimitable piano enlivened their original rendition of "Sometimes I'm Happy," while "the dry bony jangle of Lionel Hampton's xylophone punctured the air" in their thrilling interpretation of "Blue Skies." In 1938 when the Goodman band played to a standing-room-only crowd at Carnegie Hall, it was evident that live music performances were America's passion once again and that "swing was the thing."[57]

Audiences were enjoying music, and people started to insist that lessons be as much fun as listening. The problem was that many of them had unpleasant memories of childhood piano lessons and teachers. They remembered the ordeal of practicing scales and then, after a few months, refusing to take lessons anymore. Few youngsters ever attained a third-grade proficiency in piano, and the instrument itself soon became a piece of furniture on which to put family photographs, waiting to torment younger siblings. Josef Hofmann, the celebrated Steinway artist, maintained that "piano study would be far more popular than it is if students, average players, would be permitted to concentrate more on the musical expression of a composition, and would be less tormented by pure finger exercises which although necessary, are but a 'means to an end,' and if overdone may often cause an 'end to one's means'—musically speaking, of course!"[58]

The 1930s saw a revolution in the method of teaching piano. The so-called Klavier Schule method, designed to produce concert pianists, was replaced by techniques whereby pupils learned to play simple tunes in one hour for their own immediate enjoyment. Rudolph Ganz, director of Chicago Musical College, reported that "the scale has given way to the melody, the tune, the music that any father and mother can understand. . . . The old-fashioned way of teaching children to play the piano has been completely discarded." Ernest Hutcheson, dean of the Juilliard School of Music, argued that the amateur did not need the skill of a professional. Amateurs did not have to be "serious musicians"; there was no need for them to practice long hours. They could have fun and use the piano as a social asset. That way they would retain an interest in the piano and in music. In 1939 *Fortune* magazine reported that "more children were learning to play the piano than at anytime in history."[59]

The piano industry was slow to respond to this new interest. People were clamoring for an inexpensive piano with more style that occupied less space. Americans had moved into smaller apartments, and budgets were limited. "Where shall we put that piano?" asked the *Ladies' Home Journal* as early as 1928. Women's magazines and movies were highlighting not only smaller and less expensive instruments, but their design, underscoring that fashionable furniture was as important as magnificent music.[60]

Even in the face of dwindling sales, piano manufacturers stuck with baby grands and ungainly uprights; they were loath to embrace the 1930s art deco style. Retooling was expensive, and during hard times a faddish piano case constituted a risk they did not wish to take. Moreover, it wasn't in the piano manufacturers' tradition to come out with new cases. They were more likely to be selling something new *inside* the piano than outside. For the first five years of the decade, at least, buying a piano remained an investment in tradition. Consequently, there was no difference between a used piano and a new one except the price. Used pianos could always be sold at a discount and were understandably preferred over new pianos. By 1937 more than half the pianos in America were more than fifteen years old, representing a replacement possibility of almost six million instruments if the industry could give their owners a reason for needing a new one. Dealers destroyed thousands of used pianos—what they labeled "jalopies"—in an anxious attempt to skew the market in favor of new pianos. While products from vacuum cleaners to pencil sharpeners became streamlined and rectilinear, pianos retained their old-fashioned design.[61] The result was that most people bought a small, stylish radio instead.

Finally, in 1935, according to *Fortune,* "the piano industry discovered style." The Haddorff Piano Company produced a fashionable upright piano[62] that was 3 feet, 9 inches high, 5 inches smaller than the conventional upright, and cost roughly $300, 25 percent less than 1924 uprights. But the real novelty was that these pianos were chic; their chromium trimmings, mirror inlays, and blond mahogany finish delighted home decorators and women's magazines across the country. Some were partially usable as a desk, a bookcase, or a bar; others were electronically wired to contain a radio and a phonograph. *American Home* approvingly declared: "gone are the 'Model

T' styled [pianos] of yesterday and in their place smaller, moderately priced types that will fit any home."[63]

Manufacturers quickly seized on the idea of a small, stylish upright, each coining its own brand name: Spinet, Pianette, Pianino, Musette, Minipiano. A new piano boom had begun, and sales during the first six months of 1936 outpaced those of all other years since 1921. *Fortune* contended that the Minipiano had revolutionized sales in the piano industry. The National Piano Manufacturers' Association reported that "in the two years following (1935), unit shipments increased by 63 percent," with Minipianos selling at twice the rate of conventional uprights. In 1934 fewer than fifty thousand pianos had been shipped nationwide; within three years that number more than doubled, with 80 percent of the new sales being the compact, highly styled upright.[64]

The piano industry had prevailed. It was surviving the depression and the spread of the radio and the phonograph. It had modernized to meet art deco fashion requirements and had even made learning to play fun. Beginning in 1935 and for the rest of the decade, piano sales increased.

But this turnabout didn't include Steinway & Sons. Henry Steinway, Theodore's son, remembered the dealers being after them, wondering why they weren't doing something to meet this new demand. At Steinway Hall, Fritz Vietor, Theodore's energetic nephew; Roman de Majewski, the new head of sales; and Paul Bilhuber were also pressing Theodore to do something. But Theodore was paralyzed—indeed, overwhelmed, according to his son—by "this horrible sort of dead hand that took place during the Depression" and was committed to a wait-and-see policy, postulating that "it was all going to go away, we just had to wait for the upturn, which of course never came."[65]

The boom in piano sales simply passed him by. Steinway & Sons had not mass-produced uprights for more than a decade (in 1932 they shipped only twelve). When it did eventually enter the new market, in the final months of 1937, it explained its late entry by claiming that it had taken "several years of research and preparation" to design "a small vertical piano of Steinway quality." But Ned Bilhuber insists that his father Paul came up with the idea of designing a spinet for Steinway & Sons as early as 1932. It was to be a small upright, with the frame and strings at an angle, so as to get longer string length and a better tone. Paul Bilhuber had this prototype spinet built by Steinway foremen still on the payroll but without work because the factory was closed. He then showed his prototype to Theodore, insisting "that there's going to be a market for a less expensive, smaller piano." Bilhuber went on to explain to Theodore that, with the depression, few people had the money to buy a nice, handsome grand, but that many people would want a smaller, less expensive piano. But Theodore apparently countered: " 'Well, we've always made the grand, you know,' and he kind of threw cold water on these ideas of my dad."[66]

In fact, Theodore had promoted the wrong piano. Vietor had convinced him that the tradition of Steinway & Sons lay with the grand piano and that what people would buy during these hard times would be smaller inexpensive grands, not uprights. Relying on his nephew's energy to develop a new model grand and clinging to his own belief in Steinway tradition, Theodore approved the production of a small baby grand in May 1935. In 1936 and 1937 Steinway hired more than a hundred and seventy workers to build this new piano. A lavish Steinway dealers' meeting in early January 1936 and a $75,000 advertising campaign the following month launched the new 5-foot, 1½-inch grand. Steinway & Sons called it the model "S."[67]

But Vietor had got it all wrong. By 1937 he recognized his miscalculation, and in October of the following year Steinway & Sons introduced a 45-inch Pianino that sold for under $500. Theodore's son Henry, then an apprentice at the factory, remembered the excitement as Steinway & Sons prepared to go back into the upright business. An initial problem was that it had been so long since Steinway & Sons produced uprights that their workers had forgotten how to build them. Charles Reger, a cabinetmaker in the fly-finishing department, was one of the few piano makers who remembered building uprights. Paul Bilhuber and Vietor were brought in to help Reger figure out how to make the new Steinway Pianino and then teach others. Henry Steinway explained that they developed machines, and jigs, and patterns, because it was going to be the first Steinway made by machine, not hand, tools. According to Henry, figuring out how to get the machinery to make the instrument the "old Steinway way" was fun. Several decades later, he acknowledged that "had they done the upright first and forgotten the 'S' we probably would have been better off" and "the whole story would be quite different."[68]

Steinway & Sons never made much profit on the new Pianino. It turned out to be an expensive piano to build, yet it had to be sold at bargain prices. But it did provide Steinway dealers with a piano they could sell, and, as Henry Steinway put it, "kept us eating until the war." The Pianino was always a loss leader for dealers, a strategy to tempt people into the showroom, in the hope that eventually they would trade up to a grand. Though Steinway & Sons shipped more than a thousand uprights in 1938 and another twenty-two hundred the following year, they continued to lose money.[69] The bottom line at Steinway & Sons was that if you were making grands you were making money, whereas if you were making uprights you were just selling pianos.

Steinway's Pianino, introduced in 1937.

Believing that recovery was around the corner, most of Theodore's energy was spent on safeguarding the Steinway name, ensuring its dignity, and protecting his family from financial hardships. Indeed, he was more concerned with preserving the Steinway legacy than with profit. To Theodore, according to his son Henry, Steinway & Sons was "a responsibility, a sacred trust that had been laid on him. After all, he's a son of William Steinway." Theodore often referred to the company as "a glorious ship," proclaiming that "if we go down, we'll go down with all our flags flying." Characteristically, he refused a million-dollar offer to place the Steinway name on a refrigerator and another million-dollar proposition to use the name Steinway & Sons on a radio, all the while appropriating close to $20,000 to place an ornate Steinway piano in the White House, as a Steinway family gift to the nation.[70]

According to Henry, the White House piano was just the kind of thing his father would have thought up, just the kind of gesture that appealed to him. It was a tradition that had started unofficially when William Steinway presented his old friend President Grover Cleveland with a piano as a wedding present in 1886. It had been continued in 1903 when Charlie Steinway presented the first official White House piano to President Theodore Roosevelt. Now, thirty-five years later, Theodore Steinway thought it was time that the White House had a new piano, the three-hundred-thousandth Steinway. He did not see it in terms of how many pianos it would sell, only as something he was proud to do.[71]

Before the piano was shipped to Washington, there was a private showing at Steinway Hall and a "Preview Luncheon for the Creators of the White House Piano" at the Lotos Club.[72] Theodore sent a special, touching invitation to Henry, who had recently graduated from Harvard and was apprenticing at the Ditmars factory. It read: "Since you have had such an interest in the piano that is going to the White House, I wish you would do me the great honor to come and take lunch with me on Saturday, December 3rd, meeting at Steinway Hall at 12 o'clock, so that we may have a look at the piano before it goes to Washington, and also to have you meet Mr. Eric Gugler, Mr. Albert Stewart and Mr. Dunbar Beck, the artists who have helped us to create this piano. Always yours, Theodore."[73]

In December 1938 the piano was presented to the nation. It was magnificent. Along the side of the grand mahogany case was a golden frieze painting portraying a series of American dance scenes: square dancers, cowboys, early settlers, African-Americans, and Indians. The piano stood on three huge gilded eagles sculpted by Albert Stewart.[74] The presentation ceremony, attended by fewer than a dozen people, mostly Steinway officials, included Josef Hofmann playing several works of Chopin.

President Franklin D. Roosevelt accepted the instrument, dedicating it to "the advancement of music in every city, town, and hamlet in the country." Theodore's remarks focused on the motive behind the gift: "a paean of thanksgiving by a family who arrived on these friendly shores from abroad" —an odd theme to highlight in 1938, with Hitler threatening world peace. In a strictly public relations sense it was no time to be romanticizing about one's German heritage. Henry, reflecting on the speech more than fifty years later, said: "It's not the right speech at all. . . . It's amazing, but it's typical of my father. . . . This is what he would sit down and write, and this is what he would get emotional about. . . . We knew there was trouble [in Germany], yes, but my father would have ignored that in this emotion. . . . It bothered me at the time, and it still bothers me."[75]

Theodore's misjudgments and mistakes were in part the result of his

The White House Steinway, no. 300,000, 1938.

profound isolation. His daughter Betty, reflecting on why her father had no one to share his problems with, why the people around him didn't provide him with better counsel, stop him from making inappropriate speeches, insist on timely and severe budget cuts, and help him out of his paralysis, judged that the people surrounding him were second rate.[76] The family had failed to provide Theodore with supportive, wise partners. In 1930, when cousin Ziegler died and brother Billie refused to return from his post as European general manager, Theodore was left without an experienced associate to help him oversee Steinway & Sons.

Cousin Teddy Cassebeer (Julia's younger brother) was the only seasoned relative. But although he became a pillar of support to Theodore throughout the 1930s, their conversations were confined to business hours. Cassebeer's wife, Clara, would leave the house only to visit her family and wanted Teddy home immediately after work. More than fifty years later, when it was pointed out to Betty that her father did in fact have a business confidant in Cassebeer, she puzzled to herself: "Why do I not remember

Theodore E. Steinway and Theodore Cassebeer in the pattern room of the Ditmars factory.

Teddy? Was he ill for quite a long time? . . . because I don't remember him at all."⁷⁷ That was because he rarely talked to her father outside the factory gates or the offices at Steinway Hall.

The people around Theodore at work were either much older (Nahum Stetson, Friedrich Reidemeister) or much younger (Paul Bilhuber, Frederick Vietor). As for the family, Theodore, the youngest son of a second marriage, was caught between generations. The only male relative near him in age was his cousin Henry W. T., who had been estranged from the family since his series of lawsuits against Steinway & Sons in the late 1890s. There were only a few Steinway women who could have been helpful, but Theodore was not progressive enough to consider taking his cousins Clarissa or Ella Steinway into his confidence. He thus became the first person to rule Steinway & Sons alone.

He was alone at work and also at home. Rather than turn to Ruth for support, he kept from her and their children the worries he faced all day. Throughout the depression, his son Henry recalled, "our life-style [did] not change at all [even] as Theodore's formerly large income shrank away." Unaware that the family income was shriveling, Ruth planned inappropriate gatherings such as the stately dinner at Lüchows to celebrate Theodore's fiftieth birthday. Their youngest son Fritz explained that Ruth's naiveté was preserved by Theodore "perhaps he didn't even want to think about [his insolvency] once he got home."[78]

Thus, while Steinway & Sons was losing thousands of dollars a day, Theodore was draining his personal savings to support a false affluence. He maintained a brownstone at 126 East 65th Street for Ruth and their six children. To help run the household, they hired Elsa Uderheart, a nurse, to care for baby Lydia; Molly, a cook, who the family still remembers for her mouth-watering "Molly cakes"; a laundress; and Margaret Armburger, "Maggie," the maid who cleaned the downstairs and served afternoon tea and dinner in the evening. During the early 1930s, according to Betty, "my mother went to this scientific housekeeping place," where they undertook to modernize your house and your life. "My mother came out of there, and from that moment on, no [servants] lived in the house," except baby Lydia's nurse.[79]

On top of this charmed life at home, all six Steinway children were enrolled in the finest schools: Loomis, Putney, or Dalton Prep, and then on to Harvard, Radcliffe, or Smith. Henry remembered going off to Harvard in 1933 with $1,200, "enough money to live like a king up there." Several decades later he resented having lived this lie, describing it as "ridiculous," insisting that "we all should have been told," and maintaining that this false sense of affluence "had to do with my father's pride, . . . that [Theodore] was going to see this thing through and give his children an education and all that sort of stuff."[80]

Theodore's provision of this privileged life for his children was paid for with his soul. Looking back on those years, his son Fritz "sometimes wondered how . . . it was possible for him to do that . . . living in the middle of New York City in a private house, with six children, and sending them to private schools." He recalled his father "looking worried, seeming down, seeming discouraged," sleeping more, and so sad that "he didn't want to go out that much." His father routinely came home at four in the afternoon, played the piano, frequently a melancholy tune like "Smoke Gets in Your Eyes," and then "walked upstairs . . . right into his study, closed the door,

. . . pulled a blanket up over him[self], and snoozed. He'd go right out . . . and if that door was closed, nobody went in there. Absolutely nobody . . . That was a sort of day-to-day kind of a system that he developed to cope with his business life, his personal life, his relationship with his wife, his relationship with his children and the household." Fritz also noticed that Theodore's time alone in his stamp room increased during the 1930s. Reviewing his father's life during the depression, Henry regretted that Theodore had no one to talk to: "He needed somebody . . . in lieu of psychiatry, he needed somebody to unload on."[81]

The depression dragged on, and when Ruth finally asked her husband whether they had enough money, he told her, "Don't worry about it, because I'm taking care of it." But he wasn't, and gradually she came to realize the severity of their financial straits and sold the expensive cars and stopped the costly parties. To help out, Ruth's mother, Gar, gave her enormous sums of cash, roughly $30,000 labeled Christmas gifts. And when Ruth's father, Howland Davis, died, the inheritance helped immensely.[82]

As Theodore became more and more despondent, he drank more and more. By the late 1930s he had aged a lot and could find pleasure and relaxation only in the bottle. Ruth did not drink and became more and more thrown by his abrupt outbursts. According to Henry, his father's drinking problem devastated the marriage. "It was difficult for [mother], and she didn't quite understand what the hell was going on." "He had a hell of a time," Henry recounted, "and yet his sense of duty was overwhelming, that he must do this. He couldn't say 'Oh, screw it all.' " In the end, "it really killed him, in the long run . . . it took all the starch out of him."[83]

New Blood and Fresh Strategies

HEODORE STEINWAY
was a broken man. Devastated by the Depression, confronted by mounting
workers' demand for higher pay and a union shop, and apprehensive about
the future of his Hamburg factory in Nazi Germany, he sank further and
further into lethargy. At a time when his business desperately needed energy
and innovative ideas, he could only come up with plans to do less.

He cut the payroll by 50 percent, reducing the factory's work force from
2,000 to 600 between 1930 and 1934. He slashed the advertising budget from
$500,000 to $55,905 and his own salary from $47,000 in 1928 to $15,000 in
1933. He even lowered the price of the less expensive pianos, hoping to
attract customers. A small grand (model M) that cost $1,550 in 1929 sold for
$1,100 in 1936. But the cost-cutting formulas didn't work.[1] Only borrowed
money kept the company from going out of business.

As fifty-two-year-old Theodore surveyed the field of younger Steinways, he saw only two possible candidates for his battered throne: his eldest
son, Theodore, just out of college, and his ambitious nephew, Frederick
Vietor. The latter, known to the family as Fritz, was the obvious choice.
Grandson of Albert Steinway and great-grandson of the founder, Henry
Engelhard Steinway, he owned a significant number of Steinway shares. He
also believed that he deserved to run the company. Moreover, it was becoming the tradition at Steinway & Sons to pass the presidency from uncle to
nephew; it had never gone from father to son. Nevertheless, his son Theodore, nicknamed Teed, was his father's first choice. Edward Peckerman, the
company's lawyer, recalled him as "a strange young man" whom no one

would have thought of as a successor. But Theodore senior was determined to hold on long enough to give Theodore junior time to mature.[2]

Teed's birth in 1914 had been cause for celebration. He was the first male Steinway in a generation. His romantic father had ordered the factory whistle blown and free beer for all the workers. Teed was named after his great-uncle Theodor and, like him, was an avid reader. His interests ranged from pianos to animals, from puzzles to geography. Bilingual in German and English, Teed was a shy boy who felt more comfortable with books than people.[3]

At a time when money was becoming scarce, Teed had the finest education that money could buy. After he graduated, a year early, from the Loomis School in Windsor, Connecticut, his parents sent him to the American Institute in Munich to continue his study of German, which his father considered useful for business. According to his younger brother Henry, the institute "wasn't really a school. . . . It was a place for overprivileged kids to be parked." Teed claimed that he learned more German from the subtitles to English-language movies than from his tutors. He spent most of his time in Munich skiing and sailing. In 1931 he returned home and enrolled at Harvard, where he scored high in subjects that interested him and barely passed the courses he deemed dull. Sometimes he didn't even bother to take the final exam. As a result, his college transcript was an odd mix of A's and D's.[4]

Although Teed rarely dated, his good looks, virile body, and Continental poise made him the romantic fantasy of many young girls at the Steinway summer home on Long Pond. Henry recounted that Teed had "an aura that made him very attractive."[5]

One of his girlfriends, Josephine, who later became his wife, described him as a very passionate man who "ran away from being the eldest son." The more Theodore tried to make his dream of Teed's future a reality, the more his son withdrew and, like his father, turned to liquor. According to Betty Steinway Chapin, her brother never conquered the two big demons in his life: a father who refused to admit that his oldest son was not going to shape up and run the business and an adoring mother about whom he was absolutely wild. Ruth and her son shared a love of books, particularly history. They had their own shorthand that excluded everyone else and could talk "a mile a minute about a thousand things." Intellectual and artistic, Teed "was the type that she instinctively liked," according to Henry. "My mother was a worshipper of the world of ideas." Here was Teed's dilemma: captivated by Ruth and frightened of "losing himself to her if he wasn't careful,"[6] he had to contend at the same time with a father striving to shape him into Steinway & Sons' next president.

To avoid both parents, Teed took refuge in his bedroom. Henry remembered that by 1938 Teed "obviously was not with it. You'd talk to him and he'd sort of not answer." He withdrew more and more until one day he could not even get out of bed. Theodore, barely functioning himself, was shattered and did nothing. Ruth, horrified, called her sister Katherine for advice. Katherine's husband was a doctor and recommended a psychiatrist connected to Silverhill Rest Home in Silvermine, Connecticut. The family drew a curtain around Teed's breakdown. Henry recalled that Theodore couldn't even bring himself to accompany Teed to the sanitarium. Teed's treatment consisted of interacting with others on crafts and various projects, very much like the skiing and canoeing he had enjoyed near Munich. After six months, he was pronounced ready to return to his family and was advised to "join something." That something was not to be Steinway & Sons. Teed spent the next few years in a volunteer cavalry lodge and then joined the United States military, rising to the rank of major by the end of World War II. Henry understood that Teed was "more social and much happier" away from New York and "the curse of the Steinway name."[7]

With Teed out of the picture, Theodore had no choice but to look to his arrogant nephew, Fritz Vietor, to rule Steinway & Sons. The trouble with Vietor was that he frightened people. Betty Steinway Chapin described him as "very austere" and "army-officerish." According to Henry, he inherited some of his abrasiveness from his father, "a very strict old German" whom Vietor called "a tyrant." His grandfather, Albert Steinway, had served in the Civil War. Fritz carried on that military tradition, fighting with the cavalry against Pancho Villa on the Mexican border in 1916 and enlisting in the Sixth Cavalry for combat in France during World War I. Vietor was more soldier than piano maker. His daughter Marjorie recalled that after the war "he had to make a decision as to whether to come back and go into Steinway, or whether to stay on in the regular Army. And I think, in a way, he would love to have stayed with the cavalry."[8]

Vietor's "military decisiveness" rankled Theodore and led to "some real knock-down, drag-out fights between them." Their wives disliked each other as much as they did. Henry remembered Marjorie Cochran Vietor as "definitely anti-Semitic, and anti-Catholic, and anti-everything else . . . just one of those miserable women." But it didn't matter that Vietor was imperious or that his wife was a bigot: he was of "royal" blood, a director of the company, and a principal owner of the firm.[9] He was family, "of the Albert Steinway lump of stock" and therefore unquestionably a suitable successor.

He was a perfectionist, both with himself and with others; he had to know every aspect of piano making. His apprenticeship included a "thorough education at the bench comprising a working knowledge of almost every operation of piano building, including research and inventions."

Added to this was a knowledge of merchandising, both retail and wholesale, buying lumber and supplies, factory administration, and liaison with pianists and artists. No one at Steinway & Sons since William had mastered as much, and no one after Vietor would even try.[10]

During the 1930s Vietor emerged as de facto head of Steinway & Sons. Theodore's lawyer, Edward Peckerman, expressed what others were slowly detecting: "Theodore wasn't the right person to be president. . . . He was a very intelligent man, but he was not a businessman." The retirement of his devoted factory manager, Teddy Cassebeer, added to Theodore's problems. Fifty years later, Henry Steinway still remembered the moment when Teddy "came over to the lunch table and said, 'Theodore, I am quitting. I'm getting too old and I can't handle it. You've got the two boys there now. I'm quitting today.' And that was it. He wrote a letter, and that was it." The following year he died of stomach cancer.[11]

This left Vietor alone in his zeal to save Steinway & Sons. While the rest of the family fretted, he worked steadily on new ideas to make money. He pressed for the manufacture of the small, inexpensive S grand with its more responsive keyboard to meet the depression market and turned to Paul Bilhuber, who had succeeded Henry Ziegler as head of engineering and experimentation, to help him perfect it.[12]

Once given the mandate to create a new Steinway, Bilhuber searched Henry Ziegler's secret closet on the top floor of the factory for notes and rough sketches of small soundboards. He found nothing very detailed. It was Steinway tradition to keep such fundamental calculations solely in the head of the chief engineer, since detailed drawings could be stolen. Whatever it was that made Steinway the standard piano was rarely committed to paper; it was merely passed down from Theodor Steinway to Henry Ziegler, then on to Paul Bilhuber. So Bilhuber started to build the model S with just a few notes and preliminary sketches by Ziegler. In any case, as Henry Steinway explained, the drawings always came after a piano had been invented. "In other words, they'd make the plate and then Bilhuber would say, change this, move this, and then after it was all through, [Frank] Walsh would get a plate and make a detailed drawing." Craft came before science. Henry emphasized that making a musical instrument had always been completely different from manufacturing, say, an automobile. "General Motors had nine million engineers drawing details of every screw that goes in the car, and then it goes to manufacturing. That's not the way it worked in the piano business. It worked the other way around. You [start] with a piano and say, oh, we'll make this here, . . . make this plate a little longer here, . . . move this one inch, and so on."[13]

For the first time, non-Steinway technicians were consulted, and detailed

Captain Frederick
(Fritz) A. Vietor, 6th
Cavalry, World War I.

sketches of the new piano were made. Steinway secrets were no longer the sole bailiwick of the chief engineer. Frank Walsh, a draftsman for Bilhuber, was instructed to commit the design to linen paper. The S represented an entirely new way of making a Steinway. Bilhuber's former professor from Columbia University worked with him on measuring the vibrations of hundreds of small soundboards. They were trying to invent a small soundboard with a grand voice. The result, Henry Steinway insisted, "was that the S grand piano, 6 inches shorter than anything we ever made, was an excellent, beautiful, wonderful piano. And you have to give him credit for that, because that was Paul's work. . . . That was, I would say, Bilhuber's signal accomplishment."[14]

The 5-foot, 1-inch S was the first Steinway grand made for a mass market, designed not only to suit smaller apartments and limited budgets but also to accommodate the new energetic technique of piano playing that was becoming the vogue. Henry Steinway maintained that "once Horowitz came in, the style of piano playing really changed. . . . He personally demanded a very responsive action, meaning the [key] came up from its rest position, and only had to come halfway up for Horowitz to give it a full blow down again. . . . He had the musculature, and he wanted those keys right under his control, so they'd follow him right up. Vietor was working with him, and with Josef Hofmann, who really understood the action, and they were working together and talking mechanically."[15]

Together, Vietor and Hofmann invented a more responsive keyboard to match the new style of playing; Hofmann named it the "Steinway Accelerated Action." The principle was simple: Vietor placed the piano keys on a rounded fulcrum, or pivot point, much like a playground seesaw, and redistributed the weight of the keys closer to the middle so that they would bounce back more quickly after being depressed. It was an elementary change; the fulcrum that the key pivoted on had been flat, and obviously a round fulcrum was an improvement. Moreover, the keys returned to their normal position two-hundredths of a second faster. For artists like Horowitz and Hofmann with fingers as fast as lightning, this springier keyboard was crucial.[16]

Vietor's invention boosted Steinway promotion. Henry proclaimed it "a wonderful sales tool," adding that "Steinway badly needed some new patent to carry on this great tradition of 'Steinway the innovator.'" Vietor's accelerated action was featured in all advertising copy and on the sales floor. The 1936 brochure highlighted the action as "the greatest improvement in pianos in the last thirty years."[17] Paderewski, Rachmaninoff, and Hofmann all issued statements to the effect that the best piano in the world had become even better.

The model S was ready for distribution by the fall of 1935 but was kept secret while N. W. Ayer planned a $130,000 advertising campaign, including an elaborate dealer convention early in the new year.[18] The day after Christmas, 207 Steinway dealers received telegrams inviting them to be the guests of Steinway & Sons in New York City on 6 January. Roman de Majewski, head of sales, who planned the gathering, remembered dealers pouring into the city: Jerome Murphy from Boston, Fred Sherman from San Francisco, Ray Durham from Chicago, and other key dealers. No one knew what to expect. "Many thought that Steinway was going out of business or wanted to borrow money from them." While in New York, they stayed at the finest hotels, drank plenty of scotch or bourbon, and gathered at the New York Athletic Club for parties hosted by Steinway & Sons. At 9:30 Monday morning, after a weekend of partying, all 125 dealers present, as well as the entire sales force from Steinway Hall, boarded five buses headed for the factory in Queens.

Theodore E. Steinway started the proceedings with a brief speech. He then dramatically pulled back a curtain to show the small grand, the new model S, mounted on an elegantly lit platform. Surrounding it were twelve more such instruments, in a horseshoe pattern, spaced far enough apart that half a dozen dealers could gather around each one. There were also exhibits of the S at various stages of construction. Theodore proclaimed: "Gentlemen, you are participating in the birth of a new Steinway." That night the dealers were guests of Steinway & Sons at a dinner of salmon and filet

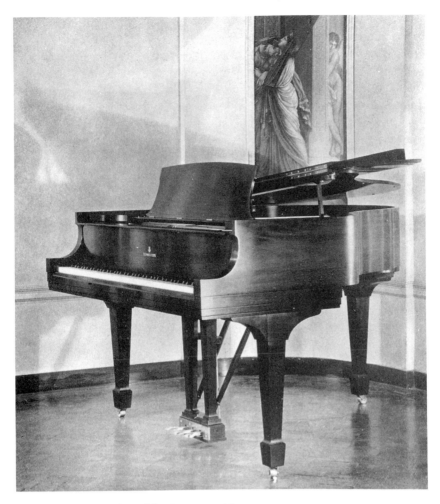

Steinway's baby grand, model S, inaugurated in 1936.

mignon at the Lotos Club. Majewski had arranged for Ray Durham, president of Lyon & Healy in Chicago, to respond on behalf of all the dealers there and present to "Mr. Steinway orders for Steinway pianos, to be filled during 1936, amounting to close to $3,000,000." It was the largest order ever given at one time in the history of the piano trade. The excitement was immense; everyone wanted Steinway & Sons to succeed. Josef Hofmann was so enthusiastic that he bought fifty such pianos for his Curtis Institute.[19]

The sales literature given to the dealers stressed that a Steinway quality grand now came wrapped up in a little package and that, moreover, you could buy this "Steinway Grand piano at the extremely low price of $885 . . . a small proportion down, and the balance distributed over a period mutually agreed upon." Theodore's explanation for having waited so long before coming out with a depression-model piano was that "Steinway had chosen to proceed slowly . . . to wait until excellence could be assured."[20]

The new model's success was part of a steady growth in piano sales since 1933. In 1936 Steinway & Sons shipped more than three thousand, six hundred pianos, up from fewer than fourteen hundred the previous year, generating an increase of more than a million dollars in sales. Vietor's dream had come true: Steinway & Sons was making money again. In 1936 profits soared to over $68,000 compared to the $300,000 loss of a year earlier. Theodore presented his employees with a Christmas bonus and increased wages for all the piano workers.[21]

But Steinway's recovery was short-lived. In June 1937 President Franklin D. Roosevelt, confident that the New Deal had worked and that the economy was ready to stand on its own, pulled back on government programs, and by the closing months of 1937 the United States economy plummeted. For Steinway & Sons, whose business was at last picking up, the bottom fell out of the market, and a million dollars in sales was lost. In an attempt to pull the economy out of its recession, President Roosevelt tried to restore some government spending, but he was limited by a conservative Congress. The recession would last until the 1939 defense buildup for war.[22]

But it was the innovative Hammond organ that dealt the final blow to model S sales. In 1935 Laurens Hammond, an electric clock manufacturer in Chicago, introduced an electronic keyboard that produced the sound of a pipe organ without pipes. The Hammond sales force went to every Steinway dealer and convinced them to carry their pipeless organ. The dealers bought the instruments wholesale for $600 apiece and sold them for $1,200, a profit margin far greater than they could realize with the Steinway S. The demand for Hammond organs spread rapidly across the nation.[23]

By late 1937 piano sales had slipped so much that the factory was practically shut down. Henry, who had just started his apprenticeship, recalled that the piano makers were working only one day a week. In 1938 the number of grand pianos shipped was less than half the number in 1936. Jess Manyoky had no work at all for almost half the year and watched his income plunge to less than $600. Steinway's losses were nearly $400,000 that year.[24]

In retrospect, Henry Steinway acknowledged that what the company needed was a small stylish upright, not a baby grand. But Steinway & Sons continued to see itself as a "grand house," and even when it started to make uprights again, their flow through the factory had to be tailored to the production of grands. But this zig-zagging through the factory was expensive.

By the time Vietor realized his mistake and Steinway & Sons started making uprights again, it was too late. Baldwin, Kimball, and other piano makers had already captured the market. Moreover, the Steinway upright was not noticeably superior to the competition. As a result, in 1939 Steinway & Sons shipped only 2,175 uprights, a modest percentage of the 88,000 uprights manufactured in the United States that year.[25]

Vietor then sought new products as a strategy for making use of over-sized facilities and a sales force that was too large. In the fall of 1939 he opened a record shop and a radio–phonograph department. The Steinway Record Shop was housed in a separate room at Steinway Hall. It had a living room atmosphere, and customers could listen to and buy a record, a Magnavox, or an RCA Victor phonograph. If that didn't work, Vietor had plans to manufacture or purchase for resale television sets, sheet music, and other musical instruments.[26]

In his tireless struggle to salvage Steinway & Sons, he eliminated outmoded departments and encouraged aging, ineffective managers to retire. His goal was to decrease Steinway's annual half a million dollar labor cost. To ferret out hidden waste, Vietor persuaded Theodore to retain a certified public accounting firm, Haskins & Sells, to audit the books. Karl Herrhammer, Vietor's fellow trooper in the cavalry and a new employee at Haskins & Sells, was asked to examine Steinway's ledgers.[27] While Herrhammer scrutinized the numbers, Vietor got Theodore to hire a consulting company from Cleveland, Robert Heller & Associates, to investigate Steinway's sales and distribution strategy. Neither of Vietor's ideas was particularly original. Both public accounting and management consulting firms had been growing in the United States since the 1920s. But for Steinway & Sons, accustomed to informal self-evaluation around the lunch table at Lüchows, it represented a radical departure.

Heller's first suggestion was that all employees over the age of seventy be retired. This venerable circle included the head of finance, Friedrich Reidemeister, longtime family friend and confidant of Fred Steinway; the imperious bookkeeper Herman Irion, self-anointed general manager, hired by William Steinway in the 1890s as a clerk; and trusted Steinway insider Albert Sturcke, employed by William as his stenographer to correspond with dealers in the 1890s. This faithful remnant was cast aside by Dudley P. Felt, a partner in Heller & Associates and overseer of the Steinway account, as representing "a major underlying weakness in the management philosophy of your Company."

Irion and Reidemeister were furious. "They thought they were just there forever," Henry declared, "and were irreplaceable and important." But Irion's and Reidemeister's old-fashioned ways irritated Vietor, according to Henry, so he was glad of the opportunity to remove them. In their place he installed five departmental managers, "all reporting directly to the general manager." Some of these new men turned out to be mistakes and were quickly ousted. The chief financial officer replacing Reidemeister was Stuart B. Miller, recognized more as a great memo writer than for what he accomplished. He tried to implement modern accounting procedures, ordering that all the old Steinway ledgers be tossed into a barrel and burned. But, as Henry recalled, a "Scotch clerk went down and actually took the barrel back and hid the books somewhere until this guy was fired, then they dragged them out again." A year later, Miller was replaced by Edward Orcutt. A short plump man with bad teeth always clenched around a cigar stub, Orcutt had been passed over initially because he had too few social graces for Felt's liking. Henry described Orcutt as "a rough cut guy, but he was pure gold. Absolutely no side to him whatever, no pretense."[28]

Felt also recommended including outsiders on the board. Two directors were added: Jerome F. Murphy, president of M. Steinert & Sons, an influential Steinway dealer in Boston, and Dudley P. Felt himself. In a Steinway publication, Theodore proclaimed that "the election of Mr. Felt and Mr. Murphy, was in keeping with the modern business policy of having on the Board men who were actively engaged in the industry and familiar with merchandising and operating problems at first hand."[29]

The Heller group then started to look beyond the boardroom in Manhattan to the factory in Queens. Ultimately, it was there that they found the most to fix. Pianos zigged and zagged through the buildings on Riker Avenue and then traveled up the hill to be finished at the Ditmars buildings. The assembly line looked like a mystery maze at an amusement park. Heller brought in his recently hired factory virtuoso, Thomas R. Harris. Only a few years older than Henry, Harris became his friend and coach in factory ways.[30]

Harris scrutinized Steinway's three plants (Riker and Ditmars no. 1 and no. 2) and reported that "the general layout of the buildings and departments was scattered and no logical or systematic flow of production had been effected." For example, a grand piano rim traveled a mile and a half from "the time the lumber was taken from the yard to the time a piano was shipped." He concluded that inefficient handling resulted in excessive costs as well as damage to materials.[31]

Harris then set about prescribing a remedy. He mapped out a path through the factory that would reduce manufacturing space by 100,000 square feet, cut down on piano travel time by 25 percent, and eliminate trucking between plants. His new streamlined factory would be able to produce 2,000 grands and 3,000 uprights a year on a one-shift schedule in 58 percent of the space. But World War II intervened, and it was to be another twenty-five years before Harris's plan was implemented. Meanwhile, Vietor became sick, and Theodore appointed Harris as acting factory manager of Steinway & Sons. For the first time in the company's history, the piano factory would be run by a professional factory man, not a Steinway man.[32]

While Vietor's driving personality had provided the spirit to prevail, it had also fed the fires of union organizing at Steinway & Sons. Peckerman, who attended all union negotiations, summed up the situation in five words: "Vietor was not Teddy Cassebeer." In contrast to Cassebeer, whom the workers saw as a guardian and helper, Vietor was regarded as the enemy, a tyrant, the villain in their fight for more money and more recognition. The difference between the two men was "like day and night," recalled one seasoned piano worker: "Vietor would always go like hell. [Cassebeer was] low key: 'If I don't come today, I'll come tomorrow, but I'll make sure I'll be there,' something like that. Very friendly . . . Cassebeer was a very, very friendly guy. . . . Vietor wasn't, he always seemed to be shouting or commanding." The old guys, according to Henry Steinway, talked about 'Vietor the Beast,' and Fritz was quite happy to be the bad guy.[33]

James Cerofeci, a filler, oil rubber, and sandpaperer at Steinway and eventually business agent for the union, recalled that Vietor once cut the wages of a fast worker who was making too much money. His salary was based on piecework. When the employee complained, "I worked very hard and the price was not high," Vietor responded, "I can get a Guinea ditch digger any time to do your job cheaper." All Steinway employees were given the same harsh message: increasing productivity would drive down the piecework rate. "I was afraid," Cerofeci explained; "I was a very fast worker, but I was afraid. At 2:00 I was finished, I had to mope around singing, fool around, in order that I didn't make too much. . . . I made about $29, now it came to me, about $29, afraid I'd make $30."[34]

On 1 January 1936 Vietor cut the piecework rates for all those working on the model S, in order to produce his new piano for under $1,000. He saw it as an extremely important marketing strategy to sell his ebony S for $885. The unpopular result was that piano makers working on the S made less than they would have made for doing exactly the same work on other grands. For example, Jess Manyoky was paid $7.16 to regulate the tone of every piano except an S, for which he earned thirty-three cents less ($6.86). Henry Steinway recalled the incensed reaction in the factory: "Here you were . . . letting the bosses piss all over you, you were getting ten percent less for identical work." Vietor's policy handed the union a perfect organizing issue— "similar work for less pay."[35]

FIFTEEN

The Rise of a Factory Union

T HE PROMISE OF STEADY
work, a commitment that united employers and workers at Steinway &
Sons, had been kept since the recession of the 1870s. It was broken in 1931.
Theodore Steinway fired 1,500 piano workers that summer. Only the highly
skilled workers were told that they might be called in part-time if orders
came in for repair work. Never before had Steinway & Sons fired so many,
and even those who were kept on (foremen and office clerks) worked for 20
percent less pay. One of the workers laid off was a Bohemian "machine
hand," Vaclav Havlena, who had been with Steinway for more than a decade.
Havlena was a joiner, which meant that he spliced strips of wood together. It
was a job that periodically resulted in his catching his hand in the splicing
machine and gashing his fingers or palm. Havlena earned a good salary for
this semi-skilled but potentially dangerous work, roughly $1,350 a year. But
in September 1931 he was given his last paycheck at Steinway for a while, $13
for the week. It would be two years before he would collect another. In 1933
a few people were rehired, including Havlena, and many more in 1936, but
their commitment to Steinway & Sons was gone. By contrast, Theodore
Steinway was proud of having managed to keep the factory open for two and
a half years into the Depression, from 1929 to 1931.[1]

Throughout these difficult years Vietor continued to threaten those with
jobs that he could easily replace them with unemployed "Guinea ditch
diggers." But the intimidation didn't always work, particularly when the
newspapers were filled with stories about ditch diggers striking to improve
their lot. Moreover, throughout the 1930s, migrant farm workers, from the

cranberry bogs of Cape Cod to the fruit groves of California, were also battling for higher wages and better working conditions.[2]

Infuriated workers went out on strike, paralyzing steel mills, automobile plants, hotels, laundries, bus depots, and department stores across the country. At the Bendix Products plant in South Bend, Indiana, 800 men and 300 women bundled together during a sit-down strike when the company turned off the heat. Striking bakery workers in Detroit threw loaves of bread at police who tried to spray them with tear gas. In Chicago, African-American wet nurses went on strike for more per ounce for their milk. At the same time, the number of unionized workers tripled, from 2,805,000 in 1933 to 8,410,000 in 1941. According to labor organizer Saul Alinsky: "Everyone wanted to hit out, employer against worker and worker against employer. . . . America was becoming more class conscious than at any time in its history . . . millions of factory workers claimed their rights to a fair share of the profits and to some control over their lives. It was the most spectacular power shift in the nation since the Civil War."[3]

By 1936 the mixture of temporary prosperity at Steinway & Sons and labor turmoil throughout the country encouraged a few piano workers to organize a union. It all began at a local Polish dance place, Busse's Hall, on Steinway Street, near the factory, where a few men met to guzzle and gripe about life at Steinway & Sons.[4] Most of the complaints were about wage cuts on the S, the lack of respect for seniority during layoffs, the diabolical Mr. Vietor, and tyrannical foremen.

Foremen were management. Their status, as well as their income, put them above the workers. There had always been tension between workers and an unreasonable foreman. He had the power of final sign-off on whether an employee would get paid. Workers, most of whom were paid by piecework, did not get new work or credit for the work they had done until the foreman said so. An oppressive or irrational foreman could make life pretty miserable for a piano maker.

Jess Manyoky remembered a couple of foremen who were resented. For example, the foreman of the damper department enjoyed reading his morning paper and telling his men: "Don't bother me." The problem, as one worker recalled, was that "when you're a piece worker, you wanted to get a job, you wanted to get work so you can make money. . . . That son-of-a-bitch, we used to say, you've got to wait until his highness gets off of that damn newspaper before you could take a piano." Another complaint was that foremen were forcing some of their workers to buy their own materials, so as to make production appear more economical. According to Manyoky, the irked crowd that gathered at Busse's grew to about a hundred.[5] As the numbers increased, dissension surfaced.

Tone regulators at Steinway & Sons in 1943, including Jess Manyoky (*middle bottom*) and (*to his right*) Jimmy Cerofeci.

Even some of Manyoky's fellow-Hungarian workers, like John Bogyos, spoke out against the incipient union. Bogyos recalled telling the crowd at Busse's that the men up front had no right to order them around. "They think they're King Tut," but they can't tell master craftsmen what to do. Bogyos described the organizers, with the exception of his countryman Manyoky, as a bunch of "lazy lousy" workers who wanted to stop others from working hard. Bogyos believed that unions were "a threat to our way of life in this country." Every time he expressed such sentiments, he was thrown out of Busse's Hall.[6] As confrontation became fierce, it became more and more critical to keep the gatherings clandestine. Manyoky recalled his concern that Vietor would discover them before the union was strong enough to fight back.

They called their budding brotherhood the "Piano Workers Organization," an independent union, not a company union, with no connection to any national union, organized solely by the employees of Steinway & Sons. Manyoky explained: "We had nothing at all, just 1937 we started the independent union, and then for two years we sweated it out, and got organized."

In 1937 they were strong enough to win a 10 percent raise. Two years later they succeeded in getting equal pay for work on the model S and called for an official vote to join the United Furniture Workers of America (UFWA).[7]

The UFWA was established in 1937 within the Congress of Industrial Organizations (CIO). Its initial leadership comprised disaffected members of the American Federation of Labor (AFL) who wanted to organize all furniture workers into one union regardless of craft. Morris Muster was the UFWA president, having been appointed by John L. Lewis. Muster was a Communist, an East European Jew, and a fighter for the seven-hour day, five-day week, social insurance, racial equality, and world socialism. By 1939 the UFWA had a membership of more than fourteen thousand and was protected by the National Labor Relations Board (NLRB) under the Wagner Act. This meant that workers could not be fired because they joined a union and that they were guaranteed collective bargaining rights. With NLRB protection the UFWA established the "Piano Workers Organizing Committee," won contracts with Pratt, Read & Company and Story & Clark, and then answered a call for help from the Steinway workers.[8] This was their first opportunity to organize piano makers in New York City.

The UFWA sent Gustave "Gus" Teunis, a former Steinway worker, to help establish links between the local union and the national organization. Teunis had started at Steinway & Sons as a porter in 1926 and after a year was sanding pianos. But, according to John Bogyos, who rubbed pianos right next to him, Teunis wanted to promote himself out of Steinway & Sons. It was obvious to Bogyos, who was against the union, that Teunis's ambition was to be a "big shot" in the CIO. In the Ditmars factory "he led everything. . . . I saw what was going on, and I mean it was right in front of me. . . . People come and go and people come to him about advice about what we're going to do." Bogyos insisted that Teunis was the "kingpin" in organizing the local union in 1937 and affiliating it with the CIO two years later. He told Teunis, "You're like a rotten apple in a barrel, you'll spoil all the apples."[9]

Henry Steinway remembered Teunis as an extremely bright, articulate fellow. He was "slim, elegant, . . . and a snappy dresser." He was from Suriname, then Dutch Guiana. He was assisted in his struggle to organize a union by an uncompromising co-worker, Milton Snyder, a Hungarian Jew who radiated a wonderfully tough aura. Teunis and Snyder even recruited a young Jewish labor lawyer, Alexander E. Racolin, to help them. Racolin was a tall, handsome, well-educated, wealthy, committed fighter for workers' rights. He represented the UFWA because he believed in the labor movement, not for the income. The rank and file only irritated him when they read the conservative *Journal American*. Racolin, known for his short temper, was constantly proclaiming: "you're in labor, men, you shouldn't read that newspaper."[10]

It was not unusual for Jews to be involved in the labor movement during the 1930s. In many unions they played a leadership role: Morris Pizer was president of the UFWA, Sidney Hillman headed the Amalgamated Garment Workers, and David Dubinsky the International Ladies Garment Workers Union (ILGWU). But there were few Jews at Steinway & Sons. Men like Milton Snyder, a grand piano fore finisher, and Morris Goldberg, a talented case maker known for his announcements before Jewish holidays that he was Jewish and wouldn't be working tomorrow, were few and far between at Steinway.[11]

Joining Snyder's and Teunis's rally for the union cause were two outspoken, ambitious, unskilled workers: William J. McSweeney, a good-looking, articulate young Irishman who worked the large drilling machine in the key-making department and mobilized the workers at Steinway's Riker factory, and James Cerofeci, Teunis's former workmate, who, according to John Bogyos, browbeat the men at the Ditmars factory into obeying him and supporting the union. Bogyos recounted: "I happened to like Cerofeci, but he used to go home with guys on a train, and he used to threaten them: 'Hey, what's the matter with you, do it for the union, this is good for you,' like that. If they didn't want to, he'd threaten them." Henry Steinway described him as "a Walter Reuther socialist, a real believer that there's no reason that the workers shouldn't own the means of production." But Cerofeci's passions went beyond workers' rights. A wiry Italian who loved to sing at his bench, he fumed about discrimination against Italian piano workers and in the same breath, in an earnest tone, proclaimed: "I'm going to tell you something, it sounds quacky, I think I'm the best dancer of the Peabody there is today, existing." Dancing at Roseland mattered to him as much as the union.

So it was that a fun-loving Italian, a tough Hungarian Jew, an articulate Irishman, and a savvy African-American from Suriname organized the predominantly German piano makers at Steinway & Sons, so forging links between groups that had little else in common.[12] The old-time German workers stood back and let the newcomers to Steinway & Sons take the lead. Henry Steinway maintained that the Germans were "not great on standing in the forefront. . . . There was a guy named [Joseph] Braun, who was a painter [a maintenance worker], who was with [Steinway & Sons] for years and years and years, and I'm sure the guy was either a Communist or . . . a socialist . . . whatever the hell you want to call it, . . . that guy was to the left of Trotsky. . . . A lot of them I know were for the union, but they were ready to let the . . . McSweeney's go in and rough up the boss."[13]

Sal Daddio, a rubber with Cerofeci, saw the German workers' passivity in more sweeping generational categories. Sal maintained that the older Europeans "done their work, they put in their hours, and they were content. . . . You know what I mean, they came from Europe . . . and if they made ten dollars they were content. But as the new generation turned out, it wasn't good enough." Bogyos, also in the rubbing department, saw it differently, arguing that the "German workers were very strong for unions, they always said, 'Why don't we have a union here? In Germany we always had a union. In Germany we had retirement benefits since I think the Iron Chancellor, Bismark.' So some Germans were for unions. I see it now as most very highly skilled people were against unions. . . . The old guys, most of the real old guys, they didn't want to change . . . no matter what."[14]

The highly skilled were the more senior workers, and this would explain the generational difference that Daddio and others noticed. At Steinway & Sons it was the younger, less skilled workers who rallied behind the union banner. But it was a more mature, politically shrewd kind of young worker who had been "burned" by the 1931 layoffs who organized this discontent. The initial organizers, James Cerofeci, Gus Teunis, and Jess Manyoky, were all in their mid-thirties and had been with Steinway & Sons for ten years or more by 1936.

To settle their differences, there was no strike, no sit-down, and no burning of pianos. Manyoky remembered "some kind of light friction, but nothing in the open that we could see, like broken windows." When they had enough enrollment cards, the UFWA proposed an election under the supervision of the NLRB. A few rumors circulated through the factory that Steinway & Sons' management was trying to sway the vote. Edward Peckerman later admitted that there was some truth in this rumor: some coaxing of undecided workers against the union did take place. But this did not stop Steinway from sending a notice to all employees denying all charges of impropriety.[15]

Throughout the entire process Theodore Steinway, Fritz Vietor, and Teddy Cassebeer expected that, in the end, most of their workers would remain loyal to the company.[16]

On 25 September 1939 workers lined up at the local public school to vote for or against joining the "United Piano Workers Union, Local 102, United Furniture Workers of America, C.I.O." According to Joe Pirola, paymaster for Steinway & Sons, "the union was voted in by one vote. . . . I and another man, the personnel director from Ditmars Avenue [William Bernauer], were on the tally so we would make sure that the men that voted belonged to Steinway & Sons. So it came down to about one vote, if I'm not mistaken. So they won out, and the union took over."[17]

Reviewing the circumstances more than fifty years later, Peckerman insisted "that the top executives of the company couldn't grasp what was happening, probably turned their backs in a sense to it. . . . There wasn't very much that a company could do, unless it wanted to play hard ball, and the Steinway people were not hard ball players."[18] John Steinway, one of Theodore's younger sons, recounted that it hit his father hard.

> My father was a tremendously emotional man, and . . . he considered it a lack of faith on the part of our employees, whom he had always sort of paternally taken care of. . . . He took it sort of personally, that they were saying, "We don't have faith in you as boss." I remember many discussions, where we tried to disabuse him of that, and [tried] to get him to understand that this was the wave of the future, this was the way life is being lived in these United States these days. But Pop was then getting along. . . . It was a blow to his sensitivity.[19]

When Cerofeci was asked how Steinway reacted to the formation of the union, his matter-of-fact comment was: "They felt terrible. But how could they stop us? We were strong then. . . . We were all sticking together. . . . We didn't like discrimination, we didn't like our wages, we had no holidays, we had nothing, absolutely nothing." Cerofeci's battle was not against Steinway personally; it was a fight for rights and benefits that Steinway was not readily providing. During the next five years Cerofeci emerged as spokesman and leader of Local 102.[20]

On 1 December 1939 Theodore was called in to sign the first union contract. It was a historic moment. For the first time Steinway & Sons acknowledged a factory-wide union affiliated with a national brotherhood. "The United Piano Workers Union, Steinway Local 102, United Furniture Workers of America, CIO" became—and still is—the sole and exclusive collective bargaining agency for all Steinway employees. "What they got," Henry Steinway declared, "was a union shop, which was what they were after."[21] Nothing was ever the same after that.

Even the pretense of paternalism was over. Vietor immediately canceled all goodwill gestures. He put an end to concerts by the Steinway Factory Orchestra during the lunch hour, personal loans to workers, and company picnics. For years Steinway & Sons had chartered two boats to ferry all the workers up the Hudson River to a park in Poughkeepsie, where the entire factory and their families—more than twenty-five hundred men, women, and children—would play all day. After a picnic lunch and dinner, several rounds of beer, free rides, and splashing about in the Hudson, they would board the boats for a summer's moonlit sail back to the city. John Steinway, one of Theodore's younger sons, wrote of the end of this paternalism at Steinway & Sons: "There was the old Steinway sick benefit fund, which was a company-sponsored thing. There was the death benefit. There were the free beds at the Lenox Hill Hospital that were available for Steinway employees. . . . All of this fell aside and was discontinued."[22]

Vietor's attitude at the time was: "Why are we doing it for these guys, and then they're giving their loyalty to this outside organization?" The rationale for ending all benefits was: "Now they got their union, no more of that." In retrospect, Henry Steinway realized that his unbending cousin Vietor made "the wrong decision. We should have done more of that, instead of less. But that's the way it was."[23]

The union was pleased to see these activities abandoned. It viewed employer benefits as covert attempts to bust the union. Walter Drasche, a young floor boy in the damper department during the 1930s, perceived the end of Steinway & Sons' benevolence as no loss. He insisted that the workers "needed a good solid hospitalization [and] medical plan, plus something for retirement, which Steinway didn't have. And they couldn't buy them with a boat ride or a picnic or a band concert."[24]

So paternalism was dead at Steinway & Sons. Drasche, reflecting on that passing, contended: "I could see that the trend was beginning." Vietor's position became: "We pay you for a day's work and if you get sick, that's too bad, and if you retire and stop working, that's too bad, too, that's your hard luck." Drasche's answer was that now "the union was going to take care of your pension, the union was going to take care of your hospitalization, the union was going to take care of your wages. Forget about it, you're not going to get any more picnics and any more boat ride and any more bands." The alliance between the Steinway family and their piano makers had been reforged.[25]

Vietor could not bear union negotiating. Nor could he handle it. His skill lay in giving orders, not compromising. After the first contract was signed, he asked his twenty-five-year-old cousin Henry, Theodore's second son, to work with the grievance committee. Within a few years Henry was handling "the whole ball of wax." He remembered sitting around at meetings with union guys making demands and discussing grievances, "and then I would report this back to Vietor, and he would say yes, no, or go to hell. That's about the way it worked."[26]

Nevertheless, within two years the union had secured eleven legal holidays, one week's summer vacation, a Christmas bonus of three full days' pay, the right to renegotiate wages "as affected by changes in the cost of living," and a 12.5 percent wage increase. A clause in the union contract also guaranteed that "the Company shall not move its three plants . . . to any place or places outside the five boroughs of the City of New York."[27] After 1939 the future of Steinway & Sons was to be defined by both the Steinway family and their factory hands.

This change to a union shop coincided with a change in piano making. Steinway & Sons stopped manufacturing iron plates and ivory keys for their pianos. Whether these changes were made in retaliation or were just good business sense is hard to determine: probably a bit of both.[28] Foundry work was a serious health hazard.

The lung disease silicosis had become unquestionably linked to foundry dust. Laid-off foundry workers were bringing silicosis cases to the courts and winning lawsuits by claiming that their lack of employment was due to physical ailments brought on by silicosis, not just layoffs due to a sluggish economy. The result was that in New York State alone during the 1930s more than $300 million dollars was awarded in silicosis-related claims. Health insurance rates on foundry workers skyrocketed. At the same time the state put pressure on old foundries like that at Steinway & Sons to update, ventilate, or shut down. In response, Steinway, like many other companies, closed its foundry, concluding that it was not worth paying the escalating insurance rates and what would have been an exorbitant renovation bill. Instead, it started buying iron plates and brass hardware from other companies.[29]

Vietor insisted that in order to keep down the price of the new upright line, he needed to modernize action manufacturing. His cousin Henry recounted accompanying him to a liquidation sale of the old New York action firm Wessell, Nickel & Gross to buy three floors' worth of action-making machinery for the sale price of $5,000. It was then, Henry reported, that Vietor decided to buy the keys for both uprights and grands. This too would save money.

Steinway & Sons would no longer make the whole of its piano. Vietor negotiated a low price with Steinway's action manufacturer to make an "action–key combination." But Henry always suspected that Vietor "was kind of sick of this whole key-making department, which was large, labor intensive and . . . quite a pain in the neck." He brought his decision before the Steinway board of directors, and it was officially sanctioned. The key-making department, Bill McSweeney's unit, and the foundry, a center of union activity, would be discontinued, thereby saving Steinway & Sons almost $30,000 per year, not to mention a fair bit of hassle.[30]

It seemed to those around Vietor that his pace, for a man of forty-nine, represented a frantic race against time. Henry Steinway remembered trying to keep up with him and always lagging behind. When they went up a flight of stairs, Vietor would always travel two at a time and yell back at his young cousin, "Come on, you lazy bastard." Vietor was the fire in the belly of Steinway & Sons. He was not revered by the men, but they all knew that he was fighting to make Steinway & Sons lucrative again. In 1941 the New York factory shipped more than five thousand, six hundred pianos, roughly seventeen hundred more than the previous year and more than any year since the record-breaking year of 1926. The company, for the moment, was operating at a profit.[31]

Vietor seemed a little weak in the spring of 1940, but he assured everyone that it was only because he had just been kicked by a horse. That summer he went off to a hospital in Plattsburgh, still claiming that his condition was due to an accident. In January 1941, when his beloved Squadron A was federalized into the United States Army as the 101st Cavalry, a military physical found that he had leukemia, and he was dropped from the company. By March 1941 it was clear to everyone that Vietor was very sick. But even when he was hospitalized at Columbia Presbyterian Medical Center, he remained active. Henry recalled that "Fritz was general manager, and still ran the factory from his death bed." Henry was Vietor's messenger boy, carrying mail to and from his hospital bed, and as such, "watched the poor guy die." Vietor died on 18 June 1941.[32]

Paderewski, that most revered Steinway artist, died less than two weeks later. For two years Greiner had watched Paderewski deteriorate. In the winter of 1939 Greiner had been at Madison Square Garden, where Paderewski was to play a recital for the benefit of the Musicians' Emergency Fund. Greiner reported that Paderewski had to be practically carried from his car to the dressing room. But the audience of twenty-five thousand people had to be informed that he would not play. Greiner, backstage, "witnessed the haggard man, sitting with bent head, staring vacantly into space. . . . It was quite obvious that Paderewski could not possibly play. Yes, there was Ignace Paderewski, world-famous pianist and statesman, but in reality it was only his shadow."[33]

At the time of his death, Paderewski was president of the exiled Polish Parliament in France. According to Greiner, it was Hitler's occupation of Poland that killed Paderewski as much as old age. The rise of the Third Reich signaled problems for Steinway & Sons as well. With a branch factory in Hamburg, Theodore now had to brace himself for a war against his own factory and workers.

SIXTEEN

Divided Loyalties in World War II

W ORLD WAR II WROUGHT
havoc at Steinway & Sons, both in New York and in Hamburg. Theodore
had finally pulled Steinway through the Depression, and just when it
was starting to make a profit again, the war began. War rationing of copper,
iron, brass, felt, and other materials basic to piano manufacturing forced
Steinway & Sons out of the piano business. At the same time Theodore
watched all four sons go off to the military. The war had robbed Theodore of
his trade; now it threatened the lives of his boys. At that point, according to
Betty, "My father, in a way, gave up. I think he said: 'I can't fight this thing
anymore.'"[1] He retreated from both his business and his family into deeper
depression and increased alcohol consumption.

It was a difficult war for a German-American family business with a
branch factory in Hamburg. Steinway had remained outside all previous
wars. It had never been called on to bend a single Conestoga carriage wheel
during the Civil War or build a rifle butt during World War I. But World War
II was different. It brought devastation and overwhelming change for the
New York piano maker. Suddenly, women dominated a work force that had
been almost all men. Moreover, in the summer of 1942, Steinway & Sons, a
company that for eighty-nine years had built magnificent musical instruments, became an aircraft manufacturer for the United States Army, while at
the same time its branch factory in Hamburg was supporting the Nazi war
machine with wooden airplane decoys, bunk beds, and rifle stock. In effect,
Steinway stayed in business during World War II by supplying both sides. It
was not the only American company with German branches. General Mo-

tors, National Cash Register, International Harvester, Swift & Company, and Standard Oil all had significant operations in Germany.[2]

The impetus for the transformation of Steinway's New York factory from pianos to planes began 4,500 miles from Queens. At dawn on 10 May 1940 German glider pilots attacked Fort Eben Emael in Belgium, taking troops and supplies inside what was once believed to be an impenetrable concrete and steel fortress encircled by a moat, barbed wire, minefields, and tank barricades. By the next day the fort had surrendered. What might have taken months was accomplished in a day with the help of Hitler's gliders. A similar German strategy of gliders and paratroopers would be used during the week-long, bloody attack on Crete in May 1941. German victories in both places, although with a high casualty rate in Crete, were ascribed to glider power and kindled American interest, albeit a bit hesitant at the beginning, in building "a combat glider corps in the shortest possible time, no matter what the cost," just like the German DFS 230 gliders.[3]

According to Theodore Steinway, United States military technocrats realized that gliders could be made out of wood, thereby reserving metals for combat planes and bombers. There was no shortage of wood, and the new phenol resin plywood hot-plate press process allowed certain products to be fabricated out of plywood and be as strong as steel, in some cases even stronger.[4] Here was a business opportunity for Steinway & Sons: to construct wooden gliders. It would enable the company to retain its workers and keep the factory open. But could it make a profit building airplanes?

By the summer of 1942 the War Productions Board (WPB) had made it impossible for Steinway and all other piano makers to buy the raw materials needed to manufacture pianos. Theodore's son John explained that "the government didn't stop us from making pianos. They said go right ahead, but you can't have any steel, you can't have any copper . . . vital war materials. So we were effectively out of business."[5]

Waco Aircraft of Troy, Ohio, designed the modern glider, a hybrid based on a captured German plane and Eldon Cessna's 1930 glider. Most people thought it looked like a boxcar with wings.[6] Waco labeled the new flying hulk the CG (Cessna Glider or Cargo Glider)-4A. It had room for fifteen soldiers or a mix of soldiers and supplies, even a Jeep. Gliders had no engines, no power source. They were towed through the air by airplanes, much the way freight cars are towed by a locomotive, and then cut loose to glide to the ground behind enemy lines.

By the spring of 1942 sixteen companies—among them Ford Motor Company, Gibson Refrigerator, Cessna Aircraft, and General Aircraft— were given contracts to build these flying behemoths. But General Aircraft, according to Joe Pirola, Steinway's payroll clerk, "had no facilities, they had

CG-4A glider during a test run, c. 1943.

no manpower, and they had no know-how." They obtained the contract only because they had friends in the Army Air Force. They then contracted with Steinway & Sons to lease them factory space, manufacture all the wooden parts for their gliders, and fill out the interminable reports, statements, and applications associated with doing business with the government. There would be three subcontracts between Steinway & Sons and General Aircraft between March 1942 and March 1944, providing 500 to 1,000 Steinway workers with something to do.[7]

Once they had signed the glider subcontract, piano making at Steinway & Sons was mothballed, packaged up, shipped out, or put down in basements, although the company continued to buy, fix up, and sell used pianos at Steinway Hall. The transition from piano maker to glider maker occurred practically overnight. Pirola remembered that "it happened in the summertime, and fortunately a lot of the men were entitled to vacation pay, so we decided that that was the proper time. . . . Then we'd call them back within two, three weeks, and bring them to this new facility to make gliders." But Theodore's youngest son, Fritz, remembered it as not such a simple, smooth transition. There "was a tremendous upheaval. . . . It was like turning your whole body inside-out, you know, just to preserve the body." And it wasn't just machines that had to be changed, it was also management. Fritz Vietor and Teddy Cassebeer had recently died, and the only piano man left, Paul Bilhuber, preferred experimentation to management, though he agreed to direct the factory for a few months. Theodore turned to the Heller consultants for advice and on their recommendation hired Justus Doane Anderson, Jr., as the new factory manager.[8] Anderson knew nothing about making gliders, but he was what the Heller group believed Steinway & Sons had always needed, a modern professional factory man.

The glider business was far from straightforward. Production was constantly frustrated by shortages of metal parts and design problems. Waiting for metal parts curbed Steinway's glider output from sixty per month to thirty and cost thousands of dollars in idle time. Moreover, the government drawings attached to the contracts were "simply terrible," according to Theodore's son Henry. However, Frank Walsh, a young Catholic from Astoria who had taken a few mechanical engineering courses in high school and had worked closely with Henry Ziegler in the 1920s, miraculously turned "vague, faulty and inadequate" Army Air Force drawings into useful blueprints. "Walsh did a hero's job," Henry proclaimed. "Walsh came in in his overalls, and crawled around with [his assistant] John Bogyos, figuring out these blueprints and making working drawings so that our guys could do things."[9]

In September 1944 Frank Walsh was promoted to acting plant manager, replacing J. D. Anderson, Jr., who was fired. The rumor was that Anderson, a handsome fellow whose family lived out of town, was drinking and carousing too much for Theodore's taste. He shared an apartment near the factory with another man and, according to local gossip, courted various Steinway secretaries. Moreover, he knew nothing about making pianos, which was a problem in 1944 when Steinway & Sons went back into the piano business.[10]

Walsh's patience was as valuable to Theodore as his drafting skills. He devised methods for teaching illiterate but highly skilled piano workers how to read mechanical drawings. Henry Steinway recounted that "Frank used to make working drawings that he would color . . . with little signs and arrows . . . because these guys had no education. He taught them how to read drawings by coloring the things so they could see the levels" of construction.

It was Walsh who in 1938 had persuaded hundreds of Steinway workers to switch from the traditional Peter Cooper no. 11 glue to urea formaldehyde, a synthetic resin glue made by Weldwood. The new glue was waterproof, rot-proof, bug-proof, and impervious to extreme temperatures, and with a quick charge from a high-frequency machine its drying time could be cut from twenty hours to four.[11]

But there were genuine problems with it. Workers found it hard to get off their tools, their wood, and their skin. Some reported allergic reactions to it. The cause was obvious. Unlike the glue it replaced, an all-natural hoof-and-hide derivative (shots in old movies with horses lined up at the glue factory were not all that wrong), the new glue was made entirely of chemicals.[12] Workman's compensation cases were filed, and Steinway was forced to pay expensive dermatologists to treat workers whose skin broke out. Steinway subsequently tested an assortment of resin glues and eventually found one that was less toxic.

The advantage for Walsh, the workers, and the company of learning all

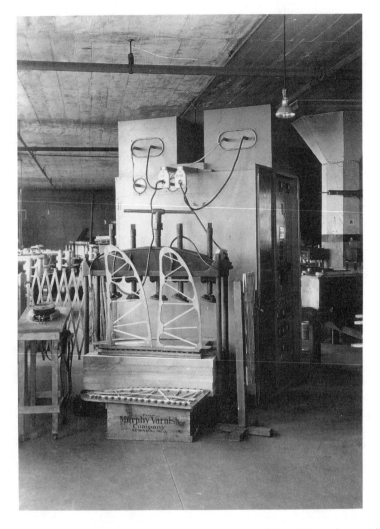

Gluing glider wing tips, using a high-frequency current of electricity and screw clamp pressure, c. 1943.

these lessons so early was that by the time they switched from pianos to gliders, an undertaking that by contract required synthetic resin glue, they had several years' experience with it.

Most of the workers using the new glue were women who had been hired to replace the young men who were drafted. These Steinway "Rosie the Riveters" worked primarily on the tails and wings. Roughly three hundred people worked the three shifts in the wing department (approximately half were women), and more than fifty women worked in the doping department, known throughout the factory as the "beauty salon." Doping consisted of sizing and cutting a thin fabric and then covering the wood frame with this fabric veneer. Then the fabric was sprayed with a highly flammable hallucinogenic dope in order to shrink it to a skintight coat. Doping was viewed as work suited to women. One newspaper account claimed that women's deftness at this job was due to their skill in painting their nails and their experience "cutting and fitting pieces to a pattern." But the women in the doping department also had to interpret and modify inaccurate patterns as they went. Walsh reported that "these women could handle these little things there. They weren't accomplished people, but they did a great job, each one." Moreover, they regularly met their quota of two planes a day, six days a week.

Although the women were part of the union and paid dues, their contract stipulated that they would not accrue seniority over men away on military service. If the returning veteran was deemed "competent to perform his prior job satisfactorily," Steinway & Sons had the right to "discharge any of his successors . . . hired in his absence." Women hired to work on the glider program were not perceived as potential piano makers, and when the war

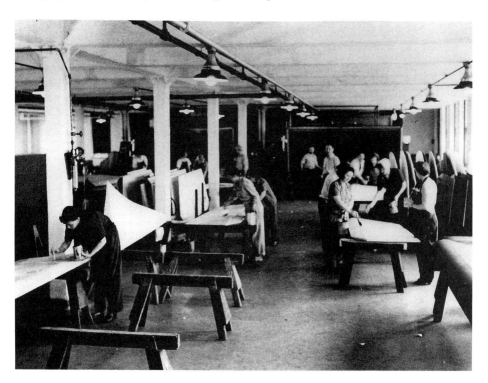

Women brushing "dope" on the glider surface, 1943.

ended, so did their jobs. Theodore's son Henry acknowledged that "all the women were pushed out without question. Today there would have been a tremendous stink about it, but I mean [back then] with everybody's agreement, out they went."[14]

The old foundry building at the Riker factory was the only place wide enough to accommodate the 84-foot span of the wings the women were building. When the wings were completed at the Riker factory, they were then hauled through the streets of Queens. Fifty years later, Henry Steinway still delighted in describing how, since those enormous wings did not fit into the regular Steinway truck, they had to construct a special tractor. It must have been quite a sight as the women glider builders daily paraded two to four of their 84-foot wings up Steinway Street and down Ditmars Avenue to the building that General Aircraft was renting from Steinway, where they were attached to the fuselage. The glider would then be ready to fly.[15]

Frank Walsh remembered the first glider to be assembled. It was taken to nearby LaGuardia Airport to be towed up into the air, then let loose for a test glide. "It was greatly voiced [a piano term for adjusting the hammers to the strings] and everything was fine," Walsh reported. "I was very happy with the fact that we were able to do this and complete it and it was one hundred percent right."[16]

To demonstrate its capacity, a CG-4A named "Voo-Doo" was towed by a twin-engine Douglas transport plane from Montreal's Dorval Airport to a landing strip in the United Kingdom—3,500 miles in little more than a day. The glider was loaded with more than a ton of cargo, including vaccines and blood plasma for Russia, equipment for the free French, and parts for B-24 bombers. It also carried parts for Ford trucks, numerous radio components, and a bunch of bananas for the pilot's family in London.[17]

But Frank Walsh's pride and the demonstrated potential of gliders notwithstanding, the whole concept was flawed. Most of the gliders were not "one hundred percent right"—not Steinway's, not anybody's. The problem lay in the design, not in the manufacturing. The standard Army Air Force gliders coming out of all the factories were plagued with technical problems and found to be dangerous in combat. The tail did not stay attached, the landing gear failed, and the towline rarely released. Regularly, more gliders (75 percent) were on the ground being fixed than were in the air. The only reason why any gliders were in the air was that new ones were being assembled and delivered all the time. By September 1944 more than thirteen thousand cargo gliders had been delivered at a total cost of nearly $275 million. The Army Air Force excused their poor performance by saying that they were designed for only one, non-return flight—an expensive throwaway machine at an average cost of $25,000 each; one company billed the government $426,000 for just one glider whose wings fell off on its first flight.[18]

There was also a human dimension to the glider's high crack-up rate. Gliders were designed to land nose first. The problem was that the pilot and co-pilot, sitting in the front of the plane in a glass compartment, had only a quarter of an inch of plywood between them and the ground as they approached a terrain frequently covered with trees and rarely perfectly flat. Heading nose first toward the ground, it was common for the pilot to pull the front end of the plane up a bit and take the landing impact in the rear, where fifteen men or the cargo were stored. But because gliders were designed to land nose first, the result was a crash landing and a high casualty rate for the men sitting in the back—so much so that gliders came to be known as "flying coffins."[19]

CG-4A gliders were used to carry troops and supplies during the invasion of Normandy, the largest sea and air assault of the war. The first glider to land at Utah beach crashed, and most gliders in that first wave missed their target because of heavy cloud cover. The airborne attack "Operation Neptune" sustained heavy losses, with most of the gliders and paratroopers harpooned in hedgerows or underwater in flooded swamp areas which had appeared as level solid land on high-altitude photographs. Soon after D-day General George S. Patton proved that tanks could do the same job faster, more efficiently, and a lot more safely.[20] By the end of the war, as soldiers came back from the field, each one had his own sarcastic glider story. Even Henry Steinway delighted in telling his story about the all-purpose wooden boxes used for shipping the gliders. "The boxes were extremely valuable because you could live in them. The box was 10 feet high and 5 feet wide, and it was a hell of a lot better than a slit trench or a pup tent or something. The thing really was good, so there was some place where they told me they took the gliders out and burned them and used the boxes to live in."[21]

No matter what their ultimate use, on land or in the air, gliders kept Steinway & Sons busy—they made more than eleven hundred. The dilemma was that, although making gliders was the company's principal work for a couple of years, it seldom made a profit. In 1942 Steinway lost more than $150,000. The following year it earned more than $200,000 but in 1944 lost nearly half a million dollars. Henry Steinway reported that, if "you look at our balance sheets through that time, there was no golden harvest there at all." His explanation was that Steinway & Sons was too naive and too fair, and that in the business of government contracts honest pricing didn't pay. The hidden costs of doing business with the Army Air Force—the added clerical labor and the delay in getting paid—should have been incorporated in the price. The first glider contract was on a "cost-plus-fixed-fee" basis, meaning that the military paid all the costs for making the glider and Steinway & Sons was guaranteed a separate profit fee, 5 percent of total costs. But part of those costs were "general and administrative expenses," and in that category Steinway charged the Army Air Force less than $5,000 when they could have charged more than $200,000. While "everybody else was loading on the kitchen sinks," according to Henry, Steinway & Sons played it absolutely straight and ended up simply spinning its wheels.[22]

To make things worse, Theodore had used most of Steinway & Sons' capital to finance the glider contract. When that money was gone, and General Aircraft did not deliver the advance in time, Theodore borrowed from the banks and absorbed the cost in his normal operations. By the end of 1942 he had invested close to a million dollars in war work.[23]

Assuming that "war work" was profitable, Theodore's cousin Clarissa inquired at one point about dividends for family members. Theodore informed her that Steinway & Sons was not making any profit on the glider contract and would not be issuing any dividends. Clarissa did not believe him. In 1943 Steinway & Sons did in fact earn more than $200,000, but Clarissa chose to overlook the losses in 1942. Incensed, Theodore responded that her "idea that vast sums of money were being made on 'War Work' was fantastic. . . . We have 190 of our employees in service, drafted or joined up! All the young were gone! Steinway Hall was now populated with old men and young women. . . . If the government ever allowed us to pursue our legitimate business again, piano making, we might again be successful and make some money and pay some dividends."[24]

After reviewing the entire glider story, what remains striking is not the financial accounts or the excessive number of reports the government required, but the fact that Theodore E. Steinway, the employer, is rarely mentioned in the records. Thousands of documents chronicle the glider contracts, yet seldom is there a memo to or from Theodore, or even an acknowledgment of his involvement on any carbon copy listings. Early drafts of the subcontracts were sent to the factory manager, J. D. Anderson, Jr., not to the president of Steinway & Sons. The infrequent note from Theodore was typically a terse sentence or two: "Re yours of July 1st on Renegotiation of Contract. It seems all right to me." According to his youngest son, Fritz, Theodore "was not the sort of person . . . who would write long, personal letters. . . . He'd just handwrite two sentences, and he'd stick it in an envelope. That's the way he corresponded."[25] But even such two-sentence notes are rare in the records. He simply did not involve himself in the glider trade—the fundamental business of Steinway & Sons from 1942 to 1944.

Instead, he was drinking in seclusion, hiding bottles of gin around the house, even filling the water pitcher with booze. On her vacations from school, his youngest daughter, Lydia, noticed that her father was "less forthcoming" and "not so willing to talk about all sorts of things" anymore. Lydia also detected changes in her parents' relationship: "I saw friction. At a certain point I realized that my mother was totally ignoring the drinking problem, totally denying, denial is the word I want. . . . People were saying to her: 'Ruth, what can we do about this?' She was saying: 'No, there's no problem, this is just social drinking.' "[26] But it wasn't. She simply didn't want to know that her husband was deteriorating.

Theodore's shunning of the glider project became a serious issue in the fall of 1943 when Steinway was notified that the CG-4A was doomed. The company would be forced to cut back deliveries and "stretch out the glider program until such time as a decision may be reached" as to the future use of gliders in the war. Drastic steps had to be taken at the factory to curtail the program, which was officially terminated the following spring. The company must look elsewhere to stay in business. But Theodore did not have the energy or interest to explore other possibilities. With no one at the helm effectively, Roman de Majewski, Steinway's wholesale manager; Edward Orcutt, head of finance; and Sascha Greiner, director of Concert & Artists, stepped in and tried to save Steinway & Sons.[27]

Majewski pushed the company back into the piano business. In June 1943 he secured an order for 405 olive drab Victory model uprights. Eight months later the War Productions Board helped his idea along when it authorized Steinway to manufacture another 800 pianos. He sold an additional 589 pianos (for $486 each, complete with tuning kit) to the United States Armed Forces so that each special service unit would have four Steinway Victory pianos. By October 1944 he had obtained the go-ahead for almost three thousand instruments. Steinway & Sons was back in the piano business.[28]

The Steinway Victory model, otherwise known as the "Olive Drab Government Issue" (ODGI) field piano, was a 40-inch upright that sat flat on the floor, with no legs, looking like a box with a shelf sticking out. It was Steinway's standard upright except that it had celluloid keys (ivory would have peeled off in tropical climates) and soft iron instead of copper wrapped around the steel bass strings (copper was a restricted metal). This 500-pound piano was transported in its own special olive-green packing case, with handles that made it easy for four soldiers to carry. The case included a set of tuning tools, a book of instructions, sheet music (ranging from Protestant hymns to advanced boogie-woogie), and some spare parts. In applauding the Victory model's sturdiness, Benjamin De Loache, a well-known baritone who toured the battlefront singing for the soldiers, reported that his Stein-

An olive drab government issue Steinway in the field during World War II. U.S. Army Signal Corps photograph.

way upright, W-672, had traveled 25,000 miles from Fort Riley, Kansas, to Port Moresby, "within eleven miles of the furthest Japanese penetration into New Guinea. . . . [It had] served soldiers, Red Cross workers, hospital patients, Australian shows, and innumerable USO Camp Shows and Concerts."29

By the time the war ended Steinway & Sons had shipped some five thousand pianos, but not all were ODGI uprights. Roughly half were sold to the United States armed forces, and the balance were bought by approved essential users: "religious organizations, education institutions, . . . hotels and other places of public gatherings." Many of these pianos came out of the extensive inventory amassed during the 1930s. But it was evident that the piano trade alone would not keep Steinway & Sons in business. Even the occasional requisition for a hundred ODGI uprights became cause for celebration.30

Desperately searching for work, Majewski investigated manufacturing bent-wood laminations for furniture, as well as floors for helicopters. He subsequently rejected these ideas, but he did launch Steinway on two new ventures. The first, selling the "Operadic Plant Broadcaster," a rival of Muzak, got started in 1943. Like Muzak, it was developed during the war to increase productivity and boost employee morale in the factory. It put out music and voice-paging throughout a building. Steinway installed an $8,000 Operadic system in its Riker factory for demonstration purposes. Its 133 speakers transmitted "six music periods during the day and at 3:30 P.M. five minutes of the latest news."[31]

The second was making wooden caskets. Queens had thrived on the cemetery trade since 1850, when the state legislature passed the Rural Cemetery Act, which, for the first time, permitted a private company to own and operate a cemetery. Three years earlier, the Common Council of New York, then only Manhattan, prohibited the taking of any new land for burials. All this made Queens, just across the East River, with its marshy, inexpensive land, a magnet for churches and synagogues searching for somewhere nearby to bury their loved ones. In 1944 Steinway & Sons became part of the local trade. Its chief customers were the National Casket Company a few miles away in Long Island City and the New York & Brooklyn Casket Company. Steinway made a full range of caskets, from a simple mahogany box to a fully upholstered couch. Gene Ayuso, who had chiseled the White House piano for President Roosevelt, was put in charge of the casket department. Theodore's son John recalled that "Gene was known around the factory as the chief of the Underground Novelties department."[32]

But the casket business was no joke as far as Theodore Steinway was concerned. It almost ruined him. Steinway's manufacturing costs were always higher than those of their competitors, while prices were held down by the market. The company lost money on every casket that left the factory and, a quarter of a million dollars in sales later, by the end of the year, was out of the casket trade altogether.[33]

But for Theodore the devastation was not only financial. He had sons in the military who might very well end up in those caskets. Teed was on General Douglas MacArthur's intelligence staff in the South Pacific, Henry on duty in New York, John in the Army Air Transport Command somewhere in North Africa or the Persian Gulf, and Fritz sailing the waters near Japan as a lieutenant in the Navy. Theodore had not heard from Teed for a while and knew only that he was a lieutenant in the Signal Corps fighting in the Philippines or somewhere in the jungles of New Guinea.[34] One day when four types of casket were on display in a showroom at Steinway Hall, ready to be inspected by the sales force, Theodore walked in. But whereas the managers and sales force saw the caskets simply as a business proposition, all Theodore could see were four caskets. And all he could think about was his four sons. According to several reports, Theodore "fell apart . . . just absolutely blew it for the day." He left the room, went back to his office, opened a bottle, and took several stiff drinks.[35]

Nor did his sons' patriotism protect him and his family from anti-German harassment. The Steinways, though native-born for two generations, were suspected of being Nazi informants and were under sporadic surveillance by U.S. intelligence agencies. In 1938 a former agent wrote a scathing letter to the FBI claiming that Steinway & Sons, which at the time was organizing White House "musicales," was bringing German spies and Nazi sympathizers into the White House. The FBI took the letter seriously and set an agent on the case to question Steinway & Sons' patriotism. The agent, working under cover, conducted extensive research and interviews, reporting the findings directly to J. Edgar Hoover. After months of investigation he found no evidence to support the letter's claims, and the inquiry remains as a thick file at the FBI, revealing more about anti-German hysteria than about any Steinway connection with Hitler.

Theodore's son Henry later wrote of his Aunt Mariechen that she had "this real kraut accent, and it was embarrassing in a restaurant because she was always not only talking in a German accent, but loud, and ordering people around, during the war, I mean, typical kraut image." A fear of being identified with the "krauts" lasted a lifetime for Henry Steinway. Only recently, when examining a 1935 photograph of a gathering of Steinway workers in the courtyard of the Hamburg factory, he acknowledged that it was "probably something Nazi, but better not to mention that."[36]

Competitors highlighted Steinway's German heritage as a reason to boycott its pianos. The word on the streets was "Don't buy from those Nazis." The response at Steinway Hall was to hang American flags all over the building. In addition, Theodore and Byron Collins, his cigar-smoking, hard-drinking retail sales manager, arranged a special display featuring GIs using a Steinway Victory piano. The front window showcased men of the Steinway family in uniform, from the Civil War, through World War I, to those currently fighting overseas. In addition, an honor roll on the entrance wall to the retail corridor listed the names of all Steinway workers serving in World War II. To highlight their Army Air Force glider work, Theodore had a new logo placed at the bottom of all Steinway letterhead: a plane arising out of the lid of a Steinway grand, beneath which were the words "Wings by Steinway." Furthermore, Steinway's advertising specified that "craftsmen in piano factories today are making gliders to carry men over the fighting front. Fingers skilled in Chopin and Schubert are now busy in war production." According to Henry, all this overt patriotism was "in response to this sort of

Steinway & Sons' factory in Hamburg in 1935.

subliminal [anti-Nazi German] thing. . . . There was a whole whispering
gallery of piano people out there."[37]

Steinway & Sons faced a similar ordeal in Germany, except that in Hamburg the whispering was that the Steinways were Jews. Walter Schwemm,
advertising clerk for Steinway & Sons in Hamburg, remembered that "there
were some problems with the Nazis. For example when we sold and transported pianos to Jerusalem. Once the Nazis wrote about that in the newspaper and remarked on it negatively."[38] Believing that the Steinways were
Jews trading with Jews, the Third Reich threatened to stop all coal delivery
and to nationalize the Hamburg factory as early as 1936.

Hitler had his preferred piano company and would not have minded if
Steinway & Sons had gone out of business. Helene Bechstein, granddaughter
of the founder of the Bechstein piano company, had close ties to both Hitler
and Goering, and Hitler considered Bechstein the official piano of the Third
Reich. "During the whole Hitler time, it was something of a problem,"
Henry Steinway explained, "because we were being described in Germany
as those Jews in New York, and we were being described in New York as
those Germans here."[39]

During the 1930s Theodore sent Teed on a mission to dig up all their birth and baptismal certificates to prove that the Steinways were Aryan. They must prove to Hitler that they were not New York Jews. On 1 March 1944 Theodore's brother Billie was issued a "Certificate of German Nationality" by the SS Main Office, verifying that he was a "member of the German ethnic group."

Steinway & Sons did not resist the Nazis. A picture of Hitler arriving at the Bayreuth festival adorned the August 1938 edition of *S&S Mitteilungen,* Steinway's monthly company publication in Hamburg, and the Steinway building in Berlin was used as a Nazi office. Theodore and Billie even discussed the possibility of establishing Steinway in Hamburg as a native German company, so as to indulge Hitler and acquire certain tax advantages. The correspondence between Theodore and his brother, who lived in Hamburg until 1939, would have revealed a great deal about the relationship between Steinway & Sons and the Third Reich—which is perhaps why all letters from the late 1930s are missing. But other letters from archives in Germany do exist, and they reveal a Steinway company eager to be seen as an important source of foreign currency for the German government, independent of the home office in New York and very much a German company with no "non Aryans as partners or stockholders." The letters concern Steinway claims for war damages to Steinway concert grand pianos destroyed in Warsaw during the German bombing. The letters are signed "Heil Hitler! Steinway & Sons."[40]

By the time the Steinways had proved they were Aryan, it was irrelevant. On 11 December 1941 Germany declared war on the United States. Almost immediately the German government seized Steinway & Sons as enemy American property and placed it under a Nazi custodian, Dr. Gestefeld, a lawyer.[41]

The Hamburg operation had been vital to Steinway's worldwide business. In the late 1930s the Hamburg factory was manufacturing between a thousand and fifteen hundred pianos a year, about 30 percent of Steinway's total production. In 1939, when the New York operation lost close to a quarter of a million dollars, Hamburg actually made a few thousand. Moreover, the Hamburg factory was the sole supplier for the London showroom, and the concert grand was in direct competition with Blüthner, Bösendorfer, and Bechstein on the London concert stage. In Germany, before the war, Steinway was not the number one piano used on the concert stage; it trailed Bechstein and Blüthner.[42]

Not too much is known about the history of the Hamburg factory, for three reasons: most of the documents were burned when Hamburg was firebombed in 1943; all communications between New York and Hamburg were abruptly cut off after 11 December; and numerous people would want

232

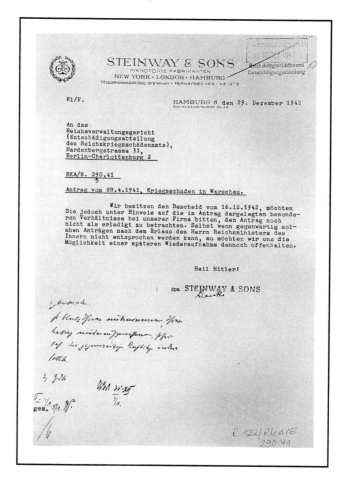

Two Steinway pianos from the Hamburg operation were destroyed during Germany's invasion of Warsaw, Poland. This letter, signed "Heil Hitler! Steinway & Sons," was sent to Germany's Department of War Compensation in an appeal for damages.

to purge all Nazi accounts from Steinway ledgers. Nor do the various accounts tally. Gretl Bruhn, the devoted executive secretary to the director of the Hamburg factory, Theodore Ehrlich, remembered Dr. Gestefeld as "easy to get along with" and claimed that he "pretty much left us alone." This hardly fits with the fact that, initially, he restricted Steinway's manufacturing to twenty instruments per month and insisted that all purchasers be screened by Otto Krause, head of the "Reichsmusikkammer" (Government Music Office), who would then decide whether the customers, mostly professional pianists and institutions, really needed a piano.[43]

Furthermore, the German government instructed Steinway & Sons to

The sawmills at the Hamburg factory, showing men cutting boards from tree trunks, 1925.

manufacture a hundred dummy wooden airplanes as decoys and almost twelve thousand beds for air raid shelters and to use their "valuable supply of seasoned Red Beechwood to build stocks for rifles." Steinway was permitted to build pianos only when Hitler made a deal with Sweden and Norway to send instruments in exchange for iron ore and cannons and when the Third Reich needed hard currency to purchase armaments, whereupon pianos were manufactured for sale to the Swiss. From 1941 to 1944 slightly more than a thousand pianos were made. Although the director of the Hamburg plant, Theodore Ehrlich, was remembered as someone who "could not cope at all with the ideas of the National Socialists," he nevertheless cooperated with them, selling pianos to whoever the Nazis told him to sell them to, and going out of his way to prove that he was not a Jew. Henry Steinway acknowledged that Ehrlich "made it his business to get along with this Doctor (Gestefeld) . . . and if this guy liked girls, he'd provide girls. If he liked American cigarettes, he'd find them. That would be Erhlich in character."[44]

A review of the documents relating to demands made by the Third Reich reveals that Steinway & Sons was "easy to get along with"—not least because Carl Koch, its corpulent factory manager *(Betriebsleiter)*, was, for a while, a National Socialist or Nazi. The record states that Steinway indulged the Nazis by sending workers to their special National Socialist training programs and disseminating Hitler's radio speeches throughout the factory. Ehrlich told Henry Steinway that "when Hitler made a speech, everybody had to listen. No matter what time of day it was, if it was working hours you shut everything down and you listened to his speeches." Koch sold Nazi badges to the men and women, claiming that he didn't want Nazi functionaries walking through the factory talking to the workers. Karl Jungnitsch, a case maker at the Hamburg factory since the 1920s, claimed that Koch became a Nazi, because it was required that one person in management be a member and Ehrlich refused.[45]

But the Nazis pushed Koch too far when they went after the very thing he loved most—his precious lumber supply. Kurt Albrecht, the chief technician and technical leader at Steinway & Sons, remembered Koch as a "fanatic about wood. . . . He was very cautious about the lumber, about its right age, its right treatment and about its stock at Steinway." Koch did not want to use good lumber for anything but pianos. He urged Ehrlich to reject all military commissions. But Ehrlich couldn't. When the Nazis insisted on Steinway & Sons making wooden swastikas, and the company complied, Koch, sick at seeing his luxury wood used for this purpose, gave up his Nazi membership.[46]

Koch was not the only Nazi at Steinway & Sons. Jungnitsch remembered "a man in the locksmith department. He was an informer and tried to squeal on everybody." Albrecht added that there were informers everywhere at Steinway. With the work force down to fewer than a hundred and fifty employees by 1942, everyone knew everyone else. Albrecht recounted a story about the foreman of the polishing department, Mr. Frees, who was sent to a concentration camp because an informant at Steinway & Sons notified the Nazis that Frees had helped a woman whose husband had been arrested by the NSDAP to get food-ration cards. Heinrich Lorenzen, who started working at Steinway in 1936 as a polisher, said that if you "disagreed with the system—either you said nothing and survived or you disagreed aloud and were punished." Lorenzen estimated that of the three hundred Steinway workers during the late 1930s, about a hundred supported Hitler, and the rest did not want to deal with the Third Reich more than was absolutely necessary.[47]

Albrecht remembered greeting a fellow worker, Quindner, one morning with "Moin" (colloquial for "Good morning"). Quindner suddenly said, "You shouldn't say 'Moin' but 'Heil Hitler Arbeitskameraden' (Heil Hitler, work comrades)." Albrecht answered him, "Oh shut up." This man then "left his working place to go to the next National Socialist office to have me arrested. I was frightened and didn't know what to do." Albrecht went to see

Koch to ask for protection. "Mr. Koch had his NSDAP badge usually laying in his screw box, he picked it out, put it on his shirt and went to the gate-keeper who was ordered by Koch to keep this man [Quindner] out of the factory." After the war, Quindner, badly injured in battle, came back to Steinway & Sons, apologized for his behavior, and was rehired. Another known Steinway Nazi, Selatschek (a Czech who changed his name to Bucholz during the war), also tried to get his job back after the war, but although Ehrlich would have taken him back, the workers didn't want him back and held a sit-down strike to make sure that he never worked at Steinway again.[48]

The city of Hamburg was bombed by Allied forces during the hot summer of 1943. On 23 and 24 July Steinway's administrative headquarters on Schanzenstrasse, near the port, where German submarines were manufactured, was burned to the ground. A fire raged through the building and through most of the area near Hamburg's harbor. Once the incendiary bombing stopped, several Steinway workers walked to the rubble that was once their work place to pick through the ashes, in an attempt to salvage an investment once worth close to $1.5 million. Hermann Keyser, head of the accounting department, described the scene in his *Memoirs:* "On the morning of this second air-raid I walked from Alsterdorf to Schanzenstrasse. The buildings were fully destroyed. An awful blaze everywhere. I could make out two or three glowing safes. After having waited two and a half hours, a female co-worker came into sight. As all public transport had stopped running, we walked to the factory in Rondenbarg. We encountered the same terrible sights."

During the following weeks, employees who had not fled the city went to see what was left of Steinway & Sons. They found the music studio at the back of the salesroom on Jungfernstieg intact and made it into a temporary office. Keyser recalled that "a number of people reported back to the factory. . . . We also hired any relatives of employees. . . . As the office-work was not of an urgent nature and could be postponed, I also reported to the factory to help save whatever possible."[49]

But the following fall, the factory on the outskirts of the city in Rondenbarg, Hamburg-Bahrenfeld, was bombed. Gretl Bruhn recorded that the "windows were all broken and parts of the wall fell down. Almost all instruments on hand were damaged." As soon as the bombing raids were over, fifty-five dedicated Steinway piano makers returned to the factory to put out the fires and salvage supplies, hardware, mechanical parts, metal fittings, felts, and lumber. They moved the pianos, which were covered with glass slivers, away from the windows, but that did not protect them. Most of the eight hundred windows, plus the roof and the heating system, remained in disrepair, and the pianos sat there, exposed to rain, wind, and the cold Hamburg winters. This exposure ruined more pianos than the blitz.[50]

On 8 May 1945 a devastated Hamburg surrendered without a fight to the Allied forces. Immediately after the armistice, a few Steinway workers, like Mr. Reichert, acquired jobs as translators for the British military forces occupying the city. Others worked in the factory building beds, chairs, cupboards, and furnishings for themselves, their families, and local companies. Jungnitsch remembered them once furnishing a restaurant. "No one bought a piano," one worker said; no one had any money. "Once we sold a piano in Fiepsen (a city) and we got paid in window glass." The employees at Steinway spent more time repairing the building than making pianos. It was not until 1948, after currency reform, that they started to make pianos again. By then, they had about thirty old men who had once made pianos and a factory full of young apprentices who knew nothing about piano making.[51]

Steinway workers in Berlin were as loyal as those in Hamburg. Berlin had been a center for European culture and the heart of Steinway's European sales, concert, and artist operations. On 2 May 1945 when Berlin fell, Elli Kuehne, wife of Paul Kuehne, Steinway Concert & Artists manager, recounted that for sixteen days during the bombing she and her husband lived in the basement of their home. When they were finally discovered by the Russians, Paul was interrogated and suspected of being a German soldier. Once they were permitted to return to their battered home, their first thought was for the Steinway stores.

Two days later, she reported, "We mustered all our courage and ran through the burning city past many dead people and horses." They found one of the Steinway stores on Lutzowstrasse still standing. They were delighted to see it; but when they came closer, they saw that it had been completely gutted by fire. Elli explained that when Berlin was taken, the Steinway building was intact, but that because it had been used as a Nazi office, it was later deliberately set on fire. When they went to inspect it, "the ruins were still smoking and we therefore did not dare to enter." A few days later they returned wearing thick gloves and rummaged through the smoldering embers picking out nails, screws, and castors, convinced that when they went back into business, metal parts would be hard to find and would be needed for repair work.

Slowly a few of the employees started to emerge from their cellars. Mrs. Krunitz and Miss Garbow walked across Berlin, not a safe thing to do in May 1945, to the Kuehne house. With a borrowed typewriter, filing cards, and some notepaper, they set up a card index from memory with the names and addresses of people who had rented pianos. They then called upon them and asked them either to pay or to return the instruments. They were surprised to find that some of them still existed. The following fall they moved from the Kuehne house to a former coal shop on Suarezstrasse, where they stored rented pianos returned by lessees who had left Berlin.

Postwar life in Berlin was difficult. During the first year, electric current was available for only a few hours at a time, and there was no public transportation. All employees who did not own a bicycle walked to work, many miles in some cases. There was no currency. An American soldier bought a piano and paid for it in cigarettes. According to Elli Kuehne, Berlin was so unsettled "that nobody could be sent to the outskirts of the city unaccompanied. People still disappeared." The city was blockaded (East and West) making it very hard for the Kuehnes to find piano parts. Elli recalled that once there was an opportunity to get some parts from a firm located in East Germany. They sent a few courageous Steinway employees to the East Station several times, to bring back parts to the West. They concealed them in briefcases and handbags, so that the Russian controllers who manned all the stations wouldn't find them.

By June 1948 the Berlin Steinway retail store was in operation and busy again. The demand outstripped their supply of pianos and parts. Most of their business was repairing, tuning, renting, and supplying concert artists with pianos for performances. There was no competition, because all the high-grade German piano manufacturers had been severely damaged or eliminated. The Berlin employees were kept alive and fed courtesy of CARE packages from Steinway people in Hamburg and New York. Elli Kuehne remembered that, hidden in piano boxes, Walter Gunther, assistant to the director of the Hamburg house, "sent coals to Berlin, which to us were as valuable as gold. . . . We had no fuel, and all the rooms were heated by stove."[52]

The news about the destruction in Hamburg and Berlin did not surprise Theodore. In September 1945 he wrote to his cousin Clarissa: "Heard from British sources . . . that our Hamburg House is pretty well shot to pieces and . . . Berlin, Frankfurt, Hamburg, are pretty well cleaned off the map. Well, they asked for it and they got it."[53] He had lost his factory in Hamburg, his retail store in Berlin, and was losing money every day in New York. But none of that mattered now, because his sons were coming home.

Teed returned from the Philippines and headed straight for the Rocky Mountains to ski and explore the Green River, so putting a few thousand miles between him and Steinway & Sons. Henry, who had secured an army counterintelligence investigator's desk job on Governor's Island and never left New York City during the war, returned to his family and, as he recalled: "Bang, they put me in charge of the factory, and that was it." As for Theodore's two youngest sons, John came back from Africa to work at Steinway Hall in sales, marketing, and advertising, and Fritz, fresh out of the navy, decided to study at Harvard Business School for two years.[54]

Almost by default, the future of Steinway & Sons fell to the lot of Henry. Two former candidates—Teddy Cassebeer and Fritz Vietor—had died, and Teed was out West riding the white water. In 1946 Henry was thirty-one years old and married with a baby on the way. He was made factory manager and then placed on the board of directors. Henry recalled that even before the war, people "started looking to me to answer questions, and pretty soon I started answering them." He recognized that he "more or less drifted into the factory management, because there was a great big fat vacuum there." But when Henry was made a director rather than his older brother Teed, that was the signal that Theodore had settled on Henry as heir apparent. All the important decisions were made at board of directors meetings. Because Henry was also the factory manager, he became the person on the board raising most of the issues, as well as the one with most of the answers. He was becoming head of Steinway & Sons. This was confirmed when Theodore had the board elect Henry vice-president. Reviewing his career fifty years later, Henry acknowledged, "I was certainly the coming guy, now that I look back, [but] I didn't think of it at that time."[55]

Henry asked Frank Walsh to be his assistant. They had an unspoken understanding: Frank would handle the factory, and Henry would run Steinway & Sons. Henry had confidence in Walsh. "He was a real factory guy, and I never was really that interested in how everything goes together." In addition, Henry started to rely on Eddie Orcutt to manage the finances, Sascha Greiner to court the artists, and Roman de Majewski to promote sales. That was his team. He described Orcutt, Greiner, and Majewski as "the three older men without whom I could have done nothing. . . . I was theoretically in charge, even though I didn't know a god-damn thing."[56]

Not included was Paul Bilhuber. Trained by the by then legendary Henry Ziegler, Bilhuber was the resident experimenter, inventor, and piano genius at Steinway & Sons. But Henry and Bilhuber were cut from different kinds of cloth and just irked each other. Henry characterized Bilhuber as a twitchy, tightly wound, nervous type. In all probability, Bilhuber was angry with Henry for keeping him on a short leash. Bilhuber wanted to continue inventing and tinkering. Henry recalled telling him that they could not just buy machines because they were nice machines; there had to be some payback. Bilhuber resigned from Steinway & Sons in 1947. Describing the friction between the two of them, Henry asserted: "They put me in charge, and he didn't like it. . . . I was the royal blood."[57]

Henry remained in control as factory manager and vice-president for ten years, then in 1955, at the age of forty, replaced his father as president. He became the youngest president Steinway ever had and the first since William to succeed his own father. When he took over the reins of Steinway & Sons, he made a solemn oath to himself that "this business is not going to kill me. . . . I'm not going to go through what my father did."[58] Nor did he.

SEVENTEEN

Steinway Celebrates Its Centennial

I N   1 9 4 6   T H E O D O R E
Steinway's report to the stockholders proclaimed: "The future looks rosy if
we can manufacture the goods that are needed and wanted. We will do our
best!" All government restrictions placed on raw materials during the war
had been removed, and the demand for pianos was three times greater than
Steinway could keep up with.[1]

The years 1946–48 constituted a fleeting period of prosperity both for
the postwar economy and for Steinway, with earnings ranging from a quarter to half a million dollars each year. Sales outpaced production, and customers had to wait for their pianos. Sherman Clay & Company, Steinway's
San Francisco dealer, complained that they could have sold a lot more pianos
in 1946 if Steinway's shipments hadn't been so slow. But this demand for
pianos fell apart in November 1948. The Steinway sales force thought the lull
would be brief, attributing it to their recent piano price increase and "a
general apathy on the part of the public in Christmas buying" that had
slowed purchasing. They expected that sales would bounce back, but they
were wrong. The national economy had withered into a recession, and shipments dropped from 163,807 pianos in 1948 to 133,401 in 1949. Profits
decreased at Steinway & Sons from more than $400,000 to less than
$160,000. The piano was competing with the washing machine and the
automobile for scarce installment dollars and with the phonograph, radio,
and television for living room entertainment time.[2]

Piano sales were so sluggish that Steinway closed parts of the factory in
June and July. That November Margaret Truman, daughter of President

Harry Truman and a singer, shocked Steinway public relations when she abandoned the Steinway as her exclusive concert instrument and adopted a Baldwin. The Baldwin company then gave a piano to the White House, promoting its gift as an "American piano," thereby insinuating that Steinway was a German piano. President Truman proclaimed on television that he never could stand that ugly Steinway piano given to President Franklin D. Roosevelt, with its great big ugly eagle legs. The Baldwin had more delicate eagle legs. The next two years saw a strike, substantial layoffs, increasing part-time work, higher taxes, price controls, discontinuance of Steinway's radio, phonograph, record, and television department, and another three-month plant closing. Theodore was frantic. He reported to his stockholders that "on the one hand more and bigger taxes are asked of us by Government, State and City! On the other hand our prices are pegged—but wages for Unions not!"[3]

In 1952 and again in 1953 sales and profits plummeted to the lowest they had been since the depression,[4] and Steinway laid off 40 percent of its work force. The nation was in a recession, and the piano trade was hampered by the raw materials they needed being diverted to the Korean War. The war ended in the summer of 1953, ushering in freedom from rationing and price controls and better times for the piano industry generally.

Steinway & Sons was not part of that boom, however, because uprights dominated the postwar market. While the national market for pianos increased from about 140,000 instruments a year during the Korean War to almost 200,000 by the end of the decade, the number of grands dropped by almost half, from 6,114 in 1950 to a mere 3,370 in the boom year of 1959, a year in which upright sales outnumbered grand sales by fifty-nine to one. Grands were Steinway's primary business. Two Steinway workers, Patsy Bionda and Jacob Pramberger, recalled that there was only part-time work at Steinway & Sons in the early fifties. In 1954 they worked one week on, one week off, until the factory shut down completely in June. Other employees reported that in some of those years they worked only six weeks.[5]

As Henry Steinway recalled, during the early 1950s the piano business shrunk away. "People would say: 'You're in the piano business? God, I thought [the piano makers] were dead.'" They were not far from the truth. During the Korean War business was so slow that Steinway turned to manufacturing helicopter floors as a subcontractor for the Piasecki Helicopter Corporation, just to keep its workers employed.[6]

The only glimmer of profit was on the other side of the Atlantic. Steinway's Hamburg branch, through rentals, tuning, concert service, sheet music, and piano sales, had been earning a small income every year since 1950. Moreover, in 1953, Walter Gunther, talented assistant to the director who four years later became director of all Hamburg operations, set up a lucrative retail outlet, called Steinway-Haus, that sold pianos, band instruments, sheet music, and records, the only full-line music store in northern Germany. But Hamburg's success was of no help to the company's operations in New York because exchange restrictions prohibited the sending of money from Germany to the United States.[7]

The New York office was badly in need of cash to meet its payroll and pay off loans. The company sold one of the Ditmars factory buildings for $725,000 and paid off the banks. But, two years later, in 1953, it had to borrow $600,000 just to cover expenses,[8] an inauspicious marker in their hundredth year in business.

It had not been this bad since the war, but Steinway & Sons decided to celebrate anyway. Putting on its best face, it presented a gala centennial jubilee extolling its contributions to the music world. It expected this year-long worldwide tribute to itself to stimulate business. Theodore named it the "Centenary: a tribute to a century of service to music." A committee of three was named to coordinate the activities: John H. Steinway, Theodore's son, who was advertising manager of Steinway & Sons, was appointed chairman of the committee, with Roman de Majewski, head of the wholesale department, and Sascha Greiner, head of the Concert & Artists Department, the other two members. John remembered his role on that committee as "madchen für alles" (handmaiden who did all the little errands and jobs). His desk was wedged between those of the other two, which, according to John, made planning this enormous event much easier.[9]

They worked with dealers across the country, who had formed their own Steinway centennial celebration committee. The agreed strategy was to use this anniversary commemorating the past to revitalize sales for the future. One dealer candidly admitted: "We want to know if this promotion will pay the rent. . . . If it isn't going to bring in sales maybe we should determine if it is feasible." Another suggested postponing the anniversary from March to September to cash in on the momentum of Christmas sales in the hope of carrying it forward into the slower spring season. Convinced that this was "a great opportunity," their "chance to clean up," 110 of Steinway's 160 dealers contributed 2 percent of the wholesale price of all new Steinway pianos billed to them from 1950 on to the promotion of the centenary. They intended to raise $100,000. John reported that, with Steinway board approval, he was planning to spend $125,000 of the company's money on national advertising. The dealers and the Steinway family had every intention of "doing it big," even though capital was scarce.[10]

In addition to a dealers' association, a Steinway artists' committee was formed, with Josef Hofmann as honorary chairman. At the artists' committee's first meeting they discussed a gala concert as part of the centenary festivities. Arthur Judson, manager of the New York Philharmonic-Symphony Society Orchestra volunteered to have the orchestra donate its services for the concert. He explained that, according to their contract, the 120 musicians were obliged to play one evening concert a year without pay for the good of the orchestra. Although the verbal agreement that had formed Steinway & Sons occurred on 5 March 1853, the concert at Carnegie Hall to kickoff the centennial celebration was put off until 19 October 1953, to anticipate the Christmas rush.[11]

The Steinway artists' committee decided to have no piano soloist but as many Steinway pianists as possible, playing in groups. After measuring the stage at Carnegie Hall, they figured out that they could have ten 7-foot model B grands in front of the orchestra. The plan was to have three groups of pianists, ten in each group.

Greiner recalled that once it was decided to have groups playing, Olin Downes, chief music critic of the *New York Times* and a member of the Steinway artists' committee, suggested that Dimitri Mitropoulos conduct the orchestra from his piano bench. The problem was that the raised top of his concert grand would block his view of the orchestra. To solve the problem, Steinway manufactured a transparent top of Plexiglas especially for Mitropoulos's piano. Greiner described Mitropoulos at rehearsals as ruling the orchestra and pianists from his piano bench like an emperor.[12]

The program would start with ten pianists, including Gary Graffman and Skitch Henderson, playing Josef Hofmann's arrangement of "The Star-Spangled Banner." The next piece, to be played by ten more pianists,[13] would be by Chopin. There was fierce disagreement as to what it should be. Mitropoulos wanted the A-flat polonaise, but Greiner, backed by Hofmann, opted for the A-major 'Military' polonaise. To conclude the concert Morton Gould composed an arrangement of John Philip Sousa's "Stars and Stripes Forever" for multiple pianos and orchestra.

The concert was sold out within two days of mailing the announcement. The dealers wanted it broadcast on radio and television, but the program was too long. There were extensive negotiations with Firestone Tire and Rubber Company to present half an hour of the concert on their weekly Monday evening television program. But when Greiner refused to start and close the program with the New York Philharmonic-Symphony Orchestra playing Mrs. Firestone's melody "Rose in the Garden," the theme song of her company, the deal went flat.[14]

That same day, Ed Sullivan, newspaper columnist and master of ceremonies of the weekly television program "Toast of the Town," called to ask Greiner if he could broadcast a live preview of the Steinway centenary concert on his Sunday night show. Sullivan came to Steinway Hall to discuss the program. He wanted to televise a six-minute piece played by one of the ten-piano groups. They agreed to the Chopin polonaise, which included some of the best-known Steinway artists, including Alexander Brailowsky and Rudolph Ganz. A few weeks later, on Sunday evening, 18 October, at 8:40 P.M., Ed Sullivan stepped before millions of Americans and announced that he "had the privilege of presenting a dress-rehearsal from Carnegie Hall of part of the Steinway centenary concert taking place the following evening." Sullivan related a brief history of the Steinway family and the founding of Steinway & Sons and introduced Theodore and Ruth Steinway, who were seated in the studio audience. The telecast then shifted to Carnegie Hall, where a battery of remote-TV cameras broadcast ten Steinway pianists playing Chopin's polonaise in A major.[15]

The following evening, thousands of people crowded into Carnegie Hall for the concert. The *New York Times* reported that the audience "included leaders in music, the other arts, industry, society and Government." The feeling in the hall was that of a lively party. People congratulated Steinway family members as if they were celebrating their personal birthdays. After the concert, men in formal dress and women in evening gowns, close to two thousand in all, enjoyed a buffet dinner in the grand ballroom of the Waldorf–Astoria Hotel. It was one of the biggest parties ever held at the Waldorf. At the end of the meal a 10-foot-high birthday cake was rolled out, and as Henry Steinway's seven-year-old son William cut the first slice, the crowd sang "Happy Birthday," accompanied by two Steinway concert grands. Speeches, champagne, and dancing followed. The crowd set an unofficial record not only for size but also for endurance, many staying until six in the morning for an unscheduled breakfast. The following day there was yet another reception at Steinway Hall, where a special "centenary grand" was unveiled. Receipts from the concert amounted to $26,875, which went to the Philharmonic-Symphony Society of New York and the Musicians Foundation. The cost of the whole event was close to $100,000 and exhausted the entire budget.[16]

It was Theodore Steinway's last hurrah. After it was all over, Josef Hofmann confided to Greiner: "I am happy that the shindig is over. The responsibility, headaches and work must have been a great strain! How has poor Theodore survived the festivities in view of his physical condition? I hope he will not suffer any consequences."[17] Theodore had in fact spent most of his time organizing a picture book on the history of Steinway & Sons.[18] He called it *People and Pianos,* and 15,000 copies were distributed.

There was a lot of fanfare at the local level throughout the year, and Greiner insisted that "the free publicity received by Steinway & Sons in hundreds of magazines and newspapers could not be paid for by hundreds of thousands of dollars." This included more than two hundred concerts at various places across the country, usually accompanied by interviews on radio and local press coverage; full-page four-color advertisements in national magazines; and a $2,000 Steinway centennial scholarship, all in celebration of the company's hundredth year.[19]

But overall, the year-long centennial was a flop. The concert at Carnegie Hall received scant press coverage and failed miserably as a sales strategy. Moreover, some famous Steinway artists—among them, Vladimir Horowitz, Arthur Rubinstein, and Rudolf Serkin—did not attend.[20] *Life* magazine sent a photographer but never ran a story. The *World Telegram & Sun,* the *Journal American,* the *New York Herald Tribune,* and the *New York Post* published only brief notices, of the length usually allocated to the debut of an obscure pianist. Only the *New York Times* made Steinway's centennial a feature story. Its music critic, Olin Downes, had become a close friend of Steinway & Sons, a relationship that was nurtured in 1948 by the free loan of a B grand piano.

None of this resulted in sales, however, and Steinway & Sons lost thousands in 1953. Fewer pianos were sold than in the previous year, making it one of the worst of their one hundred years in business.[22] Henry Steinway acknowledged that the centenary celebration had been a mistake. A month after the gala celebration at Carnegie Hall, the board of directors admitted that instead of investing in celebrating Steinway & Sons' past, they should have been investing in its future by figuring out how to manufacture and market an inexpensive upright. But, according to Henry, "my father couldn't bring himself to do that."[23]

In the fall of 1955 Theodore Steinway was seventy-two. His son Henry recounted his frustration during Theodore's last years: "We didn't know just where we were going and what we were doing . . . and I could see my father was getting sicker. . . . He was running Steinway, but it was a weak hand." Henry, as factory manager, had been telling his father that his lethargy was bankrupting Steinway & Sons. According to Betty, "Henry by that time had very strong feelings about what my father was doing wrong." Theodore's decision to retire, Betty judged, was in direct response to his son's prodding. She maintained that her father decided that "the best thing to do was to wake up one morning and say, Henry, the ball game is yours, and get out of the way."[24] He did just that.

Without warning, Theodore started the October 1955 board of directors meeting by announcing that he was retiring—immediately. He explained: "I'm sick and I'm not able to run this business anymore, and so I'm going to retire." He cited his constant fatigue and suggested that when the directors went out for lunch they select a new president. As for Theodore, he went home, sorted some stamps, had a drink, and went to bed. This abrupt departure, according to one board member, left them all sitting there "with egg on our face."[25]

During the directors' lunch at the Lotos Club, across the street from Steinway Hall, Jerome F. Murphy, the most influential voice on Steinway's board, looked across the scattered dessert dishes toward Theodore's forty-year-old son and said: "Well, Henry, I guess you've got to do it."[26] Henry was a towering, good-looking man, well over 6 feet tall and weighing more than 200 pounds, the kind of person who grabbed everyone's attention when he entered a room. His frank personality gave him a presence. His conservative dress and hairstyle made him look like a president of Steinway & Sons. The only other candidates were his older brother Teed, who did not want the job, and Uncle Billie, who was too old. That left Henry, who had been shadow president of Steinway & Sons since 1945.[27]

The vote for Henry was unanimous. Steinway had by now become atypical as far as American family businesses were concerned. By 1955 it was unusual to find a family member still active in such a business and the company still owned by the family and manufacturing the same product. Typically, in the words of the *New York Times,* "old-line companies fell into mergers and, consequently, very often abandoned the products which started them on the road to success. But the Steinway piano was different."[28]

Henry maintained that his father had held onto the business long after he should have given it up and that he, Henry, became president of Steinway & Sons simply because he was the only one in the family who knew how to make a decision and get things done. For several years Theodore's devoted secretary Rosabelle Cooke had helped fill the void created by her very sick boss. As assistant secretary to the board of directors, she had the power to sign checks and legal documents. She also kept the (confidential) payroll. Cooke, or "Cookie" as she was known to her friends, was a small, smart Jewish woman, who was divorced and never told Theodore about her baby girl, because women with children at Steinway & Sons were fired. She sat outside Theodore's office and decided who would get in to see him and who could talk to him on the telephone and covered for him when he was drunk or out sick. "He always called her Ms. Cooke, and she called him Mr. Steinway." She was the guardian of the gates, the de facto powerhouse, and the highest-ranking woman at Steinway & Sons.[29] Shortly after Theodore retired, she too retired, after marrying Eddie Orcutt.

Henry's first act as president was to create a new post for his father:

chairman of the board. It was a salaried position with one ceremonial duty: to start the monthly board meetings. Within six months even that became too much for Theodore.[30]

He died within two years. Son of William Steinway, he had worked at Steinway & Sons more than half a century. He was worth almost $200,000. When he retired, *Steinway News* aptly paid tribute to the man who had "served the firm as president for a longer period of time than any of his predecessors and steered the House through some of the most difficult years of its history." Future Steinway presidents would not match this record of duration and endurance. His son Henry often acknowledged that "Theodore was handed this ugly mess. If I'd been in charge, I'll bet in 1932, I would have closed the god damn place, sold the real estate, got out, as many piano people did."[31]

On the day of Theodore's funeral the factory and salesrooms were closed. Six hundred people packed into the Church of All Souls to pay their last respects. Van Cliburn, in a letter to Ruth, summed up what was in most friends' hearts: "The end must have been in a sense, a release and a relief on both sides—but that is cold comfort for such a loss. . . . He was a singularly patient mentor and a remarkably reliable confidant. I truly loved him."[32]

EIGHTEEN

A Businessman Takes Over

T HEODORE HAD STAYED
at the helm too long, twenty-eight years, and it was a leaky ship that he
passed on to his son. Moreover, Henry was scared of the enormous responsibility he was inheriting.[1] He was a businessman, and projected the image of
being more interested in charts, tables, and labor issues than concerts, tunes,
and pianists. Unlike his grandfather, William, who could spot a Paderewski
in London, Henry's talent lay in making a profit, not in picking artists. All
previous Steinway presidents had seen themselves as bearing a tremendous
responsibility to the music world. Henry, by contrast, described himself as
knowing nothing about music. His sister Betty portrayed him as lacking the
temperament and sensitivity of an artist. She believed that such sensitivity
was crucial to the success of Steinway & Sons, where art and business were
inseparable. But Henry saw artists as "always sort of above money in that
strange way"[2] and his own job as concerned with survival and profitability.
"Then, once you've made it profitable, you put your head up and look
around and say, what's next?"[3]

All Steinway's past presidents had reigned from the hall and been passionately involved in New York's music world. Henry made his preference
for business over art obvious when, barely three months after he took over,
he announced that he was moving the president's office and the administrative and accounting personnel from palatial Steinway Hall to the factory.
Henry had always regarded the factory and the wholesale trade as the most
important parts of Steinway's business. He insisted that Steinway invest

most of its money in the factory, where "it can be the biggest loss producer and the biggest profit producer."

By the summer of 1956 Henry was directing Steinway & Sons from the Ditmars factory in Queens, signaling his goals of cutting costs and getting the company out of debt. He preferred to keep his eye on production rather than the paintings at the hall. There were also advantages to being close to LaGuardia Airport, as dealers took to flying rather than traveling by rail. Furthermore, he made some money by renting the fourth floor of Steinway Hall to Manhattan Life Insurance. He saw his mission as making money, or "the damn thing wouldn't survive."[4]

In his new Astoria office he gathered his team together and issued his initial marching orders. Taking his cue from the Heller Report of 1941, Henry separated management from the board of directors by creating well-defined executive posts. He announced: "Freimuth, you're in charge of the store; that's your responsibility. Now you have to make a profit. Walsh, you're in charge of the factory. Majewski, you're in charge of selling. Orcutt, you're in charge of administration . . . and so on." These men became Henry's cabinet. He met with them regularly, and within ten years he had made them all vice-presidents, thereby giving his nonfamily management team control over Steinway's board of directors.[5]

In due course Henry increased their autonomy by establishing a separate annual capital expenditures budget for each department. Department heads no longer had to go to the board each month for modest purchases. He also raised their salaries to the point that they were making more money than Steinway family members, declaring: "I was not going to have Theodore, John, and Fritz get salaries because their name was Steinway, while Orcutt, Majewski, and Greiner were doing the work."[6]

He gave power to his friends and seized power from people he did not trust. He always had misgivings about Bilhuber, especially his monopoly of Steinway's technical information. To diminish his authority, Henry decided, even before he officially became president, to codify just how a Steinway was made. Never before had anyone written a manual on how to make a Steinway. It was the tradition at Steinway & Sons, going back to C. F. Theodor, Henry Ziegler, and Fritz Vietor, that all technical information resided in little private books kept by the foreman and in the minds and hands of the chief engineer. Henry wanted the design to be on record and accessible. He recounted: "Walsh and I decided we were going to make, as far as we could, detailed drawings of everything in the factory, including detailed descriptions of the operations, which we didn't have either. In other words, stand behind each man and write down what he's supposed to do."

Frank Walsh and two assistants produced a twelve-volume "Bible" documenting how a Steinway piano was made.[7]

But Henry soon discovered that manufacturing pianos was simple compared to riding herd on the Steinway family. "It sounds ridiculous," he recalled, "but in the old family set-up everybody had something to say about everything."[8] Of all his brothers, only John made Steinway his life's work. John, an attractive, debonair, mustachioed bachelor, was an amateur actor with a deep baritone voice made for telling absorbing stories. Everyone liked John. He enjoyed fancy cars, a good cigar, and recounting his version of Steinway's history. He was a performer.[9]

He became head of advertising and public relations. He was groomed to take over Uncle Billie's traveling glad-hand show as "Mr. Steinway, the piano maker." John also arranged musical performances, "musicales," after State dinners at the White House, a service Steinway & Sons performed for United States presidents from Theodore Roosevelt to Dwight Eisenhower. John liked to consider himself Henry's assistant, which he was. Henry made John secretary at board of directors meetings.[10]

Henry did not have to contend with his sisters, Betty and Lydia, because they were discouraged by their parents from even trying to work at Steinway & Sons.[11] As Betty pointed out, not only was Steinway a male-dominated institution with no place for women; there was not much room for the other brothers either.

Her older brother Teed worked in engineering. He had been trained by Paul Bilhuber and, when Bilhuber retired, became chief engineer. He was a piano expert, remembered by all as brainy, intelligent, thoughtful, and very much like his father. According to his brothers and sisters, Teed had no wish to head Steinway & Sons. All he wanted to do was design the perfect piano, and he was constantly experimenting with new notions about sound.[12]

Henry acknowledged that Teed "had read every book that they've still got out there on scales and on acoustics and all that, and could speak enormously knowledgeably about tone, piano construction and acoustics." The problem was that Teed would rarely finish a project. For example, when ivory was getting scarce, Teed spent months reading book after book about plastics and attempting hundreds of experiments with ivory substitutes. Experimental keyboards covered with a variety of plastics lay all over the factory. When Henry finally asked Teed one day, "When will you be done?," Teed answered that he was not ready yet. Eventually, Henry gave up on his older brother. In 1956 he met with other American piano manufacturers, and they all agreed to abandon ivory and start using plastic.[13]

Like his father, Teed drank a lot. Not only did his drinking keep him

The Steinway men in 1960. *Standing, left to right:* John, Fritz, Henry, Daniel, William, Charles F. G. *Seated, left to right:* Teed with his son on his lap, Robert, Christian, Henry E., and Billie. Behind Robert and Christian is Frederick E. The paintings on the wall are of the founder, Heinrich Engelhard Steinway (*right*), and his wife, Julianne (*left*).

from finishing projects; it also drove a wedge between him and Henry. Henry slowly moved Teed into a consultant position with no responsibility for everyday procedures. It suited them both just fine. As Betty explained: "My oldest brother didn't want one touch of major responsibility for the company at all, and I don't think Henry wanted him around with any major responsibility."[14]

During the 1970s Teed became more and more withdrawn and turned more and more to drink for comfort. He lived in fear of the government finding out that he had not filed his 1974 and 1975 income tax returns. In 1976 he received overdue notices from the Internal Revenue Service. Alarmed, he hired a tax consultant who advertised in *New York* magazine that he specialized "in serving clients whose tax payments were overdue."

Nicholas J. Laszlo convinced Teed that the only solution to his problem was to sign over all his money and stocks before the IRS confiscated them. Teed signed 95 percent of his wealth, more than a million dollars, over to Laszlo for safekeeping, believing that his money would be used to pay back taxes and transferred to a tax-free investment account. In fact, Laszlo used the money to pay off his own creditors and finance a lavish life-style. Records of the trial that ensued report that, "with Steinway's money, Laszlo bought a car for his wife, took a $20,000 vacation in Europe and a trip to Colorado, gave cash gifts to his two former wives, and bought a town house on East 79th Street, a building on First Ave, and a photo finishing business." He spent over a million dollars within a year. All Teed's money was gone. The irony was that the one thing he had always tried to escape—the Steinway name—became his sole asset.[15]

A different fate awaited Henry's younger brother, Fritz. Henry saw Fritz as a factory man. Fritz had a mechanical bent and the affable personality so crucial in a factory where tempers are always on the boil. People appreciated Fritz's warmth and charm. Henry described him as "an extremely attractive, likable fellow, . . . a great personality." Fritz enjoyed his factory job. Looking back on his years of running the factory, he recalled that what he wanted was to be "vice-president of manufacturing, the person who had complete administrative responsibility for all manufacturing. That's what I wanted." But it was never offered to him. Henry and Frank Walsh shared that job.[16]

In 1954, feeling stymied, Fritz moved out of the factory and became Majewski's assistant in the wholesale department. He went on the road promoting Steinway pianos. Fritz remembered how people were in awe when they met him, a real live "Steinway in captivity." One tale he loved to tell was about a dealer out West who insisted on meeting him at the airport. After five minutes of conversation during the car ride to Fritz's hotel room, the bright-eyed dealer stared at young Fritz and said: "You're a funny-looking Steinway. I expected somebody about twice your age with a beard."[17]

When Greiner, head of Concert & Artists, died suddenly in 1958, Fritz, then only thirty-seven, jumped at the opportunity and said he would take on the job.[18] It was the task of the person holding this position to assist the president of Steinway & Sons in binding the immortals to Steinway. Rubinstein, Rachmaninoff, Paderewski, Hofmann, or Horowitz had to be made to feel that Steinway & Sons sincerely adored them. In return, when these artists went on stage or gave an interview, they were expected to extol Steinway. Henry appreciated the importance of artists' endorsements for the prestige of the house and for piano sales, so he went to concerts. But he had been delighted to delegate relationships with Steinway artists to Greiner.

Greiner had been with Steinway & Sons since 1926, and, because of his apprenticeship under the venerable Ernest Urchs and his credentials from the Moscow Conservatory, he had a certain eminence that the managers of Concert & Artists after him would never possess. With his facility in languages and ability to understand people's problems and figure out how best to solve them, he was superb at the job.[19]

Henry supported and applauded Greiner's performance. According to Harold Schonberg, a Horowitz biographer, "you had to accept Horowitz for what he was . . . entirely self-centered, in love only with himself and the piano." Henry was always gracious to Horowitz. If Horowitz, one of the most influential pianists in the world, were merely to imply that the Steinway piano was not as good as it used to be, it could ruin the company. As Henry put it, Horowitz "would know how to shove it to Steinway in a very newsworthy way." If he never did, it was because Henry was cordial to him and Horowitz adored his Steinway piano and his other "inseparable friend," Greiner.[20]

Horowitz had been under Greiner's wing since he first stepped off the boat at New York's harbor in 1928. Although, with the exception of a recital at President Dwight D. Eisenhower's inaugural, he stopped performing in public in 1953, Greiner's secretary, Alice Jordan, recalled that "pianos still kept coming in and going out of (Horowitz's) house." He was constantly studying music he had not played for many years or had neglected to play at all, much of the classic repertoire. In 1955 he started recording his new repertoire with RCA but demanded that the recording studio come to his house. He had enough clout to get his way. RCA brought the equipment, and Greiner arranged for the pianos. Greiner also visited Horowitz regularly, staying at his home on upper Park Avenue into the early morning hours, drinking and listening to music.[21]

During one of these visits, Horowitz asked Greiner to build him a special piano. Horowitz was enamored of bel canto singers and particularly adored the Italian baritone Mattia Battistini (1856–1928), who had been popular in Russia in the late nineteenth century. Horowitz wanted Steinway & Sons to make him a piano that would sound like the voice of Battistini. Greiner tried to convince Horowitz that only the artist, not the instrument, could produce the beautiful singing voice, delivery, and phrasing associated with bel canto. Greiner compared the Steinway piano to the voice of Battistini, emphasizing that the beautiful tone was there to be molded by the artist. Eventually Horowitz agreed to visit Steinway Hall and select a new piano which, he hoped, would have a voice like Battistini.[22] When Horowitz finally returned to the concert stage on 9 May 1965, he told a *New York Post* reporter just before the recital: "For 20 years I played on the same piano [CD 347] and I wanted most, most, most to choose a new one. I will be playing a new

Steinway [model CD 186] for the first time. I love it more than any other. It is more mellow, more like the human voice."[23]

Arthur Rubinstein was also a Steinway superstar of the 1950s and 1960s. In the minds of many he was second only to Horowitz. To Greiner they were both eminent artists, and their loyalty to Steinway & Sons was crucial. Rubinstein, unlike Horowitz, whom he disliked, maintained a whirlwind of public performances. Although in his seventies, he played "five, sometimes even six concerts a week, going by plane from city to city, . . . as fresh after the sixth concert as after the first." He would perform eighty concerts in three months in the United States and then board a plane for Europe or South America to play another fifty or sixty concerts. Greiner made sure that, wherever the aging but peripatetic maestro played, he always had his favorite piano. On one unanticipated trip Rubinstein rushed down to Rio de Janeiro for a concert and asked Greiner to ship his beloved Steinway concert grand without delay by air express. Greiner reported that "Rubinstein got his piano all right, but it set him back three thousand dollars—a consequence that might have led a lesser man to take up the piccolo!"[24]

Rubinstein cherished his relationships at Steinway Hall and, most of all, his piano. He delighted in telling one of his dreams, to highlight his reverence for the Steinway piano:

> I had died and, reaching the Gate of Heaven, I asked St. Peter, who was guarding the entrance of Heaven, to admit me.
> "Who are you?" asked St. Peter.
> "I am Artur Rubinstein, the pianist," I replied.
> "What piano did you play on earth?" asked St. Peter.
> "The Steinway, of course," I told St. Peter.
> "No admittance!" said St. Peter.
> I was naturally surprised and most unhappy. While I was standing at the heavenly gate not knowing what to do, my colleague, Mr. X, the well-known pianist, approached the heavenly gate. St. Peter asked him the same question, but when my colleague told St. Peter he had not played the Steinway but a piano of another make on earth, St. Peter opened the gate and said: "Come right in! You deserve to be in heaven. You have suffered hell on earth!"[25]

Greiner helped Van Cliburn obtain a $1,000 grant from the Martha Baird Rockefeller Aid to Music Program and encouraged him to go to Moscow in 1958. Van Cliburn was relatively unknown at the time and in debt. He later recalled: "Sascha took me to lunch three times and, in his inimitable fashion, he said, 'Dear Van, I beg of you, please go. You should.' He seemed so confident I would win that he had a great deal to do with making up my mind." Greiner, and the rest of the country, was overjoyed when the lanky blond from the dusty East Texas town of Kilgore (population 10,500) won first prize in the Soviet Union's international Tchaikovsky piano competition playing on a Steinway. The twenty-three-year-old American's victory took on special significance because of the cold war hostilities, and he became an American hero overnight. He was described by reviewers as Horowitz, Rachmaninoff, Liberace, and Presley "all rolled into one."

Greiner died just a week after Van Cliburn had conquered Russia. He had a heart attack while sitting at his desk at Steinway Hall one Saturday afternoon. By Sunday morning he was dead. A month later, his young protégé was welcomed home with a New York ticker-tape parade. Around a hundred thousand people cheered for the first musician ever to ride the hero's route up lower Broadway, from the Battery to the steps of City Hall, where he was greeted by Mayor Robert F. Wagner.[26]

Greiner's death was a serious loss for Steinway & Sons. He had a powerful personality and a profound understanding of piano playing. He recognized potential musical talent and convinced Henry that the company should turn itself inside out and jump through hoops for relatively unknown pianists who, someday, in Greiner's view, would be important champions of Steinway & Sons. Greiner was irreplaceable.[27]

Fritz didn't have Greiner's European background or his facility with languages, although that didn't matter very much in 1958, because the up-and-coming pianists were American: Leon Fleisher, Gary Graffman, and Van Cliburn. Nor did he enjoy Greiner's intimacy with the artists or influence with Henry. But, as a longtime jazz devotee, he was enthusiastic about Greiner's undeveloped proposal to add modern jazz pianists to the Steinway artists list. Through his friend John Hammond, a legendary figure in promoting African-American musicians, he became friends with Ahmad Jamal and signed him up as a Steinway artist. "It never would have occurred to Sascha Greiner," according to Fritz, "to seek out and find out what the problems or interests were of [African-Americans] who were pianists who were absolutely in leadership positions in their own fields." Fritz made African-American musicians feel welcome and appreciated at Steinway Hall, and African-American artists started dropping in just to say hello and talk about music. They also helped him to sell pianos. Fritz recalled: "I used to get [Fats Waller] to come into Steinway Hall with some people that he knew, both black and white, who were affluent and who wanted to buy a piano. He would be the one who would say, I'll pick one out for you. That worked very well."[28]

He enjoyed being head of Concert & Artists and saw himself as good at it. It was very time-consuming, especially during the concert season, but during spring and summer he had very little to do and could spend time with his family.[29] Fritz, in his new-found confidence, started to recommend changes at Steinway & Sons, some minor, some major. For example, he endorsed abbreviating the stencil on all pianos from "Steinway & Sons" to "Steinway." As he explained to an irate Majewski, most people were calling their piano a "Steinway" anyway, so why not us? The name "Steinway" was copyrighted and appeared on one upright model and all concert grands, but Majewski and Henry were not about to use it on all their pianos. Fritz thought Majewski had no concept of marketing and should be retired. Henry disagreed.

At the same time Fritz started urging Henry to open an iron foundry in Connecticut, to supply the Steinway factory with accurate, quality castings. But his suggestion fell on deaf ears. Opening a foundry would mean borrowing money, and Henry was against going into debt. Fritz, having attended Harvard Business School, was more Keynesian in his approach and was not scared of debt if it meant expansion. He told his older brother: "For God's sake, what's a bank for? You go to a bank. You need a million dollars, you need five million dollars, go to a bank. Borrow from the bank; float the money. No problem at all." Henry was not going to the banks at all. He was from the old school—"You don't spend what you don't have." Moreover, his sole interest was piano making. Fritz slowly began to realize that although he had royal blood, he had limited jurisdiction.[30]

He was frustrated. In November 1963 he announced that he was leaving Steinway & Sons to join the celebrated Arthur Judson, Judson's longtime associate Ruth O'Neill, and his own friend from the Boston Symphony, Harry Beall, to set up an artists management firm. Fritz reckoned: "If I couldn't do what I wanted to do in Steinway & Sons and if Steinway & Sons was going to go in the direction that seemed to be indicated at that time, I didn't want to have any part of it."[31] In addition, it was an exciting opportunity to link up with the impresario Arthur Judson.

The firm Judson, O'Neill, Beall, and Steinway later became a nightmare for Fritz. It evolved into exactly the situation he sought to escape when he left Steinway & Sons, a business that he partially owned but did not control. It was Arthur Judson's company. When Fritz realized that Judson "was really not that interested in letting Harry Beall and I run it," he moved on, ending up at the University of Massachusetts at Amherst.[32] There he was the executive director of the fine arts center. When that didn't work, his mother, Ruth, asked Henry to find a place in Steinway & Sons for "Fritzy." But Henry was not willing to take him back into the business. He recalled that his mother viewed this as mean and that some family members judged him as "very stiff-backed" about Fritz. But Henry did not feel that he could just create a place for him.[33]

David Rubin, who succeeded Fritz, was not of Greiner's stature either. Nor could Henry look to him, any more than to Fritz, to be the musical soul of Steinway & Sons, as he had to Greiner. Henry's own concerns were primarily financial. On becoming president, his first thought was to cut overhead, which by 1955 was inflated through having factory buildings spread out all over Astoria. The two factory sites, one on Ditmars Avenue, the other about a mile down the hill on Riker Avenue, made sense during the first quarter of the twentieth century when demand for pianos was surging. In addition, the Ditmars site was better for finishing, because it was on higher, drier land.[34] Henry declared that he was stuck with an overhead of more than four million dollars for the two sites, which "was killing us." He wanted to cut the operation in half. With one factory, not two, Steinway could save money by eliminating the duplication of maintenance, security, shipping & receiving, office staff, electricity, telephones, insurance, and taxes.[35] Half as many pianos could be built in half the space at half the cost. This was the goal he set himself: to make Steinway & Sons smaller.

Henry had been charting ways to consolidate the two factories since 1941. The way the work was divided up was that all the piano pieces were cut and shaped at Riker and were then sent a mile up the road to the Ditmars factory to be glued and screwed together. The raw piano was then regulated, polished, and shipped from Ditmars.[36]

Consolidation would be expensive and therefore unattractive to a board of directors overseeing a company that had been barely breaking even since 1951.[37] The blueprint was detailed in Henry's 1950 "Report on Factory Consolidation." In it he argued that, "to make money, and to put Steinway and Sons back into a strong, sound financial position," manufacturing costs must be reduced. This could be done by consolidating the two factories. The decreased costs would be reflected in a reduced piano price, which, he hoped, would increase sales and ultimately profits. Who could argue with that logic? But Jerome Murphy was skeptical and didn't buy it. He assured Henry that "some time in the future a miracle may happen and you will be able to acquire a modern plant," but not now.

Anticipating opposition, Henry had prepared a list of alternatives to consolidation: to give up manufacturing pianos and sell instruments made by others, to merge with another piano company that had better facilities, or to "abandon our current quality standard and enter the medium or low-priced field." He also offered a list of alternative factory sites that Steinway & Sons might consider purchasing, including a new site either within or outside the New York area, referring to a plan to move to Roosevelt Field in the New York suburbs or to North Carolina.[38]

Rather than any of the above, he asked the board of directors to approve his plan to consolidate all operations on the Riker site. The advantages of staying in Queens, Henry maintained, were that they already owned the land, that some of the buildings at Riker were still valuable, that moving the Ditmars operations to a site down the street would cost less than moving all operations to the South or the suburbs, that they would be able to keep the same skilled labor force, and that they would remain close to Steinway Hall, where they sold 20 percent of their pianos. Henry acknowledged that his "new consolidated factory would not be as ideal as a brand new plant because of the necessity of conforming our operations to presently existing structures." While most piano manufacturers had abandoned New York City, Steinway & Sons had been in New York for 100 years and in the same factory since the 1870s. As it turned out, however, a new factory would have been the more economical option.[39]

In 1954 Henry's consolidation plan was approved by the directors with a

Left to right: Roman de Majewski, Henry Z. Steinway, Frank Walsh, and Charles F. Steinway, planning the consolidation into the Rikers factory, 1955.

price tag of $600,000. They would have to mortgage and sell properties to raise the cash. The money would be spent on several new buildings and additions to old buildings at Riker, in order to accommodate the lacquer, belly, string, case parts, and upright departments, the general offices, and a cross-cut and pre-mill storage area. As part of the deal, Henry promised to scale down production to a more realistic 2,500 instruments a year, rent out part of the Ditmars factory, and "establish a policy of offering retirement to salaried employees over 65 years of age."

Given their qualms and their bank account balance, the board's support for consolidation was a strong vote of confidence in Henry and a tribute to his lobbying skills. But it also revealed how desperate the board was, allocating half a million dollars when Steinway & Sons hadn't made any money for years. But Henry reassured and convinced them that it was worth the gamble. His frank, simple, logical, and direct approach evoked trust. He was a master at convincing people that he was right.[40]

One year later, as president of the company, he won approval for additional funds to build an enormous covered woodshed next to an open lumberyard, to be filled with more than a million feet of lumber. Here Steinway would store hard maple for action parts, clear Sitka spruce for the soundboard, American black cherry, black walnut, and mahogany for the cabinet, sugar pine for the ribs of the soundboard, yellow birch for the legs, and yellow poplar, a core wood, for the tops, key lids, and desks.[41] All this wood could be stacked for one to five years on Steinway property before being kiln-dried.

The work went ahead, and by the time of the end-of-the-year stockholders' meeting, Henry was ready to show off his new facilities. He rented a bus and took them all out to Queens "for lunch and an inspection of the new buildings at the Riker Avenue Plant." A few months later he notified them that sales had increased by more than half a million dollars, and that the company was once again profitable; net income was $90,788 that year. Henry explained that a prosperous United States economy had stimulated a strong demand for pianos toward the end of 1955. Now, he proclaimed, the biggest problem facing Steinway & Sons was how to use its assets wisely and "find a way to take advantage of the prosperity now so evident in our country." He outlined his goals: to increase shipments of pianos by 20 percent, to reduce costs, to increase profits, and to hold the price of the piano steady. He promised to accomplish all this by building 200,000 more square feet of factory and office space at the Riker site and closing down the Ditmars buildings. The cost would be an additional $1.3 million.[42]

John Reed, lumberyard foreman.

The following year net income increased almost 50 percent, thanks to an impressive $5 million in sales. Henry's delight in Steinway's success was evident in the new glossy "President's Report" he published in 1957. His accomplishment in making Steinway & Sons profitable at long last emboldened him to make more major decisions, one of which was to abandon the use of ivory as a piano key covering. Even though pianists still waxed eloquent about ivory's yielding yet firm touch, cool but never cold feel, smooth but never slippery texture, most American piano makers had switched to plastic. By 1956 Henry agreed that it was time for Steinway to join them.[43]

To provide ivory, thousands of elephants had been slaughtered for their tusks. During the height of the ivory trade, 1860–1930, between twenty-five and a hundred thousand elephants were killed each year. One tusk yielded between fifty and fifty-five piano keyboards. But it was not animal rights activists who drove Henry to abandon ivory, nor any laws—importation of ivory remained legal in the United States for another thirty-three years. Ivory had its own problems. Keys split when subject to large shifts in temperature or humidity and changed color when exposed to light or to certain acids in perspiration—indeed, some pianists' fingers even made ivory turn blue! The tusks, like most teeth, were naturally yellow and had to be bleached to the required rich creamy white color by Steinway's suppliers. This involved soaking thin slabs cut from tusks in hydrogen peroxide, then laying them out in a greenhouse, turning them periodically, and letting them bleach in the sun for weeks, sometimes months. No chemical was ever found that could do the job better than sunshine. According to Henry, ivory was more a symbol of quality than a material possessing intrinsic advantages, even if some artists disagreed, preferring ivory's rough surface texture to plastic's cold, slippery feel. Henry had been searching for a substitute ever since he joined the company and in 1956 decided to use plastic instead of ivory on all pianos manufactured in New York. Hamburg continued to use ivory, but in New York, Steinway piano keys were "ivories" in name only.[44]

Although the New York factory was cutting costs by using plastic for the keys and by operating out of one consolidated factory, the 1955 productivity was not maintained. It cost more than two million dollars to bring all the operations from several buildings into one integrated factory capable of producing twelve pianos a day. Henry expected the company to show a slight increase in profits on a smaller volume of sales. But his hopes were quickly dashed. If 1958 was a profitable year, it was only because Hamburg was included in the calculations. The New York factory lost $60,000. The company's profit of $115,406, as Henry acknowledged in his annual report to the stockholders, "came entirely from overseas operations." Hamburg had been "our real steady profit center," a source of cash since 1954, and it continued to pour money into Steinway & Sons into the 1960s. After the war Steinway was the first piano manufacturer in Germany to resume business. They would even take old Bechsteins from concert halls and replace them with Steinways. Their near monopoly on new pianos, combined with Walter Gunther's venture, a full-line music department store in the city, made Steinway in Hamburg very lucrative.[45]

The problem in New York was that the factory was inefficient. The combination of old factory buildings and new structures was inevitably a hodgepodge. Although pianos were no longer hauled up the street, there was still plenty of wasted effort moving work back and forth in the new space. Each piano had to travel a maze of corridors and floors, up and down freight elevators, through an assortment of attached buildings, before its completion. John Bogyos, a Steinway production engineer at the time, called the new work flow "helter-skelter."[46]

Steinway's factory engineers and managers were perpetually moving operations to different floors, trying to figure out how to use the mixture of multi-story buildings better. According to Fritz Steinway, "there was always a frustration when you had to work with older buildings, simply because the physical layout had its limitations. There was always constant thinking and constant discussion about well, . . . if we move the Cross Cut Department from here to there, does that make any sense?"[47]

There was another problem with the newly consolidated Riker factory. It was built on the shores of Bowery Bay, so the foundation of the buildings rested on swampy land. The humidity from the bay and the surrounding tidal swampland was why they had built the Ditmars factory, up the road on higher ground, in the first place. Now that all operations were back at Riker, the humidity was again a problem. According to Bogyos, "the worst thing you can do is to build fine pianos when there's a lot of humidity. What you want is reasonably dry conditions at all times, so I think it was a bad move [to Riker]. . . . I remember their trying to disprove the fact that Riker was more humid than Ditmars. The fact was that Riker was built on swampland, and it stayed that way."

For piano making the wood must be bone-dry, with no more than a 5 percent moisture content. Otherwise the soundboards will crack eventually, and ultimately, as the wood dries out, all the joints and veneers will become loose, and the instrument falls apart. The water content of the wood at the Riker site was edging toward 15 percent. It would have been better to have moved the factory to Ditmars, where it was drier and the factory space was more efficiently laid out.

Frank Walsh dealt with the humidity problem by keeping the windows closed, turning up the heat, and turning on the fans, thereby transforming the Riker factory into a kiln. Bogyos looked back at the scheme with regret, ashamed that he was part of Walsh's plan to overheat the buildings and then not "allow the people to open the windows." The result was that the wood dried out, but the piano workers got awfully hot and were always thirsty. After several grievances about the heat were filed by the union, Steinway & Sons provided bamboo shades to keep the sun out, little window fans to pull fumes out of the tone regulators' booths, and water coolers to quench the thirst of the workers.[48]

The consolidation was one of the most expensive and elaborate construction projects in the piano industry. It cost more than twice what the entire piano trade spent on "new capital expenditures" in 1958. To finance some of the construction, Henry doubled the mortgage on Steinway Hall to $850,000 and sold the second factory on Ditmars Boulevard for $1 million. But it wasn't enough. Henry assured the stockholders that he would get the "additional funds required . . . from current profits or from loans to be negotiated." But "current profits" started to drop in October 1957, and Henry, who had an aversion to bank loans, refused to borrow more or increase the mortgages. The only financial reservoir left was property.[49]

Henry and his chief financial advisor, Eddie Orcutt, decided that Steinway Hall was a luxury that the company could no longer afford. Since the war, profits on the hall had increased steadily to roughly $50,000 a year, but this was less than a 2 percent yield on a $3 million investment. John and Fritz Steinway explained that Henry wanted to get their money out of Steinway Hall and into a more remunerative venture. "We had many tenants up there who were rent-controlled statutory tenants [approximately 40 out of 100 tenants], paying ridiculously small amounts. Legally we couldn't toss them out or increase the rent. But if we sold the building, . . . the new owners could do what they like." Henry added that many of the tenants were piano teachers, who would cry on his shoulder when the rent was due, while expecting free pianos on loan and free tuner service.[50] So when the president of Manhattan Life Insurance Company, who happened to be Henry's cousin, offered to buy the hall, Henry was glad to sell it. No real estate agent was involved, hence no commission, so Steinway & Sons netted the full sale price of $3 million. Thirty years later he proudly proclaimed that the selling price was about $100,000 over the market value and that with that money "we came out free and clear. . . . We were out of the banks for the first time since 1930."[51] Moreover, the sale included a twenty-year lease-back agreement on salesroom space, so Steinway still had a Manhattan showroom.

The consolidation limited Steinway's earning power, but did not affect the quality of its piano. But when the decision was made to change materials in order to speed up production and save money, it proved to be a perilous undertaking. Steinway replaced the traditional wool felt cloth used in all the action bushings with TFE-fluorocarbon resin, the DuPont product known as Teflon. Although developed for space exploration, Teflon became best known as a nonstick coating for frying pans. Steinway decided to avail itself of Teflon's nonstick quality in its action bushings.

The problem with bushings made out of wool felt was that they swelled in damp weather and contracted in dry weather. The result was that the action either became very tight or too loose, which in turn made the corresponding piano key either stick, lose all sensitivity, squeak, or fail to function, a condition termed "out of regulation."

Steinway had been having problems with felt bushings since the end of the war. John Bogyos recalled inspecting felt bushings and finding some too tight, others too loose, and none that were just right. According to Bogyos, bushings were routinely noisy, inaccurate, glue-soaked, and uneven. It was so bad that when Walter Drasche became foreman of the action department, he stopped production altogether. Drasche recalled that "they were having action troubles you wouldn't believe after the War. . . . I told Henry, I'm going to stop making pianos until I find out what's wrong with them. So I stopped." Drasche solved some, though not all, of the problems, but complaints continued about actions with jerky movements throughout the 1950s. Part of the problem, according to Drasche and Bogyos, was that the felt cloths they were getting were not as good as before the war. "We didn't have the influence with the manufacturers that we did," they said, and American Felt Company, Steinway's principal supplier, had sold out to a low-grade felt maker.[52]

Henry and his brother Fritz added that working with felt bushing cloth was an expensive operation. Each little wool circle had to be cut by hand and fitted in place with a dab of glue. Sixty-five percent of this costly material ended up on the factory floor, because to fill the tiny action joint hole, cloth had to be cut away on either side.

A simple one-piece Teflon bushing, that looked like the cross-section of macaroni, had no waste and "eliminated twelve to fifteen manufacturing steps necessary with cloth." In addition, Teflon's moisture absorption rate was below 1 percent, as compared with 8 percent moisture picked up by felt bushings. Other advantages of Teflon were an "imperviousness to household chemicals, corrosion, oxidation and fungus" and "no perceptible wear or looseness through use."

By 1962 all the action centers in Steinway grands were bushed with Teflon bearings. Steinway's advertisements promised a piano free of maintenance problems in all climates. They called their friction-free bushings "Permafree bushings."[53]

Ironically, the very reason why Teflon was chosen over felt turned out to be the reason why it did not work: it did not respond to changes in humidity. The problem was that the wood surrounding the Teflon bushing did respond to the climate, whereas the Teflon did not. In the dry winter the wood would shrink, making the bushing hole smaller, thereby squeezing the bushing so tight that the action became sluggish. In the humid summer months the wood would swell with water, making the bushing hole bigger, so leaving room for the Teflon bushing to knock around.

There was a flood of complaints, but not right away. As late as 1965 Henry was still informing his directors that the New York experience with Permafree Teflon bushings was excellent. It was not until about three years after the Teflon bushings were introduced that news of the problem started to drift back to the factory. Pianists complained that in winter the piano's action became sluggish, while in summer they could hear the bushings knock at every bearing point. Piano tuners, called in to stop the noise, had the horrendous job of trying to locate which of the 1,130 little joints was clicking. Henry Steinway remembered "endless arguments about what caused the noise, whether it was the pin banging against the Teflon, or whether it was the Teflon banging against the wood, or whether it was both. But you could hear a little click."

The grievances grew over the years, and everyone came to Henry with a different idea about how to solve the Teflon problem. Some people suggested relocating the center of the bushing; others maintained that the pianos were traveling through the factory too fast, not allowing the bushings to reach their final "at rest" position until after the piano has been delivered.

Everyone agreed that Teflon "if it's done right, it's beautiful. If it isn't done right, it's horrible." The problem was that the company had rushed into it too quickly. But now that Steinway was using it, the engineers had to make it work. It would have been ridiculous, in Henry's view, to go back to the traditional wool cloth, now that "space-age" Teflon had been introduced. He was convinced that Teflon would work if they could just figure out how to use it properly.[54]

But complaints continued to come in, a few from artists, but most from self-employed tuners, whose gripe was that Steinway had never introduced them to the new technology. Drasche reported that "nobody, no repairman on the outside was able to cope with this," because they were all used to working with cloth. Teflon was entirely new, "and it was a substance which didn't lend itself to easy manipulation. Felt cloth was very easy to manipulate one way or the other. Plastic was not."[55] Tommy Martino added that the real problem was, as the tuners themselves said, that Steinway did not educate the outside tuners. So, when a tuner went into a customer's home and could not fix the bushings, he "lambasted the Steinway piano" rather than admit that he really didn't know how to do it. That was why tuners objected to Teflon. One tuner declared: "Why should Teflon bushings need all that attention? Wool didn't. We have an 1898 piano in the shop which needs all kinds of work, but its bushings are still in fine shape. A brand new Steinway I saw a few weeks ago had thirty defective bushings that needed to be replaced. If Teflon is so good, why aren't the other companies using it?"[56]

The Teflon battle was fought more in the living rooms of America than on the concert stage, where pianos were tuned and regulated daily. In private homes, where a piano was tuned maybe once a year and regulated perhaps once every ten years, the clicking sound or the sluggishness became a constant, annoying problem.

Switching to Teflon proved more difficult in Hamburg. The Hamburg factory did not make its own actions. It bought them already-made from Renner & Company. Dr. Renner sent a letter to Walter Gunther, director of Hamburg operations, outlining the problems with installing Teflon bushings. Gunther decided not to change over to Teflon right away but rather to continue the discussion about its advantages and disadvantages. Henry put intense pressure on Gunther to "start seriously experimenting with this bushing with an eye to conversion to Permafree as soon as is practical." But Renner and Gunther determined that Teflon bushings made noise. Renner did not want to lose Steinway's business, but he was not convinced that Teflon bushings would be as good as his cloth bushings. In the end, he convinced Gunther that Teflon was trouble, and the Hamburg factory never switched. Moreover, Walter Gunther managed such a profitable operation that Henry was prepared to let him go his own way on the Teflon issue.[57]

In New York the battle raged for twenty years. Steinway & Sons finally admitted defeat in 1982; but first it had to figure out what type of bushings to go back to. To return to felt after two decades would be to admit that Teflon was a mistake, not a good idea when there were already more than 60,000 Steinway pianos with Teflon bushings out there. The problem was finally resolved, after Henry's tenure as president, by his son Bill and Walter Drasche. They came up with "an impregnation of the felt cloth with a Teflon liquid which coated the fibers of the cloth, and made them slippery without losing the flexibility of the cloth." Steinway diplomatically labeled the new cloth "Teflon-impregnated felt."[58]

Meanwhile, in the 1960s, the demand for music exploded in the United States, requiring an expansion in manufacturing. The baby boom had grown into a teenage boom, creating a huge pool of customers. Their parents, profiting from economic prosperity and tax cuts under President Kennedy, were buying musical instruments for their children to play in the school band or in after-school group music lessons. Not since the 1920s had Americans poured so much money into the music business. Rock 'n' roll sent electric guitar and drum sales soaring, while other instruments, such as the grand piano, also flourished. From 1960 to 1969, grand piano sales more than doubled; and the combined upright and grand trade swelled from $400 million to $1.1 billion. "People have money, and we just can't keep them from throwing it at us," was the way the president of the National Association of Music Merchants portrayed the industry in the 1960s.[59]

The decade included the birth of the Beatles and their dramatic arrival at JFK Airport, where a passionate crowd screamed and cried at the first sight of the boys from Liverpool; the opening night of *The Fantasticks,* a musical with piano instead of orchestra, with a story and a score that would make it one of off-Broadway's longest-running shows; the glorification of folk music and folk singers like Pete Seeger, Peter, Paul, and Mary, and the Kingston Trio; the extraordinary Arthur Rubinstein, at the age of seventy-three, playing ten Carnegie Hall recitals in forty days to a standing-room-only crowd which went wild when he announced that they had not seen his "final touch"; the idiosyncratic Vladimir Horowitz, after a twelve-year absence from the concert hall, returning to electrify a Carnegie Hall audience that had waited two days in line before tickets went on sale; flower children, counterculture groups, and music lovers—almost 450,000 people—swarming to Max Yasgur's dairy farm in upstate New York for the Woodstock Music and Art Fair and a summer weekend that the world would never forget; and the young pianist superstar Van Cliburn, who caused audiences to swoon before, during, and after his performances. In 1964 Henry Steinway entertained some eight hundred friends at Steinway Hall to honor the tenth anniversary of Van Cliburn's debut with the New York Philharmonic.[60]

It was also a decade of dramatic gains in civil rights, which helped integrate and popularize Steinway's artists list. By the end of the decade Steinway was highlighting African-American artists: Duke Ellington, pictured in *Steinway News* "before an enthusiastic audience of 1,600 people in the nave of Coventry's new Cathedral" and a few years later at an informal jam session on a Steinway grand at the White House after receiving the presidential Medal of Freedom; Ahmad Jamal and Roberta Flack, portrayed at Steinway pianos during a series of free concerts in Newark, New Jersey; and Earl "Fatha" Hines, at a magnificently decorated Steinway grand with a dedication plaque inscribed "Presented by jazz lovers from all over the world. This piano is the only one of its kind and expresses the great genius of a man who never played a melancholy note in his lifetime on a planet that has often succumbed to despair."[61]

This increase in music interest and the spread of the piano from the

Ramsey Lewis at Avery Fisher Hall in 1978. Standing left to right: Robert P. Bull, president of Steinway & Sons, Vivian Rubin, Connie Bull, David W. Rubin, head of Steinway's Concert & Artists.

concert hall to the rock concert stage translated into sales. Nationwide, piano shipments went up 25 percent in five years. Steinway grands were gobbled up by hotels, churches, and schools expanding programs to meet the flourishing interest in music. For families with limited budgets yet eager for their children to play the piano, Steinway introduced a very popular upright, the "Contemporary Vertical," that boosted business from three hundred to eight hundred uprights a year.[62]

In 1963 the Steinway factory increased its shipments by 15 percent over the previous year yet was unable to cut into the backlog of orders for grands. At that time Steinway & Sons was making thirty-one different models, some of which were more back-ordered than others. The board of directors was troubled. One member of the board of directors remembered that "there was a long time when we would have meetings mostly devoted to our inability to deliver orders . . . we weren't solving that problem. That was one of my worries, that we were so limited in our ability to produce more." Henry admitted that there were years when the company was out of certain models, and "I didn't feel good" when we couldn't fill orders.[63]

Henry had tried to solve his overhead problem by consolidating the two factories, but now he needed more space to make more pianos. At the time, his idea to consolidate made sense, but, as it turned out, with hindsight, it had been the wrong way to go. So he decided to expand the factory. He sent an apologetic letter to his board of directors acknowledging that although they had spent more than $2 million consolidating in 1958, "the time has come to build more factory space . . . to assemble more grands."[64] He emphasized that all the recent buildings had footings for additional floors.

Like the consolidation, the expansion was given to Frank Walsh to plan. Walsh recommended the construction of two additional floors, which would give Steinway 60,000 square feet more of manufacturing space at a cost of $450,000. He estimated that this additional space would increase grand production by 20 percent. By the time the expansion was complete, it would have cost more than a million dollars, however.[65] Opening day, 31 January 1967, was marked by a press gathering at which politicians, journalists, and artists were given tours of the new factory and a gala party to celebrate the improvements.[66]

But the expansion did not solve the backlog problem. Tommy Martino recalled that the factory went on a forty-eight-hour work week, and that there was pressure to "try to go faster, try to get more work out." Al Daniels, in the stringing department, remembered a lot of overtime: "You stayed at night, and you came in Saturdays." But no matter how much overtime they did and how much pressure there was to pick up speed, it never worked. The real problem was the space. The production ceiling was roughly 3,600 pianos a year (2,000 grands, 1,600 uprights). From 1965 to 1972 Steinway remained back-ordered for a year or more on grands, averaging 3,366 unfilled grand orders a year.[67]

More disturbing, net profits started to dwindle again. Although sales, as measured in dollars, not units, were increasing, from $12.6 million in 1967 to $14.1 million in 1969, net profits were decreasing. In 1967 manufacturing profits before taxes were $449,000. By 1969 they were down to $314,000, and in 1972 to $120,000. Oddly, the more sales dollars increased, the less profit was made.[68]

Sales were up and profits down, Henry explained, because costs went up faster than prices. Inventories of materials expanded to more than half a million dollars' worth, which was necessary if more pianos were to be made; but swollen inventories consumed Steinway's cash flow. At the same time, the cost of nearly everything in America went up because of the war in Vietnam. The U.S. military was a drag on the country's lumber and hardware, making it more expensive to build everything, including pianos. In addition, Steinway workers were putting in longer hours, thereby requiring more overtime pay.[69]

Excessive operating costs forced Henry to borrow $400,000 in 1968. It was what he had always dreaded. He had sold Steinway Hall to get free of the banks, and now he was back to them "for the indefinite future." Like his father in the 1930s, he rotated the loans, paying one bank off in three months, then borrowing from the next. He went from First National City to Chase Manhattan, then on to Chemical.[70]

The shrinking profits were caused by a combination of inflation and an inefficient factory. The predicament, Henry's cousin Ziegler explained, was that "if you can't produce when times are good, by the time you can produce, maybe the orders have left you. I think it was very important to be able to produce, and it was a problem." Henry acknowledged that Steinway was "bumping up against a capacity ceiling" and that output could not "be increased substantially by 'better management' . . . but only through more plant and more people, and all that this involves." It would have been better, he admitted, to have taken a level piece of ground and built a new factory.[71]

NINETEEN

"A Fine Way to Treat a Steinway"

H ENRY STEINWAY SAW
his negotiations with the union as one of his crowning achievements. As he
tells the story, there were moments of disagreement and a brief strike every
now and then, but, by and large, it was a contented factory busy making
pianos that he presided over. Some of the long-term workers go along with
that story. Joseph Bisceglie, an affable fellow with a pleasant smile and an
engaging personality, who worked for Steinway for almost forty years, recalled that when he needed boards to finish his house, all he had to do was
say, "Mr. Steinway, I need some lumber," and Henry would go right over to
the yard foreman, John Reed, and tell him: "Take care of Joe, he needs
something."[1]

Joe was foreman of the tone regulators and perhaps as foreman obtained
privileged treatment. Joe's brother Ralph, who became active in the union,
also enjoyed Henry's informal patter and friendly nature but, unlike his
brother, assumed that it was all a ruse to make employees work hard for low
wages. Ralph tells a very different tale, recalling that "there was that family-
type orientation that you were getting, which . . . you didn't know how you
were getting it, you understand. It made you even try harder. But you didn't
know it, but that's what they were doing. They were like hypnotizing you,
mesmerizing you. That's the way they were. . . . The money wasn't great."[2]

John Bogyos was a Henry Steinway devotee, a supporter of company
policy, and a rabid anti-union man since the day he started working at
Steinway & Sons in 1929. He remembered telling a story about his assistant,
Walter Neu, a stocky, blond, blue-eyed German, who had been at Steinway

since 1906. Neu was a key maker but was working for Bogyos in the machine shop. Bogyos was designing new piano parts, and Neu would make the metal pieces. One day Neu came to Bogyos and asked for "a little more money." So Bogyos went to Walsh and asked him to give Neu a raise. Walsh suggested that Bogyos go to his fellow Hungarian, Mike, who was still working at Steinway past his retirement, and ask him to give up 10 cents an hour from his pension for Neu. Bogyos followed Walsh's advice. When Cerofeci heard about it, he went to Bogyos and yelled at him for trying to take money from an old man. Reviewing this story thirty years later, Bogyos admitted: "That's the stupidest thing I ever done."[3]

James Cerofeci was the business agent for United Furniture Workers Local 102. Cerofeci had consolidated his power in Local 102 during the war and maintained control over it until 1970. His power base was the old-timers, mostly Italian employees who, like him, had been with the company for twenty years or more. He was a good talker, not afraid to say what was on his mind. He was also shrewd, always aware of who was his friend and who was not. At Steinway & Sons, the union was "strictly Jimmy."[4]

In 1946 Henry tried to fire the entire upright finishing department (five workers) at only four hours' notice. Cerofeci directed the union's lawyer to bring this violation of the contract to arbitration. Henry backed down but soon gave about a hundred workers a week's notice. He claimed that most of them were people whom his father had felt sorry for and had kept busy with idle work, sweeping the floors and painting the walls, "just to keep them warm." He said he could no longer finance his father's charity.[5]

Only the rubbing department, where Cerofeci once worked, was spared. Though Henry argued that this was because "there was sufficient work to keep the rubbing department busy," he later admitted that part of his motive was "political." It didn't work. Cerofeci was outraged at the mass layoffs and published a passionate letter in the union newsletter *Piano Key* inviting Mr. Henry Steinway to an upright worker's home to meet the "children crying for milk, and the landlord tapping at the door—so he could really know the feeling of the men he laid off . . . [who are] trying to make ends meet." Cerofeci told his fellow workers that Henry was like all employers, he didn't give a damn about them.[6]

Henry recalled his initial negotiating style: "I was young then, too, . . . and if they want to walk, let them walk." William McSweeney, president of Local 102, added that Cerofeci "and the officials of the union were merely listened to, and then their requests were politely tossed aside [by Steinway]." Union leaders became callous in response to Henry's hard line. Cerofeci wrote in the union newsletter that "the name-calling and insults with which Mr. Steinway greeted the negotiating committee in previous years" no longer intimidated the workers and would be useless in settling contract differences. In the same newsletter a cartoon portrayed Henry as a fat ogre with a Porky Pig hat, dark mustache, and scowling eyes standing on a ladder posting a sign that said "Piece Work Prices." The words ballooning out of Henry's mouth were "Take it or Go Home!"[7]

The first strike that Henry had to deal with was in 1950. Walter Drasche, the tone regulators' union delegate, started it when he convinced Cerofeci that it was time to fight for a pension plan. Drasche was a small wiry fellow with a dependable air and an appealing smile. His relatives had been part of Steinway management for generations, which explained his cockiness in bargaining with Henry. When the 1950 contract came up for negotiation, Drasche argued that "when it came to the pension . . . there's no way we're going to get anything here unless we hit the bricks. So let's do it."[8]

Drasche chaired the negotiating committee and led the ensuing three-week strike. There were two issues to be settled: one fiscal, the size of Steinway's annual contribution, the other political, who would control the funds. The union and Steinway each wanted to establish itself as the source of worker benefits. Tommy Martino recalled that it was a rough three weeks. "It was raining, and I walked for that, and boy, I'm telling you, I needed the money so bad, but I walked." And they won. The new contract provided for "a general 10 cents an hour pay boost, two additional paid holidays, and a pension plan."[9] The pension plan would be financed entirely by Steinway but governed by both Steinway and the union, each with three trustees on the board. The money would not be transferable to another pension if a worker left before retiring. Steinway's annual contribution was roughly $65 per worker, based on 2 percent of the payroll. To apply for a pension, a worker must be seventy years old and have worked for Steinway & Sons for thirty-five years. The maximum payment was "$50 a month to start."

In 1953 the first six men qualified, and their careers reflected the hard times they had endured during the depression and the war. During many of the years from 1930 to 1945 they had worked only a few months. For example, Louis Bieler had started varnishing and then lacquering pianos at Steinway in 1897, but there was no record of him working at the factory from 1931 to 1940. Herman Gregory began commuting from the Bronx to regulate pianos at Steinway in 1901 but worked only part-time for most of the 1930s and was laid off for several months in 1945. Yet when these men retired, the union leadership—Cerofeci, Drasche, and Manyoky—joined Steinway management at a celebratory dinner in recognition of "an unusual example of employer–employee cooperation," the Steinway pension plan.[10]

Drasche emerged from the 1950 strike as a trustee on the pension plan board, with a reputation for being an articulate, powerful shop chairman.

During the pension negotiations he showed himself to be a man of reason and thoughtfulness, and he again joined Cerofeci in negotiating the 1954 contract. Sensing that such a man could become very powerful and self-reliant in the union, Henry offered Drasche the job of foreman of the action department, with a $10 a week increase in pay. Drasche accepted the job and, like his uncle Frederick Speyrer and his cousin Fred Speyrer, Jr., who followed in each other's footsteps as factory superintendent, became part of Steinway management.[11]

But Henry still had to negotiate with Cerofeci. There was another two-week strike in 1955, and the union won a wage increase of 10 cents per hour. But by 1957 Henry had finally convinced Cerofeci that "wage increases now mean higher prices for our pianos, and, as a result, fewer sales, smaller production for next year, layoffs, and eventually [Steinway's] withdrawal from piano manufacturing in New York City." Henry pointed to the gains made by the 1955 strike when wages went up by 6 percent to $1.97 an hour, forcing him to increase the tag on the low-priced S grand from $2,585 to $2,735. Henry maintained that this did not "cover all the increases in costs since 1950" but that he wanted to keep prices down as much as possible to encourage sales. An upright in 1957 sold for about $1,500, an ebony M grand for around $3,000.[12]

Cerofeci bought Henry's message and sold it to the four hundred workers at Steinway & Sons. He told them: "Don't ask for too much money. Don't forget this: your jobs are at stake. . . . Pianos are not a necessity. Therefore if they are priced too high, the people can live without them, and you'll be without a job." Berta Kolb, an action maker and one of the few women at Steinway, remembered Cerofeci calming the waters in 1957 and averting a strike at the last minute by telling people: "We should not demand [the raise now], because they're really in bad shape. The sales were not very good." The workers were swayed and accepted a twelve-and-a-half-cent raise this year and twelve and a half next year. As he had threatened, Henry raised the price of the piano to cover these costs. The average cost of an upright increased to $1,674 and an ebony M grand to $3,350.[13]

In 1958 Steinway wages, which since the war had averaged twenty cents an hour above the average for the industry, were for the first time below the average national wage for piano workers, $2.11 per hour, and equal to the average wage for a New York State furniture worker, $2.09 per hour. The following year sales looked shaky, and Cerofeci persuaded his workers to sign a two-year contract with no raise and a 1 percent increase in the company's pension contribution, making it 3 percent of the payroll. Ralph Bisceglie was irritated by Cerofeci at the time and thought he was being too easy on Henry. "I was impatient then, I was a young bull," he recalls, but now I "understand where Cerofeci was coming from. . . . The piano industry was falling apart in New York" in the 1950s. Richard Sera insisted that Cerofeci "did things that was good for the company, because it had to be done. So a lot of times people said: 'He's making another deal.' Maybe he did. I'm sure he did at times." Tim Gorman, a polisher, remembered that right after the contract without a raise had been signed, "the company came and gave a lot of these foremen bonuses. That really ticked the union membership off."[14]

By 1957 Cerofeci had become a man of compromise, not conflict. He had come to believe that it was better to settle for less rather than strike for more. During the rest of his career as business agent, which ended in 1970, there would be only one more strike, and it was brief. He won accolades from both labor and business for his flexibility, leadership, and commitment to cooperation. Henry reported to his board of directors that "there appeared to be a spirit of cooperation between management and the union officials and a

Signing a union contract in 1961. *Seated at the table, left to right:* Roman de Majewski, Edward Orcutt, Mike Vacca, Jimmy Cerofeci, and Henry Z. Steinway. *Standing, left to right:* A. Calandra, Jess Manyoky, Joe Bisceglie, Tony Vacca, Gerry Koester, Tony Biamonte, Frank Walsh, and Ralph Bisceglie.

resultant increase in understanding the nature of the company's problems by the union." In 1957 some four hundred people gathered at the testimonial dinner to honor Cerofeci. Civic officials, industry executives, and labor leaders praised his accomplishments. The mayor of New York City, Robert F. Wagner, sent his congratulations.[15] The piano market had been shrinking during the 1950s, and Cerofeci was seen as a model for how to minimize the pain for both workers and the industry.

By the mid-sixties Steinway sales had surged, and profits swelled. In September 1964 the company's bank balance rose to roughly a million dollars, with a second million in outside investments. The factory shipped 3,729 pianos in 1966, as compared with only 2,205 pianos in 1959.[16]

But the prosperity of the 1960s for Steinway & Sons did not translate into prosperity for the piano makers. In 1963 Steinway piano workers averaged $5,366 per annum, while Henry made $43,000, and the company cleared $620,951. During the opening days of the decade the workers were earning $2.25 per hour, less than the "average hourly wages [of $2.50] paid to workers in fourteen U.S. piano firms." By the end of the decade the average hourly wage at Steinway & Sons was $3.30, still below the average, now $3.50 per hour, in the piano industry, and Steinway workers had no paid sick days. "It was hard work" reported Al Daniels, and "at the time I wasn't getting paid that much." Cerofeci had held wage demands down each time the contract came up for renewal, still advising the workers: "I think you should take it, it's the best you can get right now." With two million dollars in the bank, Henry negotiated a three-year contract in 1964 which gave the workers ten cents per hour the first year, nothing the second year, and five cents the third year, while Steinway & Sons' profits for 1965 and 1966 surged to over $1 million. Workers pointed out that with these wage increases they had "just enough to buy a soft drink." The increases won Cerofeci the nickname "Coca-Cola Kid."[17]

During the 1960s Henry increased the price of pianos between 10 and 16 percent, depending on the model. Surprisingly, the higher prices did not dampen sales, as he had feared. Henry Ziegler, Henry's cousin and Steinway board member, maintained that "we never seemed to have a problem when we raised prices." Each year, until 1967, the factory shipped more instruments than the previous one, despite price increases. The interesting part of this success was that it contradicted the assumption that had been at the heart of all labor negotiations for the past twenty years: that stable prices were essential if Steinway were to remain competitive, and that the only way to keep prices down was to keep wages down.[18]

This was the way Henry and Cerofeci had played the roles of employer and union leader, and by the 1960s it came to seem as if they had worked out the scripts before the bargaining began. The workers lost all faith in Cerofeci when the logic for keeping wages down proved false.

Henry acknowledged, in later years, that the union negotiations looked as if he had orchestrated them with Cerofeci; but, he maintained, there was no collusion, simply mutual respect. "We were guessing what each other was thinking, and we were fortunately thinking the same things with the same motivations, so that's a lucky thing for both of us. But it looked from the outside as if we cooked this all up ahead of time, which was not so."[19] Henry insisted: "I have nothing to be ashamed of on that score. Nor has Cerofeci. . . . I never could give him one dime in any way whatsoever. . . . He did everything he could to preserve Steinway within the framework of doing the right thing for the men." Henry underscored Cerofeci's ability to conserve assets in Local 102, build up reserves, and buy a building during the 1950s when the piano industry was dying. Henry recognized that he couldn't "have operated Steinway without a union like this." It was what made it possible to keep Steinway & Sons profitable.[20]

In the late 1960s Steinway workers, led by the tone regulators, finally woke up to the fact that they had been had: piano prices were rising, sales were outstripping production, and their salaries did not reflect that prosperity. They reasoned that Steinway & Sons was doing so well because Cerofeci was asking for so little. Tommy Martino insisted that there were some "open and shut" grievances that Cerofeci helped the company win. "We always thought that he was in cahoots with the company." Al Daniels, one of the few African-American workers at Steinway, added that "there were a lot of rumors about it. Henry was a very friendly person, . . . and some say he had deals and deals and deals."[21]

Indignant workers expressed their rage in a variety of ways. Martino explained that there were unwritten laws on the shop floor, with people making agreements not to work fast or hard. Frank Walsh recalled that "after a while they didn't have that old, basic feeling about their work. It used to be the guy would cry if he saw the foreman come in and complain about his work, you know, that type of thing. But I think some of these people lost their feeling about it, their urge to be 100 percent."[22]

The apathy and lethargy were symptoms of revenge, not laziness. Most of the men worked elsewhere at night and on the weekend. Henry estimated that about half his factory workers had second jobs. They could always find work tuning, regulating, or rebuilding an old piano. In the past they did this for extra cash; now they were doing it to pay the bills. "Most of us did some work outside," John Bogyos explained. "You tune, regulate, you fixed up a piano and sold it." Tommy Martino maintained that "the only reason I made real money in the piano business was because I went out and worked on moonlighting. . . . The take-home pay was just enough to get on, to make ends meet." Ralph Bisceglie added that he knew workers with three different jobs.[23]

The "homey" atmosphere, the family feeling, where workers felt some allegiance to Mr. Steinway and comfortable enough to have a coffee pot or hot plate at their bench to cook breakfast, lunch, or a snack was no longer enough to keep them at Steinway & Sons. Many quit to start their own businesses, and several left for jobs at higher salaries. Martino quit after twenty-three years to start his own piano repair business, A & C Piano. Former Steinway workers were always in demand because of the prestige of the company. Martino and others soon discovered that having worked at Steinway could net them more than actually working at Steinway.[24]

By 1969 so many old-timers had left that Henry was in dire need of skilled workers. The board of directors asked him for an attrition study and subsequently made the progressive proposal that "the firm should seek more women for working areas which up until this time [have] been predominantly male." The attrition study revealed some astonishing facts. During a six-month period, January through June, 72 people had left, 51 of them skilled workers. There were only 273 skilled workers in the entire factory. This amounted to a projected 40 percent turnover of skilled workers for the year, surprisingly high, given the myth that the Steinway factory was filled with Old World woodworkers who came to the factory through their fathers, possibly their grandfathers, and stayed for life, eventually training their own sons. This was not the reality by 1969. Steinway piano makers did not stay long.

Old-timers were training new people and then retiring; but the new people were leaving after only a few months. Daniels explained that tuners would come in, learn the trade, and then quit.[25] Martino said that of every twenty people he broke in, only about five would stay for more than a few months. "They didn't like the work, had no interest in the work, and it was very difficult to get people to work on such a time-consuming, tedious job." Henry Ziegler recalled that the biggest problem for Steinway at that time was that people no longer had the patience to apprentice. "You come into the factory, you spend twenty hours doing a piece of woodwork, and the foreman comes in and says, 'piece of junk,' throws it away, says 'start all over again.' That was easier to sell in the twenties than it was in the sixties." Ralph Bisceglie acknowledged that in the 1960s the "whole old school" disappeared, and high worker turnover became a permanent state of affairs at the Steinway factory.[26]

Henry Ziegler acknowledged that, even during times of great difficulty, women weren't brought into the factory as quickly as he'd hoped, because the response to the board's proposal was only "Yes, let's look at it." It was not Steinway tradition to allow women in the business. Betty Steinway Chapin remembered how hurt she was when the door to her family's business "was just absolutely shut in my face. It was 'Go away, little girl.' . . . I resented that. . . . There was always that thing, where this door was open to the males in the family, but it was not open to the females." Betty's response was to distance herself: "I do not feel a part of the mighty house of Steinway at all. And I think a little bit of my feeling is, you didn't want me. OK, I went elsewhere." She married Schuyler Chapin, an English-language newscaster for NBC's international department who went on to become dean of the School of the Arts at Columbia University and general manager of the Metropolitan Opera Company. Betty went on to become a champion of the arts and education as a member of the New York State Council on the Arts, creating the Volunteers of the New York Public Library and becoming a founding trustee of the Harlem School of the Arts.[27]

Henry Steinway acknowledged that until the late 1960s, when his daughter Kate came back from college and started talking to him about discrimination against women, he had never given the absence of women in the factory any thought. He admitted to Kate that "we were definitely anti-woman for years. . . . I mean, there weren't women's toilets in the plants" until World War II, when thousands of women worked on gliders. He recalled discussions about employing women and breaking the unspoken male barrier by trying "to get women into regulating," a job in "which every other piano factory in the world had used women for years."[28]

Cerofeci never fought for women's rights or encouraged women to become active in the union. After the war Steinway & Sons, like most American manufacturers, fired hundreds of women, including Cerofeci's wife, Jane. It had been written into the 1941 union contract that all employees were guaranteed their jobs back after military discharge. Seniority was guaranteed, if the employee was "still competent to perform his prior job satisfactorily." Upon rehiring him, the company could let go any of his successors, and of course those successors were mostly women. In 1946 only thirteen women remained at Steinway & Sons. Jane Cerofeci had been "reinstated" to do hammer work a month after she was laid off with "no loss [to her] seniority." Rose Steinberg, also in the action department, where most of the thirteen Steinway women worked, tried for a promotion to hammershank gluing. She put in her bid for the job and later learned that "they hired a man instead of giving me a trial." Rose protested, but when she filed a union grievance, she was notified that "a man was required for this type of work." As late as 1968, a time of civil rights mandates and rising social consciousness about discrimination, when 29 percent of the nation's piano

Jane Cerofeci working on hammers at the Steinway factory, c. 1965.

workers were women, Steinway & Sons had only 7 percent (thirty-two women), and they were either in clerical jobs or in the action department.[29]

Inequality was also evident in the ethnic breakdown of the factory population. One of the few African-Americans hired after the war was Al Daniels, whom John Bogyos regarded as "one of our top people." Daniels was born in Bermuda, son of a stone mason from St. Kitts, the only one of eleven children to follow his father into a skilled trade, and the only one to emigrate to the United States. He got his training as a carpenter on a British military base in Bermuda and started work at Steinway & Sons in 1957, after a one-year apprenticeship at Winter Pianos in the Bronx. At that time, there were only two other African-Americans: "one guy was in repairs [Edgar Silvero] and one guy ran the elevator."

Bogyos maintained that Daniels was resented because he was so fast, so good, and African-American. "The fact that nobody could keep up with him, that's the thing; some people couldn't cope with that." Bogyos remembered picking Daniels for a job because he was the best man and the other workers being annoyed and remarking: "Why did you give it to the nigger?" Daniels was rarely insulted to his face. He remembered Cerofeci telling him,

"If you have any problems, if anybody gives you any problems, I want you to come to me." Cerofeci probably passed the word along not to harass Daniels, and it worked: Daniels never had to go to Cerofeci with any complaints about racism. He liked bowling on the Steinway team and enjoyed "hanging out at night" with his best friend on the job, Harry Boot. He stayed at Steinway & Sons for twenty-two years.[30]

Steinway's doors were finally thrown open by the civil rights movement, affirmative action and equal opportunity legislation, the aging of Steinway's labor force, the scarcity of skilled labor, and the 1960s boom in the piano business. A number of African-Americans and Hispanics were hired in 1970, many from Janssen Piano, which went bankrupt in 1969. Some started in stringing, like Daniels, or in the mill, sorting lumber, but most were in the finishing department as polishers and rubbers, unskilled jobs that required working in spray booths and inhaling noxious fumes. African-Americans and Hispanics with skills regulated actions on uprights. According to Gerald

Steinway lumberyard workers, 1980. The man at the bottom is holding a lumber rule, a symbol of his trade, used to measure the number of board feet of lumber.

Koester, African-Americans were hired in part because "Steinway didn't want to be the only one that didn't have any African-American people" but also because it "couldn't get white people to do those jobs." It wasn't until the 1970s, however, that African-Americans were hired in significant numbers, and most of them were from Haiti, Jamaica, or Guyana. Frank Urich recalled that "they still had old [world] skill." Berta Kolb agreed that "there were a lot of Haitians there in Steinway, and they all are very, very, very good workers."[31]

Cerofeci blamed the new people coming into the factory, especially the Hispanics, for whittling away at his power. But in fact he was deposed by some of his fellow Italian workers: John Coffrini, Mike Vacca, Al Compareti, and Tony Biamonte. Biamonte was a cousin, and Compareti a nephew. Cerofeci had gotten both of them, as well as Biamonte's father, their jobs. Martino acknowledged that Cerofeci had been "a good man for the thirties, the rabble-rousing and things like that, and into the fifties. Then later on, they needed new blood."[32]

Cerofeci himself insisted that he lost the election for business agent because of the increasing number of Hispanic employees and because he had foolishly put his name second, instead of first, on the ballot. But in reality, he lost the election because most of his co-workers felt that they had been "nickeled and dimed" long enough, and worker consciousness had been growing since the late 1960s. Cerofeci's power base, those hired in the 1920s or earlier, had taken their pensions and retired. There was a new group at Steinway & Sons, and they, like most Americans at the time, were demanding more rights. That Cerofeci was still in power was mainly the result of inertia and because of the support he had from union members outside Steinway & Sons. Even though the ballots were secret, many workers feared Cerofeci's revenge if he won and they had voted against him. Richard Sera remembered that to get rid of Cerofeci took two ballots, and that the first count revealed only one vote difference. Curiously, Cerofeci himself hadn't voted, he was so sure that he would win. But on the second ballot, when it was clear that Cerofeci was vulnerable, "he lost by a landslide."[33]

A fellow named Tomasello promised that he could do better than the "Coca Cola Kid." He would seek a dollar-per-hour raise, paid sick days, and more pension rights. He convinced the workers that if they went on strike they could win back all that Cerofeci had given away. The strike started on 1 October and went on and on and got uglier and uglier. Henry remembered going to meetings to try to settle it and Tomasello just sitting there, not prepared, usually drunk, and unable to respond to questions. Cerofeci sat on the sidelines and gloated: "They had a seven-week strike, they didn't know what to do."[34] In the middle of it all Henry walked out on the frustrating

Picket line in front of Steinway Hall in 1970.

negotiations and went to Europe to visit the London and Hamburg operations. When he came back, the strike was still on.

In the end the 1970 strike was "terrible for everybody." The union didn't get anything out of it, and the piano workers lost seven weeks' pay. Jess Manyoky recalled: "We were out seven weeks, and after it was all over, most of us felt, for what? . . . We used to say 'For nothing.' "[35] According to Richard Sera, who became union secretary, the union signed a three-year contract, three days before Thanksgiving, providing "the usual crummy raise that Steinway always gave, a nickel and dime. . . . We didn't get much more than that. I think we got one sick day. We were supposed to get a new pension plan, and the union was completely bamboozled in that respect, because we never got the pension plan." Within a year Tomasello was forced to resign when he was caught misusing union funds.[36]

Although Henry won, the negotiations with Tomasello had been draining. He increased piano prices to cover the cost, but he couldn't recover the loss of his alliance with the union. He knew that Steinway & Sons' wages had been kept low only thanks to Cerofeci.

Henry would always consider his influence over Cerofeci a personal triumph and in a purely commercial sense he was right. He saved the company money and increased profits by suppressing wages, which was how most American manufacturers measured their success with labor at the time. But, as with most companies, it turned out to be a triumph in the short term but a failure in the long run. Henry had traded off worker loyalty and continuity with past craftsmanship for short-term profits and had lost a large portion of his work force in the process.

TWENTY

Steinway versus Yamaha

CONFLICT WITH THE piano workers may have been draining, but it was competition from the Japanese, particularly Yamaha, that destroyed Henry's will to lead. Henry, like so many Americans, could not forget the attack on Pearl Harbor, and he believed that Yamaha wanted to destroy Steinway & Sons in much the same way. He was scared "to death of them," and the combination of fear and hate determined his reactions to Yamaha.[1]

As early as 1960 the president of the National Piano Manufacturers Association, W. W. Kimball, alerted the industry that foreign piano makers, especially Japanese makers, were for the first time trying to break into the American market. At the same time, union leaders were becoming aware that imports were taking jobs away from American workers. But the response of Steinway & Sons and other American piano manufacturers was somewhat complacent. Although they lobbied to maintain protective tariffs, they ignored Kimball's admonition and remained convinced that the Japanese did not know the American market and did not have the skills to make a good piano. They were wrong.[2]

Like Sony in electronics and Toyota in automobiles, Yamaha was poised to transform the American piano business. It had taken the company seventy years to get to that point. Torakusu Yamaha, educated son of a prominent Samurai, was first a watchmaker, then a medical equipment repairman before he built his first musical instrument in 1887, now designated as the founding date of Nippon Gakki Seizo Kabushiki Kwaisha (Japan Musical Instrument Manufacturing Company), known worldwide as Yamaha.

By 1890 Torakusu Yamaha employed 100 people and produced around 250 reed organs a year. Carried on the tide of a rapidly expanding Japanese economy, Yamaha shipped 600 pianos, 8,000 reed organs, and 13,000 violins in 1911. During this period Steinway was exporting pianos to Japan for the concert stage through a local dealer in Tokyo, and held onto that market.[3]

In the 1920s a series of disasters almost put Yamaha out of business. The yen increased in value against the dollar, making Yamaha no longer competitive in the world market; the Japanese economy went into a recession; in 1922 fires devastated Yamaha's factories; a year later the great Kanto earthquake, which claimed 130,000 lives and millions in property damage, reduced what was left of the Yamaha factory to cinders; and in 1926 a 105-day strike brought Yamaha to its knees. Chiyomaru Amano, who had been head of the company since 1916, was no match for all these disasters, and in 1927 Yamaha's board of directors asked Kaichi Kawakami, a well-educated graduate in applied physics, to come in and salvage its dying musical instrument company.[4]

Kawakami hired skilled managers, attracted new investors, gave high priority to research and development, brought in technical advisors from Steinway & Sons and Bechstein, and built an enormous factory. Japan's emphasis on music education, in 30,000 schools, provided an expanding domestic market for pianos. By 1939 Yamaha employed 2,000 people to produce 4,000 pianos, 20,000 organs, and 2,900,000 harmonicas, but only for the domestic market.[5]

World War II brought a hiatus in piano production. Two months before the attack on Pearl Harbor the Yamaha company was nationalized and put to work manufacturing propellers, fuel tanks, and wing components for the Japanese air force. Like the Steinway factory in New York at this time, it stopped making pianos and was busy making weapons. During the final months of the war, American planes firebombed Hamamatsu, destroying the city and most of Yamaha's factories. But after the war American aid rebuilt Japan back to its prewar level. Yamaha benefited enormously from this American largesse, and within two years pianos were once again rolling off its assembly line.[6]

Kaichi Kawakami was disabled by a stroke in 1950, forcing him to hand over Yamaha's leadership to his "brash, enthusiastic, outspoken," and exceptionally intelligent thirty-eight-year-old son, Genichi Kawakami. Genichi, frustrated by Japan's sluggish musical instrument market, decided to go into the motorcycle business. In 1954 he persuaded the Japanese government to return metalworking machinery used by Yamaha during the war to make airplane components. The equipment had been confiscated and warehoused by Occupational Forces at the end of the war. Genichi used the metalworks to start a motorized bicycle business. In 1955 the Yamaha "Red Dragon" was introduced, a 125 cc motorbike, and Yamaha Motors was founded. It became an independent affiliate with sales approaching $3 billion, manufacturing motorcycles, golf carts, outboard motors, and lawn mowers.[7]

With the income from motorcycles, Kawakami established a chain of music schools for Japan's budding middle class, to promote interest in piano playing. He also persuaded the Ministry of Education to expand music education in all the schools. John McLaren, head of Yamaha U.S. sales in the late 1960s, claimed that Kawakami "had a very deep philosophy that music played a uniquely important role in the life of the individual and the family and the community. . . . [Kawakami] brought music to more people than any other human being who ever lived." At the same time Yamaha, taking its cue from Steinway & Sons, promoted the piano as a sign of middle-class status. The Yamaha Music Foundation trained music teachers, marketed piano lessons for children, and on the main floor of the music school sold Yamaha pianos. Fortunately for Yamaha, its program to promote piano playing coincided with a rapid growth of Japan's per capita income. This Yamaha music education system generated a huge market for musical instruments in Japan. The music schools and the domestic market would be the basis for Yamaha's prosperity.[8]

In the summer of 1950 Kawakami sent representatives to the United States to survey business prospects and the lumber supply. In July they visited the Steinway factory and told Henry's older brother Theodore, then head of engineering, that Yamaha was "making about 20 [grand] pianos a month but that Japan needed at least 300 pianos per month." Yamaha wanted to sell Steinways to capture the high-end market in Japan. But Steinway already had a dealer in Tokyo and referred the Yamaha representatives to him. Two years later T. Matsushita, chief of engineering at Yamaha, came back and told Steinway that the company was still interested in selling Steinway grands, but if that were not possible, Yamaha would go ahead with plans to make its own grand piano. Matsushita asked for a factory tour but was kept at Steinway Hall discussing wood finishing and wood gluing. Steinway & Sons was not interested in any dealings with Yamaha, which it perceived as an obscure, inferior manufacturer in a distant corner of the world.[9]

In 1958 Yamaha was still unknown in the United States, exporting fewer than 275 pianos. At the same time it had become one of the leading instrument makers in Japan, selling 30,000 pianos that year. Kawakami hired Jimmy Jingu, a Texas-born Japanese, to help Yamaha establish an American presence. Jingu struck a deal with a Los Angeles retailer, Sam Zimmering, and sold him more than a thousand instruments. The pianos had Zimmering's name stenciled on the fall-board because it was assumed that the Yamaha name would be too strange for American tongues.

The following year Kawakami founded his own subsidiary, Yamaha International, a big name for a small office in downtown Los Angeles. In its initial advertisements, it unthinkingly labeled its piano the "pearl from Japan," unwittingly reminding American customers of the Japanese attack on Pearl Harbor. Yamaha needed an American to manage its sales and advertising.

At that time Everett Rowan, who had been working on commission for Zimmering, fell out with him and went to Yamaha to make a deal. Rowan walked into Yamaha's small office on San Pedro Street and said: " 'Look, why don't you sell these pianos direct to music dealers under your own name, Yamaha?' They thought that that wasn't very practical because of the name being so peculiar. . . . [He] persuaded them that they could do it. So to stick it back to Sam Zimmering, he got Yamaha to cut out Sam and go direct. . . . Ev became the [national] sales manager [for Yamaha]."[10] Rowan launched Yamaha in the United States and in the process revitalized the market for larger uprights and inexpensive, but quality, grand pianos.

He worked this miracle by establishing regional sales meetings with dealers, twice a year at five different locations, rather than following the conventional traveling salesman routine of visiting every retailer individually. At these gatherings Rowan would sit down with about fifty people and discuss the future of the piano market, how to sell pianos, and how to manage a small music business. He taught dealers to operate in a more organized, disciplined way and thus to become more profitable. Moreover, he guaranteed every Yamaha piano, and when there were problems, "if any needed fixing, Yamaha fixed it." McLaren maintained that "in a sense those early service problems and the very forthright way that [Rowan] dealt with them, kindled more loyalty on the part of the dealers than had been the case before." Rowan mesmerized the dealers—impressive for a fellow who didn't smile very often, and when he did smile you got the feeling it hurt him a little bit."

Henry Steinway recognized that the tuners had fallen in love with Yamaha because it was the first time that piano manufacturers had ever paid any attention to them. Rowan grasped the importance of this forgotten group and cultivated their loyalty. The Piano Technicians Guild held regional and national events, and Rowan made sure that Yamaha always had a booth demonstrating service and maintenance techniques. He also established the Yamaha Service Bond, which required the dealer to service a piano six months after purchase, impressing customers and providing work for piano tuners. Pleased with the attention, the work, and the piano, tuners advised potential customers to buy Yamaha. Henry admitted that Yamaha's "cocktail parties and stuff like that" for tuners took Steinway & Sons by surprise.[11]

But Rowan was not after the Steinway trade. Customers willing to pay— and wait—for Steinway status and quality seldom thought of a Yamaha as an alternative. Rowan rarely invited "old line" Steinway dealers to his parties. They were too well fed and too well established in their downtown stores for him. He was looking for young, aggressive, hungry dealers willing to set up stores in suburban malls and scramble to build a market for larger uprights or quality grands at attractive prices for the living rooms of suburban tract homes.[12]

This was the niche for Yamaha. Its competition was secondhand, rebuilt, good-quality grands and uprights, not new Steinways. Steinway & Sons wasn't competition; it was like the tide for boats anchored in the harbor: Steinway's reputation lifted the status of all pianos. It made buying a piano— any piano—prestigious. All pianos basked in the reflected glory of Steinway. Kawakami appreciated this and recognized "that Yamaha would never be a threat to Steinway. McLaren, who spent a fair amount of time with him, insisted that "Kawakami felt that Steinway was the pinnacle. He always was striving to make better and better Yamaha pianos, but never felt that 'Hey, we've got to knock off Steinway.' I never heard Kawakami say anything in an adverse way about Steinway." Far from competing with Steinway & Sons, it was to Yamaha's advantage to become associated with it and to distance itself from the other Japanese piano manufacturer, Kawai.[13]

But Henry Steinway never saw the relationship that way. "The implacable, growing and relentless" Yamaha was selling a good piano at a fraction of what it cost to buy a Steinway. Henry assumed that cost-conscious customers would buy a Yamaha over a Steinway. He saw Yamaha as the enemy he had fought against in the war. He believed that Yamaha had "targeted us for extinction from the position as the standard piano of the world."[14]

Still, Yamaha wanted to be partners. In 1960, it tried once again to become Steinway's agent in Japan. In a letter to Walter Gunther in Hamburg, Yamaha pointed out that the current Steinway dealer in Tokyo, Mr. Matsuo, was selling Steinway pianos for so little, at a 23 percent discount, that there was no profit to pay for "after services" to maintain the piano. Yamaha then made its pitch: "Frankly speaking, we are the largest piano maker in Japan. Through our distributors, over 350 scattered throughout Japan, we have exclusive control on piano business" and prices. This enabled Yamaha to finance a service contract for many years after the sale of its pianos. Yamaha underscored the significant differences between Yamaha and Steinway customers, the former wanting an inexpensive but good-quality instrument, the latter the best piano that money could buy. Therefore, it argued, it made good business sense for Yamaha to sell Steinways to up-market customers and its own pianos to price-conscious ones. Furthermore, Yamaha promised that it would "maintain the reputation and dignity of Steinway." In a postscript it added some gossip—that Mr. Matsuo was "trying to sell his Bösendorfer piano" while representing Steinway in Tokyo. Walter Gunther, who had visited Japan in 1960, replied on behalf of the company that he was impressed with Yamaha's stores but was going to continue to "entrust Mr. Matsuo with our sole representation." Steinway did not shift dealerships just because there was a new aggressive music store in town. It was loyal to its long-term agents. Yamaha later capitalized on Steinway's allegiances to well-established stores, usually located in deteriorating downtown areas, and set up dealerships with energetic merchants in suburban stores.[15]

A few years later, Rowan had conversations with several American Steinway dealers "regarding the feasibility of placing Yamaha on the same floor with the fine Steinway products." In exchange for the prestigious link to Steinway & Sons, Rowan proposed to his home office in Hamamatsu that Yamaha agree to never solicit a Steinway dealership to become part of the Yamaha franchise, refer all interest in Yamahas from Steinway dealers to Steinway's home office, discourage the importation and sale of Yamaha concert grand pianos, not use the name of any professional artists unless they have purchased a Yamaha, maintain Yamaha sales below 5 percent of annual American production, and not lower the Yamaha retail price even when the tariff is lowered. Rowan really wanted that Steinway connection.[16]

But Henry didn't believe that Yamaha would back Rowan's plan, because at the very time that Rowan was trying to smooth the waters in the United States, Yamaha was hustling concert grands throughout Europe. Henry's response was: "Obviously they're just biding their time. The history of Yamaha, over and over again [was that] they creep in like the camel, stick their nose in the tent, and then they take over. . . . Yamaha. You don't fool around with guys like that."[17]

In 1964 Henry bought a Yamaha piano for the engineering department to appraise. It reported that the Yamaha grand had a nice matching walnut veneer case, solid brass hardware, clean, evenly filed hammers, heavy but effective dampers, good regulation, and an even touch. In general the piano had a "clean, round, undistinguished" tone with some strength but "no real character." It was a good piano for the price, but it was not a Steinway.

John Bogyos recalled that the first time he tuned a Yamaha he concluded that it was "a very well-made piano, except it did not have the tone of a Steinway." If you want a true Steinway tone, then "you've got to buy a Steinway, not a Yamaha." Bogyos explained that, "as a matter of fact, our piano didn't hold its tune as well as the Yamaha, but that's natural, because our soundboard was more flexible. That's why it sounded better, too."[18]

Henry knew that Yamaha lacked that elegant Steinway sound. He also realized that even if a customer bought a Yamaha, there was a good chance that his or her second piano would be a Steinway. He had read the market surveys which found that Steinway "was rarely the first piano in the family." Yet Henry still perceived Yamaha as a threat. It had a modern factory, expert engineers, inexpensive labor, and access to capital. Compared to Yamaha, Steinway & Sons had an old, inefficient factory and limited access to capital. Moreover, as Morley Thompson, president of another American company, Baldwin, stated: "Where automation was unfeasible, Japanese labor rates permitted enormous savings over their U.S. counterparts." Twenty-five years later Henry had no memory of Rowan, but still passionately rejected the idea of placing a Yamaha on a Steinway showroom floor. He explained that to him it would be like a mouse, Steinway, trying to eat an elephant, Yamaha. He pointed to England and France, where Yamaha became a part-ner and then tossed the partner out and "ran it their way." Henry's policy was: "Don't have anything to do with them, keep them out."[19]

But no one had—or has—ever described Steinway as a "mouse" in the music trade. Steinway & Sons has always been a giant in the music world, even though the number of pianos it produces has been relatively small. McLaren insisted that "on a quantitative basis, [Yamaha] did not have any impact on Steinway. Steinway continued to make the number one piano that they had traditionally, and were usually back-ordered on the more popular models by a considerable amount. . . . What turned out to be the real threat was the decline of the overall piano market."[20]

After many attempts over several years to form an alliance with Steinway & Sons, Yamaha gave up and decided to compete. In 1966 Genichi Ka-wakami announced that "we have now succeeded in manufacturing a test model of what we believe will be the world's finest concert grand piano." According to a Steinway tuner in Tokyo, Yamaha had improved the quality of its piano by reproducing the Steinway concert grand, "even in every minor part." Three former Steinway tuners and Klaus Fenner, a "piano scale designer and big theoretical technical man in Germany," had dissected sev-eral Steinway pianos and integrated the best of Steinway into the new Yamaha concert grand. Yamaha even claimed to be buying its lumber from the same mills that supplied Steinway. A Steinway executive would later admit that "if a quiz on Steinway pianos were given to Yamaha and Steinway engineers, I'm not sure who would score higher."[21]

It was an improved instrument with an incisive, brilliant tone. Eventually Yamaha added insult to injury by advertising Steinway inventions as if they were their own. In a full-page ad in *Music Trades* Yamaha proclaimed: "You get resonance in a piano by designing it so the sound vibrations keep traveling for a long time inside the sounding structure. In our standard size grand pianos, we do it with a mirror. It's (a) hollow, wedge-shaped casting. . . . That mirror is something new in pianos, but it's not the only new thing in a Yamaha." That "mirror," a "wedge-shaped casting," that connected the frame of the piano was nothing new; it had been patented by Theodor Steinway in 1878 and used in every Steinway grand ever since.[22]

Yamaha had done what Henry most feared. It had moved onto Steinway sacred ground, the concert grand market, and with that transgression had introduced an aggressive sales policy aimed at the institutional market—schools, churches, and music academies. Yamaha vowed to "catch up and pass up Steinway." Henry read the vow as "we are going to destroy Steinway." Yamaha had already outpaced Steinway in production, so this threat was a challenge to Steinway's "prestige, glamour, reputation, name or whatever it was [they had] built in 120 years." Yamaha intended to overtake Steinway as the premier piano in the world.[23]

In 1967 the "Yamaha Conservatory-CF" concert grand piano was demonstrated at the Chicago Trade Fair, the Frankfurt Fair, and a special gathering in New York. The piano brought to New York for the occasion was expertly tuned, carefully voiced, and exquisitely positioned in the Terrace Room of the Plaza Hotel, just around the corner from Steinway Hall. Rowan, in his introductory remarks, announced that Yamaha had spent about a million dollars to build forty-seven concert grands just like this one and that money was no object to their intention to make the best piano in the world. This was not an assembly-line piano; it was made by hand in a series of workshops, just like a Steinway. He closed his remarks by pointing to his new Yamaha concert grand, shimmering in all its ebony glory, and proclaiming to all the piano makers present, especially to Dave Rubin, head of Steinway's Concert & Artists department, that Yamaha was here to stay and was moving into the most prestigious end of the piano trade—the concert grand market.

Rowan had carefully assembled a select group of about a hundred people, mostly pianists, dealers, piano manufacturers, music publishers, journalists, and concert managers, to judge his new concert grand. A Juilliard student performed two Scarlatti sonatas, a Chopin mazurka, and "Forlane" by Ravel. The program highlighted the new piano's attributes: "lyric line, articulation of pitch and sustained continuity." Rubin maintained that "no effort was made to demonstrate range of volume, power or response to technical virtuosity," which he believed must have been by design, to cover up the instrument's shortcomings. Rubin did acknowledge, however, that the new Yamaha "sounded far more agreeable than the concert grands of Baldwin, Bechstein or Bösendorfer."[24]

As part of its promotion, Yamaha negotiated with the Metropolitan Opera House in New York City to become its official piano. Yamaha agreed to lend the Metropolitan forty pianos free of charge, a new set of forty instruments each year, and make a significant cash contribution—about $10,000—to the opera house in exchange for the Met's endorsement. To benefit Yamaha, the forty pianos were marked with a specially forged medallion proudly stating that Yamaha was the choice of New York's Metropolitan Opera House. After a year at the Met the pianos were sold through Yamaha dealers who promoted the medallion and the impressive link with the opera house.

Yamaha was acquiring glamour for its grand piano in order to compete with Steinway's prestige. It was not replacing Steinway at the opera house, however. Knabe Piano had been the official piano of the Met since the 1890s. It was Knabe's one high-culture arrangement, like Baldwin pianos with the Boston Symphony at Tanglewood. Henry Steinway had always thought it a worthless investment to place pianos at the Met.[25]

At the same time Yamaha started a piano bank, like Steinway but on a much smaller scale. It stationed ten concert grands in major cities across the country. Rowan notified Columbia Artists Management, Incorporated (CAMI) that "these pianos will be available for concert use on the payment of moderate charges sufficient to cover delivery, service and return of the instruments to dealers' stores." He added that if any of its artists were interested "in concertizing on these instruments," Yamaha would be glad "to make suitable arrangements." Yamaha was invading Steinway's turf. Steinway's proof that it made the best piano was that artists selected a Steinway for their concerts. It was the central theme of Steinway advertising. Now Yamaha was trying to capture some of its thunder.[26]

Yamaha then took its gloves off and published, not always accurately, promotions by Steinway artists: Rudolf Serkin, Andor Foldes, Arthur Rubinstein, Wilhelm Kempff, and others. Serkin's statement was about how impressed he was with "the quality of your instrument, the Yamaha Piano. The sound in all registers is very even, and the accuracy of the mechanism is remarkable." Wilhelm Kempff, according to a Yamaha press release, "performed a concert program on the new CF and made a 10-minute voluntary speech, quite off the ceremony schedule, and acclaimed the piano as 'The world's first-class concert grand.'" Kempff was astonished when he read the quote. He insisted that on a tour of Japan he "found magnificent Steinway grands at all points. It was only at one lecture for students which was totally unadvertised that he had to play the Yamaha which was on hand." Yamaha derived the endorsement from statements he made at the lecture.[27]

Andor Foldes toured Japan in 1969 and played Bartók's Piano Concerto no. 1 on a Yamaha CF grand in the Tokyo Cultural Center. Foldes said, according to a Yamaha press release, that " 'Japan makes very good pianos. When I looked inside one I found that the design is quite different from American ones, but the tone quality is the same. This is particularly evident when playing Bartók. I would be frightened if I were the manager of the Steinway company.' He then capped his remarks by using Yamaha pianos for the rest of his concert tour."[28] In a telephone conversation with Walter Gunther, Foldes insisted that the Yamaha press "release does not agree with the facts." When Foldes toured Japan, he was under constant pressure to play the Yamaha piano, "so he consented for the Bartók concert." During his concert tour he played a Yamaha only once and a Steinway thirty-seven times.[29]

According to the *Japan Music Trades* magazine, Rubinstein endorsed the quality of the Yamaha concert grand after it was introduced in the United States in late 1967. A year later a Yamaha distributor in Venezuela quoted Rubinstein, in an eye-catching advertisement that ran in several major Caracas newspapers and was displayed in all Yamaha showrooms, as saying that the Yamaha "piano is beautiful. I am a Steinway artist, so I wrote to the USA asking for permission to give a concert on a Yamaha piano." The implication was that Rubinstein played on a Steinway because they paid him but that he would much rather play on a Yamaha. It was reported by a Steinway dealer that a German pianist visited the Yamaha Caracas showroom and purchased a piano, proclaiming that he "had to agree with Master Rubinstein."

Steinway was incensed, questioned whether Rubinstein wanted "to break with Steinway," and demanded that Yamaha withdraw the "propaganda." Rubinstein "denied, in very strong words, that he ever said anything of this kind and that [Steinway] could use his denials in any way [they] wanted." Yamaha apologized to Steinway and cabled its Venezuelan dealer to pull the Rubinstein quote from the advertisements. The Venezuelan dealer wrote back to Yamaha that he had taken the Rubinstein quote "from the publicity material that you sent to us and we thought that if you have published it we also could do it." Yamaha acknowledged that Rubinstein had commented favorably on its piano, though whether he had understood that his words would be used for publicity purposes remained unclear. They did not wish to embarrass him, however, so were withdrawing all references to Rubinstein in Yamaha advertisements while he was a Steinway artist.[30]

The propaganda, the price, the improved quality, and the ability to deliver were all translating into sales of Yamaha grand pianos. By 1968 44 percent of grands purchased in the United States were imported, most of them Yamahas. The Japanese firm was doing so well that Steinway's advertising house of sixty-nine years (the longest relationship in advertising history), N. W. Ayer, left it for the more lucrative Yamaha account. Yamaha's best customers were major universities like Stanford, Michigan, and California and music institutes, conservatories, and academies in such cities as St. Louis, Philadelphia, and Toronto. These institutional customers were less concerned with the style of the case and more concerned with the lowest bid, good quality, and prompt delivery. Yamaha's quality, endorsements by other schools, and its ability to deliver within the school's budget year provided a crucial edge. Its success in sales provoked Henry Steinway to alert his board of directors that "for the long range our competition is Japan, with particular emphasis on Yamaha."[31]

To fight back, Henry brought together the National Piano Manufacturers Association to lobby Washington. The association started to have regular informal meetings to discuss industry problems and particularly the importation of pianos from Japan. Looking at the numbers since 1964, they noted that sales of their own pianos had declined 6 percent, while sales of imported pianos were up 316 percent. The charts and graphs over which they pored indicated that within a few years the imported piano would capture more than a third of the entire American piano market.[32]

The piano makers believed that the only way to stop this debacle was to convince President Nixon to reinstate the 40 percent piano tariff of 1930. In October 1969 Henry Steinway joined Morley P. Thompson, president of the National Piano Manufacturers Association and vice-president of D. H. Baldwin, to head a delegation, representing piano manufacturers, retail piano stores, and woodworking unions, to petition the Tariff Commission for an increase in import restrictions.[33]

The piano tariff had been decreasing since 1951 and was scheduled to be reduced again in 1969 under the Trade Expansion Act signed by President John F. Kennedy in 1962. The piano manufacturers lost the battle against the 1962 Act and knew that it was going to be an uphill fight in 1969, because the past thirteen petitions to increase tariffs, on goods ranging from fur hats to barber's chairs to canned sardines, had all been turned down.[34]

Henry remembered the enormous hearing room, with members of the Tariff Commission sitting at the front. The American piano manufacturers sat on one side, the Japanese businessmen on the other. Henry's testimony before the commission was brief. He spoke of Steinway's leadership in piano making and "our nation's cultural life." He claimed that "Steinway [was] not

The Tariff Commission hearing room in 1969. *Left to right:* John McLaren, head of Yamaha sales in the United States; Henry Z. Steinway; and Hiroshi Kawashima, president of Yamaha International Corporation.

affected by imports," but that he was concerned for the other seventeen domestic manufacturers. Steinway & Sons had more orders than it could fill. When Henry was asked "if any imported or domestic piano competes with Steinway in quality," his reply was: "Not in our opinion." This led to the cross-examiner representing the Japanese to ask him: "How come you're here complaining about tariffs, when you're sold out and you have more orders than you can deal with?" The cross-examiner then introduced a series of articles about Steinway being back-ordered for two years. He proposed to the commission that "if the major player, the highest priced of the domestic grand pianos was not affected by imports, then how could anybody claim substantive injury?" Henry explained that Steinway & Sons was sold out because they manufactured the best piano in the world (which explained the demand but not the limited supply). He added that the short supply was due to "the long years required to develop fine craftsmen."[35]

The testimony lasted five days, and in the end the American piano manufacturers won a meager victory. President Nixon signed a proclamation keeping the tariff at 13.5 percent for three years. The piano manufacturers did not get the increase they wanted, but they at least stopped the tariff from decreasing any further. Moreover, never before had the United States government acknowledged that Asia posed a threat to domestic manufacturing. The *Wall Street Journal* reported that this was the first "clear-cut example of a reversal of past commission policies." Prior to this decision, postwar U.S. trade relations with Japan had been based on a patronizing view of a war-devastated country and the need to have an ally in East Asia.

But there was no benefit for Steinway. The only surprise in the proclamation was that grand pianos were not included. Tariff reductions were to continue on grands and were set to decline to 8.5% by 1975. The tariff slowed Japanese upright sales for a while but not the sale of grands. So Steinway & Sons gained nothing.[36]

In 1972 Yamaha finally found a way onto some Steinway dealers' showroom floors and a permanent base on American turf. It bought the Everett piano factory and started manufacturing uprights in South Haven, Michigan, 90 miles across the lake from Chicago. It was a powerful statement to American music dealers that, no matter what happened to the tariff, Yamaha was here to stay. The problem for Steinway was that almost every Steinway dealer was selling either a Sohmer or an Everett as its second piano. The Everett piano was a good inexpensive alternative for customers who did not want to invest in a Steinway. It would be difficult for Steinway & Sons to object to a Yamaha made at the old Everett factory as the second piano, to sit alongside a Steinway grand in dealers' showrooms.[37]

The Japanese, with Yamaha in the lead, were manufacturing more pianos per week (4,627) than Steinway made per year (3,032); most (80 percent) of the Japanese production continued to be sold in Japan. The Japanese hourly wage was about 77 cents per hour, whereas the average American piano worker made $3.50 per hour. The combination of assembly-line manufacturing, a high degree of vertical integration, low wages, and a strong domestic market—all this enabled Yamaha in 1971 to sell its uprights in the United States for an average price of $791, whereas the Steinway average price was more than twice that amount at $1,700. In 1971 the Japanese shipped 50 percent of the grands sold in the United States.[38] Yamaha was shipping an improved grand piano in sufficient quantities (capitalizing on Steinway's ongoing backlog problem) and was enjoying "a growing reputation among people who know and like pianos, everywhere." By 1974 it was apparent that more and more Americans were buying, and telling their friends to buy, a Yamaha.[39]

After an industry sales meeting in Philadelphia in 1978 Henry jotted down a few notes about the Yamaha. He recognized that Yamaha grand scales were "all newly designed." The "rim was narrower and more attractive." The action was faster, and the felt centers of the bushings were "impregnated with a secret substance." When Henry asked Yamaha people whether they were using Teflon, they smiled and made no comment. At the meeting he viewed slides of Yamaha's "new $10 million foundry using new dry-sand plastic semi-permanent mold process." The foundry capacity was 1,000 plates a day, operated by only six workers. Yamaha bass strings were made by a new machine that controlled the "winding tension and eliminated rattles and dead ones."[40]

In 1980 Steinway & Sons shipped slightly more than three thousand pianos, and Yamaha sold more than twenty thousand instruments in the United States. Within five years Yamaha, Kawai, and a Korean piano maker, Young Chang, had captured 75 percent of American grand piano sales. They had taken over the school market, and a generation of young artists was growing up with the name Yamaha in front of them. Once it was a Steinway grand in the auditorium and Baldwin's upright in the classroom; now it was almost all Yamaha. Japan had become the largest piano-producing nation, manufacturing 273,000 instruments a year (one-third of the world's output). The United States was second. Steinway & Sons was no longer the "only truly international piano house, able to supply all over the world wherever there was a community with musical interests." Yamaha was as much a threat to Steinway sales in South Africa as in the United States. By 1987 Yamaha was producing almost every musical instrument known. Every day its global network of factories manufactured "900 pianos, 900 woodwind and brass instruments, 6,000 electronic keyboards, and 1,500 guitars, as well as a vast array of sound reinforcement equipment." Yamaha would become the world's largest music education institution. The number of Japanese households with a piano would swell to 19 percent by 1987, making Japan the largest piano market.[41]

Steinway, along with the rest of the American piano industry, had peaked for the decade in 1966. Henry explained: "Our costs were projected on making so many pianos, and we made that number, not more, not less . . . Everything was working right, and so we were able to make money. Not big money, but it was for us big money. . . . The next year, about the same. . . . Towards the end of the sixties you're going to see a sort of leveling out." But in capitalism success is measured by rate of expansion, not leveling off. If you stay the same, you lose.[42]

In 1970 Henry notified his stockholders that "there seems to be a downturn in the piano business, as in many other businesses." Steinway dealers were reporting that business was off both at home and abroad. Henry blamed the decline in sales on the factory strike of 1970, claiming that Steinway sold all it could make.[43] He was right; but the reason why it couldn't make more pianos was because of having an inefficient factory.

As these problems started to show up on the balance sheet, Henry found himself confronted with questions from his major stockholders. It was clear that something had to be done.

Epilogue: The CBS Sale and
Its Aftermath

In 1971 Steinway & Sons with its fine reputation was not lucrative. Henry knew that his company was not earning much on invested capital. It was assessed at $19 million and generated a profit of only $691,000 (3.6 percent). The return on a stockholder's investment was an anemic 7 percent. Henry recognized that "we could get as much in a government bond as we can from this." His cousin Henry Ziegler, one of the largest shareholders, asked Henry how he planned to get Steinway & Sons out of the doldrums.[1]

Ziegler was "anxious to get his money out." He recalled that one of the problems with Steinway & Sons at that time was the split within the family between the cousins who were not in the business and those who were running the company. The cousins in the business, Henry and John, had "a lot of psychic income that comes from being able to run the company, and especially in a business like Steinway, which had a lot of sex appeal." The rest of the family were left holding stock in a "company that didn't have much growth potential unless you diversified, and my concern was that we didn't have the expertise to diversify. . . . And so I was afraid we were either simply going to do exactly the same thing forever, which would have no growth and perhaps the risk in bad times of getting into trouble, or that at some point somebody would get tempted to diversify and do it wrong."[2]

Ziegler wasn't the only one complaining. Helmut Friedlaender, a shrewd German-Jewish investment banker who came to New York from Berlin in the early 1930s, represented William Rosenwald's 13 percent of Steinway stock. Friedlaender was not satisfied with the investment. In the spring of

1966 Henry offered to buy him out at $120 a share. Friedlaender smiled and replied: "Henry, you're trying to steal it. Now, I'm not that dumb." Henry asked how much Steinway stock was worth to him. Friedlaender jumped on that question and said, "Let's work on that value. . . . What are we going to do, what kind of things? Should we sell it? If so, who are the possible customers?" Henry, startled, tried to calm the waters by inviting Friedlaender to join the Steinway board. Friedlaender replied, "No, I don't want to be on any boards. But," he said, "I want you to answer my questions."[3]

Henry admitted that he had neither the interest nor the energy to take the company to another level. He recognized that "a business of our size and our ownership cannot survive in the long run. You have to either be small . . . privately owned, by one or two people, or a great big giant public corporation." Steinway & Sons was floundering somewhere in between. He also maintained that Steinway & Sons had too many family members looking for income but unwilling to plow profits back into a capital expansion. His brother John, as secretary of the company, was concerned that some of the major shareholders were into their eighties and that when they died, their stocks would have to be sold off to pay their estate inheritance tax. In other words a bulk of Steinway stock had to be evaluated, no easy task given how few stocks were traded, and would then go into non-family hands. It was only a matter of time, Henry speculated, before someone would buy enough shares to take over the company. There had already been at least twenty-five serious offers since Henry became president, including propositions from Wurlitzer, Beatrice Foods, and Magnavox.[4]

Henry was frustrated and began to drink. One martini before dinner had become two and was edging toward three.[5] Terrified that he would come to the same end as his father, Henry vowed that he wasn't going to let this business get to him, that Steinway & Sons wasn't going to kill him the way it had Theodore.[6]

Henry, then in his fifties, was too young to retire but too tired to continue. He claimed that there was no talent in his own family to succeed him. As he saw it, there was "my brother Theodore, my brother John, my cousin Charles, . . . all of whom were ready to do what I said, but not really movers and shakers. . . . They were just riding along being Steinways." Henry's children were either too young or not interested at the time in piano making.[7]

Henry's sister, Betty Chapin, believed that her boys' leadership abilities had been underestimated. Her sons felt that efforts had not been made to interest their generation in piano making. Henry would say to Betty when she raised this point that "if anybody wanted to work there, all they have to do is come see me." Henry insisted that the boys never expressed any interest to him. Betty never bought that answer; she always had "the feeling that anybody named Chapin was not going to get quite as warm a welcome as somebody named Steinway." As it turned out, even the Steinway name wasn't a passport to the head of the boardroom.[8]

Henry had been thinking about selling Steinway & Sons to a large wealthy company since 1966. Beatrice Foods had offered him $21 million in 1968, but at that point he was not ready to sell. But by 1970, with no successor in sight, the union slipping out of his control, complaints about Teflon, Yamaha looming larger than ever, and no energy to set a new course, Henry was ready to sell Steinway & Sons.[9]

Friedlaender and Ziegler had kept up the pressure on him either to take Steinway in a new direction or sell. They met with Henry, they met without him. Henry recalled a lunch meeting with Friedlaender, when he was, as usual, leaning on Henry, "in a nice way," to make something of Steinway assets. Henry finally said: "Well, Helmut, I really think that we've got to sell the business." Friedlaender said, "All right, now let's talk about to who." Their first try was a "super secret" meeting in July 1970, arranged by a friend of Friedlaender's, in a downtown New York club with the Kawai piano makers from Japan.[10]

In May 1971 Henry, with support from his board of directors, initiated more formal, but still confidential, inquiries into selling Steinway & Sons. Several months later Robert G. Campbell, president of the Musical Instrument Division of the CBS Columbia Group asked Henry to join him and Harvey L. Schein, president of CBS–Columbia Group, for lunch at the Oak Room in the Plaza Hotel. CBS was putting together its own musical instrument division which already included Fender Guitars, Rodgers Organs, V. C. Squire (string makers for musical instruments), and Electro Music (manufacturers of speakers for electric organs and guitar). Now they wanted Steinway pianos.[11]

Just after New Year Henry attended a meeting with Friedlaender and Ziegler, at which they "agreed to ask for 500,000 shares of CBS (stock) in a tax-free exchange (for Steinway stock), valued at $23 million." By 3 February there was an agreement with CBS, in principal, to a price of $20,437,750 (375,000 CBS shares at $54.50 per share), with Henry remaining president of Steinway & Sons. Six days later Henry waited tensely for the final call proclaiming it a fait accompli. Henry was in a board of directors meeting when it came. He was so anxious that he asked Eddie Peckerman to answer the phone. Peckerman took the call and signaled Henry that the CBS directors had met and approved the purchase.[12]

Henry went home and made a series of phone calls to dealers, "which meant a long, emotional chat with each one." That night he boarded a Lufthansa flight for Hamburg. He had told Walter Gunther why he was coming, emphasizing that "it will be a very quick trip" and referring to it being "the correct time to come and see Mr. Gunther," who was recovering from a heart attack.[13] He added that he would visit the London house briefly on his way home. Henry remembered that trip as "the worst two or three days I ever spent." He recalled the flight over, sitting "on the plane all night and cogitating" about what he had just done and how he would "tell these guys we've sold the business."

The following morning Gunther picked him up at the airport and convened a small group at his office. Henry made a brief speech to the five or six in the room. As he reported the sale, they all looked at him without expression and without a word. Gunther later noted the irony that the sale would be announced 175 years, almost to the day, from the birth of the founder, Heinrich Steinweg.

Next morning Henry boarded a plane to London, where he was met by Lionel Squibb. As he told Squibb the news, on the car ride from the airport, he watched him sink to the floor. Squibb asked Henry not to tell anyone at dinner that night, since it would spoil a festive Friday night's fun, and said that he would break the news the following day. That night, Henry recounted "we had a dinner, we had sherry and . . . sat around, and I'm dying. Then I don't get on a late plane, I go to bed and take the first plane home in the morning," never telling anybody the real reason for my visit.[14]

On Monday Gunther sent out a letter to Steinway dealers, workers, and the music trade announcing that "the family council has come to the decision to accept an offer from the CBS . . . to merge with them in order to ensure that also in the future the Steinway pianos will keep their dominant position." The letter, signed by Walter Gunther, claimed that the aging of the Steinway brothers and the lack of interest in piano making on the part of the next generation of Steinways were the reasons for the sale. He assured the music world that "CBS will guarantee the continuity of the Steinway tradition not only in regards to cultural, but also to economical aspects."[15]

The sale wasn't official until the Steinway board meeting more than two months later. But there was no doubt that it would be approved and that those who wanted to sell—Henry, Ziegler, and Friedlaender—were in control. Henry choreographed the final stockholders' meeting to be a happy event. He invited them all to a meeting and a buffet lunch afterwards. About seventy people, mostly family who had not seen each other for years and some who had never seen the factory, crowded into the top floor of the factory in Queens. Henry explained the financial advantages to them. They were getting a nontaxable exchange of 7.1159 shares of CBS stock for one

John Steinway announcing the acceptance of the CBS offer to buy Steinway & Sons in 1972. Reproduced by permission of *The Music Trades*.

share of Steinway & Sons stock, free of any restrictions and immediately negotiable with any stockbroker. One Steinway & Sons share, which never sold for more than $200 and had recently been trading for about $135, was now worth about $370. CBS stock had come down a few dollars since February, resulting in a loss of over $1 million to Steinway stockholders, but it was still a good deal. The vote (by shares, not by person) was overwhelmingly in favor of the merger with CBS. The papers were signed by Henry and John. Henry then announced to his New York and European workers that they were all now working for CBS.[16]

Not everyone was happy with the sale, however. A few people were concerned about "continuation of quality" under CBS. Betty's son Samuel had written a letter to "dear Uncle John" to let him know that his "immediate reaction was that it would be a shame if this had to happen." He wanted to know how John personally felt "about the proposed merger, questions of fiscal practicality and necessity aside." John wrote back to his nephew that he thought the sale to CBS was a "bloody shame." He blamed "outside investors as well as quite a large proportion of 'outer' family and, of course, some of the 'inner' family [who] were more interested in making a fast buck than in preservation of a tradition of four generations." John ended his note to Sam acknowledging that "I feel a little like an unwilling funeral director!"[17]

Sam and his twin brother Theodore then sent a personal letter to all the stockholders. They disputed Henry's claim that the next generation had no interest in continuing the business, stating their own interest and saying how "unenthusiastic"—not to say discouraging—Henry had been when they worked at the factory. Both boys emphasized that their generation had not yet "committed themselves to other vocational interests" and that several of them could be part of the company's future. They were concerned about what CBS would do to the quality of the Steinway piano.[18]

Henry also received complaints from other family members, including his brother Fritz, who voted against the merger, and his mother Ruth, who "felt that (Henry) had betrayed the faith." Her husband had given his life to save Steinway & Sons, and now her son was selling out. Betty described her mother as "very, very strong-willed, very conscious of her place as wife of Theodore Steinway and then mother of Henry Steinway," but not a member of the company in any way, shape, or form." This made it all the more surprising when she stood up at the stockholders' meeting and condemned the sale. "She just wanted to go on record as feeling that this was a shame, and perhaps there might have been another way to go about it." She charged CBS to continue to "make the finest damn piano that can be made," sat down, and voted with her son to sell.[19]

In the final years of family ownership there had been little investment in new equipment. So when CBS acquired Steinway & Sons, the factories in New York and Hamburg needed millions of dollars' worth of capital improvements. CBS decided to modernize the equipment and the buildings but wanted a 10 percent return on their investment, counting on profits coming from increased efficiency and production. From the beginning some feared that CBS would compromise quality for quantity. Henry Steinway periodically reminded Robert G. Campbell, president of CBS Musical Instruments, that the piano business was not a high-profit or high-return industry. What CBS wanted was possible in broadcasting but not in pianos.

CBS cut inventory as a means of reducing its investment. It also accelerated the passage of lumber from the yards, cutting into the required one-year drying time. Henry tried to point out to Campbell that, unlike other industries, piano manufacturing did not have an inventory that would become worthless because of changes in product or consumer preference, and that it could not cut inventory and expect to increase production. It needed about three months of supplies on hand to run the factory at full speed. Henry also argued that, relative to other companies, Steinway & Sons' inventory as a percent of assets, at 13 percent, was much lower than General Electric's, at 23 percent, or General Motors, at 25 percent. Henry warned Campbell that orders to increase production, cut inventory, and reduce payroll "will destroy Steinway."

CBS decided to concentrate production and sales on the more profitable larger-size grands, abandoning the smaller-grand market to the competition. But it soon realized that production was limited by the same obstacle that had restricted Steinway in the past—an inefficient old factory with a capacity production ceiling. This could only be remedied by building a substantial modern one-floor physical plant. Henry reminded Campbell that this was one of the reasons why he had sold the business.[20]

Although production wasn't as high as CBS wanted it to be, profits, relative to past years, soared. In 1974 Steinway sales were the highest ever in America and Europe, almost $10 million, yielding a pre-tax profit of $2.5 million. It was the best year Steinway ever had, despite a long strike in Hamburg. Inflation was driving sales. Customers recognized that the durable value of a Steinway piano was a hedge against the decreasing value of the dollar.[21]

But in November 1976 Henry reported to Campbell that the retail trade was weakening. Part of the problem, he thought, was that "the word going around in music lovers' circles [was] that Steinway is not what it used to be before CBS."[22] While Steinway sales were slipping, the business in repairing used Steinways was booming. Even the Juilliard School was opting to repair used Steinways. The work was being done by ex-Steinway employees in their own shops, plus current Steinway employees at night and on the weekends.

Henry had been telling Campbell to watch the quality, and periodically he would invoke the name of Chairman Paley, referring to Paley's promise "to put quality first." No wonder tension increased between Campbell and Henry. The latter was trying to hold on to his power and his heritage. As far as he was concerned, Steinway & Sons was still his company, and he wasn't going to listen to Campbell or follow a lot of the CBS procedures. Campbell wanted monthly reports, but what Henry sent him were in effect personal accounts of what he believed was right and wrong about the company and the piano trade. Each report contained a history lesson for Campbell and some warnings about the future of the business. The reports were critiques of quality and bureaucracy, not detailed progress reports on how Steinway & Sons was carrying out Campbell's directives.[23] In May 1977 Campbell called Henry to Chicago and told him that he was replacing him as president of Steinway & Sons with Robert Bull. He asked Henry to remain as chairman of the board, with limited responsibilities.

Bull, the first ever non-Steinway president of Steinway & Sons, had been active in the piano industry and had been running the Fender (guitar) division of CBS Musical Instruments. His Steinway presidency was stormy. Artists continued to question the quality of the piano, and now that Henry was no longer president, their concern escalated. They started to refer to Bull's regime as the "dark period" in Steinway's history. Steinway critics claimed that, due to pressures to increase production, the quality of the workmanship was suffering, and there was no Henry Steinway to stop CBS. Al Daniels agreed that CBS hurt the piano by rushing production and at the same time cutting back on the number of people at the bench. In 1978 he quit because "it was not like a piano factory, it was not like Steinway."[24]

While trying to increase production, Bull was given the nod, according to Henry, to ignore him. Henry's recourse was to go above Bull's head to John Phillips, a CBS vice-president. The friction between Henry and Bull came to a head when Bull fired Henry's son Bill, who was working in the engineering and design department, and Henry's friend Henry Bamman, sales manager at Steinway Hall. Henry threatened to quit and as a parting gesture presented Phillips with a list of ideas and complaints about the way Bull was managing the company. Henry claimed that this list was instrumental in getting Bull fired in December 1978.[25]

The next president, Peter Perez (January 1978–May 1982) brought Henry's son Bill back but could not quell rumors about the declining quality of Steinway pianos. There was grumbling about inferior materials and fewer good craftsmen at the factory—"Steinways [did] not seem to be up to snuff anymore." Perez was replaced by Lloyd Meyer (May 1982–September 1985), who had been with Lowrey Organ and was running Guibrensen Organ, part of CBS Musical Instrument Division. With Meyer's appointment, CBS had named more presidents to Steinway & Sons than the company had had since the turn of the century.[26]

In the mid-1980s CBS was engaged in trying to fend off a takeover bid by Ted Turner and needed to raise $1 billion to repurchase CBS stock. It won that round, but, to replenish its coffers, started selling off assets. In December 1984 CBS announced its intention to sell all its music companies, including Steinway & Sons. It would later insist that the sale of its Musical Instrument Division had nothing to do with being starved for cash and more to do with corporate policy to focus on their basic interests: broadcasting, recorded music, and publishing.

Although Steinway & Sons was making money (1983 pre-tax profits were $7.5 million on about $50 million in sales), CBS's Musical Instrument Division had been operating in the red since 1980, with accumulated losses of more than $40 million. In 1985 a group of Boston investors bought some of the companies that made up CBS Musical Instrument Division and set themselves up as Steinway Musical Properties, Incorporated. The principal owners were John P. and Robert Birmingham, brothers whose family had owned the White Fuel Company, the largest distributors of oil in New England before it was bought out by Texaco in the 1960s.[27]

In 1992 the Birminghams did something that Steinway & Sons had resisted throughout its history. They introduced a mid-priced piano. Every time the idea had been raised before, it had been rejected because Steinway wanted to stay in the exclusive niche, selling only a top-of-the-line prestige piano. The Birminghams believed that they could retain the high end of the market while providing a lower-priced Steinway for "customers who [were] not yet ready to acquire a Steinway." They named their new piano after their hometown of Boston.

Further, the "Boston" would be manufactured by Kawai. New Steinway designs were given to Kawai to produce pianos in Japan, using sophisticated technology. As recently as 1973, Henry had warned CBS that "cooperation between Steinway and Kawai will do us harm." Less than twenty years later, in 1992, Kawai was building a piano for Steinway & Sons under the name "Boston."[28]

The Birminghams could not shake the bad publicity that had started under CBS. The question remained: were they making the same-quality Steinway as when the family owned the company? Some reviewers said no. Edward Rothstein, music critic for the *New York Times*, has been very critical of the recent Steinway. He reported that although hopes were raised when the Birminghams bought Steinway & Sons, "there are those in the musical world who still harbor misgivings about its current management and direction." In 1988 he openly cautioned the owners that "the Steinway, with its bright upper notes and clear projection, has come to define the modern 'public' piano sound. If the Steinway declines, so will the sound we hear from recordings and concert halls, the expectations we have of compositions, and even the very desire to hear the instrument that defines our musical heritage."[29]

Steinway & Sons president Bruce Stevens responded to the Rothstein criticism by assuring him that "the quality of today's Steinway pianos, far from being in decline, is in fact universally acclaimed. For example, 93 percent of all piano soloists performing with major orchestras in North America during the 1994–95 season played exclusively on Steinways. The instruments they are playing were manufactured not in previous decades but within the last five years. Similarly, virtually all finalists in the world's major piano competitions insist on playing on today's Steinway." In "a recent tour of the Steinway factory" even Rothstein had a better impression of the Steinway. He was struck by the "serious effort to improve the instrument." Rothstein reported that "the final stages of manufacturing received more attention than they did a few years ago. Outside technicians have also reported improvements in Steinways, a heartening sign."[30]

While manufacturing and sales improved, the entire industry was surprised in April 1995 when the Birminghams announced that they were selling Steinway & Sons for $100 million to the Selmer Company, manufacturer of clarinets and saxophones. Selmer is owned by Dana Messina and Kyle Kirkland, former Drexel Burnham Lambert investment bankers.[31] The Birminghams sold Steinway & Sons because it made good business sense and they wanted to pursue separate investments. Robert and John Birmingham were not planning to oversee Steinway & Sons together, forever. John explained that "it had become clear that for us Steinway was never to be a family business, passed along to sons and daughters. . . . Moreover, at my age, if I did not act soon, the proceeds from a sale might not be so easily invested in some enterprise which could involve my children." It was an excellent time to sell. Steinway revenues and sales had never been this good. Sales for fiscal year 1 July 1994 to 30 June 1995 were $125 million, up from $102 million in the previous year, and the number of grand pianos shipped was up to 2,829 from 2,569.[32]

The piano is still manufactured in Queens, at the same site, and also in Hamburg. Steinway Hall on West 57th Street remains the New York showroom. Henry is the only remaining Steinway at Steinway & Sons. It was part of his 1972 agreement with CBS that he would retire at age sixty-five. He sat in the chairman's seat until 1980 and after a series of gala parties retired on a CBS pension. He is now perched in a large office on the second floor of Steinway Hall, busy preserving his father's and grandfather's papers and looking through the piles of Steinway memorabilia, artifacts, photographs, and documents that his father, Theodore, and brother John accumulated. He has become the organizer, filer, and keeper of Steinway's past. The company provides him with office space in exchange for his promotional appearances at conventions, dealers' meetings, and important sales, replacing his late brother John, who once covered most of the "meet Mr. Steinway" functions.

Henry's role is purely ceremonial. The craft tradition includes a signature of the artisan somewhere on his work. But Henry is brought out by Steinway salespeople to sign pianos manufactured in a factory he rarely visits. Still, customers feel honored to meet a real live Steinway, to see the tradition embodied in a flesh-and-blood person. In a world in which there is no Mr. Kellogg and no Ms. Pillsbury, it is moving to meet the last Mr. Steinway at Steinway & Sons.

Notes

The following abbreviations appear in the notes.

AS   Albert Steinway
BD   Board of Directors
BD Min   Minutes, Board of Directors, Steinway & Sons
BS   William R. Steinway (Billie)
CFTS   C. F. Theodor Steinway
CHS   Charles H. Steinway
CS   Charles G. Steinway
FTS   Frederick T. Steinway (Fritz)
HES   Heinrich Engelhard Steinweg
HSJr   Henry Steinway, Jr.
HWTS   Henry W. T. Steinway
HZS   Henry Z. Steinway
HZSF   Henry Z. Steinway's personal files
JS   John Steinway
LWA   Steinway Archives at LaGuardia and Wagner Archives, Queens, N.Y.
Min   Steinway & Sons Minute Books
MR CBS   Monthly report to Robert G. Campbell, president, CBS Musical
            Instruments
MT   *Music Trades*
NYT   *New York Times*
PI   Personal interview with the author
S Min   Minutes, Steinway & Sons stockholders' meeting
S&S   Steinway & Sons
TES   Theodore E. Steinway
WS   William Steinway

WSD   William Steinway diary
Yale   Oral history, American Music Series, Steinway Project, Yale University
School of Music

CHAPTER 1. THE AMERICANIZATION OF STEINWEG

1. On the April 1860 factory opening see Supreme Court, *Henry Steinway & William Steinway* v. *Sophie Steinway et al.*, 4 Aug. 1870, in "Steinway Real Estate History," HZSF. On the 30 Aug. 1860 press party see *Frank Leslie's Illustrated Newspaper* (New York), 22, 29 Sept. 1860; *NYT*, 16 Sept. 1860. See also letter from CS to CFTS, 16 Oct. 1860, F34 L1, LWA. On the number of Steinway workers and the average pay per year see Bureau of the Census, *Products of Industry, New York State*, Schedule 5, Ward 19, Division 1, 1 June 1860 (Washington, D.C.), p. 3.

2. HES was born on 22 Feb. 1797 or 15 Feb. 1797, depending on which source one refers to. See *Church Book of Wolfshagen*, 1825, p. 426, no. 3, and "Biographical Sketch of Henry Engelhard Steinway," in *Encyclopedia of Contemporary Biography of New York*, vol. 2 (New York, 1882), p. 1.

3. Elbert Hubbard, *The Story of the Steinways* (East Aurora, N.Y., 1921). "Henry Engelhard Steinway," pp. 1–2. Daniel Spillane, *History of the American Pianoforte, Its Technical Development and the Trade* (1890; rpt. New York, 1969), pp. 213–216. On church records in Wolfshagen see file "Grotrian Name Change Documents," no. 9093/III A, p. 5, LWA. Ronald F. Ratcliffe, *Steinway* (San Francisco, 1989), pp. 15–18. On Elbert Hubbard see Nancy Jackson, "From the Sublime to the Lucrative: Elbert Hubbard's Career in Culture," *Discovery* (special supplement of the *Harvard Magazine*), Sept.–Oct. 1984. On HES's instrument making, see the testimony of his army roommate, CFTS to his parents and siblings, 25 Dec. 1855, F29, LWA.

4. For one version of HES's life after serving in the military, see Alfred Dolge, *Pianos and Their Makers* (1911; rpt. New York, 1972), pp. 299–300. See also Fanny Morris Smith, *A Noble Art, Three Lectures on the Revolution and Construction of the Piano* (New York, 1892), pp. 110–111. On the Brand story see the Seesen newspaper *Beobachter*, 5 Nov. 1886. According to Andor Izsak of the Hochschule für Musik und Theater Hannover, European Center for Jewish Music, "The greatest era of synagogue music originated [in Seesen and] influenced the music of synagogues all over the world. . . . Seesen was the place where the first organ was introduced into a temple in 1810" (letter to HZS, 14 June 1894, LWA). On his apprenticeship in Goslar see HES obituary in *NYT*, 8 Feb. 1871, p. 5.

5. On HES's property in 1829 see "What Actually Happened, Our Version, in More Detail than 'Bits of History,'" typescript for *Grotrian* case, n.d., "HZS: Bits of History," HZSF. On Julianne's family see her birth certificate, LWA. On life in Seesen see "Henry Engelhard Steinway," p. 2. John F. Majeski, Jr., "Steinway, A Century of Distinguished Family Enterprise," *MT*, 10 Oct. 1953. The population of Seesen in 1857 was 2,834.

6. On HES founding his business in Seesen and reasons for leaving after 1845 see WS, "An Exposition of Facts," for the court case *Steinway & Sons, New York, Hamburg* v. *Grotrian, Helfferich, Schulz, Successors to Th. Steinweg*, Brunswick, Jan. 1893, in "HZS: Bits of History." On HES's success in Seesen see *NYT*, 1 Jan. 1886. On CFTS at the Brunswick fair see Smith, *Noble Art*, pp. 26, 113. On early nineteenth-century piano making in England, France, and Germany see Arthur Loesser, *Men, Women and Pianos: A Social History* (1954; rpt. with new foreword and preface, New York, 1990), pp. 586–587, and Cyril Ehrlich, *The Piano: A History* (London, 1976), pp. 16–20.

7. On CS and the 1848 revolution see TES, *People and Pianos* (New York, 1953), p. 11. On the zollverein see "Henry Engelhard Steinway," p. 3; HES obituary, *NYT*.

8. On CFTS's 1847 trip to American see *Wochenblatt*, Region Gandersheim, "Auswanderung" no. 62, 11 Aug. 1847. On CS's voyage see manifest of passengers, District of New York, Port of New York, on English bark *England's Queen*, 13 June 1849, which included under

"Steerage" "Carl Steinweg, Age 20, Male, Instrumentenmacher." Dolge, *Pianos and Their Makers*, p. 301. "Henry Engelhard Steinway," p. 3. CS arrived in New York in 1849; *Henry Steinway & William Steinway*, v. *Sophie Steinway et al.*, June 1870, HZSF. On German piano makers and professional music making in New York see Loesser, *Men, Women and Pianos*, pp. 493, 497; Nancy Jane Groce, "Musical Instrument Making in New York City during the Eighteenth and Nineteenth Centuries," vol. 1 (Ph.D. diss., University of Michigan, 1982), pp. 45–46, 114–116, 185. On shipwrecks and pirates as a supply of pianofortes see Rosamond E. M. Harding, *The Piano-Forte* (1933; rpt. New York, 1973), p. 80. Also see I. N. Phelps Stokes, *The Iconography of Manhattan Island* (New York, 1967), 5:1814–1816, 1820, 1823–1824.

9. WS, "American Musical Instruments," in *1795–1895, One Hundred Years of American Commerce*, ed. Chauncey M. Depew (New York, 1895), p. 513; "Henry Engelhard Steinway," p. 3. On the Astor Place riot and the cholera epidemic see Stokes, *Manhattan Island*, 5:1820–1823; Peter George Buckley, "To the Opera House: Culture and Society in New York City, 1820–1860" (Ph.D. diss., State University of New York, Stony Brook, 1984), pp. 3–6.

10. The Steinwegs left Seesen on 7 May and arrived in New York on 9 June 1850: "What Actually Happened," HZSF. On the sale of the house in Seesen see Actum in the ducal office of Seesen, 10 Jan. 1850, in "Seesen House and Shop Contract," HZSF. See also "CFTS's Notebook, 1851–1858," LWA. On CFTS see WS, "Exposition of Facts," HZSF.

11. In 1850, 212,796 immigrants, including 45,535 Germans, arrived at the port of New York: Stokes, *Manhattan Island*, 5:1823. In 1850, 82,000 people left Germany: Theodore S. Hammerow, *Restoration, Revolution, Reaction, Economics and Politic in Germany, 1815–1871* (Princeton, 1958), p. 83. On German immigration see Stanley Nadel, "Kleindeutschland: New York City's Germans, 1845–1880" (Ph.D. diss., Columbia University, 1981), pp. 1, 48, 81. On German immigration and music societies see Howard B. Furer, ed., *The Germans in America, 1607–1970: A Chronology and Factbook* (Dobbs Ferry, N.Y., 1973), pp. 36–37, 40–44. On German musicians coming to the United States in the 1840s see Loesser, *Men, Women and Pianos*, pp. 490–494; Groce, "Musical Instrument Making," p. 114.

12. Of the 204 musical instrument establishments in the United States, 58 were in New York; see Groce, "Musical Instrument Making," pp. 45–46, 135, 353, 354, 393, 394, 409. On their employees in 1850 see HSJr and CS to CFTS, Oct. 1850, F1 L1, LWA.

13. On HES working for Bacon & Raven see advertisement for Francis Bacon's "Paragon" pianos in *American Musician*, 10 Mar. 1888. On 1850s salaries see Groce, "Musical Instrument Making," pp. 135–137. On HES's illiteracy see HZS to the family, 11 Mar. 1971, LWA.

14. On Pirsson see R. M. Bent, typescript from *MT*, 30 Dec. 1893, and Harding, *Piano-Forte*, pp. 109–110.

15. CS to CFTS, 1853, F2 L2, LWA. CS admitted that "nobody can live here for under $2.50 to $3 a week."

16. On the "truck" system see WS, "American Musical Instruments," p. 513. "Our Piano & Organ Makers," *New York Herald*, 13 Feb. 1887, p. 17.

17. The first copartnership agreement was not signed until 30 Apr. 1861; but many later documents specify 5 Mar. 1853 as the date on which S&S was founded. The agreement was never filed in the county clerk's office, but a note appended to it states that on 28 Mar. 1876 it was Plaintiff Exhibit no. 1 in a lawsuit. WS claimed: "we commenced operations on the 1st of May 1853, but did not enter into a written copartnership until the 1st of May 1856." See *Henry Steinway & William Steinway v. Sophie Steinway et al.*, 4 Aug. 1870, HZSF. On initial investment and import business in 1853 see R. G. Dun & Company, Baker Library, Harvard University Graduate School of Business Administration, vol. 376 (1853), pp. 288, 509.

18. On small imported instruments see Groce, "Musical Instrument Making," p. 81. On the 1850s piano trade see Ehrlich, *Piano*, pp. 48, 50, and advertisement for "Paragon" pianos; Edward Rothstein, "A Piano as Salvation, Temptation and Star," *NYT*, 4 Jan. 1994. On the piano in the home see Craig H. Roell, *The Piano in America, 1890–1940*, pp. 5, 8, 15–18, 23, 26. See also Clifford E. Clark, Jr., *The American Family Home* (Chapel Hill, 1986) pp. 17, 18, 34, 67.

19. Bechstein and CFTS were friends; see letter of 20 Aug. 1868, LWA. On Chickering (1823–1908) see E. F. Brooks, Jr., "Aeolian American Division of Aeolian Corporation, East Rochester, New York," typescript, n.d., LWA. On Chickering after 1853 see Spillane, *American Pianoforte,* pp. 260–269. On the Chickering fire see "Destructive Fire on Washington Street," *Boston Daily Evening Transcript,* 2 Dec. 1852. On his business 1852–53 see Richard G. Parker, *A Tribute to the Life and Character of Jonas Chickering* (Boston, 1854), pp. 77–78, 83–84, 112–113. The Chickering building, now converted into artists' housing, still exists on Tremont Street in Boston. This is cited in Gary J. Kornblith, "The Craftsman as Industrialist: Jonas Chickering and the Transformation of American Piano Making," *Business History Review* 59 (Autumn 1985): 349, 365–367.

20. The first recorded sale, on 16 Sept. 1853, was piano no. 483, to Griswold in Brooklyn. On the 1853–54 business see "Henry Engelhard Steinway," p. 3. On square piano production in the United States see WS, "American Musical Instruments," pp. 511–512; Cynthia Adams Hoover, "The Steinways and Their Pianos in the Nineteenth Century," *Journal of American Music* 7 (1981): 52–53. By the end of 1859 S&S had made 2,912 pianos, only 103 of which were grands. The first grands were nos. 791 and 792, 19 Apr. 1856. See Steinway Number Books, LWA, and Roy Kehl, "Steinway & Sons First Grand Pianos," typescript, 12 Feb. 1994, LWA. WS was a bellyman until Mar. 1854; HSJr did finishing work until Dec. 1853; and CS did regulating until Aug. 1854. According to the Number Book they made 11 pianos in 1853 and 74 in 1854.

21. CS to H. Gaehl, piano maker in Baltimore, 17 Feb. 1854, F30, LWA. On Doretta see *S&S Mitteilungen* 63 (Jan. 1923): 338. On the use of the home as a salesroom see Groce, "Musical Instrument Making," p. 80. R. G. Dun and Company, v. 376, pp. 288, 509.

22. CS to CFTS, 1 Dec. 1854, F31, LWA. On 1850s economy and marketing see Wayne G. Broehl, Jr., *John Deere's Company: A History of Deere & Company and Its Times* (New York, 1984), pp. 118, 120. On employment and production figures for piano makers in 1855 see Groce, "Musical Instrument Making," pp. 66–67.

23. On the 1855 fair in New York see Loesser, *Men, Women and Pianos,* p. 496; Hoover, "Steinways and Their Pianos," pp. 52–53; HES obituary, *NYT.* On the New York Crystal Palace exhibition and fire see *NYT,* 11 May 1864, p. 4; 6 Oct. 1858, pp. 4, 8; 7 Oct. 1858, p. 1; Stokes, *Manhattan Island,* 5:1878. On London's Crystal Palace exhibition of 1851, see *The American System of Manufactures,* "The Report of the Committee on the Machinery of the United States 1855 . . ." (Edinburgh, 1969), introduction by Nathan Rosenberg, pp. 3, 19. On the 35 U.S. prizes see *Progress Commerce 1893* (London). See "First Prize Medals Awarded to Steinway and Sons' Pianos in This Country," Steinway catalog, 1866, LWA.

24. On business in 1855 see CFTS to his parents and siblings, 25 Dec. 1855, F29, LWA. See also Groce, "Musical Instrument Making," pp. 51, 66–67, and Broehl, *John Deere's Company,* p. 124. The "Statement of Stock, Assets, & Liabilities of Messrs Steinway & Sons, New York, May 1st, 1856," reveals that manufacturing expanded throughout the 1850s. See Balance Sheet, 1 May 1856, LWA. On the panic of 1857 see Stokes, *Manhattan Island,* 5:1870. On bank failures in Philadelphia see CFTS to parents and siblings, 12 Oct. 1857, F23, LWA. On R. G. Dun and Company reports see R. G. Dun and Company, v. 376, pp. 288, 509. See Groce, "Musical Instrument Making," p. 139. On yearly draw for the partners see "Rough Attempts by HZS: Growth in Early Years," typescript, n.d., HZSF. On yearly production numbers for 1853–60 see Number Books 483–4093. On Steinway factory wages see Joseph D. Weeks, Bureau of the Census, *The Statistics of Wages in Manufacturing Industries, 1880,* vol. 20, "Pianos and Organs" (Washington, D.C.), p. 292. On new consumers see Stuart Blumin, *The Emergence of the Middle Class, Social Experience in the American City, 1760–1900* (New York, 1989), pp. 138–139, 149, 158, 159, 162, 184–185.

25. With regard to the various factory and showroom sites, the company started in 1853 on Varick Street, then moved to 88 Walker Street in 1854. In 1856 the factory was at 91 Mercer, at the back of 85 Varick (used only for making keys), and the showroom was at 84 and 86 Walker. In 1857 space was rented at 96 Crosby and 113 Walker. There was also a lumber storage site on

23rd Street. In 1858 the showroom expanded to include 82 Walker. The family's home, at 199 Hester, had also been added to the operation by 1858. In 1859 the 91 Mercer factory was expanded to include 87, 89, 90, and 109 Mercer. The properties at 82 and 84 Walker remained the main showrooms and WS's headquarters, until Steinway Hall, on 14th Street, was built in 1864. The key-making department moved from 85 Varick to 83 Walker in 1859. For references to all these sites see Stock Books for 1857–60, LWA.

26. On the movement of piano manufacturers uptown see Groce, "Musical Instrument Making," pp. 81–82. On WS's purchase of the property 1858–59 see Supreme Court, Special Term, Hon. Charles Donohue, Justice, *William Steinway et al.* v. *Julia Steinway et al.,* 1 Feb. 1876. In two years Steinway would outgrow this building and add another 75,000 square feet, changing the **L** to a **U**: CS and HSJr to CFTS, 23 Sept. 1859; S&S to Messrs. Kinyoun & Newton, 2 June 1859, found in stamp collection of Albert Spencer; copy in LWA. On the factory see *Frank Leslie's Illustrated Newspaper,* 22, 29 Sept. 1860.

27. On the $150,000 cost and details of the new factory see WS, "Wholesale Price Lists and Circulars," Apr. 1860, p. 5, LWA. S&S catalog, 1881, LWA.

28. On Chickering's 1853 factory see Parker, *Jonas Chickering,* pp. 83–84, cited in Kornblith, "Craftsman as Industrialist," pp. 366–367. On outside milling and the cost of connecting a machine to a power source see Polly Anne Earl, "Craftsman and Machines: The Nineteenth-Century Furniture Industry," in *Technological Innovation and the Decorative Arts,* ed. Ian M. G. Quimby and Polly Anne Earl, Winterthur Conference Report 1973 (Charlottesville, Va., 1984), pp. 309, 311, 315, 316, 318. On the woodworking industry in America see Nathan Rosenberg, *Perspectives in Technology* (Cambridge, 1976), pp. 32–49; Merritt Roe Smith, "From Craftsman to Mechanic: The Harpers Ferry Experience, 1798–1854," in *Technological Innovation and the Decorative Arts,* pp. 120–126; David A. Hounshell, *From the American System to Mass Production, 1800–1932, The Development of Manufacturing Technology in the United States* (Baltimore, 1984), pp. 125–151. On the 1860 engravings of the inside of the factory see *Frank Leslie's Illustrated Newspaper,* 22, 29 Sept. 1860. On the use of steam power in furniture factories see Page Talbott, "Shop and Factory, Philadelphia Furniture Makers and Manufacturers, 1850–1880," typescript, n.d., p. 5, LWA.

29. By 1864 some finer machines were added to do scroll work and round corners; see *Frank Leslie's Illustrated Newspaper,* 28 May 1864. On machines and piano production see Groce, "Musical Instrument Making," pp. 90, 128, 133–134, 154–158. On machines replacing 900 men, see S&S catalog, 1881. In 1850 HSJr wrote to CFTS (Oct. 1850, F1 L1, LWA) that ten workers made one piano per week. On making a Steinway in 1853 see Smith, *Noble Art,* p. 46. On learning by experience see Nathan Rosenberg, *Inside the Blackbox, Technology and Economics* (Cambridge, 1982), pp. 120–121. Alfred D. Chandler, Jr., cited in David A. Hounshell, *From the American System to Mass Production, 1800–1932* (Baltimore: Johns Hopkins University Press, 1984), p. 127.

CHAPTER 2. INVENTING AND MARKETING THE MODERN PIANO

1. On Henry's fear of conscription and plans for one visit see HSJr and CFTS, 30 Mar. 1861, F35, LWA. On CFTS's wife's quibbles with his brothers see Johanna Steinweg to CS, 22 Feb. 1864, F41, LWA. On their trip, which in fact lasted from 10 May, the day of the inauguration of Steinway Hall, to 2 July 1864 see "Biographical Sketch of C. F. Theodore Steinway," in *Encyclopedia of Contemporary Biography of New York,* vol. 3 (New York, 1883), p. 1. On family reunion see WSD, 24 May 1864, LWA.

2. On one of the many references to CFTS using HSJr's inventions see CFTS's letter to his parents, brothers, and sisters, 12 Oct. 1857, F23, LWA. All seven Steinway patents before HSJr's death in 1865 were in his name. His three most important were no. 20595 (15 June 1858) for the invention of a grand piano action, no. 26300 (29 Nov. 1859) for a better-fitting iron plate, and no. 26532 (20 Dec. 1859) for over-stringing.

3. On S&S's iron frame see Ehrlich, *Piano,* p. 50. On the effect of North American climate

on pianos see WS, "American Musical Instruments," pp. 509–511, 515. On larger concert halls, changing tastes in music in the 1850s, and cast-iron plates see Hoover, "The Steinways and Their Pianos," pp. 50, 58. On size of the concert halls and piano accompaniment see *New York Herald,* 15 Mar. 1863. S&S catalog, 1866, LWA. HSJr to CFTS, Oct. 1850, LWA. On Conrad Meyer's iron plate see Albert B. Faust, *The German Element in the United States,* vol. 1 (New York, 1969), pp. 114–115. On Babcock's and then Chickering's iron plate see Keith G. Grafling, "Alpheus Babcock: American Pianoforte Maker (1785–1842): His Life, Instruments, and patents" (D.M.A. thesis, University of Missouri at Kansas City, 1972), pp. 14–19, 39–64; see also Edwin M. Good, "Theodore Steinway and the Late 19th Century Piano," lecture given at Steinway Hall, 24 Oct. 1991, p. 9; Harding, *Piano-Forte,* p. 202; Smith, *Noble Art,* pp. 78–85, 104–105; Edwin M. Good, *Giraffes, Black Dragons, and Other Pianos: A Technological History from Cristofori to the Modern Concert Grand* (Stanford, 1982), pp. 126–136; Loesser, *Men, Women and Pianos,* pp. 462–463, 494. For a drawing of Chickering's frame and a full discussion of the metal frame see Harding, *Piano-Forte,* chap. 3 and p. 212. For comments on the relationship between Beethoven's music and complaints about the thin tone see ibid., p. 178.

4. The first S&S overstrung grand was no. 2522; see Roy Kehl, "Steinway & Sons Pianoforte Manufacture: Production Highlights," typescript, 12 Feb. 1994, LWA. On HSJr's work on the overstrung design see CS & HSJr to CFTS, 23 Sept. 1859, F33, LWA; Dolge, *Pianos and Their Makers,* pp. 51–52, 62, 70. On the agraffes and downward flange on the plate see TES, *People and Pianos,* p. 18. S&S catalog, 1888, LWA. See also Harding, *Piano-Forte,* p. 187. On soundboard see HSJr to CFTS, 17 Mar. 1863, LWA. On cross-stringing and the Steinway piano see Good, *Giraffes,* pp. 119, 175–177. Loesser, *Men, Women and Pianos,* p. 496.

5. On the action see CFTS to his parents, 21 Aug. 1857, F21, and HSJr to CS, 20 Sept. 1864, F43, LWA. See also Michael Lenehan, "Building Steinway Grand Piano K 2571, The Quality of the Instrument," *Atlantic Monthly* 25, no. 2 (Aug. 1982): 42; E. Donnell Blackham, "The Physics of the Piano," *Scientific American,* Dec. 1965, pp. 91–93; "The Piano's Rise and Decline," *MT,* Nov. 1954, pp. 23–24; Harding, *Piano-Forte,* pp. 5–9, 27–29, 42, 74, 156–161. HSJr's action patents were no. 17238 (5 May 1857) for "Piano-forte Action" and nos. 32387, 32386 (both of 21 May 1861), and 34910 (8 Apr. 1862), all for "Improvement in Piano-forte Action." On comparison of HSJr's action with Erard's see *Frank Leslie's Illustrated Newspaper* (New York), 22 Sept. 1860, cited in Hoover, "The Steinways and Their Pianos," p. 57.

6. HSJr and CS to CFTS, 23 Sept. 1859, F33. On praise for the Steinway at this time see *Frank Leslie's Illustrated Newspaper,* 22 and 29 Sept. 1860.

7. Loesser (*Men, Women and Pianos,* p. 564) writes that, once the Steinways had perfected their system in 1859, "further improvements were either trifling, impractical, or of insufficient value." On the modern piano see also Good, *Giraffes,* pp. 177–179; Ripin et al., *The Piano,* Grove Musical Instrument Series (New York, 1988), pp. 51–56. On the Steinway system see WS, "American Musical Instruments," p. 511; J. B. Burr and Hyde, *Great Industries of the U.S. 1871–72* (Hartford, Conn., 1872), pp. 320–321; Broehl, *John Deere's Company,* pp. 124, 252.

8. On testimonials see Ehrlich, *Piano,* pp. 15–18; Roell, *Piano in America,* pp. 6, 143–146; Dolge, *Pianos and Their Makers,* p. 386; Smith, *Noble Art,* pp. 20, 34, 108; R. Allen Lott, "The American Concert Tours of Leopold de Meyer, Henri Herz, and Sigismund Thalberg" (Ph.D. diss., City University of New York, 1986), pp. 489–507. On Thalberg see Loesser, *Men, Women and Pianos,* p. 501. On Beethoven and Broadwood see "The Piano's Rise and Decline," *MT,* Nov. 1854, p. 26; Dieter Hildebrandt, *Piano Forte: A Social History of the Piano* (New York, 1985), p. 139.

9. CS and HSJr to CFTS, 23 Sept. 1859. On sending a piano to Liszt see HSJr to CFTS, 30 Mar. 1861, F35. On Liszt and piano donations see Hildebrandt, *Piano Forte,* p. 142.

10. On advertising see Roell, *Piano in America,* p. 174; Majeski, "Steinway." On meeting Gottschalg, CS to family, 6 Sept. 1864, F44, LWA. HSJr's response, 20 Sept. 1864, F43, LWA. On CFTS missing the meeting with Henry Litolff see HSJr, CS, and WS to CFTS, 16 Oct. 1860, F34, LWA.

11. On letter to agents and dealers see WS, "Wholesale Price Lists and Circulars etc. etc. sent to our agents from 1853 to Nov. 15 1878," 31 Dec. 1864, p. 12, LWA.

12. On packing and shipping the pianos to England in 1862 see WSD, 7, 8, 15 Mar., 13 Oct. 1862. On the exhibition see *NYT*, 1862: 15 May, p. 5; 22 May, p. 2; 2 June, p. 2; 7 June, p. 3; 26 July, pp. 5, 10; 31 July, p. 13; 13 Aug., pp. 2, 13; and 12 Oct., pp. 4 and 19; exhibition pamphlet (1862), p. 4, LWA; Ehrlich, *Piano*, pp. 56–58; Good, *Giraffes*, pp. 180–181. On the U.S. official report see Hoover, "The Steinways and Their Pianos," p. 58. On 1855 Crystal Palace fair and 1862 London fair see *NYT*, 10 May 1864. "Jurors Reports," in *Class XVI, Musical Instruments, International Exhibition, 1862, London*, pp. 4–5, 11–13. On press praise after the 1862 exhibition see Steinway catalog, 1866. On HSJr's sickness, starting on his trip to London, see *Western Musical World* 2, no. 4 (Apr. 1865), p. 53.

CHAPTER 3. RIOTS, STRIKES, AND DOMESTIC TRAGEDIES

1. On the loss of Southern business during the Civil War see Majeski, "Steinway." WSD, 29 Apr. 1861, LWA.

2. On prices see "Description of Styles and Schedule of Prices," 1859, and "Schedule of Retail and Wholesale Cash Prices," 24 Apr. 1865, in WS, "Wholesale Price Lists and Circulars etc. etc.," LWA.

3. CS to CFTS, 27 Apr. 1861, F40 L1, LWA. CS's regiment left for Washington on 28 Apr. 1861 and served at Hagerstown, Martinsburg, Charlestown, Bolivar Heights, and Knoxville, Md. See Civil War muster rolls. On 5th Regiment see "Registers and Sketches of Organizations," p. 531.

4. HES and his sons CS, HSJr, and WS signed their first formal partnership agreement on 30 Apr. 1861. It was a 5-year pact with only a vague reference to the oral agreement several years before. A copartnership agreement was signed on 30 May 1863.

5. AS had enlisted on 19 June 1863. He was mustered in with the National Guard, 5th Regiment, Company B, on 3 July 1863. He left New York on 22 July 1863. See James M. McPherson, *Battle Cry of Freedom* (New York, 1988), p. 658.

6. Ibid., pp. 600–611.

7. WSD, 13 July 1863.

8. Ibid., 13, 14 July 1863. Twenty-seven years later S&S donated "to Miss Mary E. O'Connor, whose father had in June [really July], 1863, during the time of the riots, rendered valuable aid in preserving the property of Steinway & Sons from the violence of the mob, the sum of Fifty Dollars ($50) to the fund to acquire an organ for the Catholic Church at Ozone, Long Island." See Min 1876–1907, 7 Apr. 1890, p. 135, LWA. On wages see David Montgomery, *The Fall of the House of Labor* (New Haven, 1987), p. 69.

9. WSD, 14 July 1863. See also Adrian Cook, *The Armies of the Streets: The New York City Draft Riots of 1863* (Lexington, Ky., 1974), pp. 193–194. Peter Quinn, *Banished Children of Eve* (New York, 1994).

10. The 65th and 152nd Regiments also arrived in the city. WSD, 15, 16, 17 July 1863. McPherson, *Battle Cry*, p. 611.

11. WSD, 17, 19, 20 July 1863.

12. On the formation and activities of the union see *New York Herald*, 23 Jan. 1860; Groce, "Musical Instrument Making," pp. 140–146. James Sigurd Lapham, "The German-Americans of New York City, 1860–1890" (Ph.D. diss., St. John's University, 1977), p. 32; Robert Ernst, *Immigrant Life in New York City, 1825–1863* (New York, 1949), p. 31. On October 1863 strike see *New York Sun*, 5, 6, 8, 29 Oct. 1863; see also Aaron Singer, "Labor–Management Relations at Steinway & Sons, 1853–1896" (Ph.D. diss., Columbia University, 1977), pp. 25–34, 60, 64; WSD, 1, 3, 6 Oct., 23 Nov. 1863. The Pianoforte Manufacturers' Society of New York was founded on 23 Nov. 1863. S&S price lists, 15 Oct. 1862 and 3 Oct. 1863, LWA.

13. HSJr to CS, AS, and WS, Havana, 21 Jan. 1864, F25 L6, LWA.

14. For the complete correspondence from Cuba, 2 Dec. 1863 to 18 Apr. 1864, see F25 L1–12, LWA. On HSJr's illness see WSD, 29 Mar., 1 Apr., 18 May, 19 Nov. 1863 (when he left for Cuba). Ernestine returned to New York on 20 Jan. 1864; see WSD.

15. HSJr to WS, 16 Feb. 1864, F25 L9; HSJr to CS, 4 Mar. 1864, F25 L10; HSJr to WS, 11 Mar. 1864, F25 L11, LWA. WSD, 3 Mar. 1864; *New York Herald*, 2, 5 Mar. 1864. On response to demand for a wage increase see *New York Tribune*, 27 Feb. 1864. WSD, 8, 13, 22, 23, 25 Feb. 1864. Singer, "Labor–Management Relations," pp. 24, 31. Clarence D. Long, *Wages and Earnings in the United States, 1860–1890* (Princeton, 1960), pp. 61–62, 111.

16. HSJr to WS, 11 Mar. 1864, F25 L11, LWA. WSD, 25 Feb., 3, 8, 14, 15, 21, 28, 31 Mar., 4, 11 Apr. 1864. Advertisement in *Philadelphia Inquirer*, "New York Piano Company," 9 June 1864. *New York Herald*, 14, 21, 22 Mar. 1864.

17. HSJr to WS, 18 Apr. 1864, F25 L12, LWA. See S&S price lists for 3 Oct. 1863, 11 Apr., 5 May, and 9 July 1864. On 17 July 1865 Steinway gave a 10% increase and again on 17 Sept. 1865; see *New York Sun*, 27 Sept., 12 Oct. 1865, and Steinway price list circular 18, Sept. 1865. In the fall of 1864 HSJr sent an enthusiastic message to CFTS in Germany: "News about the war are very favorable. Therefore let's soon have peace through the subjugation of the rebels." See F43, 20 Sept. 1864, LWA.

18. On CS's illness see WSD, 25 Dec. 1863 to 11 Jan. 1864, and 6, 7, 27, 28 May 1864. CFTS to WS, F49. CS to his family, 14 July 1864, F42, and 6 Sept. 1864, F44, LWA. On his health, the use of Nitschkes salves and elixirs, and his brothers' health, see CS to family, 29 Nov. 1864, F45, and 11 Mar. 1864, F25 L11, LWA. On death rate of Germans in New York see CS to CFTS, 1852, F2 L2, LWA.

19. "Mr. Henry Steinway," *NYT,* 15 Mar. 1865, p. 8. On Henry's 2-year illness see *Henry Steinway & William Steinway* v. *Sophie Steinway et al.,* 4 Aug. 1870, HZSF. On the return of his sickness as soon as he returned from Cuba see WSD, 27–29 May 1864. On his deterioration see WSD, 14, 25, 28 Dec. 1864; 1, 11, 15 Jan., 2 Feb. 1865. The Steinway mausoleum in Greenwood was not built until 1869–70. On consumption as the cause of death and a description of the funeral see *Western Musical World* 2, no. 4 (Apr. 1865), p. 53.

20. Ernestine Hildegarde Miller Steinway married Charles Oaks on 30 Oct. 1865 and departed for Europe on 4 Nov. 1865. See marriage certificate of Charles James Oaks and Ernestine H. Miller, issued by Henry E. Montgomery, rector of the Church of the Incarnation, New York, 30 Oct. 1865. WS knew about the marriage by 28 Nov. 1865. See C. Koch to CFTS, 14 Dec. 1865, F50 L1, and 18 Dec. 1865, F50 L2; C. Koch to Mr. Grund, landlord, 25 Jan. 1866, F50 L3; C. Koch to Marie Muller Linden, 18 Mar. 1866, F50 L7, and 27 Apr. 1867, F50 L11, LWA. On cost of boarding the children at Koch's house see F50 L15 and 18, 1866–67. On Ernestine giving up the girls see her letter to WS of 26 Jan. 1866. On her return to New York see her letter to WS of 26 Feb. 1866. On her anger with WS and the rumors see Oaks to WS, 21 Feb. 1866, and a more apologetic letter dated 5 Mar. 1866.

21. "Henry Steinway Jr. died in N.Y. City on the 11th of March 1865 and Chas. Steinway died in the city of Brunswick, Germany on the 31st of March 1865." *Henry Steinway & William Steinway* v. *Sophie Steinway et al.,* 4 Aug. 1870, HZSF. CS obituary, *NYT,* 27 Apr. 1865, p. 4.

22. On the election and assassination of Lincoln see WSD, 9 Nov. 1864 and 15 Apr. 1865.

23. CFTS to WS, n.d., probably May 1865, F49, LWA. On help from CFTS's father see CFTS to his family, 25 Dec. 1855, F29; 12 Oct. 1857, F23; 24 Mar., c. 1862, F26, LWA. See also HSJr to WS, 23 Dec. 1863, F25 L3. Henry Kroeger started at S&S in 1855 as a tone regulator and became foreman of tone regulators in 1860 and superintendent in 1864; see HZS, "Henry Kroeger," typescript, 5 Dec. 1989. On Kroeger "getting an interest" in S&S see WSD, 24 Mar. 1865; on WS's decision to pay him a royalty of $1 for every square piano and $21 for every grand sold instead see 30 Apr. 1865.

24. CFTS to CS, ca. 1859, F19. On the Grotrian partnership and the Steinweg reputation in Germany see CFTS to his family, 18 Oct. 1857, F23. On CFTS's 1 Apr. 1858 and 11 Oct. 1861 contract with George Karl Friedrich Grotrian and his heirs see "What Actually Happened,"

HZSF. On the sale of CFTS's Brunswick firm and the Grotrian story up to 1893, see WS, "An Exposition of Facts," for court case *Steinway & Sons, New York, Hamburg* v. *Grotrian, Helfferich, Schulz, Successors to Th. Steinweg,* Brunswick, Jan. 1893; "HZS: Bits of History," HZSF. On resolution of the issue in 1975 see *Grotrian, Helfferich, Schulz, Th. Steinweg Nachf., Plaintiff-Appellant,* v. *Steinway & Sons, Defendant-Appellee,* 523 F. 2d 1331 (2d Cir. 1975); argued 10 Jan. 1975; decided 9 July 1975.

25. AS died on 4 May 1877. See Herman Ludwig Ferdinand Helmholtz letters of 9 June 1871, 13 Aug. 1873, 16 Mar. 1885, 6 Oct., 4 Dec. 1893. CFTS is still promoted as the founding Steinway wizard; see "What Can One Expect from a Quality Instrument?" in S&S's Hamburg magazine *Lyra,* May 1993, pp. 8–9, and "A Lifetime for the Piano," *Lyra,* Jan. 1994, pp. 6–7. HZS, PI, 7 Dec. 1993, pp. 13–14, LWA. HZS memo to Leo Spellman, 28 Dec. 1993, questioning the continuation of the myth about CFTS.

CHAPTER 4. *STEINWAY* BECOMES A HOUSEHOLD WORD

1. On WS and Liederkranz see Dolge, *Pianos and Their Makers,* p. 310. See also "William Steinway," p. 5; Louisa Ziegler diary, 7 May 1868, LWA. On WS and the Metropolitan Opera see Paul Eric Eisler, "History of the Metropolitan Opera from 1883 through 1908" (Ph.D. diss., Boston University, 1965), p. 502.

2. On WS's generosity to musicians see Henry T. Finck, *My Adventures in the Golden Age of Music* (New York, 1926), pp. 185–187. On WS helping Abbey, Schoeffel, and Grau see Eisler, "Metropolitan Opera," p. 502. CFTS did not support the concert business; see his letter to John F. Petri (1867, F28 L2, LWA) insisting that "that whole concert business does not appeal to me, one should think it over very carefully."

3. The salesrooms were finished by 29 Feb. 1864. See description of Steinway Hall in *Frank Leslie's Illustrated Newspaper* (New York), 28 May 1864, p. 157. See also WSD, 27 Dec. 1862, LWA. On changes in location of music making in New York see Groce, "Musical Instrument Making," pp. 81–82. See also Sam Franko, *Chords and Discords* (New York, 1938), p. 67. On the Steinway private box see Ziegler diary, 8 Jan. 1869.

4. WSD, 26 May, 31 Oct. 1866. See also Groce, "Musical Instrument Making," p. 82. Piano sales in 1866 were 1,747 and in 1867, 2,153. The three slumps were in 1870, 1876, and 1882.

5. "France, Opening of the Great Exhibition," *NYT,* 16 Apr. and 1 May 1867. Merle Curti, "America at the World Fairs, 1851–1893," *American Historical Review* 55 (1950):842.

6. CFTS to John F. Petri, 1867, F28 L2, LWA. "Oscar Paul relates that at the Universal Exhibition in Paris in 1867, Steinway and Chickering each spent in 2 months the sum of 400,000 francs": cited in Classon Ernest, *History of the Piano* (New York, 1944), p. 108. On wages in 1867 see Weeks, *Statistics of Wages,* p. 292; the average salary at the Steinway factory in 1867 was less than $800 a year.

7. WSD, 17 May, 29 June, 11 July 1867. On Chickering's awards see 2 July 1867. On start of advertising war see 3, 5, 22 July, 4 Aug. 1867. See also *Boston Post,* 16 Aug. 1867. On the jury's support of Steinway see Ehrlich, *Piano,* pp. 59–60. On Liszt and Chickering see Loesser, *Men, Women and Pianos,* p. 513.

8. S&S catalog, 1869; the letter from Wilhelm Kruger was dated 12 Nov. 1867. See also Dolge, *Pianos and Their Makers,* p. 71.

9. Letter of 5 July 1884, F24 L18, LWA.

10. R. G. Dun and Company, v. 373 (18 Oct. 1871), p. 1266. On death of HES see letter to dealers 13 Feb. 1871. On S&S wages in 1871 see Weeks, *Statistics of Wages,* p. 292. On the 1873 Vienna exhibition see Steinway catalog, 1888, LWA.

11. Contract between Anton Rubinstein, Maurice Grau, and Steinway, 8 June 1872. On serenade see "Serenade to Rubinstein," *NYT,* 13 Sept. 1872. On 23 Sept. debut see letter "To our Dealers and Agents," 31 Aug. 1872. "The Rubinstein Concert," *NYT,* 24 Sept. 1872. On ventilation problems see *NYT,* 27, 28 Sept. 1872. WSD, 16, 20, 30 Aug., 11, 12, 23, 27, 28 Sept.

1872. Rubinstein's letter of 24 May 1873 was published in Steinway's 1874 catalog. On never coming back to the United States see Min, 10 Oct. 1892, p. 259. On the tour see WS, "Personal Reminiscences of Anton Rubinstein," *Freund's Musical Weekly* 8, no. 3 (28 Nov. 1894): 5. See also Milton Goldin, "The Great Rubinstein Road Show," *High Fidelity Magazine,* Sept. 1966, pp. 60–62. For a biographical sketch of Rubinstein see Harold Schonberg, *The Great Pianists* (1963; rev. New York, 1987), pp. 269–280.

12. On making pianos in London versus Hamburg see interview with Rodge Allen, June 1987. The agreement with Anglo-Continental Pianoforte was signed on 4 Sept. 1875 and canceled on 26 June 1877; see also WSD, 12 Sept., 9, 13 Nov. 1874; 6 Aug., 4, 7 Dec. 1875. The London partnership with William M. Yandell Maxwell creating Steinway & Sons was signed on 8 Sept. 1877. On Maxwell see WSD, 14, 23, July 1875; 24 Jan., 17 Feb., 2 Mar. 1876; 27, 29 Aug., 4, 8 Sept. 1877; 12 Feb., 19 July 1878; 30 Apr. 1879. On Maxwell and Blüthner see WSD, 20, 24, 29 Apr., 12 Oct. 1879; 19 May 1885. On Maxwell's misappropriation of funds and the dissolving of the partnership on 30 Apr. 1884 see WSD, 2 Dec. 1882; 1, 2, 7–28 Mar. 1884; 26, 28–30 May 1885; and Directors Minutes, 2 Dec. 1884. On lack of profit in London see "William Steinway Wins," *NYT,* 7 Mar. 1896, p. 3. In 1925 Steinway & Sons left Lower Seymour St. and acquired the lease on the old Broadwood showrooms on St. George Street, the current site of one of Sotheby's buildings. In 1982 it moved to the showroom on Marylebone St. On Steinway and national pride see CHS, "Building Up Prestige and What It Entails," *Printer's Ink* 81, no. 6 (7 Nov. 1912): 6; Min, 18 Mar. 1884, p. 54.

13. Charles Tretbar was in charge from 20 Jan. 1865 to 1906. See Spillane, *American Pianoforte,* p. 223.

CHAPTER 5. STEINWAY & SONS IN AMERICA'S CENTENNIAL YEAR

1. CFTS to family, c. 1859, F19; to WS, 16 June 1877, F68, LWA. Response from HSJr and CS to CFTS, 23 Sept. 1859, F33 LWA. For earlier letters on the upright, see CFTS to CS, 26 Dec. 1857, F22, and CFTS to his parents, 21 Aug. 1857, F21, LWA. On the first successful uprights see Good, *Giraffes,* pp. 102–118. See also Smith, *Noble Art,* pp. 28–30. Steinway's first uprights were nos. 5451 and 5452, Apr. 1862; see "Original Serial Book of Steinway Pianos, as Manufactured," recorded by WS, LWA. On CFTS bringing over upright specialists see "C. F. Theodore Steinway," p. 4. The improved boudoir piano was introduced in the 1872 catalog and lasted six years. On upright sales see CFTS obituary, *NYT,* 3 Mar. 1889. On limited upright popularity in 1867 see Burr and Hyde, *Great Industries,* pp. 320–321.

2. On the scientific aspects of CFTS's work see Smith, *Noble Art,* pp. 148–154.

3. S&S catalogs, 1872, 1874, and 1888, LWA. U.S. Patent no. 126,848 (14 May 1872), for grand duplex scale. Letter from Helmholtz, 9 June 1871, in 1872 catalog; 13 Aug. 1873, in 1874 catalog. Letter from Liszt, Nov. 1883, in 1888 catalog. On examining CFTS's new concert grand see WSD, 25 Apr., 21 Oct., 25 Dec. 1875; 23 Jan., 17 Apr. 1876.

4. CFTS's formula for cast iron included carbon, manganese, and sulphur. S&S catalogs, 1876 and 1888. Dolge, *Pianos and Their Makers,* pp. 304, 305. On CFTS's research and his stronger iron plate see Smith, *Noble Art,* pp. 119–120, 124.

5. S&S catalogs, 1876 and 1888. *Flushing Times,* 21 Aug. 1876, p. 2, cited in Vincent F. Seyfried, *300 Years of Long Island City: 1630–1930* (New York, 1984), p. 101. HZS, 1 Nov. 1988. On shipping the pianos see WSD, 24 Apr. 1876. On the 1874 economy, piano slump, and mortgages see R. G. Dun and Company, 24 Jan. 1874 and 4 Oct. 1878. On 1876 incorporation and initial shareholders see R. G. Dun and Company, 17 May 1876, and Min, 17 May 1876.

6. For a description of the fairgrounds and piano popularity in 1876 see William Peirce Randel, *Centennial: American Life in 1876* (Philadelphia, 1969), pp. 292–293, 345. On the opening see Ezra Schabas, *Theodore Thomas* (Urbana, Ill., 1989), p. 73.

7. WS was very much in love with Regina. See HSJr and CS to CFTS, 30 Mar. 1861, F35, LWA. The morning after Albert told him what was going on, WS wrote in his diary (18 Sept.

1875) that he had "suffered all the tortures of hell and passed a perfectly sleepless night. The most terrible I have ever lived through." See also WSD, 5 July 1875.

8. Alfred was born on 12 Oct. 1869. In 1875 Regina was 32, WS was 40, George was 12, Paula 9, and Alfred 7. The secret codes are really not so secret—William left a decoding chart with the diary. Moreover, the purpose of all of this tracking was probably not to spy on his wife but to limit the number of pregnancies. See "Diary Code" in a letter from HZS to author, 26 Oct. 1983, LWA.

9. See divorce proceedings, 28 July 1876, Minna Roesen, LWA. Louise Krusi, Steinway servant, testified that on 20 Apr. 1876 Regina confessed to her that she had been "improperly intimate" with Stern for more than 3 years.

10. Divorce proceedings, testimony by Augusta Krauss on 8 Aug. 1876. See also WSD, 4 Aug. 1876.

11. Divorce proceedings, testimony of Louise Krusi, 28 July 1876.

12. WSD, 5 Apr. 1873; 31 Aug., 15, 18, 29 Oct., 6, 9 Nov. 1875; 4, 22 Mar. 1876.

13. WSD, 10 July 1876. On their first trip back to New York, Reinel "behaved in the most indecent manner. She had improper relations with a young man named Albert Hardt, Jr., and also with the ship's doctor": WSD, 15 Dec. 1876. On the attempted blackmail see WSD, 21, 23 Mar. 1876.

14. WSD, 5 Apr., 3, 4 May 1876.

15. WSD, 4 May, 30 Aug., 19, 20 Sept. 1876.

16. *NYT,* 24 Mar. 1877, 19 Aug. 1878.

17. WSD, 21, 25, 29 Mar., 1, 9, 11, 20, 29 Apr., 3, 4, 15 May 1876. On divorce decree see New York Supreme Court, City and County of New York, County Court House, *William Steinway* v. *Regina Steinway,* filed 25 Aug. 1876, Hon. Charles Donohue, Justice. The decree permitted WS to marry again as if Regina "were actually dead," but said "it shall not be lawful for the defendant Regina Steinway to marry again until the plaintiff is actually dead." The care and custody of their children, George and Paula, went to WS. When Louis Dachauer, with whom Regina was living in Nancy, was sued for divorce by his wife Marie, the news about the adultery appeared. See *NYT,* 19 Aug. 1878. See also WSD, 24 Mar. 1877, 20 Sept. 1879.

In 1881, Alfred was taken by Regina's sister to a monastery (Kloster Merienthal) "near Strassburg and was baptized Alfred Charles Marie Roos." WS reported that "he looked dreadfully Jewish . . . small and puny." They did not lose contact; WS treated Alfred as a nephew though at times like a son. See WSD, 15 Mar., 17 Sept. 1882; 15 Sept. 1890; 30 July 1891. Alfred became an engineer and ended up surveying for mining companies in the Black Hills of South Dakota. See interviews with people who knew him in Deadwood: Audrey Balcom, 9 Jan. 1892; Sam Kirk, Martha Lynde, and A. I. Johnson, 17 Jan. 1992, LWA.

Louis Stern developed a brain disorder in 1881 and went insane. He died, perhaps of syphilis, but according to the death certificate of "General Paralysis, Epileptiform Convulsions," on 19 Dec. 1881. See WSD, 6 Oct. 1875; 10, 16 Dec. 1881. Three weeks later Regina died of typhoid fever in Nancy. She had converted to Catholicism in 1881 and was buried as Regina Bergtold (her mother's maiden name), wife of William Roos (a fictitious name). On her conversion from the "Lutheran heresy" to the Catholic faith, see document in Latin, Diocèse de Strasbourg, Maison de retraite des prêtres âgés et infirmes, Marienthal, 10 June 1881. In this document Regina is listed as the Wife of Jacob Roos and takes the name Maria Joseph Regina. On Regina's death see certificate of the Registers of Births, Marriages and Deaths of Nancy, Department of Meurthe-et-Moselle. WS went to Nancy and settled all her bills and "ordered a nice tombstone" inscribed "Regina Roos." See WSD, 30 Aug., 19, 20 Sept. 1876; 21 Dec. 1881; 2 Jan., 15, 20 June 1882.

18. WSD, 15, 20 May, 22 Aug. 1876.

19. On AS and WS going to the fair see WSD, 11, 24, 25 May.

20. On Weber emerging as a major rival see WSD, 7, 8 June 1876.

21. On the workers' trip see WSD, 19 Aug. 1876. On the awards system and the jurors' biographies see Cynthia Hoover, "The Great Piano War of the 1870s," in *A Celebration of*

American Music, Words and Music in Honor of H. Wiley Hitchcock, ed. Richard Crawford, R. Allen Lott, and Carol J. Oja (Ann Arbor, 1989), pp. 132–138, 141–142.

22. On the role of fairs in marketing and exchange of ideas see Robert W. Rydell, *All the World's a Fair* (Chicago, 1984), pp. 10–13, 17, 33. On the $1,000 paid to Boscovitz, the resulting bad press, and WS's response, see WSD, 9 June, 16, 17, 19, 20 July, 1 Aug., 11 Sept. 1876. See "The Exhibition: Are the Judges of Awards Guilty of Corruption?," *New York Herald*, 16 July 1876, p. 4; also WS's response, "Explanation of Steinway & Sons," *Herald*, 19 July 1876, p. 3. On S&S winning see *Herald*, 8 Dec. 1876. See also Henry K. Oliver, "Musical Instruments," in *International Exhibition 1876: Reports and Awards, Group XXV,* ed. Francis A. Walker (Philadelphia, 1878), p. 146.

23. The awards were announced on 16 and 17 Oct. 1876; see WSD. On Weber's claim to victory see *New York Tribune*, 2 Feb. 1877; *NYT,* 27 Oct. 1876; Weber ad in playbill for St. James's Hall, Buffalo, 14 Jan. 1878, HZSF. On Weber falsifying the final report and Steinway protests see WSD, 30 Sept., 11 Nov. 1876, and *NYT,* 11 Nov. 1877; also James C. Watson, secretary to Group 25, to Charles Tretbar, 9 July, 13 Aug., 6 Nov. 1877; Watson to Hilgard, Henry, Barnard, and Oliver, 1 Aug. 1877; Watson to Tretbar, 6 Nov. 1877; "Tretbar files on matter of Weber having a 'False Certificate,'" all in HZSF. "Piano Awards: Weber, of New York, Receives the Highest Award at the Centennial Exhibition," *Harper's Weekly,* 14 Oct. 1876, p. 838.

24. On Weber's response to judges' support of S&S, Weber agent Charles C. Mellor to the public, in "Philadelphia 1876," HZSF. On the 1876 certificate see any catalog between 1877 and 1896. On claims by Herbert VanDyke see *MT* 1, no. 1 (7 Feb. 1880): 3. For the truth of VanDyke's charges see WSD, 9 Nov. 1876: "In evening, Herbert VanDyke calls, give him $100"; 16 Nov.: "In evening meet Herbert VanDyke at my house give him the 3rd hundred dollars." The following week (29 Nov.) WS noted: "Herbert VanDyke reports progress with Jones, asks for further loan of $350," which WS gave him (1 Dec.) "to save his house in Harlem." On 28 Dec. VanDyke delivered "two more affidavits."

25. Loesser, *Men, Women and Pianos,* pp. 557–558. On the Steinway–Weber battle see WSD, 29 Dec. 1878 and 4 Jan. 1879 and 23 Feb. 1879. See also James Henry Mapleson, *The Mapleson Memoirs,* vol. 1 (London, 1888), pp. 214–216. On Weber see Dolge, *Pianos and Their Makers,* pp. 296–299.

CHAPTER 6. ESCAPING THE "ANARCHISTS AND SOCIALISTS"

1. WSD, 13, 17, 20, 23, 24, 27 May 1872. *NYT,* 14, 15, 24, 30 May 1872; *New York Tribune,* 24, 29 May 1872; cited in Singer, "Labor–Management Relations," p. 65; *New York Sun* and *New York Herald,* 30 May 1872; cited in ibid., pp. 64–66.

2. On WS's worth see Supreme Court, *Henry Steinway & William Steinway v. Sophie Steinway et al.,* 4 Aug. 1870, HZSF. In 1872 S&S's net assets, including real estate, totaled $1,219,979, of which WS owned almost half. His salary in 1872 was $59,517. "Rough Attempts by HZS: Growth in Early Years," typescript, n.d., HZSF. On workers' salaries 1853–80 see Weeks, *Statistics of Wages,* p. 292. On 1871 sales and demand see Burr and Hyde, *Great Industries,* p. 322. WSD, 28, 29 May 1872. On "school" piano and "one piano every working hour" see Steinway advertisements in *Harper's Weekly* 15, no. 732 (7 Jan. 1871), and 17, no. 854 (10 May 1873).

3. Confidential circular to agents, 29 May 1872, LWA. See *Henry W. T. Steinway, Plaintiff, Appellant, against William Steinway and Steinway & Sons, Defendants Respondents,* New York Court of Appeals, 1896, p. 222. See also WSD, 29, 30 May 1872. S&S's net assets for 1869 were $562,609.02. On wages see Montgomery, *Fall of Labor,* p. 69.

4. Actually, 250 of the 600 Steinway workers tried to go back to work, but strikers scared away 100 of them. See WSD, 1, 3, 4, 5 June 1872. See also *NYT,* 7 June 1872; cited in Singer,

"Labor–Management Relations," p. 71. On deal with returning workers see letter to dealers, 11 June 1872.

5. WSD, 7–10 June 1872. On the proportion of returning workers and the use of police, see letter to dealers, 11 June 1872. All but 50 S&S workers were back at their benches 14, 15 June 1872: *NYT,* 13–16 June 1872; cited in Singer, "Labor–Management Relations," p. 73.

6. WSD, 15 June 1872.

7. *NYT,* 16 June 1872.

8. WSD, 15, 16, 19, 22 June 1872.

9. On settling of the 1872 strike see *The World,* 23 June 1872, p. 5; *New York Sun,* 19 June 1872, p. 2; 18 June 1872, p. 8; *NYT,* 17 June 1872, p. 8; *New York Evening Post,* 17 June 1872, p. 3; 24 June 1872, p. 4. WSD, 24 June 1872. On daily wages at S&S see Weeks, *Statistics of Wages,* p. 292, and Montgomery, *Fall of Labor,* p. 69. On 18 Sept. 1873 bank panic and ensuing depression see William S. McFeely, *Grant* (New York, 1981), p. 392.

10. Senate Committee upon the Relations between Labor and Capital, 1883.

11. WSD, 8, 11, 12 July, 6, 24 Sept. 1870; 3 Apr. 1871. See also S&S catalog, 1888. On the decision to move to Queens see Singer, "Labor–Management Relations," pp. 87–89.

12. Seyfried, *Long Island City,* pp. 89, 98. WSD, 2, 8, 11, 12 July, 21 Dec. 1870; 15, 24, 25 Feb., 2, 20, 21 Mar., 3 Apr., 5 Aug., 29 Dec. 1871. S&S catalog, 1888, LWA. Singer, "Labor–Management Relations," p. 89.

13. *South Side Signal,* 18 Nov. 1871, p. 2; *Hempstead Inquirer,* 19 July 1872; *Flushing Journal,* 13 July 1872, p. 2; *Flushing Journal,* 15 Apr. 1871, p. 2. *Brooklyn Times,* July 1870. WSD, June–Sept. 1870. See also Singer, "Labor–Management Relations," p. 89. the mansion became a Steinway presidential privilege on 1 May 1882; see Min, p. 43, LWA.

14. Seyfried, *Long Island City,* p. 99. Singer, "Labor–Management Relations," p. 90. See also *Flushing Times,* 29 Jan. 1876, p. 2. The S&S 1872 catalog lists "Saw Mill, Iron Foundry [not finished until 8 Mar. 1873], and Metal Works, Astoria, Long Island" as part of their address. On building the mill and foundry see WSD, 28 Dec. 1871; 22 Feb., 23, 25 Apr., 22 Oct., 24 Nov. 1872; 8 Mar., 6 May, 20 June 1873; on naming of Steinway Avenue see 5 Nov. 1872, 20 July 1873. See also *Flushing Journal,* 6 Sept. 1873, p. 3; cited in Seyfried, *Long Island City,* p. 100. On lithograph see letter "To Our Dealers and Agents," 25 Nov. 1873. On Steinway's boast see 1874 catalog. See also the 1876 and 1888 catalogs for descriptions of the Astoria Works. On keyboard parts from Pratt, Read & Company see Min, 3 Dec. 1879, p. 24.

15. In 1877 the keyboard-making and wood-carving departments were transferred to Queens. The case-making building was almost 250 feet long and 60 feet wide. All the case were now constructed in Queens: see catalog, 1888. On approval to build case-making factory see Min, board of trustees of S&S, 5 May, 12 July 1879. Seyfried, *Long Island City,* p. 103. Singer, "Labor–Management Relations," pp. 91–92. On building of the Astoria site see Min, 29 Sept. 1881, p. 35.

16. According to an R. G. Dun and Company report in 1878, the company owned 3,000 lots in Astoria, with factory and cottages claimed to be worth $500,000 free and clear. But Dun's investigators uncovered mortgages and estimated the real estate to be worth only half that amount. Some family members thought that almost $750,000 had already been lost, "squandered without much regard for profit." On company towns see Singer, "Labor–Management Relations," chap. 4. On 1878 real estate see R. G. Dun and Company, 18 Mar., 23 June 1878. WS was also trading extensively in Manhattan properties around the factory on the Upper East Side; see Min, 30 Dec. 1882. On establishment of real estate office at Queens factory see Min, 9 Dec. 1887, p. 87.

17. On one of WS's rail deals see WSD 17 Apr., 1 May, 6 June 1883, and Min, 3 May 1886, p. 72.

18. The tunnel was, as WS predicted, a major boon for Queens real estate and manufacturers. Grand Central Station was now four minutes away from downtown Long Island City. On WS and the tunnel see Clifton Hood, *722 Miles: The Building of the Subways and How They Transformed New York* (New York, 1993), pp. 163–166, 168, 172.

19. *Flushing Times,* 3 May 1876, p. 2; cited in Seyfried, *Long Island City,* p. 102. Catalog, 1888. On the firehouse see Min, 26 Dec. 1894, p. 318. Two lots worth $800 were donated to the church; see Min, 19 Nov. 1879, p. 24. On the dedication see WSD, 23 Nov. 1879. On the second land donation and the kindergarten and library, see letter to the Trustees of the Protestant Union Church, 26 Oct. 1889, in Min, 9 Nov. 1889, p. 120. See also Min, 28 June 1890, p. 137, and 31 Dec. 1890. Joseph J. Duffy, letter to the author, 20 June 1981, and Singer, "Labor–Management Relations," pp. 38–42. On the organ see Min, 7 Apr. 1890, p. 134. On the library's temporary quarters at 890 Albert Street, see Min, 26 Dec. 1889, p. 123. S&S to Long Island City Public Library, lease, 1 July 1897. On donation of books and teacher salary contribution see S&S to Dr. Walter G. Frey, President of the Public Library, L.I.C., 21 Apr. 1897.

20. *Flushing Journal,* 14 June 1879; cited in Seyfried, *Long Island City.* TES, *People and Pianos,* p. 32. Duffy, letter to author, 20 June 1981. On the wire sign see Min, 2 June 1887, p. 81. On 1881 population and houses see 1881 catalog. On Germans in Steinway Village see Lapham, "German-Americans," pp. 15, 164.

CHAPTER 7. THE PIANO WORKERS STRIKE BACK

1. On 1880s prosperity see White, "American Piano Industry," p. 210. On piano and vocal music in the late nineteenth century see Loesser, *Men, Women, and Pianos,* pp. 545–546. Spenlow, "Decorating and Furnishing," p. 5. See also CHS, "Building Up Prestige," p. 10. The "A" grand, a 7-octave parlor grand, was in the 1878 S&S catalog. Steinway had been making art-case pianos since 1857. Starting around 1889, they "maintained a special department for the designing and manufacture of pianos in period and art cases, to harmonize with any plan of architecture or decoration." See reference in S&S catalog, 1914.

2. WSD, 24 Jan., 5 Feb., 11 Sept., 31 Dec. 1879. On "revolution" see WSD, 14–16 Nov. 1878. On 11 Sept. 1879 strike see WSD and S&S letter "To Our Dealers and Agents," 12 Sept. 1879, LWA. On wage increase see Min, 1 Oct. 1879, p. 23, LWA. See also "To Our Dealers and Agents," 12 Sept., 6 Dec. 1879; 1 Jan., 26 Mar. 1880; 21 Sept., 22 Nov. 1882, LWA. Average daily wages at S&S were $2.48 in 1878, $2.66 in 1879, and $2.77 in 1880: Weeks, *Statistics of Wages,* p. 292. See also Montgomery, *Fall of Labor,* p. 69. On the keymakers' strike and subsequent manufacturers' meeting see WSD, 30 Nov.–10 Dec. 1879. On purchasing from Pratt, Read & Co. see Min, 3 Dec. 1879, p. 24, and WSD, 4 Apr. 1880.

3. WSD, 13 Feb.–29 Mar. 1880. References to varnishers' strike, "To Our Dealers and Agents," 21 Feb. 1880. *New York Star,* 12 Mar. 1880; *New York Herald* and *New York Sun,* 14 Feb. 1880; Min, 23 Nov. 1885, p. 66; 18 Oct. 1887, p. 84; 31 Dec. 1890, p. 148. Letters from Polishers Union to S&S, 17 Nov. 1885, F70 L7, F70 L8, 24 Sept. 1887, LWA.

4. Letter "To Our Dealers and Agents," 26 Mar. 1880. *NYT,* 28 Feb., 12 Mar. 1880. Min, 24 Mar. 1880, p. 25. See also Weeks, *Statistics of Wages,* p. 292.

5. Min, 9, 24 Mar. 1880. WSD, 17, 24 Mar. 1880. See check no. 1 for $8,489.90, in WS's handwriting, to HWTS, 17 Mar. 1880. They were able to sell the remains of the factory to an F. G. Smith for $9,000. See R. G. Dun and Company, N.Y., 30 Sept. 1881.

6. Min, 18 Mar. 1884. On dividends 1880–93 see Exhibit G1, *Henry W. T. Steinway Plaintiff, Appellant, against William Steinway and Steinway & Sons, Defendants Respondents,* New York Court of Appeals, 1896, p. 127. WS owned 6,250 shares.

7. On Steinway strike see *NYT,* 19 Sept. 1882. For battle in the carpet industry see Susan Levine, "Honor Each Noble Maid: Women Workers and the Yonkers Carpet Weavers' Strike of 1885," *New York History* 62, no. 2 (Apr. 1981): 154–164.

8. *NYT,* 20 Sept. 1882. WSD, 24 May, 14–21, 27 June, 13 July, 16, 17, 21 Sept., 3 Oct. 1882.

9. *NYT,* 19 Sept. 1882. WSD, 20 Sept. 1882.

10. *NYT,* 20, 21, 22 Sept. 1882. CHS was holding the fort while WS was en route from Berlin to Paris. See WSD, 21, 22 Sept. 1882.

11. WSD, 23 Sept.–1 Oct. 1882.

12. WSD, 18–20, 23, 26 Oct., 6 Nov. 1882.

13. Ibid., 7, 9 Nov. 1882. On Sommer's resignation see Min, 7 May 1883.

14. WSD, 9, 11, 12, 16, 17 Nov. 1882.

15. *New York Star,* 17 Nov. 1882, pp. 2, 3. WSD, 11 Nov. 1882.

16. WSD, 20, 22 Nov. 1882. Reports of how many ringleaders Steinway refused to rehire range from 15 to 28 to 80; see e.g. *NYT,* 25 Nov. 1882, and *New York Star,* 24 Nov. 1882, p. 1. See also "To Our Dealers and Agents," 22 Nov. 1882.

17. Editorial, *New York Star,* 24 Nov. 1882, p. 2; *NYT,* 25 Nov. 1882. On rewarding the police see Min, 30 Dec. 1882. On CHS's motion see Min, 7 May 1888.

18. "To Our Dealers and Agents," 22 Nov. 1882. WSD, 28 Nov., 9, 11, 18, 19 Dec. 1882.

19. "To Our Dealers and Agents," 22 Nov. 1882. Number of pianos manufactured in 1865, 1,810; in 1882, 1,823. After 1879 the numbers include Hamburg. Calculations based on Number Books, LWA. See also Min, 30 Dec. 1882. R. G. Dun, N.Y., 20 Nov. 1882, reported that S&S "probably lost some money by their recent strike which was settled in their favor."

20. On the switch from rosewood to ebonized cases see circulars "To Our Dealers and Agents," 15 Aug., 15 Nov. 1878; 1 Sept. 1884; 1 Jan. 1886.

21. For a discussion of CFTS's voyages to Europe between 1865 and 1889 see HZS, PI, 15 June 1990, pp. 1–2, LWA.

22. In 1880 WS and CFTS opened a factory at Schanzenstrasse 20–24 in Hamburg. On CFTS's early proposals for a branch in Germany see WSD, 15 Oct. 1874 and 5 Mar. 1879. For first advertisement of the Hamburg "Depot" see S&S catalog, 1881. On other U.S. firms in Europe, see Mira Wilkins, *The Emergence of Multinational Enterprise: American Business Abroad from the Colonial Era to 1914* (Cambridge, Mass., 1970), pp. 44–46, 59, 65–69, 101–103, 108–109. On German patent law see WS, "An Exposition of Facts," in *Steinway & Sons, New York, Hamburg v. Grotrian, Helfferich, Schulz, Successors to Th. Steinweg,* Brunswick, Jan. 1893; "HZS: Bits of History," HZSF. On CFTS's move back to Germany in 1884 see *S&S Mitteilungen* 43 (May 1921): 179. On the plans for and operation of the Hamburg factory see *Henry W. T. Steinway Plaintiff,* pp. 183–186, 190–192, 194, 198–200, 203, 216–217, 235. *NYT,* 7 Mar. 1896, p. 3. *S & S Mitteilungen* 163 (July/Sept. 1932): 1144. On CFTS's power of attorney in Europe and Great Britain see Min, 2 Dec. 1884. For official proclamation of Steinway's Pianofabrik see WSD, 29 Nov. 1880. The factory was purchased for 450,000 marks ($150,000): WSD, 17–22 Apr. 1885; TES, letter to Paul T. Culberton, U.S. State Department, 6 Apr. 1942, National Archives. In 1907 the Hamburg factory was permitted to buy plates locally and thus became independent of New York: Min, 28 Jan. 1807.

23. Doretta to WS, 17 Dec. 1889, F60 L12, LWA. On CFTS's private life see Smith, *Noble Art,* pp. 129–137. *Musical Courier* 18, no. 13 (27 Mar. 1889): 248.

24. CFTS to WS, 13 Sept. 1887, F69, LWA. Fred to CFTS, 16 Sept. 1887, F69.

25. Doretta to Steinway, telegram, 27 Feb. 1889. CFTS to Arthur von Holwede, 23 Feb. 1889, F20 L6. See also Dolge, *Pianos and Their Makers,* p. 305; *Musical Courier* 18, no. 13: 248; von Holwede to WS, 23 Feb. 1889, F61 L6; WS to von Holwede, 25 Feb. 1889, F61 L8, LWA.

CHAPTER 8. FAMILY FEUD

1. On George's illness see Min, 25 Oct. 1894. WSD, 20 Sept. 1879, 24 Oct. 1894. On George's divorce see *New York World* and *New York Herald,* 25 Sept. 1895, and *Brooklyn Eagle,* 2 Oct. 1895. See also George A. Steinway obituary, *NYT,* 22 Sept. 1898, p. 7.

2. WSD, 8 Dec. 1877.

3. On CHS in London see Min, 5 May, 2 Dec. 1884. Annual meeting of stockholders of Steinway & Sons, 6 Apr. 1891, LWA.

4. CHS recorded some of his music on Welte–Mignon piano rolls: no. 3014, Four Album Leaves; no. 3012, Polke Mazurka in A flat major; no. 3002, and no. 3007, Valse Lente in F major. On CHS's love of music see Byron H. Collins, letter to JS, 16 July 1961, LWA.

5. WSD, 21 Feb. 1878. On HWTS feeling cheated see *Henry W. T. Steinway Plaintiff, Appellant, against William Steinway and Steinway & Sons, Defendants Respondents,* New York Court of Appeals, 1896, pp. 109, 111, HZSF.

6. WSD, 19 Feb., 4 May 1885; 17 Apr., 30 Aug. 1887; 28 Apr. 1888; 22 Nov. 1889; 23 Jan. 1891. TES to Henry Ziegler, 4 Nov. 1885, F24 L22, LWA. On HWTS's tirade and his living above WS's office see *Henry W. T. Steinway Plaintiff,* pp. 179, 192, 196. On the complaints about Hamburg vis-à-vis London see TES to WS, 31 Aug., 13 Sept. 1987, F69 L4, L6, LWA.

7. Min, 30 Dec. 1890; 23 Jan., 12, 26 Feb., 15 July, 19 Dec. 1891. HWTS's resignation letter is in Min, 5 Jan. 1891. WSD, 11 July, 19 Dec. 1891. *NYT,* 30 Jan. 1895, p. 14. See also HZS, PI, 31 Dec. 1887. *Henry W. T. Steinway Plaintiff,* p. 179.

8. Tretbar was in charge of C&A from 20 Jan. 1865 to 1906. Tretbar "had bank signatures," but "as Nephew Charles came in and grew Tretbar receded to C&A and publishing": typescript, 17 Nov. 1988, 5 Dec. 1989, HZSF.

9. On HWTS's request for a desk and stables see his letter of 4 Jan. 1892 and Tretbar's reply in Min, 5 Jan. 1892. On his ejection see Min, 31 May 1892. On examining the books see Min, 11, 27 Apr. 1892. For a complete list of HWTS complaints see "Petition of Henry W. T. Steinway for an inspection of the books and records of Steinway & Sons," New York Court of Appeals, 17 Apr. 1899, pp. 14–19.

10. Min, 31 Dec. 1890, 6 Apr. 1891, 4 Apr. 1892. On complaints about WS see letter from FTS to Henry Ziegler, 10 Jan. 1890, F72 L11, LWA.

11. The *Fabrik* case, Supreme Court, *Henry W. T. Steinway* v. *William Steinway and Steinway & Sons,* lasted from 27 Aug. 1892 to 18 Feb. 1895. See Min, 27 Feb. 1895, 6 Apr. 1896. See also *Henry W. T. Steinway Plaintiff,* p. 72. The "Will" suit lasted from 29 Apr. 1893 to 22 May 1900. On CFTS's death see Min, 1 Apr. 1889.

12. On the start of the lawsuits see Min, 10 Oct. 1892. The "Will" suit lasted from 29 Apr. 1893 to 22 May 1900. On CFTS's death see Min, 1 Apr. 1889.

13. On banking business complaint see "Petition of Henry W. T. Steinway," p. 31. On questioning HWTS's timing see *Henry W. T. Steinway Plaintiff,* pp. 103, 177. On contributions to artists and politicians see "Musical Money-Makers," *NYT,* 20 Feb. 1895, and "Cigarettes for Paderewski," *NYT,* 30 Jan. 1895. On WS's relationship with President Cleveland see WSD, 9 June, 15, 17 July, 5 Aug. 1869; 8 Jan. 1886; 11, 13, 15, 22, 24 June 1887; 20–22 Feb. 1888; 10 Jan. 1889; 13 Dec. 1890; 23 Apr. 1891; 23 Jan., 16 Sept., 17 Nov. 1892; 9 Jan. 1893; 10 Jan. 1894. *NYT,* 28 Oct. 1892, p. 2. *Journal of Commerce and Commercial Bulletin* (1910), p. 740, cited in J. W. Leonard, "History of the City of New York, 1609–1909." On Cleveland's counsel, see his letter to WS, 5 June 1869, HZSF. On the wedding gift see thank you note from Cleveland to WS, 14 Aug. 1886. It was no. 55,405, a 7-octave, style B, ebonized piano shipped to showroom 16 Apr. 1886. A new plate and new duplex scale were installed between 23 June and 31 Dec. 1890; see S&S Number Books. On the 1888 Democratic Convention see WSD, 20–23 Feb. 1888. On reimbursement see Min, 31 Oct. 1888, p. 98.

14. On WS and the German hospital see his letter to von Holwede, 25 Feb. 1889, F61 L8, LWA. On WS's support of everything German see "William Steinway," *Magazine of Western History* 10, no. 6 (Oct. 1980): 669. On WS's views on Blue Laws see *NYT,* 24 Nov. 1895, p. 16. On contributions to Tammany Hall see "Musical Money-Makers," *NYT,* 20 Feb. 1895. For a brief but detailed biographical sketch of WS see J. S. Kelsey, *History of Long Island City, N.Y.* (Long Island City, 1896).

15. On cross-examination about loans to Gleason see *NYT,* 19 Feb. 1895. On William and transit see Hood, *722 Miles,* pp. 57–61, 66, 68, 69, 163–166, 168, 172. On one of WS's rail deals see WSD, 17 Apr., 1 May, 6 June 1883, and Min, 3 May 1886, p. 72. On Gleason see WSD, 29, 30 June, 18 Aug. 1883. See also Seyfried, *Long Island City,* chap. 15. On purchase of Astoria & Hunter's Point railroad from Gleason see WSD, 31 Oct. 1884.

16. On steam power at cost see Min, 7 May 1888, p. 94; 27 Dec. 1893, p. 299.

17. The "Trustee" suit lasted from 10 June 1893 to 7 May 1896: Min, 27 Feb. 1895, 11 May 1896. HZS, "Historical Notes on the Family Law Suits in the 1890s," 1987, p. 3, HZSF, lists all the sources for these lawsuits. On WS's amazing memory see "William Steinway's Memory," *NYT,* 31 Jan. 1895, and *Henry W. T. Steinway Plaintiff,* p. 179.

18. The debate became more public after WS's death. The debt he left was not covered by the estate, and there was a question of the company's liability for his investments which, because of the economy, were losing money. See "Town Topics," *Musical Courier,* 1 June 1898, p. 22.

19. HZS, interview, 8 May 1990, p. 6. HWTS's will, 4 Dec. 1835, was probated on 14 July 1839, State of New York file no. 1752/1939. See HZS, "Family Law Suits," 15 Oct. 1987. See also "Steinway Leases Henderson Home," 20 May 1939, and "Expires, Aged 83," 27 June 1939, *Watertown Daily Times.*

CHAPTER 9. PADEREWSKI: SUPERSTAR AND SUPER SALESMAN

1. "Letters," *MT,* Dec. 1953. Paderewski's London debut was 16 May 1890. WSD, 12 July 1890. Min, 12, 25 Mar. 1891.

2. Min, 16 Mar., 2 Apr., 10 Oct., 30 Dec. 1892; 11 May 1896. On Paderewski's arrival and impressing WS, see WSD, 11, 12 Nov. 1891. On the Union Square Hotel see Edwin Bolito, ed., *The Columbus Historical Guide for the City of New York,* Real Estate Record and Builders' Guide (New York, 1891). WSD, 7, 30 Jan. 1892. On hotel prices see *The Sun's Guide to New York, 1891.* On Paderewski see also Harold C. Schonberg, *The Glorious Ones* (New York, 1985), p. 216, and *Great Pianists,* pp. 301–309.

3. On the 1891 tour see Ignace Jan Paderewski and Mary Lawton, *The Paderewski Memoirs* (New York, 1938), pp. 189–222; Loesser, *Men, Women and Pianos,* pp. 534–535. On overhauling Paderewski's piano see telegram to Paderewski, 10 Mar. 1892. On leaving without a testimonial see Paderewski to WS, 7 Apr. 1892, trans. in circular "To Our Dealers and Agents," 18 May 1892.

4. On the Chicago fair see WSD, 1–4 May 1893. Paul and Ruth Hume, "The Great Chicago Piano War," *American Heritage,* Oct. 1970, pp. 16–21. On withdrawing from the fair see Min, 1 Apr. 1893. On 1895 contract and 1896 trust fund see Hugo Gorlitz to Eshelby, 8 Aug. 1895, and Paderewski to WS, 21 Apr. 1896.

5. Net profit in 1893, $247,500: Min, 31 Mar. 1894; in 1894, $231,558: Min, 1 Apr. 1895. See Number Books for manufacturing figures and Min for shipping figures. On credit to dealers and the mortgage see Min, 28 July, 22 Aug. 1893. On Hamburg, London, and New York profits see Min, 25 Oct. 1893, 6 Apr. 1896. On the panic see WSD, 28, 29 June, 26 July, 15, 26 Aug. 1893. On death of Elizabeth Ranft Steinway see *NYT,* 5 Mar. 1893, p. 5.

6. On death of WS see Min, 4 Dec. 1896. Letter from FTS to his mother, Sophia Millinet Steinway Fricke, 4 Dec. 1896, in FTS's copy book, p. 194, LWA. See also WS's "Certificate and Record of Death," no. 38934, State of New York, Albany.

7. "An Address by Ex-Senator Carl Schurz, at the Funeral of William Steinway" (privately printed, London, Dec. 1896). *NYT,* 1, 2, 3 Dec. 1896.

8. "William Steinway Estate Involved," *New York Herald,* 19 May 1898, and *NYT,* 20 May 1898, p. 2. Net profits had been coming down since 1892; in 1895, they were $307,750: Min, 30 Dec. 1895; in 1896, $100,000: Min, 5 Apr. 1897. For a list of stockholders see Min, 28 July 1893. For an inventory of WS's investments see "Astoria Homestead Co.," personal files of HZS. On Grotrian story see WS, "An Exposition of Facts," HZSF. See also *Grotrian, Helfferich, Schulz, Th. Steinweg Nachf., Plaintiff-Appellant,* v. *Steinway & Sons, Defendant-Appellee,* 523 F. 2d 1331 (2d Cir. 1975); argued 10 Jan. 1975, decided 9 July 1975. On the London sale attempt, see "Petition of Henry W. T. Steinway for an inspection of the books and records of Steinway & Sons," New York Court of Appeals, 17 Apr. 1899, pp. 49, 93. See also CHS to "Dear Boys," 13 Aug. 1897. Broehl, *John Deere's Company,* pp. 258–260.

CHAPTER 10. FROM NEAR BANKRUPTCY TO FABULOUS WEALTH

1. On trust for Mary Claire Osgood see "Trust Deed," CHS to William A. Mertens, 14 Dec. 1918, LWA. After CHS's death, his girlfriend inherited a trust of Steinway stock, and Marie married her French lover.

2. On election of CHS see S&S Minute Books, 4 Dec. 1896. On FTS's vote against dividends see e.g. Min, 5 Apr. 1897, 3 Apr. 1899.

3. On introducing Ziegler's "B" grand see Min, 27 Apr. 1891.

4. Min, 5 Apr. 1897, 27 Mar. 1902, 16 May 1904, 29 Mar., 3 Apr. 1905. On ragtime see Roell, *Piano in America*, pp. 32–36, 50–51.

5. Net profit in 1900 was $460,000: Min, 29 Mar. 1901; in 1901, $500,000: Min, 27 Mar. 1902; in 1902, $540,000: Min, 6 Apr. 1903. On salary increase see Min, 21 Apr. 1898, 29 Mar. 1901. On rent and wages see Elizabeth Ewen, *Immigrant Women in the Land of Dollars, Life and Culture on the Lower East Side, 1890–1925* (New York, 1985), pp. 112 and 116–121. On other prices see Sears Roebuck catalog, 1902.

6. In 1899 S&S in New York sold 1,008 grands. In 1911 they sold 2,444 grands. In 1899 Hamburg sold 909 pianos, and in 1911 they sold 2,338. Net profits in 1904 and 1905 were $400,000 each year. On the value of WS's estate in 1904 compared to 1896 see *NYT*, 31 Jan., 3 Feb. 1904. On the land sale that saved "the bacon for Father's estate," see letter from TES to BS, 21 May 1921, HZSF.

7. On White House piano see Min, 16 June 1902, and Jia-Sun Tsang, Nancie Ravenel, Johanna Bernstein, and Scott Odell, "The Conservation of the 100,000th Steinway Piano," Smithsonian Institution. Joseph M. Hunt and Richard H. Hunt executed the design, and Thomas Wilmer Dewing decorated it. On price of D grand see price lists 1 Nov. 1902, 1 Feb. 1904, LWA.

8. On CHS's deals with artists see Min, 4 Oct. 1897, 25 July 1900. On Moritz Rosenthal see Min, 27 Dec. 1897.

9. On Paderewski threatening to go to another firm see letter from W. Adlington, agent, to CHS, 10 May 1903. On correspondence between Sherman, Clay & Co. and S&S see "Paderewski, 1904–1905, Flap over Piano," HZSF. Clay was former Confederate Colonel Philip T. Clay. On Paderewski's move to a Weber see Paderewski and Lawton, *Paderewski Memoirs*, pp. 364–365. It is uncertain how they eventually got back together, but evidently Paderewski was satisfied a few years later (by 1908) that "perfect harmony" had been restored. Alexander Greiner, "Memoirs," unpublished MS, 23 Aug. 1957, pp. 31–32.

10. "Messrs. Urchs and Steinway Back," *Music Trade Review*, 1907, Urchs's scrapbook.

11. Roell, *Piano in America*, pp. 42–43, 98, 316n. See also HZS, interview with author, 22 Feb., 8 May 1990, pp. 5, 35, 36, 43, LWA. *NYT*, 20 Feb. 1909. On Duo-Art Steinway pianos see JS, interview by Elizabeth Harkins, 7 Nov. 1978, p. 38, Yale. In Europe Steinway shipped pianos to Welte-Mignon (Freiburg), Orchestrelle (London), Choralian (Berlin), and Pianola (Melbourne) for outfitting with player mechanisms. See Roy Kehl memo, "Outline of Steinway Piano Manufacture, Hamburg—Steinway's Piano-Fabrik and Branch Factories, 1880 to present," 21 July 1993. Min, 9 Mar., 5 Apr. 1909.

12. Min, 4 Apr., 16 Dec. 1910. On piano purchasing in 1870 and 1910 see Loesser, *Men, Women and Pianos*, p. 521. On Midwest stores see Min, 19 Jan. 1911; 29 Apr. 1912; 27 Mar., 7 Apr. 1913. On the growing piano market 1900–15 and the rise of Mason & Hamlin and the American Piano Co. see Loesser, *Men, Women and Pianos*, pp. 548–551, 570, and 572. See also Roell, *Piano in America*, pp. 87–90.

13. On 1910–13 profit see Min, 3 Apr. 1911; 29 Mar., 1 Apr. 1912; 27 Mar. 1913; 6 Apr. 1914. On Hamburg making their own plates see Min, 28 Jan. 1907. On the new M and 1911–12 sales see Min, 1 Apr. 1912, 27 Mar. 1913. On the 6-foot model A see letter "To Our Dealers and Agents," 15 Aug. 1978. See also CHS, "Building Up Prestige," pp. 4, 6.

14. On women employed during the war see Joseph D. Duffy, letter to the author of 20 June

1981; see too Steinway personnel cards, 1917–20. Henrietta Kammerer obituary, *NYT,* Oct. 1932.

15. On the war see Min, 31 Dec. 1914. On 1914 and 1915 profits and losses see Min, 1, 3 Apr. 1915; 14 Mar. 1917. Letter from BS to TES, 5 July 1916, HZSF. S&S kept up production throughout the war but could not meet demand. On CHS's health see letter from Edward T. Bates to CHS, 26 July 1916, after a dealer luncheon: "We all appreciated your presence with us, and especially because, we were aware that you at that time were recovering from a long illness."

16. Memorandum, 20 July 1917. Letter re Chas. H. Steinway, to Commanding Officer, Police Department, Bomb Squad, from Michael Santaniello, 28 Aug. 1917. Letter to File, subject: Mrs. Charles Steinway, reported by Mr. Gray, 26 Sept. 1917. RG 165 (Records of the WDGS), Mil. Intell. Div. Corresp., 1917–44, 9728-34, box no. 2172.

17. Min, 5 Apr. 1920. On CHS's worth see *NYT,* 26 Nov. 1919, p. 17. HZS to FTS, 4 Feb. 1991.

CHAPTER 11. THE "INSTRUMENT OF THE IMMORTALS" GOES NATIONAL

1. Roell, *Piano in America,* p. 186. See letters from TES and BS, 23 Aug., 22 Oct. 1921, in personal files of HZS. Ehrlich, *Piano,* p. 176. Robert S. and Helen Merell Lynd, *Middletown, A Study in Modern American Culture* (New York, 1929), p. 244, n. 35.

2. Roell, *Piano in America,* pp. 191, 192, 198, 199.

3. Ibid., pp. 151, 154, 156, 200, 216, 217.

4. The Ampico building is still on the north side of West 57th Street, between Fifth and Sixth avenues. HZS, PI, 8 May 1990, p. 5, LWA. Roell, *Piano in America,* pp. 42–44.

5. Steinway sales in 1923, 7,217; in 1924, 7,420; in 1925, 8,141.

6. FTS to Ziegler, 20 Nov., 4 Dec. 1889, LWA. On FTS's conservative nature, TES to BS, 23 Aug., 13 Sept. 1921; 9 June 1922, HZSF.

7. WSD, 28 Mar. 1867; 23–25, 31 July 1868; 1 July, 31 Aug., 24 Nov., 7 Dec. 1870; 4 July, 31 Aug., 4, 5, 7 Sept. 1871; 22 July 1872. See also "Manifest of All Passengers Taken on Board the S.S. Otendorf," which arrived in New York 1 July 1870, and "Manifest of All Passengers Taken on Board the S.S. Hermann," which arrived in New York 16 Sept. 1871. HZS, PI, 25 Apr. 1990, pp. 11–12.

8. WSD, 1–14 May 1877, 17 Oct. 1978. HZS and JS, PI, 1 Nov. 1888, p. 14. HZS, PI, 25 Apr. 1990, pp. 11–12, and 15 June 1990.

9. HZS, PI, 8 Dec. 1989, pp. 30–33, and 17 Nov. 1989, p. 1.

10. HZS, PI, 22 Feb. 1990, p. 36, and 25 Apr. 1990, p. 18.

11. FTS diary, 1, 6, 9, 13, 15, 16, 17, 20, 21, 23 Jan. 1895, and letter to "My dear Henn," 11 Sept. 1988.

12. FTS diary, 16, 17 Jan. 1895.

13. Ziegler to FTS and CHS, 19 Oct. 1900, Wiesbaden.

14. The letter is to "My dear cousins Henry & Addie," from "Yours most affectionately Fred T. Steinway," 19 Dec. 1889.

15. For their 1925 salaries see State of New York, Taxation of Manufacturing and Mercantile Corporations; for the tax year beginning Nov. see State Tax Department, Albany, N.Y., 1925.

16. HZS, PI, 22 Feb. 1990, p. 32.

17. Ibid., p. 48.

18. Ibid., p. 36. The L replaced the model O. The New York retail price for the L was $1,575–1,700, $25–50 more than the O. See typescript, "New York Retail Prices of Steinway Pianos," prepared by JS and HZS, LWA.

19. See Min, 10 Oct. 1922. On Henry Ziegler see JS, 7 Nov. 1978, Yale, p. 18. HZS interview, 22 Feb. 1990, pp. 33, 34, 72, 73.

20. S&S catalog, 1888. HZS, PI, 18 Mar. 1994. On the straight-grained soundboard and case see Richard Spenlow, "Decorating and Furnishing," *NYT,* 4 Sept. 1887, p. 5. On the advantages of CFTS's new rim see circular "To Our Dealers and Agents," 1 Jan. 1881. See also Smith, *Noble Art,* pp. 84–85. Grand piano case construction: U.S. Patent nos. 204,106 (21 May 1878) and DES10740 (2 July 1878). Rim-bending screw: no. 229,198 (22 June 1880). On history of bending wood see Carolyn C. Cooper, *Shaping Invention, Thomas Blanchard's Machinery and Patent Management in Nineteenth-Century America* (New York, 1991), pp. 3, 211–213, 229–233.

21. JS, Yale, p. 38.

22. FTS diary, 3 Jan. 1895.

23. Frank Lehecka to TES and sons, 21 Sept. 1953. Lehecka, "My Forty-eight Years with Steinway & Sons (1905–1953)," in "Employee Memories of Steinway: Frank Lehecka," HZSF. HZS, PI, 22 Dec. 1989, pp. 1, 2.

24. HZS, PI, 22 Jan. 1988, p. 2.

25. Edward Bilhuber (Ned, son of Paul), 27 Mar. 1990, pp. 3, 18–19. HZS, PI, 8 Dec. 1989, p. 15.

26. HZS, PI, 8 Dec. 1989, p. 15, and 22 Feb. 1990, p. 37.

27. Bilhuber, 27 Mar. 1990, pp. 6, 10.

28. HZS, PI, 8 Dec. 1989, pp. 35–41.

29. Franchise Tax on Business Corporations, State Tax Department, Albany, N.Y., reports for 1921, 1923, 1925, 1926. Min, 27 Mar. 1922 for 1921 net profit, 28 Mar. 1927 for 1926 net profit. HZS, "Factory Shipments from 1891 through 1980," handwritten chart produced in 1980 from shipment records once kept at the factory and now gone.

30. The factory at 43-02 Ditmars Blvd. was completed in 1927 at a cost of $937,000: HZS, "Historical Notes on Steinway Factories," typescript, 28 Jan. 1985, pp. 3–4, HZSF. See also Min, 26 Mar. 1928. Sales of $7,861,627 in 1925 were comprised of roughly $5.7 million in New York, $1 million in Hamburg, $500,000 in London, and $500,000 in Cincinnati: Min, 1 Apr. 1926.

31. Profits for 1921–26 were $74,081 in London; $290,134 in Hamburg; $5,684 in Cincinnati. See Min, 27 Mar. 1922; 21 Mar. 1923; 3, 26 Mar. 1924; 30 Mar. 1925; 1 Apr. 1926; 28 Mar. 1927; 26 Mar. 1928.

32. Min, 21 Mar. 1923, 1 Apr. 1926.

33. Leslie Savin, "In for Repairs: Ayer's Image," *NYT,* Business World section, 10 June 1990. HZS, PI, 25 Apr. 1990, p. 4.

34. Roell, *Piano in America,* p. 175. HZS, PI, 25 Apr. 1990, pp. 3–5. "Raymond Rubicam: My Years at N.W. Ayer & Son," *Advertising Age,* 7 July 1975, pp. 21, 25. Allen Sommers, "Value of Steinway Name Estimated to Equal All Its 50-Year Ad Investment," *Advertising Age,* 24 July 1950, pp. 46–47.

35. Sommers, "Steinway Name." Roland Marchand, *Advertising the American Dream, Making Way for Modernity, 1920–1940* (Berkeley, 1985), p. 265.

36. "Raymond Rubicam." HZS, PI, 25 Apr. 1990, p. 5.

37. Sommers, "Steinway Name." Marchand, *Advertising,* pp. 5, 8, 121, 122.

38. "Raymond Rubicam." Marchand, *Advertising,* p. 14.

39. Roell, *Piano in America,* pp. 180–181. Marchand, *Advertising,* pp. 4, 10, 12.

40. See Min, 14 Nov. 1923. Agreement to purchase, Hermann M. Biggs and Frances R. Biggs (his wife) and S&S, 29 June 1916, file "S&S Real Estate." "Steinways to Move," *Musical Courier Extra,* 8 July 1916, pp. 9–11. "Transfer of Steinway Hall Will Mark Passing of World-Famous Piano Center," *MT,* 15 July 1916, pp. 8–9. The 14th Street Steinway Hall was sold for $475,000: BS to TES, 28 Apr. 1923, HZSF.

41. Norval White and Elliot Willensky, *AIA Guide to New York City* (New York, 1978), p. 20. Edward M. Bassett, "Control of Building Heights, Densities and Uses by Zoning," in *Regional Survey of New York and Its Environs,* vol. 6 (New York, 1931), pp. 362, 369, 375, 383.

42. Typescript marked "Copy, Received from Mr. Solinger [Steinway lawyer] Oct. 8th (1917)," probably a press release sent to *MT.* See also copy of Building Zone Resolution and Use

District Map, section no. 8, adopted by the City of New York, Board of Estimate and Apportionment, on 25 July 1916, LWA.

43. Bassett, "Building Heights," p. 362. The zoning resolution of 1916 was based on a report by the Building Commission, 23 Dec. 1913. See also Hermann M. Biggs to S&S, 29 Aug. 1916.

44. Bassett, "Influential Zoning Cases in the U.S., *Biggs* v. *Steinway & Sons; Anderson* v. *Steinway & Sons,*" in *Regional Survey of New York and Its Environs,* 6:17. S&S also lost a second suit to Anderson, owner of the other two houses. The court order came on 7 July 1920. In 1922, a profitable year, S&S bought more parcels of land on West 58th, and in 1923 another two, on the advice of architects Warren & Wetmore, to "give us great light benefit." See Min, 14 Nov. 1923. Court of Appeals, State of New York, *Hermann M. Biggs and Frances R. Biggs (Plaintiff-Appellants) against Steinway & Sons (Defendant-Respondent),* New York, 1918.

45. On 1919 strike see Min, 21, 24, 26 Apr., 5, 27 May, 25, 30 Sept., 23 Dec. 1919.

46. Min, 14 Nov. 1923, 24 Oct. 1924, 1 Apr. 1926. The construction contract was given to Thompson–Starrett Company. On relaxation of zoning legislation from 1916 to 1919 see Bassett, "Building Heights," p. 383. Cost of the new Steinway Hall: $2,418,888.18 .to Thompson–Starrett; $145,558,84 to Warren & Wetmore; $547,500 for the land. "Toward the cost of this investment they [S&S] have taken a loan from the Metropolitan Life Insurance Company for $1,000,000." On 15 Oct. 1924 S&S received the $475,000 due on the old hall and transferred the title to Samuel Klein, who kept only the back entrance on East 15th Street. Klein's department store remained there until recently, when it gave way to a condominium development. See also HZS, interview, 22 Feb. 1990, pp. 44, 45, 48, 50, 61–67, 72.

47. TES, "The History of the Building of Steinway Hall," Min, 14 Nov. 1923. White and Willensky, *AIA Guide,* p. 173.

48. Specifications for New Building for Steinway & Sons, 109–113 W. 57th and 106–114 W. 58th streets, New York City, Architects Warren & Wetmore, "Limestone," division no. 7, and "Marble and Terrazzo," division no. 13, job no. 1357, 11 Oct. 1923, LWA. See also W. L. Hopkins, "The Steinway Building, New York, Warren & Wetmore, Architects," *Architectural Record* 58, no. 3 (Sept. 1925): 201. "The New Steinway Hall in New York Is Formally Opened to Public," *Music Trade Review,* 20 June 1925, p. 25. HZS, PI, 22 Feb. 1990, pp. 36, 63. HZS, interview with Elizabeth Harkins, 21 Dec. 1978 and 19 Jan. 1979, p. 21, Yale.

49. Hopkins, "Steinway Building," p. 201. "New Steinway Hall Is Opened," p. 23. The sculpted pieces were the work of Leo Lentelli. HZS, PI, 15 June 1990.

50. "Steinway Hall New York—Piano Mecca," sales brochure, c. 1989. The painter was Paul Arndt. See also Specifications for New Building, "Plastering," division no. 12. "New Steinway Hall Is Opened," p. 23.

51. The marble was real up to a certain level; then the walls and columns consisted of wood and plaster painted to look like marble—"imitation Tinos marble." Specifications for New Building, "Marble and Terrazzo" and "Plastering." Brochure, "Piano Mecca." The rug was designed by Ginskey; rpt. in Mullensdorf, "Czecho-Slovakia," "New Steinway Hall Is Opened," p. 23.

52. "New Steinway Hall Is Opened," p. 23. HZS, PI, 22 Feb. 1990, p. 53.

53. Specifications for New Building, "Carpentry Work," division no. 16. "New Steinway Hall Is Opened," pp. 23–24.

54. Hopkins, "Steinway Building," p. 210. "New Steinway Hall Is Opened," pp. 24–25. HZS, PI, 25 Apr. 1990, p. 30.

55. Rent from cash tenants at Steinway Hall in 1925 was $75,600.19: Min, 1 Apr. 1926. Net rent in 1926 was $40,964.22 (gross rent $220,400.56): Min, 28 Mar. 1927. Net rent for 1927 was $58,410.72 (gross rent $248,214.29): Min, 26 Mar. 1928.

56. "New Steinway Hall Is Opened," p. 25. Specifications for New Building, "Plumbing," division no. 22; "Plumbing Accessories," division no. 23; "Finished Wood Floors," division no. 18; "Cast Stone," division no. 23. HZS, PI, 25 Apr. 1990, p. 25. In fact, FTS and Julia never lived in the penthouse. It was rented to William Paley's WEAF radio station.

57. The opening day of the new Steinway Hall at 109 West 57th Street was 15 June 1925: see Min. See also S&S rpt. of "Steinway Appreciations," *Musical Courier Extra* 41, no. 17 (24 Oct. 1925).

58. "Steinway Appreciations." See also paid advertisement in the *NYT*, 18 Oct. 1925, p. 28. HZS, PI, 8 Dec. 1989, p. 34. *NYT*, 12 Oct. 1925, p. 25. "Steinway Start Broadcasting Series," *Musical Courier*, 15 Oct. 1925, p. 8.

CHAPTER 12. A MARRIAGE OF MUSIC AND COMMERCE

1. *S&S Mitteilungen* 63 (Jan. 1923): 339. WSD, 14 Sept. 1883. WS hired Stetson on 20 Nov. 1876. See HZS, "Nahum Stetson," typescript, 7 Mar. 1985, HZSF. Stetson was a Steinway director from 1891 to 1927 and corporate secretary from 1892 to 1926: HZS, "Brief Biographical Notes on Steinway Employees," typescript, 5 Dec. 1989, HZSF. HZS, PI, 25 Apr. 1990, p. 4, LWA.

2. Stetson retired on 31 Mar. 1930: HZS, "Nahum Stetson."

3. Death certificate for Ernest Urchs, Department of Health of the City of New York, registration no. 18975. See also "Francis C. Urchs, Father of Ernest Urchs of Today," *MT*, 8 Dec. 1917. WSD, 8, 13, 22, 24 Apr., 5, 10, 27 June 1862. Urchs was born on 10 Aug. 1864. See obituary, *NYT*, 22 July 1928. Paul Degavre, "Three-Minute Music Chats For Beginners," *Newark Ledger*, 10 Apr. 1927.

4. Chickering died on 23 Mar. 1891. Urchs was hired by S&S that September. See WSD, 23 Mar. 1891. See also Chickering obituary, *NYT*, 25 Mar. 1891. HZS, PI, 8 May 1990, pp. 10–13. See also HZS, "Biographical Notes"; *S&S Mitteilungen* 52 (Feb. 1922): 248.

5. Min, 11 May, 8 Oct. 1896; 28 Mar. 1899. See also HZS, PI, 1 Aug. 1990, pp. 16–18. Ernest Urchs & Co. advertisement, Cincinnati Symphony Orchestra program, 1897–98 season, Ernest Urchs scrapbook, LWA.

6. Min, 28 Mar. 1899. FTS diary, 18 May 1898; 23 Jan., 21 Mar., 15 July 1899, LWA.

7. *MT*, 13 Feb. 1926, Byron H. Collins letter to JS, 16 July 1961, HZSF. HZS, PI, 1 Aug. 1990, p. 8.

8. Ernest Urchs correspondence, Library of Congress, Music Division, report card, 3 June 1978.

9. His scrapbook is filled with thank-you notes from people he sent notes or gifts to. *S&S Mitteilungen* 74 (Dec. 1923): 423–424.

10. *S&S Mitteilungen* 52: 248. HZS, PI, 8 May 1990, pp. 11–13, and 25 Apr. 1990, p. 24.

11. Greiner, "Memoirs," pp. 33, 41.

12. Ibid., pp. 32–35. *S&S Mitteilungen* 74: 423–424.

13. Greiner, "Memoirs," p. 161. *S&S Mitteilungen* 109 (Aug. 1926): 703, 706. Vladimir Horowitz, interview by David Dubal on WNCN radio station, New York, Feb. 1980, cited in Glenn Plaskin, *Horowitz: A Biography* (New York, 1983), p. 76. HZS, PI, 8 May 1990, p. 11.

14. Plaskin, *Horowitz*, pp. 77–79.

15. Albert Chasins, *Speaking of Pianists* (New York, 1958), p. 138; cited in Plaskin, *Horowitz*, pp. 82–84n.

16. Judson Radio Program Corporation rented space in Steinway Hall, and Arthur Judson paid $14,446.50 in 1927 and $14,552.70 in 1928 for the Steinway Concert Hall: S&S general ledger, 1927–28, pp. 144, 151.

17. Arthur Judson, "The Making of a Name," *Etude*, June 1940; cited in Plaskin, *Horowitz*, p. 93. Judson and George Coats created United Independent Broadcasters, in which Columbia Phonographic Company invested $163,000 in 1927 with the proviso that the network be renamed the Columbia Phonographic Broadcasting System. In 1928 William Paley became president of Columbia: William S. Paley obituary, *NYT*, 28 Oct. 1990, p. 39.

18. Henry Prunières, *La Revue musicale* (Apr. 1926); cited in Plaskin, *Horowitz*, p. 90. *Courier*, 29 Dec. 1927.

19. "Ernest Urchs Visits Steinway Representatives and Musical Celebrities Abroad," *Piano Trade*, Dec. 1927.

20. *Hamburger Nachrichten*, 10 Oct. 1927; cited in Plaskin, *Horowitz*, p. 103n. Urchs scrapbook. "Ernest Urchs," *Piano Trade*.

21. Linton Martin, *Philadelphia Inquirer*, 11 Dec. 1928, in *Arthur Judson Press Book* (New York, 1940); cited in Plaskin, *Horowitz*, pp. 105–106n.

22. Urchs scrapbook. Greiner, "Memoirs," pp. 113–114.

23. Barbara Amiel, "Horowitz on the Road," *Canadian*, 10 July 1976; cited in Plaskin, *Horowitz*, p. 109n.

24. Urchs scrapbook.

25. Pitts Sanborn, *New York Telegram*, 13 Jan. 1928; cited in Plaskin, *Horowitz*, p. 108. Urchs scrapbook.

26. Greiner, "Memoirs," p. 52; Urchs scrapbook.

27. Urchs scrapbook. Plaskin, *Horowitz*, p. 110.

28. Urchs scrapbook.

29. *NYT*, 13 Jan. 1928, p. 26.

30. Urchs scrapbook, 23 Feb. 1928.

31. Olin Downes, "Music," *NYT*, 21 Feb. 1928, p. 19.

32. Horowitz's fee would go up to $1,000 per performance, less the 20% commission to Concert Management Arthur Judson: Urchs scrapbook, 23 Feb. 1928.

33. Urchs died on 12 July 1928; see death certificate, Department of Health of the City of New York, registered no. 18975. HZS, PI, 8 May 1990, p. 13. HZS, "Biographical Notes," 5 Dec. 1989. *NYT*, 16 July 1928, p. 25.

34. John Higham, *Strangers in the Land: Patterns of American Nativism 1860–1925* (New York, 1969), p. 208. See also Mary Beth Norton et al., *A People and a Nation: A History of the United States*, vol. 2 (Boston, 1982), p. 656.

35. Higham, *Strangers in the Land*, pp. 219, 222, 223.

36. Interview with JS, Yale, 7 Nov. 1978, pp. 71, 72, 75, 82, 83, 230, 231. Greiner was fluent in his native Russian and Latvian and also adept in German, English, and Polish.

37. Plaskin, *Horowitz*, p. 107.

38. Greiner, "Memoirs," pp. 142–143, 222.

39. Alice Jordan, PI, 30 Apr. 1990, p. 20. B. Chapin, PI, 18 Apr. 1990, p. 33.

40. Jordan, PI, p. 19. Greiner, letter to Jordan, 26 June 1956, Vatican City.

41. FTS, interview by Vivian Perlis, Yale, 8 Apr. 1979, p. 62.

42. About Greiner, "Memoirs," HZS wrote in 1987: "I don't see any useful purpose in having it published. . . . The put down of Paderewski the most unnecessary, if that is the right word." In 1990, however, he wrote: "It contained so many intimate details of Steinway's operations, and his experience with renowned figures in the musical world, that I decided not to publish it in any way. Now that the years have passed, I think it is time to make this available to those interested." But although available to researchers, it has never been published. See also Jordan, PI, p. 44.

43. Greiner, "Memoirs," p. 35.

44. Ibid., p. 78.

45. Ibid., p. 87.

46. Ibid., pp. 77, 99.

47. Julia Dorothea Hermine Cassebeer Steinway, known as Julia D., was born on 12 Oct. 1873. She was the daughter of Henry A. Cassebeer and Louisa Ziegler, daughter of Doretta Steinway and Jacob Ziegler. Julia was named after her great grandmother Julianne Thiemer, wife of HES, and her grandmother Doretta. Julia died on 21 Feb. 1958. JS, family genealogy, HZSF. See also FTS diary, 26 Mar. 1878, 27 Mar. 1899.

48. WSD, 4 Oct., 11 Nov. 1887; 7 Apr. 1890.
49. FTS to Julia, 20 Mar., 30 Apr. 1896, LWA.
50. FTS diary, 10 Mar. 1899.
51. Ibid., 28, 29 Mar. 1899.
52. Ibid., 27, Apr. 1899.
53. Ibid., 28–30 Apr. 1899. Philip H. Sheridan, a courageous Union general, was remembered for regrouping his army in Washington after defeat at Cedars Creek, Va., and then launching a successful counterattack on Confederate forces.
54. Ibid., 1, 2 May 1899.
55. Ibid., 20 Mar., 5, 7 Apr., 25 Aug. 1899.
56. Ibid., 24 Aug. 1899. On Pottier, Stymus & Company see *King's Handbook of New York* (New York, 1893), p. 854.
57. FTS diary, 3 Aug., 14 Dec. 1899.
58. Ibid., 7 Mar., 27, 28 Dec. 1899.
59. HZS, PI, 8 Dec. 1989, p. 42. Florence was born 11 Apr. 1913 and died 7 Jan. 1977. Chapin, PI, p. 38.
60. Chapin, PI, pp. 37–38.
61. Julia and FTS lived at the Dakota, 1 West 72nd Street, in the early 1920s. The maintenance on their cooperative apartment at 420 Park Avenue was $1,416.66 in 1927: general ledger, 1927–28, p. 277. After FTS's death, Julia spent the rest of her life at 555 Park Avenue: Julia Cassebeer Steinway obituary, *NYT,* 22 Feb. 1958, p. 17. Chapin, PI, p. 31.
62. Chapin, PI, p. 13.
63. HZS, PI, 22 Jan. 1988, p. 1. See HZS, Yale, 21 Dec. 1978 and 19 Jan. 1979, p. 4.
64. Greiner, "Memoirs," p. 146.
65. HZS, Yale, p. 2.
66. FTS obituary, *NYT,* 18 July 1927, p. 17.
67. FTS loved golf and was a member of the Oakland Golf Club: obituary, *NYT.*
68. Bob Pyle, librarian at Northeast Harbour, telephone interview by author, 17 Apr. 1990.
69. Hotel register for Kimball House, 29 June 1927; Marian Kimball, telephone interview with author, 17 Apr. 1990; general ledger, 1927–28, p. 277.
70. *NYT,* front page, 14, 15, 16 July 1927; FTS obituary, *NYT.*
71. Min, 25 July 1927.
72. HZS, PI, 25 Apr. 1990, pp. 28, 42. HZS, Yale, 21 Dec. 1978, p. 20.

CHAPTER 13. A RELUCTANT LEADER

1. This note is scribbled in pencil on a small "Memorandum from Theodore E. Steinway." TES used little notes like this as reminders and outlines for after-dinner speeches: "Theodore E. Steinway," under "Speeches & Jokes TES," Family Members file drawer, HZSF.
2. "William R. Steinway, December 20, 1881," typescript, p. 1, probably by HZS, HZSF. B. Chapin, Yale, 12 Oct. 1978, pp. 8, 48.
3. HZS, Yale, 21 Dec. 1978, pp. 2, 18.
4. Paula von Bernuth to Mr. J. Browning, 28 Aug. 1894; "Theodore E. Steinway: TES MSC," HZSF. "Theodore E. Steinway: A Personal Memoir," Oct. 1983, p. 6. *The Collectors Club Philatelist* 36, no. 3 (May 1957): 110. HZS, Yale, pp. 25, 29, 37.
5. Ruth Davis Steinway and JS, Yale, 31 July 1978, p. 7. HZS, Yale, pp. A–D, 3. See also "William R. Steinway," p. 1, HZSF. Legal letter of "Testamentary Guardianship," 9 Jan. 1897, signed by the clerk of the Surrogate Court and sealed on 12 June 1900, HZSF. But, because Paula "failed to qualify as guardian by taking the oath of office within 30 days after the probate of [WS's] will," it was declared on 6 Jan. 1903 that she was not "now and never has been the guardian of her brothers and sister." See Fernando Solinger, letter to Louis von Bernuth, esq.,

6 Jan. 1903, in "Steinway (Von Bernuth) Paula," HZSF. *Strumpfel Peter* fairy tales by Heinrich Hoffman were turn-of-the-century, typically frightening, German children's stories. FTS, interview by Vivian Perlis, Yale, 8 Apr. 1979, pp. 32, 42. See also TES obituary, *NYT,* 9 Apr. 1957, p. 33; HZS, "Theodore E. Steinway," p. 6; FTS, Yale, 8 Apr. 1979, pp. 28, 32.

6. HZS, PI, 25 Apr. 1990, p. 28

7. Ibid., pp. 22–23, 32, 46, and HZS, PI, 8 May 1990, p. 3. HZS, "Theodore E. Steinway," p. 6.

8. TES to Ziegler, 23 Aug. 1915, under "Henry Ziegler," Family Members file drawer, HZSF.

9. HZS, "Theodore E. Steinway," p. 6. HZS, PI, 25 Apr. 1990, p. 42. B. Chapin, PI, 18 Apr. 1990, p. 8.

10. TES, "Address to the Players," Founders' night, 1941. "Theodore E. Steinway," HZSF.

11. HZS, PI, 8 Dec. 1989, p. 44. See also TES, typescript of 1953 *Variety* article, pp. 2–3. On the typescript TES noted that "they cut out all the nice theatre stuff." "Theodore E. Steinway," HZSF. FTS, Yale, p. 14. B. Chapin, PI, p. 10. See also Ruth McAneny Loud, obituary for Ruth Gardner Davis, "Brearley School Bulletin," class of 1906, Fall 1978, HZSF. Ruth Davis Steinway, Yale, pp. A–B.

12. B. Chapin, Yale, p. 47. Ruth Davis Steinway, Yale, p. 2.

13. FTS, Yale, p. 40. Every summer, starting in 1890, the Davis family took up residence at their country property at Long Pond, halfway between Plymouth and Buzzard's Bay, Mass. See Ruth Gardner Steinway, *Plymouth's Ninth Great Lot and the Six Ponds, 1710–1967: A Chronicle* (Kingston, Mass., 1976), p. 36. Ruth Davis Steinway, Yale, 31 July 1978, pp. 5, 8.

14. B. Chapin, PI, p. 7.

15. *MT,* 12, 19 Apr. 1913.

16. "Theodore Steinway and Bride Home from Honeymoon," *MT,* 9 Aug. 1913. See also letters from "Your loyal Friend, A. von Holwede" to "My dear Henry [Ziegler]," 17 June and 25 July 1913.

17. HZS, PI, 8 Dec. 1989, p. 44; interview with Michael Kushner, 6 Jan. 1987, p. 12; and Yale, 21 Dec. 1978, p. 2. B. Chapin, PI, pp. 9–10.

18. TES, "The Book of Long Pond," notes found in 1990 and typed up by Samuel Chapin, p. 1. FTS, Yale, p. 48.

19. HZS, "Theodore E. Steinway," p. 4. R. G. Steinway, *Plymouth's Ninth Great Lot,* pp. 47–48.

20. B. Chapin, PI, p. 19. TES, "Book of Long Pond," p. 5. HZS, "Theodore E. Steinway," p. 4.

21. HZS, PI, 8 Dec. 1989, p. 45. See also HZS, Yale, p. 61. Robert Sellmer, "The Fortune a Piano Built," *Collier's,* 23 Oct. 1948. "375 Park Avenue . . . an apartment building that is now torn down, and the Seagram's building has replaced it." HZS, Yale, p. 2.

22. On TES's continued love for Hadley's music see B. Chapin, Yale, pp. 32, 34. See also "William R. Steinway, December 20, 1881," typescript, p. 2, HZSF, HZS, "Theodore E. Steinway," p. 3. FTS, Yale, p. 11.

23. HZS, "Theodore E. Steinway," pp. 1, 7.

24. State of New York, Franchise Tax on Business Corporations, Department of Taxation and Finance, Albany, N.Y. S&S Annual Report, income for fiscal year starting 1 July (rounded off to nearest thousand): 1915, $609,000; 1916, missing; 1917, $520,000; 1918, $128,000; 1919, $147,000; 1920, $588,000; 1921, $361,000; 1922, $412,000; 1923, $1,067,000 (net); 1924, $1,081,000 (net); 1925, $951,000 (net); 1926, $1,123,000 (net); 1927, $646,000 (net); 1928, $759,000 (net); 1929, $602,000 (net); 1930, $128,000 (net loss).

25. In 1925, 306,584 pianos were produced in the United States; by 1927, the number had already slipped to 218,140, and by 1932, it was down to 27,274. See Bureau of the Census, *Biennial Census of Manufacturers, 1932* (Washington, D.C.), pp. 1122, 1126. There were 142 piano factories in 1925, 124 in 1927, 81 in 1929, and 50 in 1931. See also *Fortune,* Dec. 1934,

p. 154. S&S general ledger, "New Pianos Sold," 1929 and 1932. Losses totaled $1,433,042 in 1932. See State of New York, Franchise Tax on Business Corporations; S&S Annual Report, 1 July 1933.

26. W. H. Strohmenger, president of the Piano Manufacturers' Association in the U.K.; cited in Ehrlich, *Piano*, p. 188.

27. Ehrlich, *Piano*, p. 187. Roell, *Piano in America*, pp. 225–226.

28. Roell, *Piano in America*, pp. 205, 219, 225, 226, 228. *Fortune*, Aug. 1939, p. 46. See also Gortun Carruth, *The Encyclopedia of American Facts & Dates* (New York, 1987), p. 465.

29. Mary Beth Norton et al., *A People and a Nation: A History of the United States, Brief Edition*, vol. B, 2d ed. (Boston, 1988), pp. 411, 703.

30. Ehrlich, *Piano*, p. 184. The logo for the Victrola was Nipper the dog looking into the horn of the machine above the words "His Master's Voice." The name Victrola soon became synonymous with phonograph. See Carruth, *Encyclopedia*, p. 433. For the full line of Victrolas see *NYT*, 16 Dec. 1924, p. 29.

31. Greiner, "Memoirs," p. 104. Ehrlich, *Piano*, p. 184. On prices of Steinway pianos in New York, see price list, 1 Apr. 1930, LWA. The price for a model A Ford in 1930 was quoted by the National Auto History Museum. Carruth, *Encyclopedia*, p. 475. Irwin Unger, *These United States: The Questions of Our Past*, vol. 2, 4th ed. (Englewood Cliffs, N.J., 1989), p. 702.

32. See *Biennial Census of Manufacturers, 1932*, pp. 1126–1127. See also *Fortune*, Aug. 1939, p. 46. Steinway Grand Duo-Art pianos cost from $3,875 to 4,675: New York retail prices, Aeolian Company. See price list for 1924 in Business Files, "Player Pianos," HZSF. For prices of radios, Victrolas, and Radiolas see *NYT*, 16 Dec. 1924, pp. 16, 18, 29.

33. Business Files, "Player Piano Contracts Aeolian, Welte," Aeolian agreement, 9 Mar. 1909 and 7 Apr. 1933, and "Player Piano" file, list of "Player Pianos shipped years 1911–1931." HZSF private collection.

34. In 1926 S&S manufactured mostly grands; only 213 of the 6,294 pianos shipped that year were uprights. In 1932 they shipped 888 grands and 12 uprights. S&S was not in the upright business. These numbers are based on a table by HZS, 28 Dec. 1989. Gross income for new pianos sold in 1929 was $5,401,009; in 1932 that number had dropped to $934,011. See S&S general ledgers, LWA. Building rental income in 1929 was $370,320; in 1933, $251,943. Piano rental income in 1929 was 64,304; in 1933, 23,699. The sale of secondhand pianos brought in $226,933 in 1929, $136,250 in 1933. General ledgers, 1929–30 and 1933–34.

35. The minutes report the previous year's Cincinnati losses: 30 Mar. 1925, 11,161; 1 Apr. 1926, 23,882; 28 Mar. 1927, 10,699; 26 Mar. 1928, 35,667; 6 Mar. 1929, 15,614. S&S subsequently sold the lease to the Cincinnati store for $160,000: Min, 14 Aug. 1929, Min, 21 Jan. 1930, refers to the closing of the Cincinnati branch on 15 Jan. 1930 and "Miss Johanna Waldhaus—our Cincinnati accountant taking charge of the accounts of all Steinway middle west branches." JS, Yale, 7 Nov. 1978, p. 92.

36. Min, 8 June, 27 Aug. 1931. Concert & Artists expense in 1929 was $153,223; in 1930, $151,307; in 1931, $122,969; in 1932, $85,037; in 1933, $85,779. The subsidy was $100 per concert. Rachmaninoff was never paid a subsidy, even during good times. Paderewski's subsidy was $3,100 in 1930, $8,000 in 1931, and $6,000 in 1932. Hofmann's subsidy was $3,300 in 1930, $1,800 in 1931, $900 in 1932, and $1,800 in 1933. See general ledgers, 1929–30, 1931–32, 1933–34. See also Greiner, "Memoirs," p. 108. According to "Levitzki," general ledger, most of the loans were 3- and 6-month notes of $2,500 or $5,000, with interest.

37. All other artists had to pay $25 for piano service in cities where S&S provided pianos; in other cities, the artist would bear all costs for delivery. Service rate for New York City was $20 for all concert halls. See Min, 27 Aug. 1931. See also Greiner, "Memoirs," pp. 108–109.

38. Greiner, "Memoirs," p. 107.

39. Ibid., p. 108.

40. Ibid.

41. Ibid., p. 109.

42. Ibid., pp. 109–110.

43. Ibid., p. 108.
44. The 1931 loss was $484,355. See State of New York, Franchise Tax on Business Corporations. S&S Annual Report, 1 July 1932. General ledger, "Advertising," 1930, $416,904. S&S advertisements, Oct., Nov., Dec. 1930; Jan., Feb. 1931.
45. S&S advertisements, same months as above.
46. *Fortune,* Dec. 1934, p. 156. Min, 1 Dec. 1930; 8, 10 June, 27 Aug. 1931. In 1930 TES's salary was $33,000; it dropped to $28,000 in 1932 and $15,000 in 1933. State of New York, Franchise Tax on Business Corporations. S&S annual reports, 1931–34.
47. In 1931 S&S lost $484,355, or $2,018 per workday. See State of New York, Franchise Tax on Business Corporations. S&S Annual Report, 1 July 1932. Payroll in 1929 was $725,531; in 1931, $528,627; in 1932, $415,432; in 1933, $298,410; in 1934, $298,310: general ledgers, 1929–30, 1931–32, 1933–34. In a random sample of one-third of the personnel cards: in 1929, 126 workers were fired or left of their own accord; in 1930, 76; in 1931, 97; in 1932, 28; and in 1933, 30. Hiring dropped off noticeably in 1930, when only ten people were taken on, and did not rise above single digits until 1936. Jess Manyoky work log 1929–41, LWA.
48. HZS, PI, 5 Nov. 1990, p. 17, and 5 Feb. 1991, pp. 17–18, 20.
49. Ibid., 5 Feb. 1991, p. 19, and 9 Apr. 1991, p. 11.
50. There is a mention of a factory closing on 1 Dec. 1930: "factory only work 12 days to end of the year restricting output to 240 pianos for December. Omit Christmas bonus of one month salary to employees." "We ceased work in our factories toward the end of [1931]" President's Report, Apr. 1932. "Our factories were re-opened Aug. 7 1933": President's Report, 1934. On 23 May 1934, "close factory for two weeks in June due to too much inventory." The factory officially closed on 2 Sept. 1931. "Depression, Factory Closed 2 Sept. 1931, Factory Reopened 7 Aug. 1933": Employees Book, Ditmars, 1928–42, back of front cover. Roughly 400 workers at the Ditmars factory were terminated between 1929 and 1934: 120 in 1929, 75 in 1930, 70 in 1931, 32 in 1932, 29 in 1933, and 70 in 1934: Employees Book, Ditmars, 1928–42. The Employees Books for Rikers, Steinway Hall, Hamburg, and London are missing. State of New York, Franchise Tax on Business Corporations. S&S annual reports, 1932 and 1933, reported that S&S employed 2,000 workers (United States and Europe) in 1931 but only 600 a year later. This number must include part-time workers.

Private payroll, books 4 and 5, S&S, Ditmars Blvd., LIC. In Jan. 1931 there were 36 foremen at the Ditmars factory earning an average salary of $45 a week. Two years later there were 30 foremen earning an average of $34 a week. In 1937 salaries start to rise, slightly. "Theodore E. Steinway shut down the factory and continued to pay his sixty-one foremen, while 1,000 workers were thrown out of jobs": *Fortune,* Dec. 1934, p. 156. S&S hired 10 people in 1930, 3 in 1931, none in 1932, 3 in 1933; 1 in 1934, 5 in 1935, and 53 in 1936.

51. To supplement his income, Manyoky worked with relatives on truck bodies. See Manyoky work log, 1929–41. See also HZS, PI, 3 Dec. 1990, p. 17, and HZS to Mrs. Katherine Ogden, 11 June 1991. On Ernest Eichenbrenner biography see *S&S Mitteilungen* 147 (Jan.–Feb. 1930): 1012, and 155 (Jan.–Feb. 1931): 1076–1077. See also his personnel card, no. 4601, LWA. On Paul Eichenbrenner see personnel card no. 7147. For other piano makers laid off on 1 Sept. 1931 see personnel cards.

52. *Fortune,* Dec. 1934, p. 156, reported that 560 Steinway workers had been reinstated. See also Employees Book, Ditmars, 1928–42, "Number changed." In 1933, 22 employees were rehired and given new time-clock numbers. In 1934, 250 were entered with a number change. The highest number was 898, but many numbers were missing. Manyoky earned $140 in 1932, $335 in 1933: Manyoky work log, 1929–41. In Sept. 1933 S&S had 32 foremen, with monthly total salaries of $3,768 in Sept., $4,880 in Oct., $4,069 in Nov., and $4,129 in Dec. The office payroll averaged $370 a week. There were no paid vacations. Payroll in 1935 was $301,738; in 1936, $341,473; in 1937, $366,125: general ledgers.

"Foremen who had been working five days [43⅓ hours] will now work for 40 hours . . . and will be paid at their 1929 *HOUR RATE* less 18¾%. Foremen working four days [34⅔ hours] will work five days at 7 hours each . . . and will be paid at their present rate. Foremen working for three days [26 hours] will work three days at 7 hours each . . . and one day at five hours . . . and will be paid at their present rate. FACTORY CHAUFFEURS will conform to the above schedule." Notice dated 1 Aug. 1933, Private Payroll, book no. 5, S&S, Ditmars.

53. New pianos sold in 1934 brought in $981,860; advertising totaled $59,565 in 1933, $106,695 in 1934: general ledgers. The piano-playing contest was under the auspices of the National Guild of Piano Teachers; see Roell, *Piano in America*, p. 246. It lost $389,238. See State of New York, Franchise Tax on Business Corporations; S&S annual report, 1 July 1935. Sales of new pianos increased significantly in 1936 to 2,633,232, but by 1940 had dipped below two million: general ledger.

54. Roell, *Piano in America*, pp. 244–247. In 1927, 124 U.S. piano makers had shipped 218,140 pianos. The 36 U.S. piano makers still in business in 1935 shipped only 65,000 pianos, up 27% from 1934. See U.S. Census Bureau, *Biennial Census of Manufacturers, 1932*, pp. 1122, 1126. Total U.S. piano production fell from 120,000 in 1929 to 30,000 in 1932, then climbed steadily to 100,000 in 1937. See Ehrlich, *Piano*, p. 265.

55. Roell, *Piano in America*, p. 248. The Federal Music Project was directed by Dr. Nikolai Sokoloff. On number employed see Carruth, *Encyclopedia*, p. 500; Unger, *These United States*, pp. 716–717.

56. Letter to Music Editor, *NYT*, 23 Jan. 1938, sec. 11, p. 8. Gama Gilbert, "Swing It! And Even in a Temple of Music," *NYT Magazine*, 16 Jan. 1938, p. 21.

57. Gilbert, "Swing It!" Letter, *NYT*, 23 Jan. 1938. Gunther Schuller, *The Swing Era: The Development of Jazz, 1930–1945*, vol. 2 (New York, 1989), chap. 1.

58. Roell, *Piano in America*, p. 207. Some 54% of all piano students stopped after 3 months, and 94% quit before attaining a third-grade proficiency; 80% of all piano music sold was at first-grade level: "Suggestions on Modern Piano Instruction," a series of articles by John Erskine, Rudolph Ganz, Howard Hanson, Josef Hofmann, Ernest Hutcheson, Olga Samaroff, published by S&S (New York, 1931), p. 10.

59. "Suggestions on Modern Piano Instruction," preface and pp. 7, 12. The Klavier Schule of Siegmund Leberr and Ludwig Stark was launched in 1858 with the publication of their *Method.* See also *Fortune,* Aug. 1939, p. 49.

60. Ehrlich, *Piano*, pp. 189–191. Roell, *Piano in America*, pp. 258–259.

61. *Fortune*, Aug. 1939, p. 119. Roell, *Piano in America*, pp. 209, 259, 263.

62. The pioneer in this development was Percy Brasted, owner of the Associated Piano Co. in England, who bought the rights for the new mini console design from Lundholm in Stockholm and manufactured small pianos under the trademark Minipiano. See Ehrlich, *Piano*, p. 190. Roell, *Piano in America*, pp. 259–260. HZS, PI, 9 Apr. 1991, p. 6.

63. *Fortune,* Aug. 1939, pp. 45–46. *American Home* 21 (Dec. 1938): 23–24; cited in Roell, *Piano in America*, p. 260, n. 86.

64. Roell, *Piano in America*, p. 260. *Fortune,* Aug. 1939, p. 45. Ehrlich, *Piano*, p. 191. Number of pianos shipped: in 1934, 47,000; in 1935, 65,000; in 1936, 90,000; in 1937, 106,000. The new uprights varied in height from 3 feet, 9 inches, to 2 feet, 10 inches; in depth from 25½ to 17½ inches; in width from 5 feet with 88 keys to 4 feet, 3 inches, with 72 keys.

65. HZS, PI, 3 Dec. 1991, p. 5, and 15 Jan. 1991, p. 5.

66. *Steinway News* no. 52 (Oct. 1938). Ned Bilhuber, 27 Feb. 1990, p. 28. N. W. Ayer was also encouraging TES to produce an upright. See Mrs. Charles Kittredge, interview by Elizabeth Harkins, Yale, 28 Nov. 1978, p. 8. Eventually Bilhuber redesigned the 45-inch upright into a 40-inch piano: HZS, 9 Apr. 1991, p. 10.

67. Personnel cards show 130 new employees for 1936 and 42 for 1937. Min, 31 May, 8 Nov. 1935.

68. The Steinway Pianino was 45 inches high, 57½ inches wide, and 25 inches deep. See *Steinway News* no. 52 (Oct. 1938). See also HZS, PI, 3 Dec. 1990, p. 5. Charles Reger was born 3 Mar. 1880 in Germany. He lived in Queens and started working for S&S as a casemaker on 10 Apr. 1917. He left S&S on 1 May 1919, returning 4 Oct. 1926 as a cabinetmaker in the fly-finishing department. He stayed in fly finishing until 1938, when he became foreman of the

upright department. See personnel cards 2378, 7553, and 8921. HZS, PI, 9 Apr. 1991, pp. 12–14; 3 Dec. 1990, p. 5; 15 Jan. 1991, p. 6.

69. The S&S factory was set up for the manufacture of grands, and even though the new uprights were produced with machines, Theodore Cassebeer never changed the flow of work through the factory. As HZS recalled, "[the flow of the uprights] had to fit in with the flow of the grands, which was expensive . . . the larger producers, Baldwin and Kimball, had two entirely separate factories," which was more efficient. See HZS, 15 Jan. 1991, pp. 1–2. S&S shipped 1,008 uprights in 1938, 2,175 in 1939. According to the "Statement of Profit and Loss" for the Ditmars and Riker factories, S&S lost $356,174 in 1938 and $201,225 in 1939. According to *NYT*, 16 July 1939, sec. 3, p. 3, S&S net loss for 1938 was $395,306.

70. HZS, PI, 5 Feb. 1991, p. 26. *Fortune*, Dec. 1934, p. 163. "Pianos in Public Places," no. 300,000; typescript, "White House Piano Costs," HZSF.

71. HZS, PI, 5 Feb. 1991, pp. 21–22, 25; and 9 Apr. 1991, pp. 3, 5. Elise Kirk, *Antiques*, May 1984.

72. The men who designed no. 300,000 were Eric Gugler (artist), Dunbar Beck (designer), Albert Stewart (sculptor); see "Pianos in Public Places"; "Preview Luncheon to the Creators of the White House Piano," pamphlet, 3 Dec. 1938; "White House Piano Costs," HZSF.

73. The letter was tucked inside the pamphlet and is dated 28 Nov. 1938 (the Monday before the Saturday event), from TES to HZS at the Ditmars Blvd. factory. "Pianos in Public Places," "Preview Luncheon," HZSF.

74. Charles Cooke, "All About 'That Gold Piano in the White House,' " *Washington Sunday Star*, 21 Aug. 1966, Arts section, p. 1; rpt. by S&S as "The Story of the White House Steinway." See also typescript "White House Piano No. 300,000 (Presented 1938)." It is a model D grand finished in Honduras mahogany. "The Dance Scenes are American: #1 on the left, square dance 'Swing your partner,' #2 Cowboy songster, #3 Colonial Minuet, #4 Darkies' shuffle, #5 Indian grass dance. The red color in the interior is taken from antique red morocco leather": "Steinway Pianos in Public Places."

75. Cooke, " 'That Gold Piano' ": "Steinway Pianos in Public Places." HZS, PI, 5 Feb. 1991, pp. 24–25.

76. B. Chapin, PI, p. 35.

77. HZS, PI, 3 Dec. 1990, p. 1, and 22 Feb. 1990, pp. 39, 47. Much to TES's dismay, Theodore Cassebeer resigned on 12 Sept. 1940. He died the following year, 11 Oct. 1941. B. Chapin, PI, p. 36.

78. HZS, "Theodore E. Steinway," p. 1. HZS, 3 Dec. 1990, p. 6. FTS, Yale, p. 23.

79. HZS, 8 Dec. 1989, pp. 45–46. HZS, Yale, p. 42. B. Chapin, PI, pp. 26–27. HZS, "Theodore E. Steinway," p. 2. Birth dates of children: Theodore, nicknamed Teed (1914); Henry, known in the family as Hank (1915); John (1917); Frederick, known to all as Fritz (1921); Elizabeth, usually called Betty (1925); and Lydia (1928).

80. FTS, Yale, p. 24. HZS, 8 Dec. 1989, p. 49. HZS, Yale, p. 23.

81. FTS, Yale, pp. 23, 25, 27. See also B. Chapin, PI, pp. 57–58. HZS, 8 Dec. 1989, p. 47. HZS, "Theodore E. Steinway," p. 3.

82. HZS, 8 Dec. 1989, p. 51. Howland Davis worked at Blake Brothers and became wealthy managing what became an important brokerage firm in New York. B. Chapin, PI, pp. 1–5. See also HZS, Yale, pp. A–D.

83. HZS, 21 Dec. 1978, pp. 22, 38; 8 Dec. 1989, p. 51; 25 Apr. 1990, p. 46. HZS, "Theodore E. Steinway," pp. 1–2.

CHAPTER 14. NEW BLOOD AND FRESH STRATEGIES

1. S&S general ledger and State of New York, Franchise Tax on Business Corporations, Department of Taxation and Finance, Albany, N.Y. To attract the individual buyer, piano prices were lowered by 29% for an M, 25% for an L, and 17% for a B (D prices were not cut). See

listing prepared by JS in 1983, LWA. Steinway Hall rental income in 1929 was $370,320, and in 1935, $227,906: see ledger books.

2. The other male Steinway in that generation was Charles F. M. Steinway, son of past president CHS. But, according to HZS, "Charles F. M. was useless. . . . He was alcoholic and really he couldn't do anything. So he was out." PI, 5 Nov. 1990, p. 19. Edward Peckerman, PI, 12 June 1991, p. 5.

3. "Theodore D. Steinway," *MT,* Nov. 1982. *S&S Mitteilungen* 175 (July/Dec. 1935): 1272. HZS, "Theodore E. Steinway, A Personal Memoir," Oct. 1983. HZS, PI, 8 Dec. 1989, p. 50, and 15 Jan. 1990, p. 14. HZS, interview by Vivian Perlis, Yale, 21 Dec. 1978, p. 47.

4. HZS, PI, 30 Apr. 1991, pp. 1–2; 15 Jan. 1990, p. 14. HZS, Yale, p. 47. Josephine Steinway, PI, 26 Apr. 1991, pp. 8–10. *S&S Mitteilungen* 175: 1272.

5. HZS, PI, 30 Apr. 1991, p. 4.

6. Josephine Steinway, PI, pp. 4, 11–14, 23, 28, 42, 50–52. Betty Steinway Chapin, PI, 18 Apr. 1990, pp. 33–34. HZS, PI, 8 Dec. 1989, p. 50; 15 Jan. 1990, p. 19; 30 Apr. 1991, pp. 5–6; 27 Aug. 1991, p. 8.

7. HZS, PI, 15 Jan. 1990, pp. 13, 14, 15, 18–19; 30 Apr. 1991, p. 5. Josephine Steinway, PI, pp. 8–9, 16–17, 20–21, 24–26, 45–46. Silverhill Rest Home is now Silverhill Hospital, still in Silvermine, Conn. "Theodore D. Steinway," *MT.* "Steinways in the Federal Service," *Steinway & Sons News* no. 85 (24 Dec. 1940). In 1941 Squadron A was "federalized," taken from the State National Guard by the United States military, and the group broke up. Teed was assigned to the 121st Signal Radio Intelligence company at Fort Meade, Md., a perfect job for him. He spent the next five years in the army, applying his language and cryptographic skills to deciphering codes and aiding MacArthur's return to the Philippines. He was stationed in New Zealand, Australia, the Philippines, and Hawaii and was all the healthier for being so far away from New York and his family. "Theodore D. Steinway," Family Files, HZSF.

8. Typescript, 15 Jan. 1942, "Vietor, Fred Albert," Family Files, HZSF. HZS, PI, 3 Dec. 1990, p. 7; 15 Jan. 1990, p. 8; 25 June 1991, p. 8. B. Chapin, PI, p. 26. Vietor was president of his 1909 class at the Collegiate School and was described in the school's 1909 yearbook as "pugilistic," p. 27. Mrs. Charles Kittredge, interview by Elizabeth Harkins, Yale, 28 Nov. 1978, p. 1. "Squadron A" grew out of a mounted political club during the Blaine-Cleveland presidential campaign in 1884; after the election, eighteen horsemen formed an exclusive cavalry called the "New York Hussars," later renamed "Squadron A." Vietor's "Squadron A" was "called into federal service in 1916 to patrol the Mexican Border, and was again mustered into service as the 105th Machine Gun Battalion of the 27th Division in World War I." See pamphlet "The Squadron A Association Fund" at the New York Community Trust. "Steinways in the Federal Service," *Steinway & Sons News* no. 85. Carruth, *Encyclopedia,* p. 436.

9. JS, Yale, 7 Nov. 1978, pp. 93, 120–121. HZS, PI, 3 Dec. 1990, p. 7; 8 Dec. 1989, p. 49; 22 Feb. 1990, pp. 15–16; 25 Apr. 1990, p. 26; 15 Jan. 1990, p. 7. B. Chapin, PI, p. 26.

10. HZS, PI, 15 Jan. 1990, p. 6; 5 Nov. 1990, p. 19; 22 Feb. 1990, p. 18. "Vietor, Fred Albert," HZSF.

11. Edward Peckerman, PI, pp. 4, 8. HZS, 27 Aug. 1991, p. 16; 5 Nov. 1990, p. 19; 9 Apr. 1991, p. 16; 22 Feb. 1990, p. 13. Teddy Cassebeer regard unionization as a betrayal. Peckerman described him as feeling "let down by people that he had been an uncle to. . . . He was very, very unhappy, and he couldn't remain in charge any longer, and resigned very shortly thereafter. Yes, he was, what do you call it, betrayed. That's a pretty strong word, but I guess it's appropriate." Christian Friedrich Theodore Cassebeer was born 9 Sept. 1879 and died 11 Oct. 1941. *Steinway & Sons News* no. 85. See Min, 12 Sept. 1940. Cassebeer's letter of resignation is on 1920s stationery and dated 11 Sept. 1940.

12. HZS, 22 Feb. 1990, pp. 18, 20; 25 June 1991, p. 12. *Steinway News,* 3 Feb. 1936.

13. HZS, 15 Nov. 1991, pp. 6–8, 10. See also John Bogyos, PI, 23 Dec. 1991, p. 24. J. Bronowski, *The Ascent of Man* (Boston, 1973), pp. 73, 74, 416, 417, 421. Editorial, *Piano Trade Magazine,* Feb. 1936, p. 6.

14. HZS, 8 Dec. 1989, p. 39.

15. HZS, 27 Aug. 1991, p. 7; 22 Feb. 1990, p. 20.

16. Joseph Hofmann letters, Book no. 6, 1932–34, HZSF. See also HZS, PI, 27 Aug. 1991, pp. 6–8; 22 Feb. 1990, p. 80. On accelerated action see United States Patent Office no. 2,031,748, registered 25 Feb. 1936; Frederick A. Vietor, "Piano Keyboard," application 18 May 1934, serial no. 726,196.

17. HZS, 27 Aug. 1991, pp. 6–7; 8 May 1990, pp. 22–23; 22 Feb. 1990, p. 80; 25 June 1991, p. 12. "A New Steinway Grand Piano for Only $885," sales brochure, 1936, LWA.

18. Jess Manyoky recorded: "made 1st Style 'S' 17 Jan. 1935" in his 1929–41 work log, LWA; by Nov. he was working on one S a week. See also Min, 31 May, 8 Nov. 1935. Advertising expenditures were $55,905 in 1935, $186,651 in 1936, $188,027 in 1937, $98,961 in 1938: ledger books. HZS, PI, 9 Apr. 1991, pp. 9–10. The model S baby grand has 7⅓ octaves. It is still manufactured by S&S but was not produced between 1965 and 1977. See Roy F. Kehl, "Outline of Steinway Piano Manufacture, New York City, 1853 to present," typescript memo to "Staff Members, Steinway & Sons Historians, Pianos made by Steinway & Sons," 5 Sept. 1991, p. 4, LWA.

19. The actual ceremony was at Steinway's Ditmars factory, 43-02 Ditmars Blvd., 6 Jan. 1936; see editorial, *Piano Trade Magazine*, Feb. 1936, p. 6. In retrospect it was unusual to introduce a new instrument in January and miss the Christmas sales. "Steinways Announce New Grand at $885; Book $3,000,000 in Orders at New York," *Piano Trade Magazine*, Feb. 1936, pp. 8–10. See HZS, PI, 22 Feb. 1990, p. 25; 27 Aug. 1991, pp. 1–4, 6.

20. The model S was introduced in 1936 for $885 in mahogany and $910 in walnut. By 1940 it was priced at $1,035 in mahogany, $1,060 in walnut, and $985 in ebony. Prices of pianos are taken from a list prepared by JS in 1983. See also 1936 sales brochure for the S.

21. S&S shipped 1,367 grand pianos in 1935, 3,620 in 1936. HZS, handwritten list of piano shipments, 28 Dec. 1989. S&S lost $570,000 in 1933, $397,000 in 1934, and $303,000 in 1935; profit was $68,713 in 1936, $26,059 in 1937: New York State Franchise Tax statements. The Christmas bonus was two weeks' wages: *Steinway News* no. 21 (Nov. 1936). Wages of factory workmen increased 10% from 1 Jan. 1937: Min, 23 Dec. 1936. Work on the S during 1936 doubled Jess Manyoky's income; he earned $802 in 1935, $1,602 in 1936. Vaclav Havlena's income went from $412 in 1934 to $721 in 1935 to $1,272 in 1936, including a $52 Christmas bonus. See Manyoky and Havlena personnel cards and work records, LWA.

22. Michael Kushner, "Paternalism and the Skilled Worker: The Rise of Unionism at Steinway & Sons" (M.A. thesis, Columbia University, 1987), p. 31. In 1935 S&S sales were $1,195,335; in 1936, $2,633,232; in 1937, $2,248,508; in 1938, $1,578,754; in 1939, $2,185,072: Steinway & Sons' Sales, Appendix F. James R. Green, *The World of the Worker: Labor in Twentieth-Century America* (New York, 1980), p. 165. Chandler, *Visible Hand*, p. 496. J. Joseph Muthmacher, *Senator Robert F. Wagner and the Rise of Urban Liberalism* (New York, 1971), pp. 235–258.

23. Min, 17 Mar. 1948. HZS, PI, 27 Aug. 1991, pp. 4–5; 6 Dec. 1991, p. 21.

24. HZS, PI, 6 Dec. 1991, p. 22. S&S shipped 1,580 grands in 1938. Jess Manyoky regulated 289 instruments in 1937 (his income was $2,209) but only 72 in 1938 (income, $558). He had no work at all from 9 June to 10 Nov. See Manyoky work log. In 1937 the piano industry made a profit, and in 1938 it broke even. See *Fortune*, Aug. 1939, p. 120.

25. In 1936 Steinway assembled a few 3-foot, 9-inch, model Ws, but the W was never marketed effectively. It is now listed as one of those rare, experimental, apparently singular Steinway uprights. In 1938 S&S was back in the upright business and sold 1,008 instruments; in 1939, 2,175 uprights. Manyoky worked on more uprights (142) than grands (135) in 1939 and earned $1,561 that year. Upright production increased to 2,231 in 1940 and 3,406 in 1941, an all-time high. Even during World War II S&S sold uprights: 1,454 in 1942, 371 in 1943, 957 in 1944. Roy Kehl, letter to Monica Blank, 7 Oct. 1990, LWA. HZS, PI, 15 Jan. 1991, pp. 2, 6; 27 Aug. 1991, p. 5. HZS, Yale, 19 Jan. 1979, p. 94. John Bogyos, PI, p. 16. *Fortune*, Aug. 1939, p. 120. The

1938 Steinway upright (manufactured until 1960) was a 7 ⅓-octave model P, the Pianino, which measured 3 feet, 9 ½ inches, high. See Kehl, "Piano Manufacture," p. 6. For national upright production numbers see Roell, *Piano in America,* pp. 264–265.

26. *Steinway & Sons News* no. 72 (20 Nov. 1939). Frank Pompa, Yale, 8 May 1979, pp. 7–8. As it turned out, the phonograph–radio venture, which lasted from 16 Oct. 1939 to 31 Dec. 1950, did not make money. See HZS, PI, 5 Nov. 1990, p. 19; 5 Feb. 1991, p. 6. Min, 7 Apr. 1941, 19 Oct. 1939. HZS, "From some of my old stuff. Sale of other than Steinway pianos at Steinway Hall," typescript notes, Dec. 1991, HZSF. See also Chandler, *Visible Hand,* p. 473. See also a report to TES by Dudley P. Felt, Robert Heller & Associates, Inc., Cleveland, 20 Feb. 1941, p. 12, LWA.

27. HZS, 15 Jan. 1991, pp. 9, 10, 43. See also Joe Pirola, 30 Nov. 1980, p. 17.

28. HZS, PI, 15 Nov. 1991, pp. 33–34, 36–37, 48–51. "Corporate History of Steinway & Sons," typescript, c. 1983, HZSF.

29. Min, 30 Dec. 1940. The Minutes for 4 Mar. 1941 reflect the appointment of a new management team at S&S. The retirement of Reidemeister, Irion, and Sturcke in Jan. 1941 would save S&S $28,000 a year: Felt report to TES, 20 Feb. 1941, pp. 2, 5, 19. Jerome F. Murphy, an accountant for Steinert who bought the company during the depression, was elected to the S&S board of trustees 18 Mar. 1941 (Min). Felt was elected on 7 Apr. 1941 (Min). HZS, PI, 15 Nov. 1991, p. 32; 15 Jan. 1991, pp. 8, 9, 11, 33, 39–42; 21 Feb. 1992, p. 1. *Steinway & Sons News* no. 90 (June 1941).

30. HZS, PI, 3 Dec. 1990, pp. 1–2; 15 Nov. 1991, pp. 13, 15. Heller Report, final draft, typescript, 18 Apr. 1941, p. 5. "Corporate History of Steinway & Sons."

31. Heller Report, pp. 1, 3, 4.

32. Ibid., pp. 2–4. Harris proposed to consolidate all operations in the Ditmars buildings and sell the factory on Riker Avenue. HZS, PI, 5 Nov. 1991, pp. 12–15. Min, 23 Apr. 1941.

33. Peckerman, PI, pp. 1, 3. HZS, PI, 5 Nov. 1990, p. 14; 22 Feb. 1990, p. 24. John Bogyos, PI, 10 Jan. 1992, p. 22. Jacob Pramberger, interview by Elliott Sparkman, 9 Mar. 1988, p. 30, LWA.

34. James Cerofeci, handwritten memoir, 1981, p. 1. Cerofeci, PI, 18 Oct. 1981, p. 16. According to Cerofeci's personnel card (LWA) there were years when he did make over $29 per week, but not by much: in 1936, he made $1,718 ($34/wk); in 1937, $1,522 ($30/wk); in 1938, $1,104 ($25/wk); in 1939, $1,452 ($29/wk); in 1940, $1,450 ($29/wk); in 1941, $1,782 ($36/wk). See also Bogyos, PI, 10 Jan. 1992, p. 3.

35. "New York Retail Prices of Steinway Pianos," typescript by JS, sheet no. 3. The first entry in Jess Manyoky's work log in 1936 was "1936, Jan. 9., 1 S Mah(ogany) $6.83." He regulated five pianos that week, four S grands for $6.83 each and one M for $7.16. In 1936 he regulated 143 S models and 92 other grands. Manyoky work records, LWA. HZS, typescript, 10 Feb. 1988, "Random Memories about Unionization of Steinway & Sons," p. 4, n. 1, HZSF. HZS, PI, 5 Nov. 1990, p. 15; 27 Aug. 1991, p. 10; 22 Feb. 1990, p. 24. Cerofeci, 20 Nov. 1991, p. 9.

CHAPTER 15. THE RISE OF A FACTORY UNION

1. The number of workers plummeted from roughly 2,000 in 1930 to just over 500 in 1931: New York State Franchise Tax reports, Albany, N.Y., 1930–34. The factory was officially closed from 2 Sept. 1931 to 7 Aug. 1933. Kushner, "Paternalism," p. 29. John Bogyos, PI, 23 Dec. 1991, p. 15. Vaclav Havlena earned $1,456 in 1929, $1,064 in 1930, $356 in 1931, nothing in 1932, $345 in 1933, $412 in 1934, $721 in 1935, $1,272 in 1936: Havlena work records, LWA. TES, letter to Edward J. Weber, acting president, United Furniture Workers of America Local 102, 9 Oct. 1944, LWA.

2. Green, *World of the Worker,* p. 143. See also Stanley Aronowitz, *False Promises: The Shaping of American Working Class Consciousness* (New York, 1973), p. 237.

3. Caroline Bird, *The Invisible Scar* (New York, 1966), pp. 186–187, 190. Green, *World of*

the Worker, pp. 133, 146–147, 172–173. Joshua B. Freeman, *In Transit: The Transport Workers Union in New York City, 1933–1966* (New York, 1989), p. 42.

4. There are no records of who attended these meetings, but from several oral history accounts it appears that some of the early organizers were James Cerofeci, William McSweeney, Milton Snyder, Gus Teunis, Jess Manyoky, Nils Anderson, and Henry Miller. Manyoky referred to the hall at 20–41 Steinway Street as Busse's, because of the two bartenders, brothers Gus and Artie Busse. In 1927 an Elizabeth Busse (personnel card no. 395, LWA) worked for several months at S&S as a lathe hand in the action department. See Manyoky, PI, 30 Sept. 1981, pp. 4–5. On Busse's Hall, see United Piano Workers Local 102 newsletter, *Piano Key* 3, no. 1 (10 Mar. 1947): 5. See also Bogyos, PI, 23 Dec. 1991, pp. 17–18; 10 Jan. 1992, p. 8. Freeman, *In Transit,* p. 54. On the role of saloons in German working-class life see Hartmut Keil, ed., *German Workers' Culture* (Washington, D.C., 1988), pp. 164–165.

5. Manyoky was recording secretary of the Independent Union at Steinway and financial secretary for Local 102 from 1940 to 1955. He voted "yes" for a 15% pay raise on a 1937 ballot found in records he donated to LWA. See *Piano Key* 2, no. 7 (Sept. 1946). See also Manyoky, PI, pp. 7–9. Manyoky, interview by Linda Ocasio, 11 Mar. 1979, pp. 1, 4–5, 16, LWA. See also "Oldtimer with Steinway Piano 41 Years, Hails Gains of UFWA," 1946 newspaper article, Cerofeci clipping file, LWA. For a similar list of grievances in another union at the same time see Freeman, *In Transit,* p. 60. See also Bogyos, PI, 23 Dec. 1991, pp. 4–5; 10 Jan. 1992, pp. 7, 13. John Furlong, Yale, 25 May 1978, p. 8.

6. Bogyos, PI, 23 Dec. 1991, pp. 17–18; 10 Jan. 1992, p. 15.

7. Manyoky, PI, pp. 7–9. Manyoky interview, 11 Mar. 1979, pp. 1, 4, 5. *Piano Key* 2, no. 7. Bogyos, PI, 23 Dec. 1991, p. 17. See also "Oldtimer with Steinway Piano 41 Years." With the 10% raise, the rate for tone-regulating grands went from $7.16 to $7.88 generally, but only $6.83 to $7.51 for the S. The pay per S remained less than that for all other types of pianos until spring 1939 (this was settled before the first union contract). See Manyoky papers. Peckerman, PI, 12 June 1991, p. 4. Cerofeci, PI, 20 Nov. 1991, p. 6. HZS, in a different interpretation, claimed that the UFWA came to S&S workers because it had "decided to go after the piano business, and naturally you want to go after the biggest and most prestigious first, and so we were it. It's true": HZS, PI, 27 Aug. 1991, p. 10, and 5 Nov. 1990, p. 13.

8. Daniel B. Cornfield, *Becoming a Mighty Voice: Conflict and Change in the United Furniture Workers of America* (New York, 1989), pp. 18, 66. "Proceedings of the Furniture Unity Committee Called by Chairman John Brophy, December 8, 1937 at Washington, D.C.," CIO memo signed by Muster et al., 9 Dec. 1937; cited in Cornfield, *Mighty Voice,* p. 82, n. 36. By 1939 Communists also controlled Mike Quill's transport workers, the Newspaper Guild, the teachers' union, the electrical workers, the longshoremen, and several other unions: Bird, *Invisible Scar,* p. 190; see also p. 184.

9. HZS, PI, 5 Nov. 1990, p. 13. See also HZS, "Random Memories about Unionization of Steinway & Sons," typescript, 10 Feb. 1988. Gustave Teunis (personnel card no. 7671, Ditmars, LWA) was born 11 Oct. 1900 in Paramaribo, Suriname, and recorded his nationality as "Hollander": Bogyos, PI, 23 Dec. 1991, pp. 2, 4, 6.

10. HZS and JS, PI, 1 Nov. 1988, p. 3; 15 Nov. 1991, pp. 56–58; HZS, 6 Dec. 1991, p. 5; 5 Nov. 1990, pp. 12–13, 20. HZS, "Unionization," p. 1. See also Bogyos, PI, 23 Dec. 1991, pp. 5, 7; 10 Jan. 1992, p. 5. Cornfield, *Mighty Voice,* p. 87.

11. On Jewish labor leaders in the UFWA see Cornfield, *Mighty Voice,* pp. 69, 81. On Hillman and Dubinsky see Green, *World of the Worker,* pp. 140–141. HZS, 22 Feb. 1990, pp. 10–12. HZS and JS, PI, p. 3. A grand fore finisher takes the raw keyboard and action and fits them together, establishing the action in the proper position above the keys.

12. William McSweeney (personnel cards 8776 and 7427) was born 9 Apr. 1910. He started working at S&S when he was 23 as a bushing machine operator in the key department. In 1941 he was transferred to the Ditmars factory to work on the gliders. He was inducted into the U.S. Army on 28 Apr. 1944. See Bogyos, PI, 23 Dec. 1991, pp. 2, 6, 19. HZS, PI, 6 Dec. 1991, p. 3; 5 Nov. 1990, p. 13; 15 Nov. 1991, pp. 60–61. HZS interview by Michael Kushner, 6 Jan. 1987,

pp. 16, 21–22, LWA. Cerofeci, PI, 18 Oct. 1981, p. 8. Also see Gary Gerstle, *Working-Class Americanism: The Politics of Labor in a Textile City, 1914–1960* (Cambridge, 1989), p. 125.

13. HZS, PI, 5 Nov. 1990, pp. 20–22. Kushner, "Paternalism," pp. 41, 43. HZS, Kushner interview, p. 16. HZS, PI, 27 Aug. 1991, p. 12. Joseph Braun (personnel card 335, Riker) was born 22 Oct. 1898. He started as a painter in the repair department at S&S on 23 Mar. 1936.

14. Salvatore Daddio, interview by Sam Sills, 16 July 1987, p. 21, LWA. Bogyos, PI, 10 Jan. 1992, pp. 12, 16.

15. Manyoky, Ocasio interview, p. 16. HZS, PI, 5 Nov. 1990, p. 14. See also HZS, "Unionization," leaflet dated 14 Aug. 1939, with a preamble: "In order to correct certain rumors which we understand have recently been circulated throughout our plants, the management of Steinway & Sons desires all employees to clearly understand."

16. Peckerman, PI, p. 4. HZS, Kushner interview, p. 16. HZS, PI, 27 Aug. 1991, p. 15.

17. The Voter's identification card read: "Place of election: Public School No. 141, Queens, 21st Avenue between 37th & 38th Streets, Long Island City, N.Y. Date of election: Sept. 25, 1939. This is not your ballot, your vote will be absolutely secret." Written in pencil: "N.L.R.B. Election." Joe Pirola, PI, 30 Nov. 1980, p. 29. Bogyos, PI, 10 Jan. 1992, p. 16.

18. Peckerman, PI, p. 4.

19. JS, Yale, 7 Nov. 1978, p. 119.

20. Cerofeci, PI, 18 Oct. 1981, pp. 2–3. Cerofeci's power skyrocketed when McSweeney was transferred to Ditmars for a year to work on uprights (26 May 1941–18 Sept. 1942) and when McSweeney was inducted into the U.S. Army (28 Apr. 1944). McSweeney personnel cards 7427 and 8776. HZS, PI, 5 Nov. 1990, p. 22.

21. Min, 1 Dec. 1939, 21 May 1941: "A contract with United Piano Workers' Union, Steinway Local 102, United Furniture Workers of America, CIO was approved." See folder entitled "Heller Report, 1941," final draft, typescript, 18 Apr. 1941, p. 14. See also HZS, 8 Dec. 1989, p. 52, and 27 Aug. 1991, p. 13.

22. HZS in 1897, cited in Kushner, "Paternalism," pp. 11, 30. A photograph of the Steinway Orchestra appeared in *S&S Mitteilungen* 99 (Dec. 1925): 628, and in *Musical Courier*, 19 Dec. 1925. The 28-piece orchestra was started in the early 1920s and was led by Heinz Horster; Jess Manyoky, John Furlong, and Frank Walsh played violin, and Michael Bogyos played clarinet. Bogyos, PI, 10 Jan. 1992, pp. 3, 20, recalled that "the only time I got to Riker (factory) was when the band played there once a month. We played at Riker once a month and once a month we played in Ditmars (factory) for the people while they ate their lunch." JS, Yale, pp. 122–123. For more fond memories of the Steinway Orchestra and other employee social events see FTS, Yale, 8 Apr. 1979, p. 68. On the Steinway outings see "Boat Ride News," bulletin no. 4, Apr. 1929, Boat Ride Committee, S&S. On the boat ride see Mrs. Charles Roach, daughter of Henry Miller (Steinway action worker 1908–68), letter to author, 7 Sept. 1982. In 1937, 2,846 workers and their families paid 50 cents a ticket for the boat ride; see S&S, "Fire Protection," bulletin no. 9, Sept. 1937. Daddio, Sills interview, 16 July 1987, pp. 6, 7, 9, 16. Charles Walters, interview by Jeffrey Kroessler, 22 Oct. 1981, p. 3, LWA.

23. HZS, Yale, 21 Dec. 1978, p. 68.

24. HZS, PI, 27 Aug. 1991, p. 13. See also JS, Yale, p. 123. Furlong, Yale, p. 13. Walter Drasche (personnel cards 7133 and 7134) was 17 in the summer of 1935, when he started his apprenticeship in the damper department at S&S. He went into the U.S. military in summer 1941 and after the war came back to S&S to apprentice as a tone regulator. He also became the "shop chairman, and chairman of most of the delegating committees, and negotiating committees" for Local 102. In the factory he was promoted to foreman of the action department. Walter Drasche, interview by Sam Sills, 4 June 1987, pp. 3–5, LWA.

25. Drasche, Sills interview, 4 June 1987, pp. 3, 4. For a different opinion of paternalism at S&S see Kushner, "Paternalism," p. 43: "The unique relationship which evolved at Steinway was based on the legacy of paternalism, which had been weakened but not entirely destroyed by the depression."

26. HZS, PI, 5 Nov. 1990, p. 16; 9 Apr. 1991, p. 15; 25 June 1991, p. 20; 27 Aug. 1991, p. 15.

See also HZS, Yale, 21 Dec. 1978, p. 67. Negotiations for the 1941 contract started with a 12-hour meeting on 20 Oct. 1941 and continued on a weekly basis. See Manyoky papers and work log.

27. See "1941 Union Contract," dated Nov. but signed 3 Dec. 1941, between S&S and the United Piano Workers Union, clauses 2 and 3, p. 2, and clause 18, p. 12, LWA. The summer vacation was for employees who had worked a year or more as of 1 June and would begin in the summer of 1942: pp. 12–14, items 17, 18, 20, 22, and Schedule A, "Wage Increases." In 1945 S&S would claim that they gave the workers a 22.5% raise in 1941. The union then reminded Steinway that the cost of living in 1941 had gone up about 40%. See "To the Members of Local 102," 10 Dec. 1945, LWA.

28. Heller Report, p. 2, refers to the "elimination of the foundry, plate, and key departments" as part of a plan to consolidate the floor space used for manufacturing pianos. HZS insisted that the union, though an annoyance to Vietor, was "not connected in any way with" the closing of the key-making department or the foundry, although both departments were centers of union ferment. See HZS, PI, 15 Nov. 1991, p. 12.

29. On the silicosis crisis see David Rosner and Gerald Markowitz, *Deadly Dust, Silicosis and the Politics of Occupational Disease in Twentieth-Century America* (Princeton, 1991). See Furlong, Yale, 25 May 1978, pp. 29–30. S&S purchased an almost finished plate from O. S. Kelly and then from Wickham, both in Springfield, Ohio; see Bogyos, PI, 23 Dec. 1991, p. 20. Joe Pirola, PI, p. 32.

30. Otto Wessel and his partners Nickel and Gross all worked for S&S as action makers before they started their own business in 1875. See Dolge, *Pianos and Their Makers,* pp. 379–381. HZS, PI, 15 Nov. 1991, pp. 11–12. "It was also resolved to discontinue the Key dept., Foundry and Plate dept": Min, 30 Dec. 1940. For calculations on savings in closing the foundry and key department see "Heller Report Worksheets," report no. 186, "Factory Costs and Expenses," and within it a sheet of paper entitled "Resumé of Savings," 28 June 1939: "Savings on plates = $16,913; Savings on keys = $10,729; Clerical savings = $1,500," for total savings of $29,142, HZSF. See also Felt, Robert Heller & Associates, Inc., report to TES, 20 Feb. 1941, p. 7. The Heller numbers all backed up Vietor's ideas. "He's the pusher in the whole thing": HZS, PI, 15 Nov. 1991, p. 12.

31. HZS, PI, 9 Apr. 1991, p. 16. Min, 12 Sept. 1940. The New York factory shipped 6,294 pianos in 1926 (6,081 grands and 213 uprights); 3,924 in 1940 (1,693 grands and 2,231 uprights); 5,601 in 1941 (2,195 grands and 3,406 uprights): HZS's handwritten list of "Factory Shipments from 1891 through 1980," 28 Dec. 1989. S&S net loss in 1940 was $39,903; net income in 1941 was $142,612; see *NYT,* 28 Apr. 1941, p. 32.

32. According to his military activities list, Vietor was "inducted in the Army on January 27, 1941, as Lieutenant Colonel in the 101st Cavalry, XR" and then, on the very same day, was relieved of his duties, SCD, and placed on an unassigned list: *Squadron "A" Association Fund,* pamphlet published by the New York Community Trust. See also HZS, PI, 15 Nov. 1991, p. 18. TES placed Paul Bilhuber in charge of the factory and created a new title for Vietor: general manager. See Min, 4 Mar., 23 Apr. 1941. HZS, 15 Nov. 1991, pp. 17–19. On Vietor's death, see obituary, *New York Herald Tribune,* 19 June 1941. "Corporate History of Steinway & Sons," typescript, c. 1983. See also HZS, PI, 15 Jan. 1991, p. 12, and Yale, 21 Dec. 1978, pp. 65–66.

33. Paderewski died on 29 June 1941 in the Buckingham Hotel, next door to Steinway Hall on West 57th Street: Slonimsky, *Dictionary of Musicians,* p. 936. See also HZS, PI, 22 Feb. 1990, p. 46. The concert was due to be played on 26 Feb. 1939. See Greiner, "Memoirs," pp. 220–221.

CHAPTER 16. DIVIDED LOYALTIES IN WORLD WAR II

1. B. Chapin, Yale, 12 Oct. 1978, pp. 49–50. FTS, interview by Vivian Perlis, Yale, 8 Apr. 1979, p. 93.

2. Roell, *Piano in America,* p. 269. TES, *Memoirs,* "War Works 1942: The Lyre Bird Soars,"

rough notes, c. 1955, in Ruth Steinway Papers, privately held by her grandson Samuel Chapin. On other companies in Germany see London Hamburg Report, suppl. 1 to Hamburg Report, memo to TES from Solinger & Solinger, 15 Oct. 1946.

3. G. M. Devlin, *Silent Wings* (New York, 1985), pp. 33–36, 42–47; J. E. Mrazek, *The Glider War* (London, 1975), cited in J. Norman Grim, "Army Glider Construction during World War II from the Pudgy Three Seaters to the Gentle Giants," *Journal of the American Aviation Historical Society,* Winter 1989, p. 298, n. 1. The victory on the hilly terrain of Crete was actually due more to the paratroopers than the gliders. Out of 53 gliders, only 9 landed on target. See G. C. Kiriakopoulos, *Ten Days to Destiny: The Battle for Crete, 1941* (New York, 1985), pp. 119–244. See also Lowden, *Silent Wings at War,* pp. 32–39.

4. HZS, 1 Aug. 1990, p. 45.

5. Ibid. Roell, *Piano in America,* p. 269. TES to Edward J. Weber, acting president, UFWA, Local 102, 23 Oct. 1944, LWA. JS, Yale, 7 Nov. 1978, p. 124.

6. Eldon Cessna of Wichita, Kans., son of Cessna Aircraft's founder, designed the CG-2 glider in 1930: Eldon Cessna obituary, *NYT,* 25 Feb. 1992.

7. Pirola, PI, 30 Nov. 1980, p. 17. HZS, PI, 21 Feb. 1992, p. 12. TES to U.S. Army Air Force, Price Adjustment Section, draft, 30 June 1943, p. 5, LWA. The first subcontract (6 Apr. 1942) was originally for $500,000 and increased on 6 Jan. 1943 to $2,750,000: Min, 6 Apr. 1942. On number of workers see Min, 16 Dec. 1942 (1,073) and 20 Sept. 1944 (540). The second subcontract was for 500 gliders and parts; $5,750,500 was confirmed on 24 May 1943. See Anderson, Jr., letter to H. J. Maynard, Jr., 24 May 1943, and Maynard letter to TES, 21 Aug. 1943. The cost dispute was finally resolved in a letter from Orcutt to E. S. Gremse, 30 Aug. 1943, LWA. The third subcontract was in Apr. 1944, when S&S added 513 CG-4A gliders to the May 1943 contract. See "Supplemental Agreement No. 1 to subcontract with S&S under Prime Contract No. W535-ac-40674," LWA. See also "1942–1944 War Work Contracts, General Aircraft and Leases," HZSF. C. E. Torrance to Orcutt, "Latest Revision of Price Distribution Schedule by Assemblies," LWA.

8. Pirola, PI, p. 17. S&S was given permission to "complete the assembly of 162 grands": see Min, 17 Mar. 1943. FTS, Yale, p. 90. For a brief period, Paul Bilhuber (4 Mar.–23 Apr. 1941), then Thomas R. Harris (23 Apr.–16 July 1941), managed the factory: see Min. On 16 July 1941, J. Doane Anderson, Jr., was appointed factory manager.

9. HZS, PI, 6 Dec. 1991, pp. 14, 30, 33; 25 June 1991, p. 27; 1 Aug. 1990, p. 45. Grim, "Army Glider Construction," pp. 298, 300, 302–303. S&S was "stopped from attaining its production goal through the inability of the prime contractor to furnish certain metal parts needed for the complete assembly of woodworker parts." See TES to U.S. Army Air Force, pp. 5–6. See also Anderson, Jr., to TES, 5 Aug. 1943, "New Proposed G.A.C. Contract," p. 2, LWA.

10. On the Anderson rumors see HZS, PI, 15 Jan. 1991, p. 3; 25 June 1991, p. 28. On the union's response to Anderson's firing see Weber, letter to TES, 20 Sept. 1944, and TES to Weber, 2 Oct. 1944, LWA.

11. HZS, PI, 9 Apr. 1991, p. 17. FTS, Yale, p. 108.

12. "Nature of Grievance: We the Casemakers are not satisfied with the time that was allowed us. . . . The glue is much harder now than in 1941, and dulls our tools more and we have to sharpen them more often, which takes quite a bit of time." Grievance adjustment form, Case Assembly Department, 8 June 1945; see also Joseph Lakner, "Loss of time sharpening tools because of the glue now being used," Case Department, 29 May 1945, LWA. But for certain parts, the hot Peter Cooper glue was not replaced—e.g., the soundboard. John Bogyos, PI, 10 Jan. 1992, pp. 23–26. HZS, PI, 25 June 1991, pp. 21–23. Paul Bilhuber was credited with bringing the new fast-drying glue into the factory in 1938 for use in the production of uprights. See also Ned Bilhuber, PI, 27 Mar. 1990, pp. 16, 28–29.

13. HZS, PI, 25 June 1991, p. 23. FTS, Yale, pp. 104–105.

14. S&S agreement with United Piano Workers Local 102, UFWA, CIO, 1 Oct. 1945, p. 11, article 14, "Veterans," LWA. Walsh, PI, 21 Apr. 1989, p. 25. HZS, PI, 1 Aug. 1990, p. 46; 26 June 1991, p. 24; 15 Nov. 1991, p. 54; and Yale, 21 Dec. 1978, p. 69. Emily Cheney, "Tunes in the Air,"

unknown newspaper, c. 1942. See also P. Zajic, Porter Group I, grievance adjustment form, 24 Aug. 1945, LWA. S&S ordered 357 women's uniforms in 1944; Anderson, Jr., memo to E. B. Ormond, 13 Jan. 1944, LWA.

15. HZS, PI, 25 June 1991, pp. 24, 27. R. B. Jones to A. G. Geiger, memo, 1 Feb. 1943, with chart attached showing 1–3.5 gliders built per day, LWA.

16. Walsh, PI, p. 21.

17. Geoffrey Parsons, Jr., *New York Herald Tribune,* 4 July 1943, cited in *Steinway News* no. 116 (July–Aug. 1943). Grim, "Army Glider Construction," p. 302, n. 22.

18. In 1944 General Aircraft sold the U.S. Army 500 gliders for $26,248 each. S&S's subcontract was $10,695 for the wooden parts of each plane. See "1942–1944 War Work Contracts, General Aircraft and Leases," HZSF. See also Lowden, *Silent Wings at War,* pp. 17, 38–39. "By September of 1944, 10,584 cargo gliders had been delivered at a total cost of $271,168,544. The average cost was $25,630." Grim, "Army Glider Construction," p. 305, nn. 38–40.

19. Lowden, *Silent Wings at War,* pp. 67–68. See also HZS, PI, 6 Dec. 1991, pp. 32–33; Yale, pp. 73–74.

20. The "Flying Falcon" was the first glider to land at Normandy on D day, before dawn on 6 June 1944; see Devlin, *Silent Wings.* Lowden, *Silent Wings at War,* pp. x, 67–73. See also Grim, "Army Glider Construction," p. 305. HZS, PI, 1 Aug. 1990, p. 45; 6 Dec. 1991, pp. 32–33. *Steinway News* no. 126 (July 1944).

21. HZS, PI, 6 Dec. 1991, p. 33.

22. The increased depreciation incurred by operating a plant and machinery on a 54-hour week, with a third of the workers on night shift, was never charged to glider operations. TES to U.S. Army Air Force, p. 7. HZS, PI, 6 Dec. 1991, p. 34; 25 June 1991, p. 27; and Yale, 21 Dec. 1978, pp. 71, 74. See also Paul Bilhuber to TES, 7, 9 Apr. 1943, LWA.

23. See TES to U.S. Army Air Force, p. 6.

24. Letter from TES to his cousin Clarissa Steinway Oaks on 17 June 1943, F14, LWA.

25. TES did participate in the endless negotiations on the second subcontract with General Aircraft during the spring, summer, and fall of 1943. It is the only time he appears regularly in the documents. TES to Anderson, Jr., 26 July 1943. See also TES to Orcutt, Renegotiation of Original Contract, 9 July 1943, LWA. FTS, Yale, pp. 88–89.

26. Lydia Steinway Cochrane, PI, 5 Oct. 1991, pp. 18–19, 23.

27. J. D. Anderson, Jr., to TES, 28 Oct. 1943, LWA. J. D. Anderson, Jr., factory manager, to W. S. Mayfarth, War Production Board, 21 Jan. 1944, LWA. See also Anderson to Roman de Majewski, 28 Feb. 1944, "Release 800 pianos by WPB," LWA: "Our mill room very shortly will need additional work because of the absence of additional glider work." On canceling the glider subcontract see "General Aircraft Corp—1942–1943, Contracts and Quotations—1944 Correspondence," LWA. TES to H. J. Maynard, Jr., 25, 26 Apr., 16 May 1944; A. G. Geiger to W. W. Bray, 4 May 1944. HZS, PI, 15 Nov. 1991, p. 42.

28. On the 405 uprights see Min, 16 June 1943, and Walsh memo to Anderson, Jr., "Order for 405 victory model Army Pianos," 22 Sept. 1943, LWA. J. Joseph Whelan, recording secretary, War Production Board, to S&S, 1 Feb. 1944, CD: 27, Musical Instruments, LWA. See also Charles Dopf to Anderson, Jr., 3 Feb. 1944, "800 Additional Grand Pianos," LWA. Majewski convinced the WPB to permit S&S to manufacture "four hundred pianos for replacement of pianos now being used for concert purposes throughout the United States (in addition to the) eight hundred pianos for sale to our dealers": Majewski to Col. William A. Peterson, commanding general, Philadelphia Quartermaster Depot, 19 Jan. 1944; 21 Jan. 1944, Schedule C, "Delivery Schedule 40 Upright Pianos," total = 589 pianos: LWA. The cost for 217 pianos was $105,354. See also Anderson, Jr., to Majewski, 28 Feb. 1944, "Release 800 Pianos by WPB." Dopf to Anderson, Jr., 5 June 1944, LWA. On permission to manufacture 2,850 pianos (1,000 of them uprights), see Min, 18 Oct. 1944.

29. HZS, PI, 1 Aug. 1990, p. 46; 25 June 1991, p. 25; Yale, pp. 71–72. JS, Yale, 7 Nov. 1978, pp. 124, 210–211. FTS, Yale, pp. 90–93. The ODGI piano (1942–45) was based on sketch 1051 (1940–41); see Kehl, "Piano Manufacture," p. 6. See also *Steinway News* nos. 106 (Sept. 1942)

and 112 (Mar. 1943). On use of iron wire see grievance adjustment form, George Guth, Spinning Department, 6 June 1945, LWA: "Due to different wire—it is harder—and more work to make the strings than in 1941. Due to no more copper wire, I have to spin all iron wire by hand. This takes more time." *Steinway News* no. 126 (July 1944).

30. S&S shipped 1,454 uprights and 1,411 grands in 1942, 371 uprights and 248 grands in 1943, 957 uprights and 462 grands in 1944, 758 uprights and 693 grands in 1945: HZS, "Shipments of Pianos—1939–1945," 28 Dec. 1989, HZSF. See also TES to Weber, 23 Oct. 1944, 20 Jan. 1945, LWA. See also TES to Maynard, Jr., 25, 26 Apr., 16 May 1944; A. G. Geiger to W. W. Bray, 4 May 1944.

31. E. B. Ormond to Majewski, "Thonet Bros. Lamination," 12 May 1944, LWA. On "Operadic Plant Broadcaster" see *Steinway News* no. 127 (Aug. 1944). See also Min, 16 June, 15 Sept. 1943; 21 June 1944.

32. JS, Yale, p. 126. HZS, PI, 1 Aug. 1990, p. 46; Yale, p. 74. On the cemetery trade in Queens see Vincent Seyfried, *Queens: A Pictorial History* (Virginia Beach, Va., 1982), p. 116. On Steinway's casket business see Min, 19 May 1943, 23 Aug., 20 Sept. 1944. See also Ormond to Anderson, Jr., re "Caskets—Priority," 2 Feb. 1944, and Anderson, Jr., to Walsh, 21 Mar. 1944, LWA.

33. TES to Weber, 9 Oct. 1944, p. 2. Price listing, "Design 3A, Half Couch Mahogany Casket," 6 Dec. 1944, LWA.

34. JS, Yale, pp. 127, 212. B. Chapin, PI, 18 Apr. 1990, pp. 26–27, 31. B. Chapin, Yale, pp. 49–50. FTS, Yale, pp. 84–87, 94, and PI 23 Mar. 1993, pp. 1–3. Cochrane, PI, pp. 18–19. HZS, Yale, pp. 23, 70, 77; 8 Dec. 1989, p. 50. See also *Steinway News* nos. 115 (June 1943), 123 (Mar.–Apr. 1944), 124 (May 1944); and Art Cohn, *San Francisco Call Bulletin*, 28 July 1943, cited in *Steinway News* no. 117 (Sept. 1943). *Harvard Class of 1935, Twenty-fifth Anniversary Report* (Cambridge, Mass., 1960), pp. 1285–1286.

35. JS, Yale, pp. 127, 212. B. Chapin, PI, pp. 26–27, 31. B. Chapin, Yale, pp. 49–50. FTS, Yale, pp. 85–86, 94. Cochrane, PI, pp. 18–19. HZS, Yale, pp. 23, 70, 77; PI, 8 Dec. 1989, p. 50.

36. HZS, PI, 21 Feb. 1992, pp. 9–10; 1 Aug. 1990, p. 43.

37. HZS, PI, 15 Nov. 1991, pp. 37–38; 21 Feb. 1992, pp. 9–10. JS, "Chronology of Steinway & Sons," typescript with pencil notations, c. 1984, HZSF. JS, Yale, pp. 135–136. *Steinway News* nos. 106 (Sept. 1942); 110 (Jan. 1943): 1; 127 (Aug. 1944).

38. Walter Schwemm, PI, Hamburg, trans. Anna-Katrin Stammer, 8 Aug. 1990, p. 22, LWA.

39. In 1933 S&S had considered merging with Bechstein and Blüthner in Germany. See "Theodore Ehrlich Minutes," New York, 1933, HZSF. HZS, Yale, p. 33. HZS, PI, 4 Oct. 1991, p. 1. On the Bechstein–Hitler connection see "Foreign Journal," *Washington Post*, 9 Aug. 1993, p. A10.

40. On 22 Dec. 1943, BS requested a copy of his marriage certificate from the "registry office Berlin-Schoeneberg," under "Steinway, William Richard," HZSF. See also HZS, PI, 30 Apr. 1991, p. 10; 4 Oct. 1991, p. 2. Ratcliffe, *Steinway*, p. 50. On the Berlin Nazi office see Elli Kuhne, "Berlin Steinway History from 1945," typescript, 17 Jan. 1975, HZSF. On the BS–TES correspondence, HZS noted that certain files had always been missing. On Steinway letters in German archives contact Bundesarchiv, Postfach 320, 56003 Koblenz.

41. Gretl Bruhn, "Short Look at the History of Steinway—Hamburg," notes edited by HZS, typescript, c. 1979, HZSF. See also Hermann Keyser, "My Life as Employee at Steinway & Sons, February, 1929 until June 30, 1972," typescript trans. Mrs. Claussen, 31 Oct. 1979, p. 2, HZSF. Kurt Albrecht, PI, Hamburg, trans. A.-K. Stammer, 15 Sept. 1990, p. 8.

42. New York loss was $217,913, Hamburg profit $6,148, London profit $6,596: Min, 30 Mar. 1939. See Concert & Artists reports from London for 1938 and 1939, p. 4.

43. Bruhn, "Steinway—Hamburg," p. 4. See also Ratcliffe, *Steinway*, p. 50. On government offices controlling each operation of S&S in Hamburg see London Hamburg Report, 11 Oct. 1945, suppl. 4, pt. II.

44. Ratcliffe, *Steinway*, p. 51. Bruhn, "Steinway—Hamburg," p. 5. See Keyser, "My Life as Employee," p. 3. See also Lorenz Mutzel, PI, Hamburg, trans. A.-K. Stammer, 4 Nov. 1990,

p. 14. On materials supplied to the German government see London Hamburg Report, 15 Oct. 1946, suppl. 3A, LWA. After 1942 S&S could ship pianos outside Germany with a permission document issued by Otto Krause. Bruhn, "Steinway—Hamburg," p. 4. On the trade agreement with Sweden and Norway see Karl Jungnitsch, PI, Hamburg, trans. A.-K. Stammer, 16 Aug. 1990, p. 22. See also TES to R. W. Flourney, acting legal advisor, U.S. State Department, 19 June 1945, citing an 11 June 1945 cable from John Ehrlich, manager of Steinway House in London, National Archives. Grand and upright production in Hamburg was 1,621 in 1939, 1,352 in 1940, 698 in 1941, 271 in 1942, 201 in 1943, 144 in 1944. London Hamburg Report, 15 Oct. 1946, suppl. 3A. HZS, PI, 8 Dec. 1989, p. 28. Richard Ehrlich, PI, 12 Oct. 1992, pp. 9–10.

45. *S&S Mitteilungen* 76 (Feb. 1924): 445. Schwemm, PI, p. 23. See also HZS, PI, 4 Oct. 1991, pp. 9–10. Ehrlich, PI, p. 10.

46. Jungnitsch, PI, 16 Aug. 1990, pp. 1, 25–26. Albrecht, PI, p. 7.

47. Jungnitsch, PI, 16 Sept. 1989, pp. 2, 25–26. Albrecht, PI, pp. 4, 11, 22. Albrecht was drafted in 1940 and served as a front-line soldier until he was wounded and captured in 1945. The Hamburg factory had 200 employees in 1941, 140 in 1942, 130 in 1943, 110 in 1944: London Hamburg Report, 11 Oct. 1945, suppl. 4, pt. 2, LWA. Heinrich Lorenzen, PI, Hamburg, trans. A.-K. Stammer, 11 July 1990, p. 15.

48. Albrecht, PI, 15 Sept. 1990, pp. 21–22.

49. Keyser, "My Life as Employee," p. 4. See also JS, Yale, p. 59. On the bombing of Hamburg see Martin Caidin, *The Night Hamburg Died* (New York, 1960), pp. 8–10, 63–119, 129. On value of Hamburg assets see TES to Paul T. Culberton, U.S. State Department, 6 Apr. 1942, National Archives.

50. The factory was built between 1923 and 1928; it was bombed 22 Oct. 1944 and 15 Mar. 1945. See Bruhn, "Steinway—Hamburg," p. 5. See also Keyser, "My Life as Employee," pp. 4–6. Ratcliffe, *Steinway,* pp. 51–53.

51. Keyser, "My Life as Employee," pp. 4–5. Jungnitsch, PI, 16 Sept. 1989, p. 2. Lorenzen, PI, pp. 13, 15. Albrecht, PI, pp. 4–5.

52. Kuhne, "Berlin Steinway History." Albrecht, PI, p. 17. See also letter to BS, 2 Sept. 1945, probably from Kuhne. On life in Hamburg see Theodore Ehrlich to BS, 8 Oct. 1945, under "Wm R. Steinway's Post War," HZFS. See also BS to TES, 13 Jan. 1947.

53. TES to Clarissa Steinway Oaks, 24 Sept. 1945, F14, LWA.

54. HZS, PI, 15 Jan. 1991, p. 3; Yale, pp. 75, 76, 107. *Harvard Class of 1935,* p. 1286. JS, Yale, p. 212.

55. HZS, PI, 5 Feb. 1991, p. 27; 15 Nov. 1991, pp. 59, 62; 27 Aug. 1991, pp. 21–22; 8 Dec. 1989, pp. 51, 53, 55, 56.

56. Ibid., 27 Aug. 1991, p. 22; 8 Dec. 1989, p. 54; 25 June 1991, p. 29.

57. Ibid., 22 Feb. 1990, p. 40; 5 Feb. 1991, p. 27; 8 Dec. 1989, p. 36; 6 Dec. 1991, p. 35. Bilhuber resigned on 14 Sept. 1947.

58. HZS became president of S&S on 11 Oct. 1955. HZS, PI, 8 Dec. 1989, p. 52.

CHAPTER 17. STEINWAY CELEBRATES ITS CENTENNIAL

1. "Report of the President for 1945," 2 Apr. 1946, LWA. In 1946 S&S shipped 1,891 pianos; in 1947, 3,234; in 1948, 3,811: HZS, "Factory Shipments from 1891 through 1980," 28 Dec. 1989, HZSF. See also "Report of the President for 1946," Min, 7 Apr. 1947. On 6 Mar. 1946 wartime restrictions on piano manufacturing were lifted, taxes decreased, and sales increased. Profits soared to $233,112 that year. The following year S&S sold more than 3,000 pianos and netted $528,790 profit.

2. In 1948 profits remained high at $434,943: S Min, 2 Apr. 1946, 7 Apr. 1947, 6 Apr. 1948, 4 Apr. 1949; BD Min, 19 Nov. 1947; 1, 31 Dec. 1948; 26 Jan., 4 Apr. 1949. Letter from Sherman Clay & Co. to Paul Schmidt, 13 Jan. 1947, HZSF.

S&S's profit for 1949 was $154,979, quite a drop from the previous year. They sold 2,541 pianos in 1949, compared with 3,765 in 1948. See "Report of the President for 1949": S Min, 3

3 Apr. 1950. Chandler, *Visible Hand*, pp. 496–497. See also Glenn Porter, ed., *Encyclopedia of American Economic History*, vol. 1 (New York, 1975), p. 152. Pizer, brief, 15 Mar. 1950. Loesser, *Men, Women and Pianos*, p. 612.

3. BD Min, 15 June, 26 July 1949. A. W. Greiner to W. P. Chrisler, Aeolian Company of Missouri, 3 Nov. 1949, LWA. HZS, PI, 25 Sept. 1992, p. 10; 12 Mar. 1993, pp. 2–3. "Piano Industry Pleads for Increased Materials," *MT*, June 1952; and "1950–1959, The Baby Boom Fuels Spectacular Growth," *MT*, 100th anniversary issue, 1990, p. 138. "Report of the President for 1950," S Min, 2 Apr. 1951; for 1951, S Min, 7 Apr. 1952; for 1952, S Min, 6 Apr. 1953. On factory week-on, week-off schedule see BD Min, 30 Dec. 1949; 25 Jan., 1 Mar., 18 Oct. 1950. For S&S 1951 was as profitable as 1948; profits were $434,486, up from $181,736 in 1950: S Min, 2 Apr. 1951, 7 Apr. 1952. HZS to Cerofeci, 18 Dec. 1953, LWA.

4. Profits were $54,275 in 1952, but 1953 saw a loss of $17,977. "Report of the President for 1952," S Min, 6 Apr. 1953; for 1953, 5 Apr. 1954. HZS to Cerofeci, 18 Dec. 1953.

5. Patsy Bionda, PI, 11 Apr. 1981, p. 34. Gerald Koester, PI, 30 Oct. 1981, pp. 13–14. Jacob Pramberger, interview by Elliott Sparkman, 9 Mar. 1988, p. 53. In Apr. 1950 S&S employed 440 workers; by July of 1955, only 265. See HZS, "Number of Factory Employees: 1947–1959," graph drawn in summer 1959. See also notice of 29 Dec. 1953 from HZS, plant manager, alerting all employees that "it will be necessary to cut back temporarily the hours of work during the new year." This notice is attached to BD Min, 31 Dec. 1953. In 1954 the factory shut down "Friday night, May 28th, to Tuesday morning, July 6th"; see BD Min, 19 May 1954. See also HZS to Cerofeci, 18 Dec. 1953.

6. On the Korean War and the piano industry see "Baby Boom Fuels Spectacular Growth," pp. 138–139. HZS, PI, 5 June 1992, p. 15. BD Min, 21 May 1952.

7. Hamburg showed small profits from 1950 to 1952. In 1950 it produced 607 pianos; in 1951, 889; in 1952, 847; in 1953, 823, with a profit of about $21,727. BD Min, 2 Apr. 1951, 7 Apr. 1952, 6 Apr. 1953, 5 Apr. 1954.

8. S Min, 2 Apr. 1951. Steinway sold the Ditmars no. 3 building on 1 Mar. 1951 to "Alstores Realty Corporation, an affiliate of the Stern Department Store, for the price of $725,000, all cash." With it, Steinway paid off its last $750,000 in bank loans: "Report of the President for 1953," S Min, 5 Apr. 1954.

9. JS, Yale, 7 Nov. 1978, pp. 213–214. S Min, 3 Apr. 1950; 8 Aug., 19 Sept. 1951.

10. The 19-member dealers' committee included Jerome F. Murphy (M. Steinert & Sons, Boston), Louis G. LaMair (Lyon & Healy, Inc., Chicago), and Clay Sherman (Sherman, Clay & Co., San Francisco): "Executive Committee for Steinway Centennial," LWA. At an S&S dealers' luncheon, George H. Beasley said, "We should have the sentiment work for commercial advantage": LaMair, president and chairman of the committee, to Majewski, 20 July 1950. Initially the company authorized $100,000 for promotion: BD Min, 19 Sept. 1951. On the $125,000, see Min, 20 May 1953. The contribution from dealer sales was 1% in 1950, raised to 2% after 1 July 1951: LaMair to Majewski, 19 July, 3 Nov. 1950; 16 Feb. 1951; letter to all dealers, 12 Oct., 7, 28 Nov. 1950; "Report of Meeting of the Members of the Steinway Centennial Committee," 17 July 1951, LWA.

11. Greiner to Orcutt, 10 Apr. 1951; Greiner to Josef Hofmann, 10 Apr. 1951; LWA. Greiner, "Memoirs," pp. 163–169. HZS memo to Carlos Mosley, 12 Dec. 1986.

12. Greiner, "Memoirs," pp. 174, 182, 186.

13. Ibid., pp. 170, 174.

14. Ibid., pp. 175–176.

15. Ibid., p. 181. "Carnegie Hall Concert Officially Inaugurates Steinway Centennial," *MT*, Nov. 1953, p. 21.

16. The evening was not without its problems. S&S drivers were members of the Teamsters' Union and were on strike; they formed picket lines around Steinway Hall and the factory in Queens. This made it impossible to move any pianos to Carnegie Hall and deliver the new "centenary model." S&S gave in to the Teamsters' demands and settled the strike just four days before the concert. Greiner, "Memoirs," pp. 178–184. See also "Carnegie Hall Concert." "Re-

port of the President for 1953." The Steinway centenary grand, designed by Walter Dorwin Teague, was priced at $3,375. It used the regular model M scale and case. See also Taubman, "34 Pianists." BD Min, 18 Nov. 1953.

17. Greiner, "Memoirs," p. 184.

18. HZS, PI, 5 June 1992, p. 16.

19. Greiner, "Memoirs," p. 187. "Carnegie Hall Concert." "News of Advertising and Marketing," *NYT,* 9 May 1954, sec. 3, p. 12, and 18 Apr. 1953, Amusements section, p. 16.

20. "Carnegie Hall Concert."

21. Taubman, "34 Pianists." Olin Downes, "Steinway Jubilee: A Family and a Piano Observe Centenary of Service to Music and to America," *NYT,* 18 Oct. 1953, sec. 2, p. 7. Downes had been "delighted" with S&S since 1948, when his Steinway piano had been put on a "loan basis instead of rental." See R. W. Freimuth, inter-office memo to Miss B. Cook, 31 Dec. 1947; Greiner to Downes, 8 Jan. 1948; Downes to Greiner, 12 Jan. 1948, LWA. *NYT,* Amusements section, 18 Apr. 1953, p. 16. See also HZS, PI, 20 Nov. 1992, pp. 25–28.

22. S&S lost $17,977 in 1953: "Report of the President for 1953." HZS, PI, 5 June 1992, p. 16. BD Min, 4 Mar., 18 Nov. 1953.

23. BD Min, 18 Nov. 1953. HZS, PI, 5 June 1992, p. 16.

24. HZS, PI, 5 June 1992, pp. 16, 20. B. Chapin, PI, 18 Apr. 1990, pp. 46, 47. HZS was appointed factory manager on 2 Apr. 1946. See BD Min, 1 Apr. 1946.

25. BD Min, 11 Oct. 1955. HZS, PI, 1 Nov. 1988, p. 28, and Yale, 19 Jan. 1979, p. 101.

26. See HZS, PI, 15 Nov. 1991, pp. 39, 40, 62; 5 June 1992, p. 27; 1 Nov. 1988, p. 28. Heller & Associates report to TES, 20 Feb. 1941, p. 2.

27. HZS, PI, 5 June 1992, pp. 23, 26; 8 Dec. 1989, p. 54; Yale, pp. 90, 101, 114. BD Min, 11 Oct. 1955. On Henry's shadow presidency see Min, 31 Dec. 1948.

28. Chandler, *Visible Hand,* pp. 451, 492. "Comments on Founders," *NYT,* 26 Oct. 1952, sec. 3, p. 3.

29. BD Min, 1 Apr. 1946, 28 Oct. 1948. HZS, PI, 20 Nov. 1992, pp. 5–9.

30. HZS, PI, 1 Nov. 1988, p. 28; Yale, p. 102. BD Min, 11 Oct. 1955; S Min, 15 Dec. 1955. After 25 Apr. 1956, TES's attendance at board meetings became sporadic. His last one was on 28 Nov. 1956, 4 months before he died, 8 Apr. 1957: BD Min, 1956. See also HZS, PI, 27 Aug. 1991, p. 26. JS, Yale, p. 233.

31. "Corporate History of Steinway & Sons," typescript with pencil updates, c. 1982–84: TES's will shows him worth $184,020.90; "TES Will & Trust," HZSF. *Steinway News* no. 262 (Nov. 1955): 2. HZS, PI, 5 June 1992, p. 32.

32. TES's funeral was on 11 Apr. 1957. The choir sang "Glorious" by TES's intimate friend Sergei Rachmaninoff, and the opening hymn was from his favorite opera, *Die Meistersinger.* Van Cliburn to Ruth Steinway, 9 Apr. 1957, under "Theodore E. Steinway," HZSF.

CHAPTER 18. A BUSINESSMAN TAKES OVER

1. HZS, PI, 5 June 1992, p. 25. BD Min, 11 Oct. 1955.

2. HZS, Yale, 21 Dec. 1978, 19 Jan. 1979, pp. 53, 55, 56, 59, 139, 140. B. Chapin, Yale, 12 Oct. 1978, p. 20. HZS, PI, 5 June 1992, p. 26.

3. HZS, PI, 5 June 1992, pp. 32–33.

4. BD Min, 18 Jan. 1956, 21 June 1950; see HZS's attached "Report on Factory Consolidation," 15 June 1950, p. 3. See also HZS, PI, 25 June 1991, p. 33; 27 Aug. 1991, p. 25; 25 Sept. 1992, p. 8. "Report of the President for the Year 1955, Future Plans," S Min, 2 Apr. 1956.

5. Chandler, *Visible Hand,* pp. 466–467. Heller Report to TES, 20 Feb. 1941, p. 5. HZS, Yale, pp. 99, 100, 103. HZS, PI, 8 Dec. 1989, p. 54; 25 Sept. 1992, p. 5. BD Min, 11 May 1962. HZS, "Officers, Steinway & Sons, Elected at Annual Meetings in April," handwritten table, HZSF.

6. The first capital expense budget was $126,000 for all departments. See BD Min, 28 Jan., 25 Feb. 1959. HZS, PI, 8 Dec. 1989, p. 59.

7. HZS, PI, 15 Nov. 1991, pp. 8–10; 25 Sept. 1992, pp. 12–13.

8. HZS, Yale, pp. 114, 118, 119; PI, 27 Aug. 1991, pp. 25–26. JS, Yale, p. 139.

9. HZS, PI, 5 Feb. 1991, p. 28; 27 Aug. 1991, p. 26.

10. John started arranging the musicales in Nov. 1957. See BD Min, 26 Nov. 1957, 31 Dec. 1953. On Greiner meeting with Bess Truman about White House musicales see BD Min, 23 Oct. 1946. HZS, PI, 12 Mar. 1993, pp. 1–2; 25 Sept. 1992, p. 9. See also *Steinway News* no. 286 (Jan. 1958): 3. Elise K. Kirk, *Music at the White House: A History of the American Spirit* (Urbana, Ill., 1986), pp. 234, 258, 309, 325, 339. HZS, "Memo for the File: Steinway and the White House," 1 May 1992, p. 2, HZSF. On 29 Feb. 1956 JS was elected secretary to the BD. "Corporate History." B. Chapin, PI, p. 48.

11. Ruth Davis Steinway, JS, and B. Chapin, Yale, 31 July 1978, pp. 19–21. For another point of view see HZS, Yale, p. 144.

12. HZS, PI, 15 Jan. 1991, p. 16. FTS, interview by Vivian Perlis, Yale, 8 Apr. 1979, pp. 168–169.

13. HZS, PI, 30 Apr. 1991, p. 5; 27 Aug. 1991, p. 23; 15 Jan. 1991, p. 16. BD Min, 26 July 1956.

14. B. Chapin, PI, pp. 48–49. HZS, PI, 15 Jan. 1991, p. 18. Mrs. Charles Kittredge, interview by Elizabeth Harkins, Yale, 28 Nov. 1978, p. 23.

15. Josephine Steinway, 26 Apr. 1991, pp. 31–33. Steven Crabill, "How a Rich Piano Maker Was Swindled," *Record*, c. 1982. On 1 Nov. 1982 Theodore D. Steinway died. "Corporate History."

16. FTS, Yale, pp. 169–170. FTS, PI, 23 Mar. 1993, pp. 13–14.

17. On 11 Jan. 1954 FTS "started in as an Assistant to the Wholesale Department." BD Min, 31 Dec. 1953. Kittredge, Yale, p. 30. HZS, PI, 5 Feb. 1991, p. 29. FTS, Yale, p. 122.

18. FTS was appointed Concert & Artists manager on 18 June 1958; see Min. FTS, PI, p. 14. FTS, Yale, pp. 148–149.

19. Greiner, "Memoirs," pp. 17–18. FTS, PI, p. 8. HZS, PI, 9 June 1993, pp. 7–8.

20. Schonberg, *Horowitz* (New York, 1992), p. 179. HZS, PI, 12 Mar. 1993, p. 18; 8 Dec. 1989, p. 68; 9 June 1993, pp. 14–15.

21. Alice Jordan, PI, pp. 22–23. Greiner, "Memoirs," pp. 117–118. Schonberg, *Great Pianists*, p. 435. On the RCA recordings see Schonberg, *Horowitz*, pp. 196, 198.

22. Schonberg, *Horowitz*, p. 193. Greiner, "Memoirs," p. 63. On Mattia Battistini see Slonimsky, *Dictionary of Musicians*, p. 83.

23. *New York Post*, 2 May 1965. See also *Steinway News* no. 320 (summer 1965). See too Howard Klein, "Vladimir Horowitz on Road Back to Concert Stage," *NYT*, 17 Mar. 1965, pp. 1, 53. CD means Concert Department, a piano bank from which S&S lends out pianos to its artists.

24. Greiner, "Memoirs," pp. 121, 191. Schonberg, *Horowitz*, p. 187.

25. Greiner, "Memoirs," pp. 126–127. See also HZS, PI, 9 June 1993, pp. 8–9.

26. "The All-American Virtuoso," *Time*, 19 May 1958, pp. 58, 59, 63. Greiner died at Steinway Hall on 20 Apr. 1958. He had been at S&S for 32 years. Van Cliburn won first prize in Moscow on 13 Apr. 1958, and the New York ticker-tape parade took place on 20 May 1958. Max Frankel, "U.S. Pianist, 23, Wins Soviet Contest," *NYT*, 14 Apr. 1958. "Van Cliburn Gets a Hero's Parade," *NYT*, 21 May 1958, p. 35. On Greiner and Van Cliburn see FTS, PI, p. 36. Howard Reich, *Van Cliburn* (Nashville, Tenn., 1993), pp. 92–94. *Steinway News* nos. 286 (Jan. 1958), 289 (May 1958). HZS, Yale, 19 Jan. 1979, p. 123. B. Chapin, Yale, 12 Oct. 1978, pp. 17–20. HZS, PI, 12 Mar. 1993, pp. 12–13. Van Cliburn, 18 Mar. 1994, discussion with author, untaped, Steinway Hall.

27. HZS, introduction to Greiner's "Memoirs." *Steinway News* no. 315 (spring 1964). On the loss of Greiner see HZS, PI, 12 Mar. 1993, p. 10; 9 June 1993, pp. 10–14.

28. BD Min, 26 June 1957. FTS, Yale, p. 148. Alice Jordan, Yale, 28 Jan. 1979, p. 3. HZS, PI, 25 Sept. 1992, pp. 11–12. FTS, PI, p. 11.

29. FTS, Yale, pp. 191–192. FTS, PI, p. 14.

30. FTS, Yale, pp. 122, 135–137, 145, 194. FTS, PI, pp. 31–33.

31. Kittredge, Yale, p. 30. FTS, PI, pp. 30–32. At a 22 Nov. 1963 board of directors meeting Orcutt reported that, while HZS was out of town, "Mr. Frederick Steinway had indicated his intention to leave the firm of Steinway & Sons within the next two or three months, in order to pursue his own career in the field of concert and management." See also "Corporate History." On 31 Jan. 1964 FTS resigned. On 1 Feb. 1964 David W. Rubin, from D. H. Baldwin, was appointed manager of the Concert & Artists department. See BD Min, 24 Jan. 1964. See also *Steinway News* no. 315 (spring 1964). FTS, Yale, pp. 170–171, 190.

32. FTS, Yale, pp. 198, 199, 200. FTS, PI, pp. 30–32.

33. HZS, PI, 8 Dec. 1989, p. 55; 5 Feb. 1991, pp. 29–30; Yale, pp. 107–111. Kittredge, Yale, p. 30.

34. HZS, PI, 12 Feb. 1993, p. 8. Heller Report, final draft, 18 Apr. 1941. HZS to Morris Pizer, international president, UFWA, CIO, 7 Mar. 1950. LWA.

35. Henry's plan was to move the main executive office and officers to the Riker factory. HZS, "Report on Factory Consolidation," 15 June 1950, pp. 1–2. See also FTS, PI, pp. 28–29. HZS, PI, 12 Feb. 1993, pp. 4, 9.

36. "Report of the President for the Year 1955," S Min, 2 Apr. 1956. "Description of Production Facilities," c. 1950, "Steinway Facilities Booklet," HZSF.

37. In 1951 net income was $434,487; in 1952, $54,276; in 1953, net loss was $17,977; in 1954, $138,510.

38. On HZS's frustration with doing business in New York see Cristopher Lydon, "Employer Balks at Cash Payroll, Steinway Fights State Rule Barring Check Payments," *NYT,* 18 Feb. 1969, p. 22. HZS to Isidore Lubin, industrial commissioner, New York State Department of Labor, 17 Feb. 1955, LWA. On possible removal of piano industry to the South see "Commissioner Leonard Urges 20% Duty," *MT,* Mar. 1970, p. 54. See also "1950–1959, The Baby Boom Fuels Spectacular Growth," *MT,* 100th anniversary issue, 1990, p. 139. Orcutt to Cerofeci, 12 Nov. 1954, LWA.

39. There were only 9 piano manufacturers left in New York by 1950, employing 2,000 workers and producing 30% of the nation's pianos. They were S&S, Winter, Hardman Peck, Sohmer, National, Melodigrand, Krakauer, Kranich & Bach, and Weser. Heller Report, final draft. Jerome Murphy, letter to HZS, 4 Jan. 1950, HZSF. HZS, Yale, pp. 31, 80. HZS, "Report on Factory Consolidation," 25 Oct. 1954, attached to BD Min, 27 Oct. 1954. For early discussions of consolidation, see Min, 3 Apr., 17 May, 21 June, 20 Sept. 1950. On thoughts of moving the factory see FTS, PI, p. 25. On organizing non-union piano workers in the South see James Cerofeci, "Report from the Business Agent," *Local 102 News* 2, no. 1 (winter 1962): 2.

40. "Plant Manager HZS requested the sum of $15,000 for Architectural Plans for the Consolidation of our two Factories on Long Island [Ditmars into Riker]": BD Min, 5 Apr., 23 June 1954. S&S raised $430,000 of the $673,761 by increasing the mortgage on Steinway Hall from $420,000 to $850,000. The "Estimate of Reduction in Factory Expense due to Partial Consolidation" was $61,855. See "Preliminary Estimate of Annual Savings Resulting from Consolidation," attached to BD Min, 23 Nov. 1954; see also BD Min, 27 Oct. 1954, 4 Apr. 1955, 18 Nov. 1958. "Report of the President for the Year 1954," S Min, 4 Apr. 1955. "Factory Consolidation, Summary of Progress Report," c. 1958.

41. Michael Demarest, "At Steinway & Sons, 12,000 Parts Add Up to a Grand Tradition," *Avenue* 6, no. 2 (Oct. 1981): 48–50. *Horizon,* Mar. 1982, p. 51. Amy Alson, "Returning a Virtuoso Sound," *Crain's New York Business* 2, no. 40 (6 Oct. 1986): 1, 30. *Sound Board,* S&S employee newsletter, Mar.–Apr. 1985, pp. 1, 3.

42. *Steinway News* no. 289 (May 1958). "Steinway Marks 105th Anniversary," *MT.* See also Edward Rothstein, "Making Music by Hand and Machine at Steinway: It Is All Craft," *NYT,*

21 Dec. 1981. BD Min, 14 Dec. 1955; 29 Feb., 24 Oct., 19 Dec. 1956; 18 Nov. 1958. S Min, 15 Dec. 1955. "Report of the President for 1955," S Min, 2 Apr. 1956. Sales increased from $4,530,000 in 1955 to $4,901,000 in 1956, when 2,535 pianos were shipped. See annual reports for 1956 and 1957, LWA. HZS, "Factory Shipments for 1891 through 1980," 28 Dec. 1989. HZS, Yale, pp. 31, 80–81. See also HZS, PI, 27 Aug. 1991, p. 25. Tim Gorman, PI, 22 Mar. 1993, p. 5.

43. BD Min, 26 July 1956. HZS, PI, 12 Mar. 1993, p. 7.

44. "Change of Keys," *NYT,* 25 Jan. 1958, pp. 25–26. George Read and Julius Pratt were Connecticut's major importers of African ivory in the early nineteenth century. See Kathryn Domrose, "Writer Explores Irony of Abolition and Ivory," *Hartford Courant,* n.d. Richard Conniff, "When the Music in Our Parlors Brought Death to Darkest Africa," *Audubon,* July 1981, pp. 77, 79, 80, 83, 85, 86, 89, 91. HZS, PI, 5 June 1992, p. 17; 12 Mar. 1993, p. 8. FTS, PI, p. 21. John Majeski, PI, 22 Mar. 1993, p. 22. On manufacturing ivory keys see David H. Shayt, "Elephant under Glass: The Piano Key Bleach House of Deep River, Connecticut," *Journal of the Society for Industrial Archeology* 19, no. 1 (1993).

45. The consolidation, involving more than six buildings, cost $2,316,267 plus in-house maintenance costs of $160,811. By 1958 S&S had 422,931 square feet of floor space in the consolidated Riker plant. "Statement of Conversion" and "Floor Space Data," c. 1958, LWA. See also BD Min, 18 Nov. 1958. "Steinway Expands Queens Piano Plant," *NYT,* 1 Feb. 1967. Rothstein, "Making Music," *World Journal Tribune,* 2 Feb. 1967. See "Report of the President for 1957." HZS, Yale, p. 82. HZS, PI, 20 Nov. 1992, pp. 9–13.

1958 was the first year in which Hamburg was included in the profit calculations. The explanation given was that U.S. and German currencies were now fully convertible. "President's Report for the Year 1958," 5 Mar. 1959. On Hamburg's profits for 1954–64 see annual reports, S Min. See HZS, MR CBS, 19 Jan. 1973, p. 2.

46. In 1948, 480 workers had enabled S&S to ship 3,811 pianos, 8 per worker. In 1958, 277 workers enabled Steinway to ship 1,936 pianos, only 7 per worker. See HZS, "Factory Shipments," 28 Dec. 1989. HZS, "Number of Factory Employees, 1947–1959," graph, 1959. HZS, "Number of Employees & Average Hourly Earnings, 1944–1978," chart, c. 1979. See also FTS, PI, pp. 27–28.

47. FTS, PI, p. 26. HZS, PI, 12 Feb. 1993, p. 3; 12 Mar. 1993, p. 22; 9 June 1993, pp. 21–23. HZS had a sense of urgency, because S&S was now "up against modern factory Baldwin, modern factory Kimball, . . . and these gigantic, extremely efficient and fully integrated European (and Asian) factories." See also HZS, MR CBS, 24 Oct. 1975, p. 2: "In manufacturing, we are looking forward to the study recently approved which will take a new look at our grand piano flow and suggest a new layout." On Steinway upright compared to others and on factory flow evaluations see HZS, MR CBS, 26 Dec. 1975, 27 Dec. 1976, p. 2.

48. Tommy Martino, PI, 29 Mar. 1993, p. 13. John Bogyos, PI, 8 Apr. 1993, pp. 1–7.

49. "Steinway Marks 105th Anniversary." According to the Bureau of the Census, *Census of Manufacturing, 1958, Pianos,* new capital expenditures for the piano industry were $1 million. See *MT,* Apr. 1960, p. 58. On 9 Jan. 1951 S&S sold the 2-story Ditmars building to Stern Brothers for $725,000: see BD Min, 29 Jan. 1951. On 1 Feb. 1957 S&S sold the 6-story Ditmars factory for $1,003,090 with right to rent (for $253,090) almost half the building for two and a half years (until 1 Aug. 1959), enabling them to take their time moving their operations down to Riker. See also annual reports for 1956 and 1957. HZS, PI, 5 June 1992, p. 29.

50. On Henry's earlier plan to sell Steinway Hall, see BD Min, 18 June 1947, 26 May 1948. On offers for it see Min, 20 Sept., 18 Oct. 1950; 21 Feb. 1951. See BD Min, 14 Mar., 7 Apr., 18 Nov. 1958. "Report of the President for 1958," 5 Mar. 1959. See also HZS, PI, 5 June 1992, p. 29; 20 Nov. 1992, pp. 3–4; 12 Feb. 1993, p. 7. See also HZS, memo to senior Steinway people, 14 Mar. 1958, "Re: Sale of 57th Street Building." "The Building 109–13 West 57th Street has been 100% rented during 1946 with the result that a profit of $10,112 was realized, which compares with 1945 profit of $6,032." "Report of the President for 1945," 2 Apr. 1946. According to the 1951 "Report of the President," S Min, 7 Apr. 1952, Steinway Hall was fully rented and showing a profit of $59,777. In the 1955 report, S Min, 2 Apr. 1956, Steinway Hall was fully

rented and showing a profit of $50,956. JS, Yale, 7 Nov. 1978, p. 142. FTS, PI, p. 29. John Majeski, PI, pp. 20–21. On "statutory" tenants see "Rent Roll," 6 Mar. 1958.

51. TES's sister Maude Paige had a daughter Audrey. Audrey Paige's second husband was Thomas E. Lovejoy, Jr., president of Manhattan Life. See JS, Yale, p. 141. HZS, PI, 20 Nov. 1992, pp. 1–2, 4; 12 Feb. 1993, p. 8; 8 Dec. 1989, p. 34; 27 Aug. 1991, p. 25; 5 June 1992, p. 29; 25 Sept. 1992, pp. 17–19. Piano shipments in 1956 were 2,535; in 1957, 2,467; in 1958, 1,936. See HZS, "Factory Shipments," HZSF. BD Min, 28 Aug. 1946, 7 Apr. 1958, 14 May 1958, 18 May 1960, 19 Jan. 1967. "Report of the President for 1958," S Min, 5 Mar. 1959. See also HZS, Yale, pp. 81, 82, 95.

52. Bogyos, PI, 10. 1992, p. 8. For a detailed description of working with cloth bushings see Theodore D. Steinway, "Steinway Grand Pianos Adopt Bushings of 'Teflon,'" *Journal of Teflon,* June 1962. See also A. Geiger memo, 28 May 1945, on poor-quality felt, resulting in extra pay ($1.88) for "extra time allowed due to extra juicing of hammers and a better standard of workmanship." The extra money on piecework was to stay in "effect until such time as we can get the pre-war standard of Grand Hammer Felt, at which time there should be less time required for juicing the hammers."

53. HZS, 30 June 1992, p. 15. FTS, PI, p. 22. The first mention of Teflon was in HZS's "Report on European Trip, Inter-House Matters, N.Y. Experiments," Apr.–May 1961, attached to BD Min, 18 May 1961. The first reference to "Permafree Bushing" was in BD Min, 11 May 1962. "Upholding tradition . . . in the modern way," *DuPont Magazine* 56, no. 5 (Sept.–Oct. 1962): 31–32. Theodore D. Steinway, "Bushings of 'Teflon.'" Eva Jacob, "Fussing Over Steinways: Not So Grand as They Used to Be," *Real Paper* 6, no. 17 (30 Apr. 1977): 26, 28–29. Bogyos, PI, 10 Jan. 1992, p. 7; on felt suppliers, PI, 26 Mar. 1993, pp. 2–5. Walsh, PI, 21 Apr. 1989, p. 30. HZS, PI, 8 Dec. 1989, p. 60; 30 June 1992, p. 15. Josephine Steinway, PI, 26 Apr. 1991, p. 30. Fred Drasche, Yale, 6 June 1978, p. 33. *Steinway News* no. 309 (fall 1962). Finston, "Happy Note," p. 19. FTS, interview by Vivian Perlis, Yale, 8 Apr. 1979, p. 129. BD Min, 18 Oct. 1965. TES, Permafree Action, no. 3240095, 15 Mar. 1966, cited in BD Min, 22 June 1966. Harry Firstenberg, Yale, 30 Oct. 1978, pp. 7–8.

54. FTS, Yale, pp. 129–130. HZS, "Memorandum of Discussions with Mr. Gunther & Mr. Squibb: Improved Action," to the directors, 25 Oct. 1965. "Upholding tradition," pp. 31–32. S&S, "Grand Hammershank—Flange Pinning, Perma Free Bushing," May 1969, HZSF. On rushing into Teflon see Martino, PI, pp. 28–29.

55. HZS, 30 June 1992, pp. 16–17.

56. Martino, PI, p. 29. See also Boston tuner-technician Frank Hanson, in charge of New England Conservatory's piano shop, quoted in Jacob, "Fussing Over Steinways," pp. 26, 28–29.

57. HZS, "Memorandum of Interhouse Discussions: Hamburg, Permafree Bushing," 25 Apr.–8 May 1963, attached to BD Min, 3 May 1963. HZS, "Memorandum of Discussions with Mr. Gunther & Mr. Squibb." HZS, "Report on Trip to London, Berlin, Hamburg," 26 Sept.–7 Oct. 1966, attached to BD Min, 3 Nov. 1966. HZS, "Report on Europe Trip: German Branch," 30 Apr.–13 May 1967, attached to BD Min, 23 May 1967. HZS, "Notes on Visit to European Branches: Hamburg," 22–28 Oct. 1967, attached to BD Min, 3 Nov. 1967.

58. Bogyos, PI, 10 Jan. 1992, p. 8. HZS, PI, 8 Dec. 1989, p. 60; 30 June 1992, pp. 16, 18, 19. Jacob, "Fussing Over Steinways," pp. 26, 28–29.

59. Robert Pace, 29 Apr. 1993, pp. 1–5. For the 1960s boom see S Min, 5 Apr. 1967. "Report of the President for 1968," S Min, 12 Mar. 1969. Russell and David Sanjek, *American Popular Music Business in the 20th Century* (New York, 1991), p. 186. John Majeski, PI, pp. 16–17. Although grand piano sales increased, total piano sales went down slightly: from 198,200 pianos in 1960 to 193,814 pianos in 1970. "Steinway & Sons," Harvard Business School, Case 0-682-025, 1981, p. 7. On grand piano sales see HZS, MR CBS, 23 Aug. 1974, p. 2. See also "1960–1969, GO-GO Sales Lure Outside Investors," *MT,* 100th anniversary issue, 1990, pp. 152, 156. In 1969, 1.4 million guitars and 175,000 organs were sold. The quote is from Jack Wainger of American Music Stores, Detroit, president of NAMM in 1967. In 1960 there were 53 million children in grades 1–12; in 1969, 68 million. FTS, PI, pp. 33–34.

60. Carruth, *Encyclopedia:* p. 648 for Beatles' arrival 7 Feb. 1964; p. 620 for "The Fantasticks," 3 May 1960; p. 622 for Arthur Rubinstein, 1961; p. 658 for Horowitz, 9 May 1965; p. 697 for Woodstock, 15–18 Aug. 1969. See also "GO-GO Sales," pp. 152, 154, 156. Schonberg, *Great Pianists,* p. 435. Schonberg, *Horowitz,* pp. 212, 213, 217. Richard F. Shepard, "Horowitz Tickets Are Sold Out in 2 Hours," *NYT,* 27 Apr. 1965, sec. 2, p. 1. Franz Mohr, "Horowitz, Exciting Years with the Great Pianist," *Piano Quarterly,* fall 1991, pp. 18, 19, 28. FTS and Cass Steinway, letter to Mr. & Mrs. Horowitz, 10 May 1965; Ruth Steinway to Wanda, 10 May 1965; Horowitz Archives, Yale Music Library. On the Van Cliburn swooners see Normal Lee Browning, "Teens Acclaim A New Idol: Van," *Chicago Tribune Sunday Magazine,* 1 Oct. 1961, pp. 7–9.

61. *Steinway News* nos. 319 (spring 1965), 323 (spring 1966), 336 (summer 1969). It was not the first time that S&S included African-American artists on their list, but it was a first in terms of the promotion and importance of Ellington, Jamal, Flack, and Hines. For an earlier African-American S&S artist see Billy Taylor, highlighted in *Steinway News* no. 291 (Sept. 1958).

62. BD Min, 4 Apr. 1960, 3 Apr. 1961, 2 Mar. 1962, 22 Nov. 1963. HZS, PI, 5 June 1992, p. 28. On churches and hotels buying grands see statements by Morley Thompson in "Raise Import Duties on Pianos," *MT,* Nov. 1969, P. 64. "Steinway Marks 105th Anniversary." On the new vertical see BD Min, 18 May 1960. Upright shipments in 1959 totaled 1,170; in 1960, 1,537; in 1961, 1,516; in 1962, 1,432; in 1963, 1,650; in 1964, 1,556; in 1965, 1,711; in 1966, 1,959; in 1967, 1,831; in 1968, 1,515; in 1969, 1,461: HZS, "Factory Shipments," HZSF.

63. Annual reports for 1963 and 1964, S Min, 5 Mar. 1964, 5 Mar. 1965. *Steinway News* nos. 321 (fall 1965), 331 (spring 1968). Mark N. Finston, "Happy Note; Jingle of Money Is Their Sound of Music," *Star-Ledger,* 1 Feb. 1967, p. 19. HZS, MR CBS, 22 Aug. 1975, p. 2. BD Min, 28 Jan. 1966. HZS, PI, 12 Mar. 1993, p. 24. For HZS's analysis of booked orders see MR CBS, 22 Mar. 1974, p. 2; 24 June 1976. On board meetings about backlog see Henry Ziegler, 26 Mar. 1993, pp. 9–10.

64. In 1963 HZS asked the board for an additional $850,000 for rough milling and storage space, 44,000 square feet on two floors. See BD Min, 21 June 1963. Part of that expense was financed by the sale of $271,260 in "investment securities." See also annual report for 1963, S Min, 5 Mar. 1964, and HZS letter of 5 Jan. 1966, attached to BD Min, 28 Jan. 1966.

65. See BD Min, 28 Jan. 1966.

66. HZS letter of 18 Nov. 1965, attached to BD Min, 3 Dec. 1965; also Min, 24 July, 25 Sept. 1964; 28 Jan., 7 Mar., 19 May, 22 June, 30 Nov. 1966. S Min, 14 Apr. 1966. Annual report, 1965, S Min, 5 Mar. 1966. *Ridgewood Times,* 16 Feb. 1967. "Steinway Opens Astoria Facility," *NYT,* 1 Feb. 1967. Finston, "Happy Note." *Steinway News* no. 327 (spring 1967). "Steinway Adds Extension to Piano Factory in Astoria," *Queens County Times,* 2 Feb. 1967.

67. On 48-hour work week see Martino, PI, pp. 7–11. Al Daniels, PI, 2 May 1993, p. 18.

68. "Statement of Figures since Consolidation of All Branches & Subsidiaries," chart of sales and net income 1958–69, attached to S Min, 8 Apr. 1970. In 1966 sales were $12.9 million, and net income was $1 million. In 1968 sales went up to $14.3 million, while net income went down to $897,955. In 1968 Henry explained that part of the decrease in income was "due to the large extra tax surcharge" in the United States and a changeover in Germany from a sales tax to a value-added tax and a 4% export tax. A year later he acknowledged that sales were slightly off but that earnings were down a severe 26%. See S Min, 9 Apr. 1969. See also annual report for 1968, S Min, 12 Mar. 1969. On factory shipments, production ceiling, and unfilled orders, 1965–73, see HZS, MR CBS, 19 July 1973, 22 Jan. 1974; on later net profits and production see monthly report, 30 Jan. 1976, HZSF. Shipments of grands increased (1,603 in 1967, 1,806 in 1969), but shipments of uprights decreased (1,831 in 1967, 1,461 in 1969), so altogether, fewer instruments left the factory. On grands being more profitable than uprights, Theodore Ehrlich to HZS, 12 May 1956, under "Ehrlich," HZSF.

69. Annual report for 1964, S Min, 5 Mar. 1965; for 1966, S Min, 3 Mar. 1967. HZS, MR CBS, 20 Oct. 1972. The entire industry stalled between 1965 and 1967, but Steinway's problems started in 1967, just when everyone else was shrugging off the mild recession. See annual report for 1969, S Min, 11 Mar. 1970. On music industry 1965–67 see "GO-GO Sales," p. 159.

70. Twenty years later Henry would remember these rotating loans but incorrectly date them as occurring during his father's presidency. S Min, 10 Apr. 1968. The $400,000 was a 3-month loan at 6% from First National City Bank. BD Min, 3 Nov. 1967, 28 Jan. 1968. See also William Leonhardt, treasurer to board of directors, 25 Jan. 1968, attached to Min, 28 Jan. 1968, and 5 Nov. 1969, attached to Min, 5 Nov. 1969.

71. "There is no doubt that this consolidation was the right move for S&S as a ten-year review of the figures will show": HZS, 5 Jan. 1966, attached to BD Min, 28 Jan. 1966. On admitting a new factory would have been better, see HZS, PI, 12 Mar. 1993, p. 21; John Bogyos, PI, 8 Apr. 1993, p. 4. See also Henry Ziegler, PI, 26 Mar. 1993, p. 9.

CHAPTER 19. "A FINE WAY TO TREAT A STEINWAY"

1. Joseph Bisceglie, interview by Sam Sills, 30 June 1987, pp. 8–9, 32, LWA. HZS, PI, 20 Nov. 1992, p. 11.

2. Ralph Bisceglie, interview by Sam Sills, 2 July 1987, pp. 3, 21, LWA.

3. John Bogyos, PI, 26 Mar. 1993, p. 8. Walter Neu personnel record no. 8817, LWA. Bogyos started working at S&S on 8 Nov. 1929; personnel record no. 7055.

4. Richard Sera, interview by Sam Sills, 6 July 1987, p. 22, LWA. Martino, PI, 29 Mar. 1993, p. 21. Daniels, PI, 2 May 1993, pp. 16, 25. All but one of Cerofeci's 19 union delegates in 1946 had been hired between 1902 and 1926; the other started in 1940. See Cerofeci to S&S, 11 Jan. 1946, LWA.

5. "Steinway Layoffs," *Piano Key: Local 102 News* 2, no. 4 (Apr. 1946), LWA. *Piano Key* 2, no. 7 (Sept. 1946). On union demand for arbitration on the layoffs of upright finishers see BD Min, 20 Nov. 1946. On "labor situation easing somewhat," see Min, 22 Jan. 1947. On HZS laying off his father's charity cases and remembering the 1946 firings see HZS, PI, 12 Feb. 1993, pp. 10, 19.

6. HZS, PI, 12 Feb. 1993, pp. 20–21. *Piano Key* 2, no. 7 (Sept. 1946).

7. Cerofeci, "Shop Talk," *Piano Key* 1, no. 5 (Aug. 1945). Joe Pirola, head of payroll, dredged up all the prewar records and added 22.5% to the 1941 piecework rates. See "Labor Increases Since the War," LWA. "On the Attitude of Steinway," William McSweeney, president of Local 102. *Piano Key* 2, no. 4. (Apr. 1946), LWA. See also HZS, PI, 15 Nov. 1991, p. 55.

8. On strike negotiations see Min, 18 Oct. 1950. Walter Drasche, interview by Sam Sills, 4 June 1987, p. 3. On Drasche as union delegate see Cerofeci, "Results of Elections Held in Local 102 UFWA-CIO," letter to HZS, 7 Jan. 1947, and Joseph Guirty letter, 28 Jan. 1949, LWA.

9. Union contract, 1950, article 10, "Wage Rates," p. 8, and article 22, "Pensions," pp. 21–22, 1 Oct. 1950. See also "First Strike at Steinway Brought Real Results for Members of Piano Local 102" and "Pensions Plus 10 Cents Boosts Top New Local 102 Pacts," *Furniture Workers Press,* UFWA, CIO, Oct. 1950, Cerofeci clippings, LWA. On pension negotiations and importance of Drasche see HZS to Cerofeci, 4 Oct. 1950, LWA. The two additional paid holidays brought the total to ten. On ratification of the 1950 contract on 18 Oct. 1950 see BD Min, 29 Nov. 1950. *Furniture Workers Press,* Oct., Nov. 1950. HZS, handwritten notes, LWA. On the strike see Martino, PI, p. 19. On the history of the battle over benefits see Gerald Markovitz and David Rosner, "Seeking Common Ground: A History of Labor and Blue Cross," *Journal of Health Politics, Policy and Law* 16, no. 4 (winter 1991): 695–718.

10. The S&S pension plan was finally agreed on 27 May 1952, retroactive to 1 Oct. 1951: HZS, handwritten minutes of the pension meeting at Steinway Hall, 27 May 1952; handwritten note to Bill Bernauer, c. 1952, LWA. HZS to Cerofeci, 27 Feb. 1951, LWA. Union contract, 1950, article 22, "Pension," pp. 21–22. BD Min, 28 Oct. 1952. Drasche, interview, pp. 3, 7, 8. Manyoky, interview by Linda Ocasio, 11 Mar. 1979, p. 23. HZS, PI, 6 Dec. 1991, pp. 35–36, 39; Yale, 19 Jan. 1979, p. 115. Drasche personnel record no. 7134. On pension negotiations see TES, "To Our Factory Employees," 26 Nov. 1951; 18 Feb., 28 Nov. 1952, LWA. On the 30 Mar. 1953

dinner to honor Herman Gregory (no. 7238), Gabor Dolgos (no. 7123), Louis Bieler (no. 7036), William Ash (no. 7011), Louis Profera (no. 7543), and William Manley (no. 1825), see *Steinway News* no. 230 (May 1953).

11. Drasche, interview, pp. 1–3, 7, 8. Manyoky, interview, p. 23. HZS, interview by Michael Kushner, 6 Jan. 1987, pp. 21–22. On Drasche and the 1954 negotiations see Labor files, 1944–70, LWA.

12. On the 1955 strike see "Report of the President for the Year 1955," S Min, 2 Apr. 1956. See also BD Min, 11 Oct., 16 Nov. 1955. HZS, PI, 8 Dec. 1989, p. 59. At a meeting in 1952 HZS alerted Cerofeci "that anything given [on wages] will go on price and probably affect employment": HZS, handwritten notes on meeting with Cerofeci, Weinstock, and Guirty at Steinway Hall, 18 Nov. 1952, LWA. On 1955 strike and HZS's argument for keeping wages and piano prices down see HZS letter "To All Factory Employees," 7 Oct. 1955, LWA. On 1954, 1955, and 1956 average hourly earnings see HZS, "Number of Employees & Average Hourly Earnings," 1944–1978, c. 1979, HZSF. In 1955 all other models either stayed the same price or increased by about 3%: "New York Retail Prices of Steinway Pianos," chart compiled by JS in 1983.

13. Berta Kolb, interview by Sam Sills, 14 Aug. 1987, p. 2. Average Steinway pay was $1.97 an hour in Oct. 1956, $2.10 in Oct. 1957, $2.23 in Oct. 1958. See "Average Hourly Wages—All Employees in Factory: 1947–1959," graph by HZS, LWA. See also HZS, "Number of Employees and Average Hourly Earnings." See BD Min, 18 Oct. 1957. *Furniture Workers Press,* Oct. 1957. On 1957 profit slump see annual report for 1957. "Current Profits" started to drop in Oct. 1957. On increasing piano prices see "New York Retail Prices of Steinway Pianos." See also annual report for 1961, S Min, 2 Apr. 1962.

14. Yearly wage increases from 1945 to 1961 were 5 or 10 cents an hour, flattening out from 1953 to 1955; the one exception was a 15-cent raise in 1946: see BD Min, 23 Oct. 1946. In 1947 S&S wages went up 8% from $1.35 to $1.45. See "Report of the President for 1947," S Min, 6 Apr. 1948. See union contract, article 10, "Wage Rates," 1 Oct. 1947. In 1949 the average increase was 10 cents, to $1.55; in Apr. 1951 wages went up to $1.70, and in 1952 to $1.80. According to New York State statistics, S&S pay was now 20 cents above the average furniture worker's wage. In 1953 pay went up 2.7% to $1.85; see union contract, article 10, "Wage Rates," p. 8, 1 Dec. 1952. Pay went to $1.95 in Oct. 1955, $2 in July 1957, $2.10 in Oct. 1957, and $2.23 in Oct. 1958. See "Average Hourly Wages—All Employees in Factory: 1947–1959." HZS, "Number of Employees & Average Hourly Earnings." See also HZS, Kushner interview, pp. 21–22. For number of workers at S&S (approx. 380) from 1967 to 1971, see United Furniture Workers, "Insurance Fund Report to the Trustees." According to Bureau of the Census, *1958 Census of Manufacturing, Pianos,* state average pay was $2.11 an hour ($19 million in total wages, 9 million "man hours"). See *MT,* Apr. 1960, p. 58. Annual report for 1959, S Min, 4 Apr. 1960. BD Min, 14 Oct. 1959. On 1959 contract, see letter of agreement between United Piano Workers Local 102, UFWA, CIO, and S&S, 1 Oct. 1959, LWA. R. Bisceglie, interview, p. 22. Sera, interview, p. 22. Tim Gorman, PI, 22 Mar. 1993, p. 12.

15. BD Min, 14 Oct. 1959. Drasche, interview, 4 June 1987, p. 5. Manyoky, interview, 11 Mar. 1979, p. 10. Cerofeci, PI, 20 Nov. 1991, p. 11. "400 Toast Cerofeci at Testimonial Dinner," *Furniture Workers Press,* Dec. 1957, Cerofeci clippings.

16. Orcutt, treasurer, letter to board of directors, 23 Sept. 1964, attached to BD Min, 25 Sept. 1964. This was the first time since World War II that profits were reported in the Minutes. S&S, "Statement of Figures since Consolidation of All Branches & Subsidiaries," attached to annual report for 1969, 11 Mar. 1970. See HZS, "Factory Shipments," 28 Dec. 1989. See also HZS, PI, 5 June 1992, p. 28.

17. HZS, "Number of Employees & Average Hourly Earnings." S&S 1963 federal income tax return, officers' salaries, p. 1, line 12, schedule E, LWA. On weekly salary ($93.96 for a 41.7-hour week) of Furniture & Fixtures Workers in New York City see U.S. Department of Labor, Statistics, "Furniture Workers, N.Y.C.," 1960. On the 14 U.S. piano firms' salaries in 1960 see "Full Text of U.S. Tariff Commission Report to Nixon." The 1961 contract provided a 10-cent raise, with a 5-cent raise in 1962. See S&S–union agreement, 1 Apr. 1961, LWA. See

letter to Cerofeci, 27 Oct. 1964, LWA. The next contract, won by a 2-week strike, included a 22.5-cent increase spread over 3 years. See "Statement of Figures since Consolidation of All Branches & Subsidiaries," attached to S Min, 8 Apr. 1970. Annual report for 1961, S Min, 2 Apr. 1962; annual report for 1964, S Min, 5 Mar. 1965. On wage increases, 3 weeks' vacation, piano prices, sales, and 3-year contracts, see BD Min, 29 June 1961, 30 Nov. 1962, 30 Oct. 1964, 3 Nov. 1967. See also Louis and Ida Jandris, interview by Elliott Sparkman, 11 Feb. 1988, p. 19. Sera, interview, p. 24. On average wage for U.S. piano workers see "Raise Import Duties on Pianos," *MT,* Nov. 1969, pp. 65, 93. Daniels, PI, pp. 32–33.

18. BD Min, 29 June 1961; 21 Sept., 3 Nov. 1966; 3 Nov. 1967; 21 Jan. 1970. In 1966 the price increase was "due to increased labor costs as well as the extraordinary increase in walnut." From 1965 to 1970 the D price increased 15%; B and L increased 14%; M increased 12%; S increased 16%; the upright increased 10%. On higher prices having no impact see Henry Ziegler, 26 Mar. 1993, p. 9. S&S blamed 1967 price jumps on the 22.5-cent pay hike; prices kept rising for the next 4 years. See "New York Retail Prices." On sales increasing see BD Min, 3 Nov. 1966, and falling off, 23 May, 17 Aug. 1967; 25 Jan. 1968. On HZS's claim that high prices would drive away customers see HZS, MR CBS, 26 Dec. 1975, 25 Oct. 1976. For a typical argument on the relationship of low wages to low prices and thus to increased sales and full employment, see HZS to Cerofeci, 2 Sept. 1959, LWA.

19. HZS, PI, 8 Dec. 1989, p. 56; Kushner interview, pp. 21–22.

20. HZS, PI, 8 Dec. 1989, p. 56; 25 June 1991, p. 34. HZS, Kushner interview, pp. 21–22. According to the *1958 Census of Manufacturing, Pianos,* there were only 20 plants with more than 20 employees. See *MT,* Apr. 1960, p. 58.

21. Martino, PI, p. 22. Daniels, PI, p. 16.

22. Walsh, PI, 21 Apr. 1989, p. 28.

23. R. Bisceglie, interview, pp. 9–10, 18, 21. Bogyos, PI, 23 Dec. 1991, p. 7. Martino, PI, pp. 25–26. HZS, PI, 12 Feb. 1993, p. 17.

24. Daniels, PI, p. 21.

25. Ibid., pp. 20–21.

26. In 1962, a third (93 out of 291) of Steinway employees, the "old school," had been with the company for 19 years or more: typed note, 4 Sept. 1962, Labor files, 1944–70, LWA. On the search for skilled workers and high turnover see BD Min, 31 Dec. 1947; 17 June, 23 July, 23 Sept. 1969; 21 Jan., 8 Apr. 1970; 27 July, 15 Sept., 22 Nov. 1971. "Employment Data, 6 Jan. 1969–30 June 1969," and "Personnel Requirements Based on Production, without Overtime," attached to Min, 23 July 1969. Martino, PI, pp. 7–12. Bernard Merolla, personnel record no. 7435. Henry Ziegler, PI, 26 Mar. 1993, p. 5. On making more money outside S&S see Martino, PI, pp. 26–28. On decreasing productivity see BD Min, 20 Oct. 1971. R. Bisceglie, interview, pp. 25–26.

27. Betty Steinway Chapin, Yale, 12 Oct. 1978, pp. 39–41. Ziegler, PI, pp. 5–6. Elizabeth Steinway Chapin obituary, *NYT,* 20 June 1993. Alex Witchel, "At Work with Schuyler Chapin," *NYT,* 8 Feb. 1995.

28. HZS, Yale, p. 144; Kushner interview, pp. 14–15; PI, 12 Jan. 1993, p. 15. Gorman, PI, pp. 6–7.

29. Union contract, 1941, pp. 10–11; union contract, 1947. Jane Cerofeci, personnel record no. 7094, worked for S&S from 28 Oct. 1942 to 5 May 1944. She was then "laid off, lack of work." See also HZS, PI, 9 June 1993, p. 3. Union contract, 1947, article 13, "Veterans," p. 13. William G. Bernauer, letter to Local 102, UFWA, 20 Mar. 1946. Kolb, interview, pp. 3–4. Rose Steinberg, grievance adjustment form, 10 Dec. 1946, LWA. See also HZS, PI, 9 June 1993, pp. 1–2. "Tariff Commission Report to Nixon," p. 92. Daniels recalled only 3 or 4 women at S&S in the late 1950s: PI, pp. 14–15. In 1965 there were 28 women out of 477 S&S workers; in 1966, 30 out of 468; in 1967, 30 out of 476; in 1969, 34 out of 463; in 1970, 47 out of 475. See "Confidential" payroll book for these years, LWA.

30. Daniels, PI, pp. 1–4, 7–8, 23, 28. Bogyos, PI, 10 Jan. 1992, pp. 30–31. Walsh, PI, pp. 27–28. Martino, PI, p. 10.

31. Daniels, PI, pp. 9–11, 13. Frank Urich, interview by Elliott Sparkman, 18 Feb. 1988,

p. 7, LWA. Gerald Koester, PI, 30 Oct. 1981, p. 11. Raymond Parada, interview by Sam Sills, 6 July 1987, p. 2, LWA. Kolb, interview, pp. 7–8. R. Bisceglie, interview, p. 17. *Furniture Workers Press,* Nov. 1970. Gorman, PI, pp. 8–9. On the training of "ten black and Puerto Rican men" and the few Black employees at S&S in the early 1970s see "Piano Workers Hit a Bright Note in Boro," n.d., clipping in the files of Colony–South Brooklyn Settlement House.

32. Martino, PI, p. 23.

33. Sera, interview, p. 23. According to Ralph Bisceglie, the first ballot was discounted because the local had not notified Washington that it was having an election. On support for Cerofeci in other piano factories see Cerofeci, editorials, *Piano Key,* Dec. 1952, pp. 3–4.

34. Cerofeci, PI, pp. 10, 11, 13, 14. Dominick Iovino, interview by Sam Sills, 22 June 1987, p. 20, LWA. Martino, PI, p. 20. Daniels, PI, p. 25. Bogyos, PI, 10 Jan. 1992, p. 32.

35. Manyoky interview, p. 9. BD Min, 10 Nov., 3 Dec. 1970.

36. In Nov. 1971 Tomasello lost his post: BD Min, 22 Nov. 1971. See also HZS, PI, 6 Dec. 1991, pp. 39–40; 25 June 1991, p. 34; 5 June 1992, p. 31. Bogyos, PI, 10 Jan. 1992, p. 33. Cerofeci, PI, p. 11. Iovino, interview, 22 June 1987, p. 21. Sera, interview, pp. 24–25. R. Bisceglie, interview, p. 22. Annual report for 1970, 12 Mar. 1971. The strike ended on 23 Nov. 1970. In Sept. 1970 average wage was $3.41; by Sept. 1971 it was $3.67; a year later, $3.84. See *Furniture Workers Press,* Dec. 1970. See also HZS, "Number of Employees and Average Hourly Earnings."

CHAPTER 20. STEINWAY VERSUS YAMAHA

1. HZS, PI, 12 Feb. 1993, pp. 25, 30.

2. *MT,* June 1960, p. 70. HZS, "Jap Imports into the U.S.," handwritten chart, c. 1980, HZSF. The Japanese manufactured 48,000 pianos in 1960. United Nations, *Growth of World Industry* (1960), cited in Ehrlich, *Piano,* appendix 2, p. 221. On labor's response see Cerofeci to Fred Fulford, secretary-treasurer, UFW of America, 6 July 1960; on piano manufacturers' response see HZS to Cerofeci, 20 July 1960, LWA. On the complacent U.S. piano industry in the 1960s see John McLaren, PI, 16 Apr. 1993, p. 2.

3. "Yamaha's First Century: The Story of How an Obscure Reed Organ Maker Evolved into a World Leader in Musical Products," *MT,* Aug. 1987, pp. 50–56, 58. Ehrlich, *Piano,* p. 196, n. 16; p. 197, nn. 20–21. Cynthia Dann-Beardsley, "Instrument of the Immortals," *Rotunda* 24, no. 3 (winter 1991): 35. *Diamond's Japan Business Directory,* 1992, Diamond Lead Co. Ltd, p. 918.

4. "Yamaha's First Century," pp. 59–62.

5. Yamaha also made airplane propellers. Yamaha's output in 1939 was valued at 8 million yen. Letter to *The Piano Maker,* Dec. 1939, cited in Ehrlich, *Piano,* p. 197, n. 23. Kevin McKeon, "Ebony and Ivory," *Sky,* July 1991, pp. 29–34. Andrew Tanzer, "Create or Die," *Forbes,* 6 Apr. 1987, pp. 52, 56. "Yamaha's First Century," p. 62.

6. "Japan Report," Japan Information Service, Consulate General of Japan, vol. 11, no. 15 (15 Aug. 1965). In 1950 Yamaha employed more than 1,000 workers, who produced 12,000 reed organs and 1,200 pianos: "Yamaha's First Century," p. 62.

7. McLaren, PI, p. 26. "Yamaha's First Century," p. 67.

8. "Yamaha's First Century," pp. 50, 64, 67. "Kawakami Retires from All Yamaja Posts," *MT,* July 1992, p. 61. Tanzer, "Create or Die," p. 52. On Yamaha music courses see "Raise Import Duties on Pianos," *MT,* Nov. 1969, p. 71. See also McLaren, PI, pp. 5, 25. HZS, PI, 9 June 1993, p. 26.

9. Theodore D. Steinway (Teed), inter-office memo to Engineering, 17 July 1950. T. D. Steinway to R. de Majewski, 29 Feb. 1952. "Contacts between Steinway & Yamaha" file, HZSF.

10. McLaren, PI, pp. 11–12.

11. "Yamaha's First Century," p. 68; "1960–1969, GO-GO Sales Lure Outside Investors," *MT,* 100th anniversary issue, 1990, p. 154. See also HZS, "Jap Imports into the U.S." and

"Steinway & Sons Factory Shipments, 1891–1980," HZSF. HZS, PI, 18 Dec. 1992, pp. 5–6. "Report on Europe Trip," Apr. 30–13 May 1967, German Branch, attached to BD Min, 23 May 1967. John Majeski, PI, 22 Mar. 1993, p. 12. McLaren, PI, pp. 10, 12–14.

12. On a similar appraisal of Steinway dealers many years later see HZS, MR CBS, 24 June 1976. On Yamaha's appeal in the U.S. market see McLaren, PI, pp. 1, 19.

13. McLaren, PI, pp. 26–27.

14. HZS, PI, 6 Dec. 1991, pp. 42, 45, 46. Letter from Everett S. Rowan, 26 Jan. 1965, HZSF. HZS, MR CBS, 23 Nov. 1976, p. 3; 27 Dec. 1976, p. 2.

15. Akio Nagaoka, business manager, Nippon Gakki, to S&S, 26 Nov. 1960. Walter Gunther to Nippon Gakki, 1 Dec. 1960. "Contacts between Steinway & Yamaha," HZSF.

16. HZS to BD, 18 May 1964, attached to BD Min, 21 May 1964. Letter from Rowan, 26 Jan. 1965, HZSF.

17. HZS, PI, 12 Feb. 1993, p. 25; 9 June 1993, p. 29.

18. Report to HZS on "Yamaha Grand no. 293814, NoG2, 66," 20 Aug. 1964. See also Bogyos, PI, 10 Jan. 1992, pp. 33–34. Martino, PI, 29 Mar. 1993, p. 30.

19. HZS, PI, 12 Jan. 1993, pp. 25–26.

20. McLaren, PI, pp. 2–3.

21. TES, memo to HZS, 21 May 1968, "Yamaha" file, HZSF. The 3 Steinway tuners were Wagner, Luderman, and Griem. HZS, "Important Yamaha Executives" and "Yamaha Executives Listed Alphabetically," typed lists, c. 1968, HZSF. S&S, Harvard Business School, Case 0-682-025, 1981, p. 8. On Steinway not being the first piano purchased see HZS, MR CBS, 21 Dec. 1974.

22. HZS to John F. Majeski, Jr., 29 June 1970. CFTS's patent no. 204,106, 21 May 1978. "Yamaha" file, HZSF. On suspected Yamaha sabotage see Gretl Bruhn, report on Roland L. L. Chou, 11 Mar. 1969, trans. HZS, HZSF. On Yamaha's inventiveness see "Raise Import Duties," p. 71.

23. Genichi Kawakami, quoted in *Seiko,* a Yamaha publication, Mar. 1966; quote is handwritten by HZS in file "C & A Activities," HZSF. On Yamaha's "catch up and pass up" statement see *Japan Music Trades,* Jan. 1968. On HZS's analysis of that statement see HZS, MR CBS, 19 Jan. 1973, and PI, 9 June 1993, pp. 28–29. On discussion of the new Yamaha concert grand and concern for its replicating a Steinway see H. Matsuo to W. Gunther, 11 Apr. 1966, and Gunther to Matsuo, 15 Apr. 1966; HZSF. See also HZS, PI, 30 June 1992, p. 19; 12 Feb. 1993, p. 26.

24. Rubin, memo to HZS, 31 Oct. 1967, HZSF. S&S, Harvard Business School, Case 0-682-025, 1981, p. 8.

25. Rothstein, "Making Music," *NYT,* 21 Feb. 1981. Dann-Beardsley, "Instrument of the Immortals." On introduction of Yamaha "Conservatory-CF" grand piano see *MT,* Mar. 1967. On Knabe's, Aeolian's, and Baldwin's contracts (with the Metropolitan Opera House in New York City and Baldwin in Tanglewood), see E. F. Brooks, Jr., "Aeolian American Division of Aeolian Corporation, East Rochester, New York," typescript, n.d., HZSF. HZS, PI, 12 Mar. 1993, pp. 5–7; Majeski, PI, pp. 14–15; HZS, MR CBS, 24 Oct. 1975; and WSD, 16 Nov. 1895, reference to Knabe's contract with the Met.

26. Rowan to Charles Jones, 18 Nov. 1966, HZSF. HZS, PI, 9 June 1993, p. 18.

27. When Alexander Brailowsky toured Japan, Yamaha arranged with Yomiuri Newspaper Company to put its name on the bottom of all his posters to imply that Brailowsky was playing a Yamaha. H. Matsuo to Gunther, 4 Feb. 1967. Gunther, memo to HZS, 14 Feb. 1967. *Charlotte Observer,* 23 Sept. 1967. JS to Rubin, 6 Oct. 1967. See also Gunther, memo to Rubin, 26 Apr. 1968. On Kempff statement to S&S see Theodore D. Steinway, memo to HZS, Rubin, and Howard Cushing, 21 May 1968. On Yamaha's interpretation of Kempff's endorsement see *Japan Music Trades,* Jan. 1968. All in HZSF.

28. "Yamaha Concert Grand Model CF: In Demand among the World's Masters," Yamaha news release, no. 14, July 1969, HZSF.

29. Notes from a telephone conversation with Andor Foldes by Walter Gunther, 8 Sept.

1969, HZSF. Howard Cushing to John McLaren, 12 Sept. 1969; McLaren to Cushing, 26 Sept. 1969; HZSF.

30. On Rubinstein endorsing the Yamaha grand see *Japan Music Trades,* Jan. 1968, HZSF. Gretl Bruhn, memo to HZS, 30 Aug. 1968, Hamburg. M. Arimoto, export division, Nippon Gakki, letter to F. Cannella V., president, Musiyama C.A., 2 Sept. 1968. Nippon Gakki, cable to Cannella, 2 Sept. 1968; Cannella response to Nippon Gakki, 5 Sept. 1968, in Spanish, trans. Eduvina Estrella. Sam Kajimura, export manager, Nippon Gakki, to Gunther, Hamburg, 22 Nov. 1968. Gunther to Kajimura, 26 Nov. 1968. All in HZSF. Conrado Insam, director of Musikalia, C.A., to S&S, Hamburg, 22 Aug., 22, 30 Oct. 1968; Gunther to Insam, 22 Oct. 1968; trans. Irene Soloman, HZSF.

31. "Raise Import Duties" and "2 Commissioners Deny Need to Shelter Domestic Industry," *MT,* Nov. 1969 and Mar. 1970, p. 60. "Commissioner Leonard Urges 20 Percent Duty," *MT,* Mar. 1970, p. 55. In 1968, 11,258 grands were sold in the United States (6,358 domestic and 4,900 imported). See "Full Text of U.S. Tariff Commission Report to Nixon," *MT,* Mar. 1970, pp. 93, 94, tables 2, 4. HZS on Yamaha competition see BD Min, 14 Mar., 24 May 1968, HZS, MR CBS, 23 Aug. 1974, p. 2; 22 Jan. 1974; 24 Oct. 1975. HZS, "Jap Imports into the U.S." *Japanese Music Trade,* 1975, p. 402. On Yamaha and the school market see Robert Pace, 2 Apr. 1993, p. 16. McLaren, PI, p. 23. On N. W. Ayer going to Yamaha see Barbara Johnson, "Ayer–Steinway 69-Year History Resulted in 'Immortal' Ads," *Advertising Age,* 2 Aug. 1969.

32. "Piano imports total about $8.4 million a year, of which Japan accounts for about $7.4 million": "Tariff Panel Supports Aid for Piano Makers, Reversing Past Policy," *Wall Street Journal,* 30 Dec. 1969, p. 7.

33. "Commissioner Leonard Urges 20 Percent Duty," p. 55. "Raise Import Duties," pp. 46, 50.

34. "Tariff Commission Report to Nixon," p. 53. Trade Expansion Act, 1962, sec. 301(b) (1). "Raise Import Duties," pp. 46, 50. "Nixon Approves Piano Tariff Increase to 13.5 Percent for 3 Years," *MT,* Mar. 1970, p. 100. On the 1962 campaign against lowering the tariff, see, e.g., HZS to Fulford, UFW, 26 July 1962, and other correspondence in Labor files, 1944–70, LWA.

35. "Nixon Approves Tariff Increase," p. 100. Commissioner Sutton was chairman; see "Tariff Commission Reports to the President on Pianos and Parts," press release, 23 Dec. 1969, White House Central Files: Subject Files (TA) Trade, Gen TA 4/CM Tariff-Imports [Oranges—Pianos], 30 Jan. 1970. "Raise Import Duties," pp. 54, 72. "Tariff Commission Report to Nixon," pp. 64, 92. See also HZS, PI, 30 June 1992, p. 21. On Japanese cross-examiner see McLaren, PI, p. 6.

36. "Nixon Approves Tariff Increase," p. 100. HZS, PI, 6 Dec. 1991, pp. 44–46; 30 June 1992, p. 21. Cornfield, *Mighty Voice,* p. 160. Alice Jordan, Yale, 28 Jan. 1979, p. 14. BD Min, 17 June 1969, 25 Feb. 1970. S Min, 8 Apr. 1970. *Furniture Workers Press,* Feb. 1970. Presidents Nixon and Carter did nothing to stop the flood of low-priced, high-quality Japanese products coming into U.S. markets. "Presidential Proclamation Excludes Grand Piano" and "Tariff Commission Report to Nixon," *MT,* Mar. 1970, pp. 52, 100, 107. On trade relations with Japan see C. Prestowitz and S. S. Harrison, "Pacific Agenda: Defense or Economics?," *Foreign Policy,* summer 1990, pp. 56–76. U.S. imports from Japan dropped in 1970 to 19,332 pianos but bounced back a year later to 25,293. On Japanese piano import numbers see HZS, "Jap Imports into the U.S." On number of Japanese grands coming into the United States from 1971 to 1974 see HZS, MR CBS, 15 Nov. 1974, p. 3. On U.S. piano manufacturers' focus on uprights see HZS, MR CBS, 21 Jan. 1974, and appendix D on grands shipped and appendix E on total number of pianos shipped 1900–73. In 1968, 6,358 domestic grands were sold in the United States, of which S&S shipped 1,932 (30%) from their New York factory. See "Tariff Commission Report to Nixon," p. 93, table 2, and HZS, "Factory Shipments." On U.S. grand shipments versus Japanese grand imports, 1970–73, see HZS, MR CBS, 22 Jan. 1974, appendix H. See also McLaren, PI, pp. 5–6. The Tariff Commission submitted its findings to President Nixon on 23 Dec. 1969; see White House Central Files. See also "Tariff Panel Supports Aid for Piano Makers, Reversing Past Policy," *Wall Street Journal,* 30 Dec. 1969, p. 7.

37. "Steinway Named Everett Dealer in New York City," *MT,* May 1954, p. 19. HZS, PI, 25 Sept. 1992, pp. 27–29; 12 Feb. 1993, p. 28; on Sohmer as the alternative second piano, see HZS, PI, 9 June 1993, pp. 17–18. On decision to sell Everett pianos at Steinway Hall see also "Report of Retail Study Committee," attached to BD Min, 18 Feb., 5 Apr., 1 May 1954. On decision to discontinue Everett at Steinway Hall see Min, 18 Oct. 1965, 28 Jan. 1966. *MT,* Aug. 1987, p. 72. McLaren, PI, p. 8.

38. In 1960 Japanese manufacturing workers averaged 29 cents an hour, compared with $2.66 in the United States. In 1963 the wage of Japanese workers was still less than 50 cents an hour, compared with 90 cents in Great Britain and German and $2.50 in the United States. See "Raise Import Duties," p. 65. On wages and labor productivity see "Japan Report," pp. 3, 4. On 1960 and 1975 wages in the United States and Japan, see HZS, MR CBS, 25 Aug. 1976, HZSF. On Yamaha production see Steinway & Sons, Harvard Business School, Case 0-682-025, 1981, p. 8. On relative prices, Yamaha and Steinway, see "The Steinway Tradition," *NYT,* 24 Aug. 1980, sec. 3, p. 1. On Japanese pianos and unit costs to the United States see HZS, "Jap Imports into the U.S." See also HZS, MR CBS, 22 Jan. 1974, appendix G. On number of Japanese grands imported 1971–74 see HZS, MR CBS, 15 Nov. 1974, p. 3. On Steinway piano shipments see HZS, "Factory Shipments." See also "Steinway Prices," 17 Nov. 1971. On Japanese piano sales to domestic market see Ehrlich, *Piano,* p. 197.

39. HZS, "Jap Imports into the U.S." See also HZS, MR CBS, 19 Mar., 23 May 1975; 25 May 1976, exhibit A; and 21 Nov. 1975, chart for shipments of grands only. The average Yamaha price in 1974 was $1,370. Average Steinway price was $5,453: "Steinway Prices," 15 Apr. 1974. For Japanese average price 1971–75 see HZS, MR CBS, 25 May 1976, p. 4.

40. HZS, "Yamaha," handwritten notes, 22 Sept. 1978, HZSF. HZS, PI, 12 Feb. 1993, p. 32.

41. Rothstein, "Making Music." In 1980 Yamaha produced 250,000 pianos; see Steinway & Sons, Harvard Business School, Case 0-682-025, 1981, p. 8. On imports capturing domestic market see *Sound Board,* S&S employee newsletter, Dec. 1984, p. 1. See also HZS, PI, 12 Feb. 1993, p. 31. In the 1960s Japanese piano makers still exported only 12% of their total output. In 1970, more than 750,000 instruments were manufactured worldwide. Loesser, *Men, Women and Pianos,* pp. 598–599. Ehrlich, *Piano,* pp. 195, 197, n. 24, 198. Dolge, *Pianos and Their Makers,* pp. 265–266. Ripin et al., *The Piano,* pp. 67, 68, 172. *Steinway News* no. 335 (spring 1969). Tanzer, "Create or Die," p. 52. BD Min, 9 July 1965. Annual report for 1969, S Min, 11 Mar. 1970. In 1970 the United States produced 220,000 pianos; Russia, 200,000; West Germany, 24,000; East German, 21,000; England, 17,000; and France, 1,000. Ehrlich, *Piano,* appendix 2, p. 221. *Diamond's Japan Business Directory, 1992,* p. 918. Edward Rothstein, "Don't Shoot the Piano," *New Republic,* 1 May 1989, p. 33. HZS, MR CBS, 21 Dec. 1974, p. 4. On S&S losing its international monopoly and thoughts on a third factory in South American or Japan, see HZS, MR CBS, July 1976. "Yamaha's First Century," pp. 50, 64, 67. In 1992 Yamaha Corporation of American estimated U.S. sales were $410 million (music and sound products only), placing it first on the list of U.S. Music and Sound Suppliers. Steinway musical properties sales (U.S.A., Germany, & Boston Piano) were $80 million, placing it ninth on the list. See *MT,* Apr. 1993, p. 67. "Raise Import Duties," p. 71. McLaren, PI, pp. 5, 25. HZS, PI, 9 June 1993, p. 26.

42. HZS, PI, 5 June 1992, p. 30. "2 Commissioners deny need to shelter domestic industry," *MT,* Mar. 1970, p. 62. Handwritten chart attached to HZS's MR CBS, 21 Jan. 1974, HZSF. BD Min, 23 Sept. 1969.

43. Annual report for 1969, 11 Mar. 1970. Annual report for 1970, 12 Mar. 1971.

EPILOGUE: THE CBS SALE AND ITS AFTERMATH

1. FTS, PI, 23 Mar. 1993, pp. 38–39. HZS, PI, 20 Nov. 1992, p. 18. On value of S&S in 1971 see HZS, "Sale of Steinway and Sons to CBS, a Chronology," typescript, 1986, HZSF. "Stein-

way & Sons Swan Song," *OTC Securities Review*, June 1972. On the Ziegler family's 6,474 stocks see S&S stockholders list, 4 Apr. 1972, in S Min, 27 Apr. 1972.

2. Henry Ziegler, PI, 26 Mar. 1993, p. 7. HZS, "Sale of Steinway and Sons to CBS."

3. Ziegler, with his brother and sister, owned 12.3% (6,474 of 52,699 shares) of S&S. Rosenwald, under various names, owned 13.3% (6,999 shares). See HZS, PI, 20 Nov. 1992, pp. 14–20. HZS, typescript, 26 Mar. 1993. HZS, "Sale of Steinway and Sons to CBS." "Steinway & Sons Swan Song."

4. HZS, Yale, 19 Jan. 1979, pp. 124, 130–131. Mrs. Charles Kittredge, interview by Elizabeth Harkins, Yale, 28 Nov. 1978, p. 34. On aging stockholders see JS, Yale, 7 Nov. 1978, pp. 175, 177. Maude S. Paige had 1,501 shares; Meta von Bernuth had 752 shares; Mariechen (BS's widow) had 1,010 shares: see S&S stockholders list, 1972. HZS, "Review of Merger & Acquisition Contacts," handwritten list, 1955–68, 15 Sept. 1973, HZSF. The offer from Wurlitzer came in 1960, from Magnavox in 1963, from Beatrice Foods in 1968. See also HZS, Yale, 19 Jan. 1979, pp. 126–127, 130.

5. HZS, PI, 8 Dec. 1989, p. 62.

6. Ibid., p. 62; 5 Feb. 1991, p. 30; 27 Aug. 1991, p. 29; Yale, p. 62. On Yamaha see S Min, 27 Apr. 1972.

7. HZS, PI, 8 Dec. 1989, pp. 60–61, 64; 9 June 1993, pp. 19–21. On HZS's reasons for selling, S Min, 27 Apr. 1972.

8. Betty Steinway Chapin, Yale, 12 Oct. 1978, p. 5. HZS, PI, 9 June 1993, pp. 20–21.

9. HZS, PI, 8 Dec. 1989, p. 62. S Min, 27 Apr. 1972. For a list of offers to buy S&S, 1955–68, see HZS, "Review of Merger & Acquisition Contacts." Bogyos, PI, 26 Mar. 1993, p. 8.

10. HZS, PI, 8 Dec. 1989, p. 62; 20 Nov. 1992, p. 15; 9 June 1993, p. 28. HZS, "Sale of Steinway and Sons to CBS." On plan to sell S&S to Kawai see HZS, typescript, 26 Mar. 1993.

11. The first meeting with Schein was on 2 Dec. 1971. HZS told Schein to talk to his negotiator, Nicholas Brady of Dillon, Reed on 10 Dec. 1971. See HZS, "Sale of Steinway and Sons to CBS." HZS, typescript, 26 Mar. 1993. In 1977 CBS acquired Gemeinhardt flutes and Lyon & Healy harps; see "Steinway & Sons Acquired by Boston-Based Investment Group," *MT*, 25 Sept. 1985. See also Alexander R. Hammer, "CBS Seeking Steinway; Expands Profit and Sales," *NYT*, 10 Feb. 1972, p. 63. On Harvey Schein see Austin Perlow, "Steinway Piano, CBS Talk of Merger," *Long Island Press*, 10 Feb. 1972, p. 18.

12. HZS, Yale, 8 Dec. 1989, pp. 65, 73; 19 Jan. 1979, pp. 131–132, 136–137. The purchase was actually a "reverse merger"; CBS Musical Instruments Inc. was merged in S&S, which became the surviving company. See JS, Yale, p. 178. See also S Min, 5 Apr. 1972. Reference to 9 Feb. 1972, date of directors' meeting, in HZS to Gretl Bruhn, 5 Feb. 1972, "Sale to CBS" file, HZSF. Charles P. Durkin (know as Pat) represented Dillon, Reed and conducted all the negotiations with CBS. On agreements in principal to the sale see HZS, "Sale of Steinway and Sons to CBS."

13. HZS, PI, 8 Dec. 1989, p. 62. On Gunther's heart attack see Gretl Bruhn, telegram to HZS, 23 Dec. 1971, and memo, 24 Dec. 1971. HZS, letter to Bruhn, 27 Dec. 1971, HZSF.

14. HZS, PI, 8 Dec. 1989, pp. 65–67, 73. HZS, letter to Bruhn, 5 Feb. 1972, HZSF. On events of 9 Feb. 1972 see HZS, "Sale of Steinway and Sons to CBS."

15. "To our friends and representatives all over the world." from Walter Gunther, 14 Feb. 1972, HZSF.

16. The closing sale price of the common stock of CBS on the New York Stock Exchange on 3 Apr. 1972 was $52.25. See Hammer, "CBS Seeking Steinway," p. 63. See also "Steinway & Sons Swan Song." In terms of stock, 375,000 CBS shares were traded for 52,699 S&S shares. The merger was structured so that taxes were paid when CBS stock was sold. "When you as a stockholder are taken over by another company and they give you their stock, and you haven't done anything, that's a tax-free event." HZS, PI, 30 June 1992, pp. 7–8; 8 Dec. 1989, pp. 63, 68; 5 Feb. 1991, p. 30; Yale, pp. 62, 131–132, 137–138. Kittredge, Yale, p. 34. JS, Yale, p. 179. S Min, 27 Apr. 1972. On value of CBS stock see proxy statement attached to S Min, 27 Apr. 1972. HZS to

Walter Gunther & Lionel Squibb, 30 Apr. 1972, HZSF. The legal merger papers became effective at midnight, Friday, 28 Apr. 1972. See also HZS, "Sale of Steinway and Sons to CBS."

17. Sam Chapin, letter to JS, 14 Feb. 1972, HZSF.

18. Samuel and Theodore Steinway Chapin, "To the Stockholders of Steinway & Son," 7 Apr. 1972, in "Chapin Objection to Merger" file, HZSF.

19. B. Chapin, Yale, pp. 6–8. FTS, PI, p. 39. S Min, 27 Apr. 1972. HZS, PI, 25 Sept. 1992, p. 23.

20. "The Steinway Tradition," *NYT*, 24 Aug. 1980, sec. 3, p. 1. Matthew Wald, "Steinway Changing amid Tradition," *NYT*, Business section, p. 1. S&S invested about $1 million per year in capital improvement, mostly in Hamburg, and Hamburg continued to deliver profits. On CBS going around HZS, see MR CBS, 18 Apr., 22 July 1975. On CBS wanting a 10% annual increase in profits, see MR CBS 27 Dec. 1975. On CBS bureaucracy see HZS, MR CBS, 21 Nov. 1972; 19 Oct., 20 Dec. 1973; 24 Oct. 1975. On CBS's cost-cutting methods see MR CBS, 23 Aug. 1974; on CBS destroying S&S, 18 Oct. 1974; on the capacity ceiling, 22 Jan. 1974; on promoting the larger grands, 22 Jan. 1974, 21 Nov. 1975. It made a 33% margin (the difference between cost and wholesale price, expressed as a % of wholesale price) on the model B grand and 42% on the model D, but only 17% on the small model S and 20% on the model M.

21. On CBS stock see Bogyos, PI, p. 8. On the high sales record see MR CBS, 15 Nov. 1974. On pre-tax profit, see MR CBS, 23 Jan. 1975.

22. On concerns about CBS Steinway, see HZS, MR CBS, 23 Nov. 1976. On improving piano quality see HZS, handwritten memos to Robert G. Campbell, 21 Dec. 1974, 22 Aug. 1975.

23. HZS, PI, 8 Dec. 1989, p. 69.

24. On the "dark period" see *New York Daily News*, "Steinway Troubles Strike Sour Note," 20 Aug. 1985. See also "Steinway," *Oakland Tribune*, 5 Mar. 1978, p. 8, Daniels, PI, 2 May 1993, pp. 26–27.

25. HZS, PI, 30 June 1992, p. 26. "Steinway Tradition," *NYT*.

26. "Perez Resigns, Replaced by Meyer. A Jarring Change at Steinway," *NYT*, 26 May 1982, sec. 4, p. 1. "For Pianists, Steinway Sale Hits a Sour Note," *New York Newsday*, 22 July 1985, sec. 3, p. 8.

27. "Bruce Stevens President, Buyer of Steinway Sees a Challenge," *NYT*, 17 Sept. 1985, sec. 4, p. 2. "Steinway & Sons Acquired by Boston-Based Investment Group," *MT*, 25 Sept. 1985. On CBS selling Steinway, see "Sale Hits Sour Note," *Newsday. MT*, Jan. 1990.

28. "Steinway Musical Properties, Inc. and Kawai Musical Instrument Mfg., Co., Ltd. Announce Agreement to Distribute New Line of Mid-Priced Pianos," press release, 16 Jan. 1992, LWA. HZS, MR CBS, 20 Apr. 1973.

29. Edward Rothstein, "To Make a Piano of Note It Takes More than Tools," *Smithsonian Magazine*, Nov. 1988.

30. Edward Rothstein, "Made in the U.S.A., Once Gloriously, Now Precariously," *NYT*, 28 May 1995, section 2, pp. 1 & 36. Bruce Stevens, letter to the editor, *NYT* Arts & Leisure section, 25 June 1995.

31. Kenneth N. Gilpin, "Steinway & Sons Is Sold for $100 Million," *NYT*, 19 April 1995, p. D5.

32. John Birmingham, letter to Bruce Stevens, 28 June 1995. David M. Halbfinger, "Steinway Is Sold to Big Producer of Instruments," *Newsday*, 19 April 1995, pp. A41 & A43. Interviews with Henry Z. Steinway, Bill Youse, Jr., and Frank Mazurco, 19 April 1995 and 15 June 1995.

Index

366

Index